ENCOUNTERS WITH ANCIENT EGYPT

# Ancient Perspectives on Egypt

Institute of Archaeology

## Titles in the series

**Ancient Egypt in Africa**
*Edited by David O'Connor and Andrew Reid*

**Ancient Perspectives on Egypt**
*Edited by Roger Matthews and Cornelia Roemer*

**Consuming Ancient Egypt**
*Edited by Sally MacDonald and Michael Rice*

**Imhotep Today: Egyptianizing architecture**
*Edited by Jean-Marcel Humbert and Clifford Price*

**Mysterious Lands**
*Edited by David O'Connor and Stephen Quirke*

**'Never had the like occurred': Egypt's view of its past**
*Edited by John Tait*

**Views of Ancient Egypt since Napoleon Bonaparte: imperialism, colonialism and modern appropriations**
*Edited by David Jeffreys*

**The Wisdom of Egypt: changing visions through the ages**
*Edited by Peter Ucko and Timothy Champion*

ENCOUNTERS WITH ANCIENT EGYPT

# Ancient Perspectives on Egypt

Edited by

Roger Matthews and Cornelia Roemer

Institute of Archaeology

First published in Great Britain 2003 by UCL Press,
an imprint of Cavendish Publishing Limited, The Glass House,
Wharton Street, London WC1X 9PX, United Kingdom
Telephone: + 44 (0)20 7278 8000   Facsimile: + 44 (0)20 7278 8080
Email: info@uclpress.com
Website: www.uclpress.com

Published in the United States by Cavendish Publishing
c/o International Specialized Book Services,
5824 NE Hassalo Street, Portland,
Oregon 97213-3644, USA

Published in Australia by Cavendish Publishing (Australia) Pty Ltd
45 Beach Street, Coogee, NSW 2034, Australia
Telephone: + 61 (2)9664 0909   Facsimile: + 61 (2)9664 5420

© Institute of Archaeology, University College London  2003

All rights reserved. No part of this publication may be reproduced, stored in a retrieval system, or transmitted, in any form or by any means, electronic, mechanical, photocopying, recording, scanning or otherwise, without the prior permission in writing of Cavendish Publishing Limited, or as expressly permitted by law, or under the terms agreed with the appropriate reprographics rights organisation. Enquiries concerning reproduction outside the scope of the above should be sent to the Rights Department, Cavendish Publishing Limited, at the address above.

You must not circulate this book in any other binding or cover
and you must impose the same condition on any acquirer.

British Library Cataloguing in Publication Data
Matthews, R.
Ancient perspectives on Egypt – (Encounters with ancient Egypt)
1 Egypt – History  2 Egypt – Civilization  3 Egypt – Historiography
I Title  II Roemer, C.
932

Library of Congress Cataloguing in Publication Data
Data available

ISBN 1-84472-002-0

1 3 5 7 9 10 8 6 4 2

Designed and typeset by Style Photosetting, Mayfield, East Sussex
Email: style@pavilion.co.uk

Printed and bound in Great Britain

Cover illustration:   Detail of the Nilotic mosaic of Palestrina (late second century BC): the hunt of Seth in the form of hippopotamus (© Stuto/Archeomedia).

# Series Editor's Foreword

This series of eight books derives from the proceedings of a conference entitled 'Encounters with Ancient Egypt', held at the Institute of Archaeology, University College London (UCL) in December 2000. Since then, many new chapters have been especially commissioned for publication, and those papers originally provided for the conference and now selected for publication have been extensively revised and rewritten.

There are many noteworthy features of the books. One is the overall attempt to move the study of Ancient Egypt into the mainstream of recent advances in archaeological and anthropological practice and interpretation. This is a natural outcome of London University's Institute of Archaeology, one of the largest archaeology departments in the world, being the academic host. Drawing on the Institute's and other related resources within UCL, the volumes in the series reflect an extraordinary degree of collaboration between the series editor, individual volume editors, contributors and colleagues. The wide range of approaches to the study of the past, pursued in such a vibrant scholarly environment as UCL's, has encouraged the scholars writing in these volumes to consider their disciplinary interests from new perspectives. All the chapters presented here have benefited from wide-ranging discussion between experts from diverse academic disciplines, including art history, papyrology, anthropology, archaeology and Egyptology, and subsequent revision.

Egyptology has been rightly criticized for often being insular; the methodologies and conclusions of the discipline have been seen by others as having developed with little awareness of archaeologies elsewhere. The place and role of Ancient Egypt within African history, for example, has rarely been considered jointly by Egyptologists and Africanists. This collaboration provides a stimulating review of key issues and may well influence future ways of studying Egypt. Until now, questions have rarely been asked about the way Egyptians thought of their own past or about non-Egyptian peoples and places. Nor has the discipline of Egyptology explored, in any depth, the nature of its evidence, or the way contemporary cultures regarded Ancient Egypt. The books in this series address such topics.

Another exceptional feature of this series is the way that the books have been designed to interrelate with, inform and illuminate one another. Thus, the evidence of changing appropriations of Ancient Egypt over time, from the classical period to the modern Afrocentrist movement, features in several volumes. One volume explores the actual sources of knowledge about Ancient Egypt before the advent of 'scientific' archaeology, while another explores knowledge of Ancient Egypt after Napoleon Bonaparte's expeditions and the unearthing of Tutankhamun's tomb. The question asked throughout these volumes, however, is how far fascination and knowledge about Ancient Egypt have been based on sources of evidence rather than extraneous political or commercial concerns and interests.

As a result of this series, the study of Ancient Egypt will be significantly enriched and deepened. The importance of the Egypt of several thousands of years ago reaches far beyond the existence of its architectural monuments and extends to its unique role in the history of all human knowledge. Furthermore, the civilization of Ancient Egypt speaks to us with particular force in our own present and has an abiding place in the modern psyche.

As the first paragraph of this Foreword explains, the final stage of this venture began with the receipt and editing of some extensively revised, and in many cases new, chapters – some 95 in all – to be published simultaneously in eight volumes. What it does not mention is the speed with which the venture has been completed: the current UCL Press was officially launched in April 2003. That this series of books has been published to such a high standard of design, professional accuracy and attractiveness only four months later is incredible.

This alone speaks eloquently for the excellence of the staff of UCL Press – from its senior management to its typesetters and designers. Ruth Phillips (Marketing Director) stands out for her youthful and innovative marketing ideas and implementation of them, but most significant of all, at least from the Institute's perspective, is the contribution of Ruth Massey (Editor), who oversaw and supervized all details of the layout and production of the books, and also brought her critical mind to bear on the writing styles, and even the meaning, of their contents.

Individual chapter authors and academic volume editors, both from within UCL and in other institutions, added this demanding project to otherwise full workloads. Although it is somewhat invidious to single out particular individuals, Professor David O'Connor stands out as co-editor of two volumes and contributor of chapters to three despite his being based overseas. He, together with Professor John Tait – also an editor and multiple chapter author in these books – was one of the first to recognize my vision of the original conference as having the potential to inspire a uniquely important publishing project.

Within UCL's Institute of Archaeology, a long list of dedicated staff, academic, administrative and clerical, took over tasks for the Director and Kelly Vincent, his assistant as they wrestled with the preparation of this series. All of these staff, as well as several members of the student body, really deserve individual mention by name, but space does not allow this. However, the books could not have appeared without the particular support of five individuals: Lisa Daniel, who tirelessly secured copyright for over 500 images; Jo Dullaghan, who turned her hand to anything at any time to help out, from re-typing manuscripts to chasing overdue authors; Andrew Gardner, who tracked down obscure and incomplete references, and who took on the complex job of securing and producing correctly scanned images; Stuart Laidlaw, who not only miraculously produced publishable images of a pair of outdoor cats now in Holland and Jamaica, but in a number of cases created light where submitted images revealed only darkness; and Kelly Vincent, who did all of the above twice over, and more – and who is the main reason that publisher and Institute staff remained on excellent terms throughout.

Finally, a personal note, if I may. Never, ever contemplate producing eight complex, highly illustrated books within a four month period. If you *really must*, then make sure you have the above team behind you. Essentially, ensure that you have a partner such as Jane Hubert, who may well consider you to be mad but never questions the essential worth of the undertaking.

*Peter Ucko*
*Institute of Archaeology*
*University College London*
*27 July 2003*

# Contents

*Series Editor's Foreword*   v
*Contributors*   ix
*List of Figures*   xi
*A note on transliteration from ancient Egyptian*   xv

1. Introduction: the Worlds of Ancient Egypt – Aspects, Sources, Interactions   1
   *Roger Matthews and Cornelia Roemer*

2. South Levantine Encounters with Ancient Egypt at the Beginning of the Third Millennium   21
   *Eliot Braun*

3. Egyptian Stone Vessels and the Politics of Exchange (2617–1070 BC)   39
   *Rachael Thyrza Sparks*

4. Reconstructing the Role of Egyptian Culture in the Value Regimes of the Bronze Age Aegean: Stone Vessels and their Social Contexts   57
   *Andrew Bevan*

5. Love and War in the Late Bronze Age: Egypt and Hatti   75
   *David Warburton*

6. Egypt and Mesopotamia in the Late Bronze and Iron Ages   101
   *David Warburton and Roger Matthews*

7. Finding the Egyptian in Early Greek Art   115
   *Jeremy Tanner*

8. Upside Down and Back to Front: Herodotus and the Greek Encounter with Egypt   145
   *Thomas Harrison*

9. Encounters with Ancient Egypt: The Hellenistic Greek Experience   157
   *Csaba A. La'da*

10. Pilgrimage in Greco-Roman Egypt: New Perspectives on Graffiti from the Memnonion at Abydos   171
    *Ian Rutherford*

| 11 | **Carry-on at Canopus: the Nilotic mosaic from Palestrina and Roman Attitudes to Egypt** | **191** |

*Susan Walker*

| 12 | **Roman Poets on Egypt** | **203** |

*Herwig Maehler*

| *References* | *217* |
|---|---|
| *Index 1: place names* | *243* |
| *Index 2: names of people, peoples and deities* | *247* |
| *Index 3: topics* | *251* |

Note: No attempt has been made to impose a standard chronology on authors; all dates before 712 BC are approximate. However, names of places, and royal and private names have been standardized.

# Contributors

**Andrew Bevan** is a Leverhulme Research Fellow at the Institute of Archaeology, University College London. His current research interests include value theory, trade and contact in the eastern Mediterranean Bronze Age, landscape archaeology and GIS. He received his PhD from the Institute of Archaeology, University College London.

**Eliot Braun** is a senior research archaeologist in the Israel Antiquities Authority and has specialized in salvage and rescue excavations in Israel and the archaeology of the southern Levant. He has taught at the University of Haifa and was Dyson Fellow at the University of Pennsylvania in 1998. His publications include *En Shadud: salvage excavations at a farming community in the Jezreel Valley, Israel* (1985) and *Salvage and Rescue Excavations at the Late Prehistoric Site of Yiftah'el in Lower Galilee, Israel* (1997). He received his PhD from the University of Tel Aviv, Israel.

**Thomas Harrison** is Lecturer in Ancient History at the University of St Andrews. His main interests lie in Greek history and historiography. He is the author of *Divinity and History: the religion of Herodotus* (2000), *The Emptiness of Asia: Aeschylus' Persians and the history of the fifth century* (2000), and editor of *Greeks and Barbarians* (2002). He received his PhD from the University of Oxford.

**Csaba A. La'da** is a Research Associate of the Austrian Academy of Sciences, Vienna and also lectures in ancient history and papyrology at the University of Vienna. His research encompasses the social and cultural history of Hellenistic and Roman Egypt, as well as Greek and demotic Egyptian papyri and inscriptions. His recent publications include *Foreign Ethnics in Hellenistic Egypt* (2002). He received his PhD from the University of Cambridge.

**Herwig Maehler** is Emeritus Professor of Papyrology in the Department of Greek and Latin, University College London. His publications include *Die Auffassung des Dichterberufs im frühen Griechentum bis zur Zeit Pindars* (1963), *Die Lieder des Bakchylides* (1982), and *Greek Bookhands of the Early Byzantine Period AD 300–800* (1987). He received his PhD from the University of Hamburg.

**Roger Matthews** is Reader in Archaeology of Western Asia at the Institute of Archaeology, University College London. He was previously Director of the British Institute of Archaeology at Ankara (1995–2001) and of the British School of Archaeology in Iraq (1988–1996). He has directed field projects on sites ranging in date from Neolithic to Middle Bronze Age in Iraq, Syria and Turkey and is interested in long-term settlement studies, the rise of complex, literate, urban societies, and the development of the discipline of archaeology in Western Asia. His recent publications include *The Archaeology of Mesopotamia* (2003), *Secrets of the Dark Mound* (2002), *The Early Prehistory of Mesopotamia* (2000), *Ancient Anatolia* (1998), and *Cities, Seals and Writing* (1993). He received his PhD from the University of Cambridge.

**Cornelia Roemer** is Professor of Papyrology at University College London. She has published widely on texts from late antique Egypt, including the life of Mani and documents from the early Christian Church. Currently, she works on annotated papyri of the archaic Greek poet Alcman which reveal scholarly interest in his poetry dating from Antiquity. She is the field director of an ongoing survey project in the Fayum to examine the places where papyri from the Greco-Roman period have been found. She studied classical philology, papyrology and art history at the Universities of Cologne and Florence.

**Ian Rutherford** is Professor of Greek in the Department of Classics at the University of Reading. His research interests include papyrology, pilgrimage in the ancient world, and Hittite religion. His publications include *Pindar's Paeans: a reading of the fragments with a survey of the genre* (2001) and *The New Simonides: towards a commentary* (1996). He received his D Phil from the University of Oxford.

**Rachael Sparks** is Curator of the Petrie Palestinian Collection at the Institute of Archaeology, University College London. Her main areas of research include interaction between Egypt and the Levant during the second and first millennia BC, the development of Canaanite cult, and issues related to stone vessel manufacture and distribution. She has taken part in a number of field projects in Jordan, including excavations at Pella and Teleilat Ghassul. She received her PhD from the University of Sydney.

**Jeremy Tanner** is a Lecturer in Greek and Roman art, and co-ordinates the Comparative Art and Archaeology MA programme at the Institute of Archaeology, University College London. He is currently completing a monograph, *The Invention of Art History: religion, society and artistic differentiation in Ancient Greece*, and he has published on the body, expressive culture and social interaction, and on portraits, patrons and power in the late Roman Republic. His current research involves comparative and sociological approaches to the art of complex societies in the ancient world. He received his PhD from the University of Cambridge.

**Susan Walker** is Deputy Keeper of Greek and Roman Antiquities at the British Museum and co-editor (with P. Higgs) of the exhibition catalogue *Cleopatra of Egypt: from history to myth* (2001) and *Ancient Faces: mummy portraits from Roman Egypt* (1997). She has also published widely on Roman art and society, including *Roman Art* (1991) and *Greek and Roman Portraits* (1995). She received her PhD from the Institute of Archaeology, University College London.

**David Warburton** has taught at universities in Switzerland, Denmark and China. He is a former Director of the American Institute for Yemeni Studies in Sana'a, Yemen. His recent publications include *Egypt and the Near East: politics in the Bronze Age* (2001); *Archaeological Stratigraphy: a Near Eastern approach* (2003) and *Macroeconomics from the Beginning* (2003). He studied Near Eastern archaeology and Egyptology at the American University of Beirut and received his D Phil from the University of Basel.

## List of Figures

| | | |
|---|---|---|
| Figure 2:1 | Map of Israel and the Palestinian Autonomous Zones with sites where Egyptian and Egyptianized artefacts have been found. | 22 |
| Figure 2:2 | Seven of the nine potsherds of Egyptian origin bearing *serekhs*, incised before firing, recovered from Tel Lod. | 28 |
| Figure 3:1 | Map of sites mentioned in the text. Ugarit covers the area of modern Ras Shamra and Minet el-Beida. | 41 |
| Figure 3:2 | The chronological distribution of stone vessels with Egyptian royal name inscriptions found in the Levant. | 47 |
| Figure 3:3 | Frequency of objects (excepting scarabs) with New Kingdom royal inscriptions found in the Levant. | 49 |
| Figure 3:4 | Stone vessels with Egyptian royal name inscriptions. a: Byblos (cat. 28, Minault-Gout 1997: fig. 3), b: Ras Shamra (cat. 51, after Caubet 1991: pl. XI.7), c: Beirut (cat. 58, after Saidah 1993-94: pl. 23.1.1), d: Gezer (cat. 69, after Macalister 1912: pl. XXIV.1). | 50 |
| Figure 4:1 | Late Old Kingdom stone vessels from Egypt and Byblos and their Cretan imitations. | 60 |
| Figure 4:2 | First Intermediate Period–early Middle Kingdom stone vessels from Egypt and their possible Cretan imitations from the Mesara. | 61 |
| Figure 4:3 | Sites with Predynastic–Old Kingdom stone vessels found in Middle–Late Bronze Age contexts (1–5 examples per site unless otherwise stated; for further information, see Phillips 1992; Sparks 1998; Warren 1969). | 62 |
| Figure 4:4 | Egyptian anorthosite gneiss bowls and Cretan imitations. | 64 |
| Figure 4:5 | Chart of the use of imported travertine for Cretan stone vessel shapes (from Warren 1969 with a few additions). | 67 |
| Figure 5:1 | Map showing the context of interaction in the Late Bronze Age: Egypt and Hatti. | 76 |
| Figure 5:2 | Egyptian version of Egyptian-Hittite peace treaty, temple of Karnak (Kitchen 1982: fig. 24). | 93 |
| Figure 5:3 | Relief scene of battle of Kadesh, Luxor temple (after Kitchen 1982: fig. 19). | 95 |
| Figure 6:1 | Map showing the context of interaction in the Late Bronze and Iron Ages: the Assyrian expansion. | 102 |
| Figure 6:2 | The battle of Til-Tuba: the Assyrian forces drive the Elamites into a river. From Sennacherib's Palace, Nineveh, ca. 660–650 BC (Reade 1998: fig. 91). | 110 |

| | | |
|---|---|---|
| Figure 7:1 | Egyptian bronze statue of a man clothed in a panther skin, from the Heraion, Samos. Late eighth, early seventh centuries BC (© German Archaeological Institute, Athens). Height 26.6 cm. | 119 |
| Figure 7:2 | Egyptian bronze statuette of Neith, from the Heraion, Samos. Late eighth, early seventh centuries BC (© German Archaeological Institute, Athens). Height 22.5 cm. | 120 |
| Figure 7:4 | Faience figurine, female servant, from Kamiros, Rhodes. Mid-seventh century BC (© British Museum 64.10-7.1334). Height 9 cm. | 122 |
| Figure 7:5 | Temple of Apollo, Corinth, with detail of Doric capitals. Sixth century BC (© Bildarchiv Foto Marburg). | 127 |
| Figure 7:6 | Deir el-Bahri, Egypt. Portico of shrine of Anubis (15th century BC) (Coulton 1977: pl. 4). | 128 |
| Figure 7:7 | 'Treasury of Atreus', Mycenae, ca. 1300 BC. Restored elevation of façade (British School at Athens). | 128 |
| Figure 7:8 | Temple of Artemis, Ephesus. Commenced mid-sixth century BC; completed fifth century. Plan and reconstruction view (after Boardman *et al.* 1967; © Hirmer Verlag). | 130 |
| Figure 7:9 | Kouros, ca. 590 BC (© Metropolitan Museum of Art, New York). Height 193 cm. | 133 |
| Figure 7:10 | Kouros from Rhodes, sixth century BC (© British Museum B330). Height 24.5 cm. | 134 |
| Figure 7:11 | 'Nikandre'. Statue of a woman from Delos, ca. 640 BC (© German Archaeological Institute, Athens). Height 175 cm. | 135 |
| Figure 7:12 | Reconstruction of the grid system used to plan archaic kouroi (after Stewart 1997; © Candace Smith and A. F. Stewart). | 137 |
| Figure 10:1 | Religious activity at Abydos. | 172 |
| Figure 10:2 | Tomb painting of imaginary journey to Abydos, Beni Hasan. | 173 |
| Figure 10:3 | The 'Mortuary Temple' and 'Cenotaph' of Seti I, Abydos. | 175 |
| Figure 10:4 | Graffiti of various types and different languages from the Ramesseum, Abydos (top: PL 334; left bottom: PL 313; right centre: PL 385). | 176 |
| Figure 10:5 | Graffito of a palm, a foot and a flask, Abydos (PL 325). | 176 |
| Figure 10:6 | Abydos catchment area. | 182 |
| Figure 10:8 | Distribution of graffiti related to Serapis: hellenistic period. | 183 |
| Figure 10:7 | Distribution of Syllabic-Cypriot graffiti: classical period. | 183 |
| Figure 10:10 | Distribution of Egyptian graffiti. | 184 |
| Figure 10:9 | Distribution of graffiti related to Bes: Roman period. | 184 |

| | | |
|---|---|---|
| Figure 11:1 | Fragment from a marble frieze: a couple make love in a boat in a Nilotic and Mediterranean setting (British Museum GR 1865.11-18.252). Height 38 cm; width 39 cm; thickness 5 cm. | 192 |
| Figure 11:4 | Terracotta 'Campana' relief: a parody of life on the Nile. Princeton University Art Museum. Gift of Edward Sampson, Class of 1914, for the Alden Sampson Collection. | 195 |

## COLOUR SECTION

| | |
|---|---|
| Figure 4:6 | Stone vessels from the Isopata 'Royal Tomb' (the tomb plan is after Evans 1905: pl. xciii). Apart from the stone vessels shown here the tomb group also included one small bowl in local calcite and several serpentine lids. |
| Figure 7:3 | Faience double unguent vase of presenting servant, from Kamiros, Rhodes. Second-half seventh century BC; ht. 9.5 cm (British Museum 60.4-4.75). |
| Figure 11:2 | Painted panel from a colonnade: a parody of an Egyptian festival (Museo Archeologico Nazionale di Napoli I.N. 113195). |
| Figure 11:3 | Painted panel from a colonnade: a parody of a festive Egyptian symposium (Museo Archeologico Nazionale di Napoli I.N. 113196). |
| Figure 11:5 | Details of the Nilotic mosaic of Palestrina: the festival of the inundations of the Nile (© Stuto/Archeomedia). |
| Figure 11:6 | Symposium at the festival of the inundations of the Nile. Staatliche Museen zu Berlin, Preussischer Kulturbesitz, Antiken Sammlung Mosaic 3 (© Christa Begall). |

# A note on transliteration from ancient Egyptian

The ancient Egyptian scripts convey 24 consonants, no vowels. Fourteen of these occur in modern English, written with one letter: b, d, f, g, h, k, m, n, p, r, s, t, w, y. Three more are also found in English, but usually written with two letters: to keep transliteration as direct as possible, these are transliterated by Egyptologists as follows:

š    'sh' as in 'sheep'

ṯ    'ch' as in 'chin'

ḏ    as in 'j' and 'dg' of 'judge'

The other seven Egyptian consonants do not occur in written English, and are transliterated by Egyptologists as follows:

ȝ    the glottal stop (faintly heard if you start a sentence with a vowel in English)

i    a sound varying between glottal stop and y

ʿ    the 'ayin' of Arabic, a deep guttural clenching of the throat

ḥ    a stronger 'h', found in modern Arabic

ḫ    found in Arabic, the 'ch' of Scottish 'loch'

ẖ    a sound varying between ḫ and š

q    a form of 'k' pronounced deeper in the throat, and found in Arabic

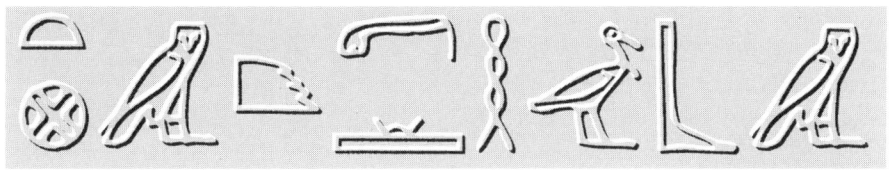

CHAPTER 1

# INTRODUCTION: THE WORLDS OF ANCIENT EGYPT – ASPECTS, SOURCES, INTERACTIONS

*Roger Matthews and Cornelia Roemer*

Through the millennia of its history, Ancient Egypt was viewed from a variety of perspectives by the peoples and states with whom it came into contact. And any given state or people could itself experience an almost limitless range of perspectives on Egypt through time, and also through its social strata, as its relationships with Egypt evolved. In this book we present a sample of those perspectives on Egypt from the ancient past, in order that we may appreciate as fully as possible the cultural, social and political contexts within which Egypt was situated. Broadly speaking, the chapters make use of two major categories of primary source, occasionally both: archaeology and written texts. A chronological dividing line between the two types of source occurs at roughly 1500 BC, so that chapters dealing with pre-1500 BC are essentially, but not exclusively, non-textual archaeological, while those dealing with periods from 1500 BC onwards rely more intensively on written sources. Any such dichotomy is at the same time a reflection of research choices leading to apparently differing availability of the sources, part of a trend whereby archaeologists have expended much of their efforts on earlier periods, electing not to invest energies in the excavation of later settlement sites, such as those of the Roman period, where rich textual sources are present.

The potential for historical archaeology in Egypt has yet to be fully realized (Funari *et al*. 1999). There exists great scope for the generation and application of approaches that tightly combine historical and archaeological theories and methods. The kinds of statements and interpretations that can be generated on the basis of the patchy and complex archaeological evidence are very different from, but often complementary to, those based on written sources, and it is important to ensure that interpretations based on one type of source are not judged by the criteria applied to another.

For the centuries after 800 BC, there is written evidence that allows different and sometimes 'closer' perspectives on Egypt. Authors from Greece and Rome reflected on Egypt and wrote down what impressed or appalled them. Their legacy has influenced the image of Egypt in ways that are different from the picture deriving from the archaeological sources alone. O'Connor (2003: 160) makes the point that 1000 BC marks a major change in the status of Ancient Egypt, with increasing dominance in subsequent centuries by external powers, including Nubians, Assyrians, Persians,

Macedonians and Romans. The fact of this dominance from outside opens up a range of sources for historians and archaeologists, many found within Egypt, that can be exploited in explorations of the nature of encounters with Egypt, and that is largely the approach employed by the authors in the second half of this volume.

In this opening chapter we explore some broad issues relating to the position of Ancient Egypt within its cultural and social worlds. In keeping with the structure of the book, the first part considers principally archaeological issues relating to ancient perspectives on Egypt, while more textual and historical issues are the focus of the second part.

## Archaeological (and textual) perspectives on Ancient Egypt

The perspectives discussed throughout this book, and indeed the book's title itself, are presented as *ancient* perspectives on Egypt. First and foremost, however, they are not ancient perspectives at all, but rather *modern* constructed archaeological and historical perspectives on how Egypt might have been viewed by a selection of its contemporaries. They are perspectives refracted through the lens of the evidence, and above all through the lens of how archaeologists and historians decide to recover, construct and examine that evidence. In this light, it becomes important to establish the nature of the lens itself, to determine how it is constructed, how powerful it is, what resolution of detail it might afford, and what distortions it might generate, as the past is examined through the looking glass. We need to consider how archaeology has approached the past of Egypt, and what perspectives it has generated, permitted and excluded through time.

The birth of Egyptian archaeology is conventionally ascribed to the Napoleonic expedition of 1798–1802 (see several chapters in Jeffreys 2003a). The discovery of the Rosetta Stone and subsequent decipherment of the Egyptian hieroglyphic script ensured that from its inception Egyptology was biased towards documentary sources. The divide between those who read texts and those who conduct archaeological investigations still characterizes Egyptology today, although there are increasingly bold attempts to transcend this artificial divide. Early Egyptology, like its sister disciplines across south-west Asia and much of the modern world, involved the unsystematic looting of rich archaeological sites, especially temples and tombs, with the aim of recovering spectacular objects and written texts that could adorn the museums of western Europe. A walk through the galleries of the British Museum in London, the Louvre Museum in Paris or the Berlin Aegyptisches Museum immediately gives some idea of the sorts of objects sought and obtained during the decades of the 19th and early 20th centuries. Weeks (1997: 68) has nicely caught the atmosphere of those pioneering, destructive expeditions:

> It was an exciting time: excavators plundered tombs, dynamited temples, committed piracy, and shot their competitors in order to assemble great collections.

At the turn of the 19th and 20th centuries, developments in the archaeology of Egypt were largely the result of the innovative work of Flinders Petrie, whose controlled excavations of cemetery and settlement sites were coupled with highly detailed analysis of excavated artefacts, especially pottery. Petrie's excavation and analysis by ceramic seriation of hundreds of graves from the predynastic Naqada period established a basic chronology for the fourth millennium BC that overall holds good to this day (Midant-Reynes 2000). An associated perspective that no longer finds adherents, by contrast, was his interpretation that the Naqada tombs represented evidence for a "New Race" or "Dynastic Race" of Asiatic conquerors who brought with them from outside Egypt the notion of pharaonic statehood.

Alongside Petrie's innovative and careful work, the first half of the 20th century saw a continuation of poorly executed and badly recorded explorations of tombs and temples, conducted within the 19th century paradigm of collecting for European museums. The development of contextual stratigraphic excavation, already well developed in Mesopotamia by German archaeologists in the first decade of the 20th century, took much longer to appear within Egyptian archaeology, partly as a result of the types of site being excavated. Deeply stratified, multi-period, mud-brick settlements such as Babylon and Assur in Iraq could be meaningfully explored only through the careful application of stratigraphic excavation and recording. While such sites did exist in Egypt, they were not the main target of excavators. A legacy of the early failure to develop contextual stratigraphic excavation in Egypt lingers on in the methodologically unsound practice of excavating in arbitrary spits, still employed on certain field projects in Egypt (Warburton 2000a: 1,734).

Changes in Egyptian archaeology came with the Nubian Salvage Campaign of the 1960s (but see Jeffreys 2003b: 6). An international appeal by Egypt and Unesco for participation in the salvage excavation of sites affected by the Aswan High Dam brought a host of new archaeologists into the country from Europe, North America and elsewhere. Egyptian archaeology was enlivened by the introduction of some new approaches to survey, excavation and analysis, rooted in the intellectual contexts of anthropological and ecological studies. Some of these proponents elected to stay on and run new projects elsewhere in Egypt. Current long-term, problem-oriented projects, such as excavations at Tell el-Amarna (Kemp 1989) and Tell ed-Dab'a (Bietak 1995), epitomize modern approaches.

Many perspectives on Ancient Egypt have undoubtedly been shaped by the particular history of the discipline sketched above. In terms of the excavated and published evidence, upon which interpretations must depend, there is naturally a bias towards tombs, temples and hieroglyphs, particularly in Upper Egypt. Baines (1988: 204) has written that "Egypt appears like an estate focused on the king and his burial, and only marginally like an urban society". But this appearance is very much the result of Egyptological focus on the elite elements of Egyptian society, the tiny minority of at most a few thousand males who attempted to impose an ideology on their own peoples, an ideology that still holds us in its power through our fascination with its surviving physical manifestations. Most of our recovered sources relate to these small elite groups, while by contrast great swathes of the population have stayed in the dark, silent spaces of history. If we excavated more settlements and private houses, explored more of how lower-class individuals, peasants, women, children, artisans and servants interacted with elite ideologies, as detectable in their material culture, we would undoubtedly find ways to see beyond the appearance of an estate devoted to the pharaoh and his mode of burial. We could at least delineate and amplify the nuances and variations in this conventional image of Egypt through space and time. More recent approaches in Egyptian archaeology, such as Kemp's excavations of the Workmen's Village at Tell el-Amarna, have started to provide some substance in this regard, for example by revealing that workers in the village continued to build shrines in their homes to the traditional Egyptian gods despite living in the new capital of Akhenaten whose sun-worship was officially viewed as the state's exclusive religion (Kemp 1989: 304; Meskell 2002: 11). Here, alongside their superficial allegiance to an elite ideology, as manifest at least in their enforced participation in the physical construction of its monuments, the workers of Amarna were at the same time sustaining and reifying, for us to discover if we look in the right places, their own side of a subtle discourse of power.

In another sense, in the context of Baines' characterization of Egypt as an estate focused on the pharaoh and his burial, Malek (2000: 111) has pointed out that such a position doubtless was the theoretical or ideological state of affairs but that produce grown, husbanded and offered to the pharaoh, his temples, and his shrines, in practice would be used to feed most of the Egyptian population. In this perspective, Egyptian non-elite elements will have been fully aware of the potential benefits to themselves of at least superficial adherence to an elite ideology, however that allegiance may have been formally expressed through rites and rituals.

The standards of survey and excavation employed, as much as the choice of site or region in which to work, have materially affected the quality and quantity of recovered sources. In connection with the failure of survey to discover evidence of Nubian Nile Valley settlements dating to the Egyptian predynastic and early dynastic periods, Baines has argued that Egyptian oppression of the local population "depressed the inhabitants' material culture below the archaeological 'threshold' for the methods of recovery used up to the 1960s" (Baines 1988: 205). We might then envisage a local Nubian population, perhaps aceramic, transhumant, and living in small dwellings built of perishable materials, whose archaeological traces will be recovered only, if at all, by appropriately nuanced, meticulous methods.

Another, broader issue of Egyptian archaeology that has been shaped by the history of the discipline is the way in which Ancient Egypt has been regarded as culturally *sui generis*. In the words of Savage (2001: 104):

> Egypt was viewed as a peculiar place, whose cultural history was perhaps so unique that it shed little new light on large theoretical issues.

Principally for this reason the study of Ancient Egypt has often stood outside the currents of theoretical developments that have swept through many other branches of the social sciences in recent decades (Champion 2003: 179–184; Jeffreys 2003b). If Egypt was unique, how could it inform on the development of civilization in the rest of the Old World and beyond? A bolder approach in recent years has at last brought Egypt into the arena of grand comparative studies, with results that are highly illuminating both for Ancient Egypt and for its selected comparanda (Baines and Yoffee 1998; Trigger 1993; Wenke 1989).

Finally, the potentials for interdisciplinary, innovative research in the field of Ancient Egypt were well stated almost 15 years ago by Wenke (1989: 132):

> If archaeological explanations can ever usefully incorporate social theory, Egypt would seem to be the ideal case to demonstrate this: its techno-environmental determinants are relatively simple, and its early evolution of a written language and elaborate material culture provide us with a long, rich record of ancient ideology. Thus, if current theoretical trends in archaeology continue, Egypt may once again become a primary data base for attempts to explain and understand cultural complexity.

The strengths of the ancient Egyptian archaeological and historical record are being exploited in increasingly holistic and interdisciplinary ways, as exemplified in the pioneering mix of textual, iconographic, archaeological and anthropological approaches employed in Meskell's (2002) study of private life in New Kingdom Egypt.

Keeping in mind these shifting archaeological perspectives, which constitute the lens through which we look at the past, how might we approach the issue of *ancient* perspectives on Egypt today? The remainder of this part of the introduction examines selected episodes in the early history of Egypt's encounters with external peoples and states, attempting to learn something of those encounters and perspectives themselves, while at the same time appreciating how the archaeological lens has shaped our visions.

## Contact: earliest encounters and the fourth millennium BC

Apart from palaeolithic encounters with Egypt, certainly as a route for migration from east Africa into the Levant and beyond (Hendrickx and Vermeersch 2000), the first major episode of external contact attested in the archaeological evidence is the adoption or introduction of agricultural practices in the later sixth millennium BC, including the husbanding of sheep and goats, and the raising of wheat and barley, at sites such as Merimda Beni Salama (Hassan 1995). The independent domestication of cattle in the Sahara region, however, indicates a strong local element in the adoption of farming and it may be too simplistic to see the introduction of farming into Egypt in the form of a complete package arriving wholesale from the Levant. In the light of the rather sparse archaeological information pertaining to this important period in Egypt, Wenke's (1989: 138) suggestion that substantial sedentary communities appear only *after* the adoption of agriculture, in contrast to the sequence in south-west Asia, may be a reflection of the fact that pre- and proto-neolithic settlements of Lower Egypt have been permanently eroded or, more probably, smothered in Holocene deposits from the Nile. Only carefully targeted future work can hope to address this issue of possible contacts between Egypt and south-west Asia in the Neolithic.

It is with the fourth millennium BC, particularly its latter part, that we are presented with a substantial body of archaeological evidence with which to consider the question of interactions between Egypt and one of its contemporaries, Mesopotamia. For a long time now there has been awareness of evidence for some form of contact between Mesopotamia and Egypt in the later fourth millennium BC (Frankfort 1941; Joffe 2000; Kantor 1992; Largacha 1993; Moorey 1987, 1998; Teissier 1987). The evidence takes the form of limited pottery parallels, a handful of cylinder seals from Egyptian tombs, a few shared artistic motifs, some rather tenuous architectural connections and, most impressively, large quantities of raw materials, such as lapis lazuli, that can only have reached Egypt through Mesopotamia from the Badakhshan region of Afghanistan. At a more structural level, it has also been argued that the idea of writing, but not the specifics, reached Egypt from Mesopotamia (Dalley 1998: 11), and that the notion of a 360-day year comprising 30-day months may also have reached Egypt from the sexagesimal Sumerians of Lower Mesopotamia (Warburton 2000b: 46).

Algaze's (1993) studies of Mesopotamia in the later fourth millennium, the Late Uruk period, while situating the so-called Uruk expansion within its international context, fail to consider the significance of the Egyptian connection. It seems clear, however, that the evidence for these early contacts is best viewed within the perspective of expanding Mesopotamian horizons through the fourth millennium, coinciding with an independent development of statehood in Upper Egypt. Interpretations of the origins and early development of social complexity in both Egypt and Mesopotamia conventionally lay great stress on the importance of trade, and control over access to raw materials, as stimulants to statehood. The shared cultural features of predynastic Egypt and Mesopotamia, as listed above, can all be viewed as elements of the 'high culture' defined by Baines and Yoffee (1998: 235) as "the production and consumption of aesthetic items under the control, and for the benefit, of the inner elite of a civilization, including the ruler and the gods".

The early development of statehood in Upper Egypt, later spreading to the north, coincided with the maximum diffusion of Mesopotamian influence, itself at least in part economically stimulated, and the assumption by the emerging Egyptian elite of the symbols and seals of a distant elite can be seen as a means, one amongst many, employed by that elite to underpin and expand its legitimacy, by importing and transforming elements of the high culture paraphernalia of a powerful but distant neighbour. The spread of Upper Egyptian complexity to Lower Egypt is likely to have been influenced by the elite's desire to control access to the raw materials and commodities reaching the Delta from a range of sources. It seems most likely that Mesopotamian influences, however diluted, were reaching Egypt by a sea route from the northern Levant, connected across land to the south Mesopotamian 'colonies' on the Euphrates (Mark 1998).

In no case is there evidence for persistent, intimate, face-to-face contact between Uruk Mesopotamians and Late Predynastic Egyptians, and all the raw materials, artefacts, motifs and intellectual notions reaching Egypt from or via Mesopotamia are transmuted into specifically Egyptian forms and contexts before they reach the archaeological record. Pittman's (1996) study of the Gebel el-Arak knife handle, with its imagery of a typical Uruk priest-king standing between two rearing lions, argues that motifs were adopted not so much for their specific Mesopotamian meanings but rather for the ways in which they operated as vehicles for the conveyance of meaning. Emergent Egyptian elites were thus adopting Mesopotamian high cultural traits, including the notion of writing, the administrative use of seals, high-status artistic motifs, and perhaps time-keeping, at structural and functional levels rather than as random pickings from the material culture of a far neighbour.

In a way this evidence tells us more about Egypt's perspective on the outside world than about external perspectives on Egypt, for no objects or commodities of Egyptian type dating to the fourth millennium have been found inside Mesopotamia.

Nevertheless, Mesopotamian traders, themselves tapping into long-established trade routes in materials such as gold, copper and lapis lazuli, must have been aware of Egypt and would have had experiences of it that have yet to be recognized in the archaeological record. Excavations of Lower Mesopotamian sites of this period have so far been extremely restricted, with the exception of Uruk-Warka itself. A resumption of excavations in south Iraq may in due course revolutionize understanding of this issue.

## Bronze Age contacts and perspectives

Through the centuries of the Bronze Age we gain more detailed and varying images of how Egypt interacted with its neighbours. Braun (Chapter 2) employs the archaeological evidence to demonstrate a hierarchy of Egyptian involvement in Early Bronze Age Levant, heavily rooted in trade in wine, timber and aromatic oils, while Sparks' (Chapter 3) study of Egyptian stone vessels found in the Levant explores mechanisms and modes of distribution of these distinctive artefacts. These forms of contact suggest a heavy exploitation of adjacent regions by a dominant Egyptian state in search of raw materials and commodities required by a well-established elite, even at the start of the third millennium or earlier. Thus, huge quantities of aromatic oils and wine attested in royal tombs of the earliest dynasties at Abydos in Upper Egypt demonstrate the importance of Levantine trade by the late fourth and early third millennia (Gophna 1998: 277–279; Shaw 2000: 321), and again stress the significance of control over that trade as a factor in the rise of the Egyptian pharaonic state. Persistent Egyptian influences attested at Byblos on the central Levantine coast indicate the importance of this port in channelling trade in timber and other commodities, and an archaeological insight into Byblos' perspectives on Egypt is vividly presented through the inclusion of Egyptian objects in the graves of the local elite at Byblos. In Marfoe's (1987: 32) words:

> The institutionalization of an Egyptian-oriented Byblian cult becomes understandable; as a guide and as a rationalization, facets of Egyptian civilization were translated into local idioms that became the cultural and ideological framework of a Byblian polity and the legitimizing prerogative of its elite.

A halt in the evidence for Egyptian-Mesopotamian contacts around 3000 BC coincides with a break in the flow of lapis lazuli into Egypt (Astour 1995: 1,405), and must be related to the collapse of the Uruk 'world system' at this time, to be replaced by a range of more local cultural entities across south-west Asia, including Jemdet Nasr in Lower Mesopotamia, Ninevite 5 in Upper Mesopotamia, and Proto-Elamite in Iran (Matthews 2002). By this stage, Egypt's well-developed political, social and cultural structures were resilient and self-sufficient enough to allow continued monolithic state development, in contrast to other regions of south-west Asia, which hosted more fragmented political entities, principally in the form of city-states. Contacts between Egypt and Lower Mesopotamia are barely attested through the third millennium, despite the fact that their spheres of interest, at least in terms of trade routes, must have intersected at many points. Rare cultural transmissions, such as that attested by the copper alloy relief of twin lions trampling naked victims found in the 'King's Grave' at the 'Royal Cemetery' of Ur (Hansen 1998: 67–68), may indicate continuing elite group interactions, or the movement of high-status goods in the form of booty in wars against intermediate states in Syria or the Levant (Reade 2001: 21).

Egyptian connections with Ebla in the third millennium are attested by stone vessel fragments, yielding a rare glimpse of Egyptian relations with north-west Syria in these centuries. In the ruins of 'Palace G' at Ebla, destroyed towards the end of the third millennium, many fragments of alabaster and diorite vessels were found, all comparable in form to well-known Egyptian types (Scandone Matthiae 1988). Two of the fragments display pharaonic inscriptions, one of Kafra (Khephren) of the fourth Dynasty, builder of the second large pyramid at Giza, and dated to the mid-third millennium, the other of Pepi I of the sixth Dynasty, of the later third millennium. Although Byblos is not mentioned in the cuneiform archives found at Ebla, it is nevertheless probable that Egyptian stone vessels were reaching Ebla through that port. As with the much earlier Mesopotamia-Egypt connections associated with the Uruk expansion, discussed above, lapis lazuli may have been an important element in these exchanges. Ebla was an important halting point along the lapis trade route from Afghanistan through south-west Asia and beyond. A total of some 22 kg of unworked lapis and many worked pieces were found in rooms of the 'Administrative Quarter' of Palace G, and it may be that precious Egyptian gifts, in the form of stone vessels and their contents, were reaching Ebla, whether or not via Byblos, in exchange for lapis lazuli and other commodities (Pinnock 1988).

A later find of an inscribed Egyptian artefact from Ebla suggests a perspective other than that of trading partner or courtly correspondent. From tombs of the Middle Bronze II period, of the 18th century BC, several Egyptian artefacts have been recovered, including faience vessels, scaraboid beads, items of gold, silver and ivory, alabaster vessels, and a ceremonial mace, adorned with applied hieroglyphs giving the name of the thirteenth Dynasty pharaoh Hotepibre. Scandone Matthiae (1988: 73) has suggested that this pharaoh, who designated himself "Son of Asia", may have had his origins in south-west Asia, perhaps at Ebla itself, and that the inscribed mace attests his desire to maintain links with his home town. However, Ryholt (1998) argues that the reading "Son of Asia" is incorrect, that the mace has no Egyptian parallels, that the reading "Hotepibre" is in doubt, and that the applied hieroglyphs on the mace came originally from another artefact. If Scandone Matthiae's speculative interpretations are correct, Ebla may have entertained a special perspective on Egypt in these years, as the birthplace of one of its pharaohs.

Egyptian interaction in the third millennium with the land of Punt, possibly located along the Red Sea coastal regions of southern Sudan and Somalia (but see Meeks 2003), was conducted on the basis of one-sided exploitation of the natural resources of Punt, including frankincense, myrrh, gold, ebony, gums, exotic animals, and slaves (Bryan 2000: 242; Potts 1995; Shaw 2000: 322–324). Expeditions to Punt were a royal prerogative, as depicted in detail on the temple reliefs of Queen Hatshepsut in the mid-second millennium BC. We have not so far recovered from the archaeological record any inkling of how the native peoples of Punt viewed their powerful neighbour to the north, but their perspective on Egypt, doubtless shared with many other of its silent partners of the past, may have consisted of terror and abhorrence. There may at the same time have been elements of Punt society who welcomed dealings and exchanges with Egypt.

With the onset of the Late Bronze Age, around 1500 BC, we are increasingly able to study relations between Egypt and its neighbours through both archaeology and documentary sources, sporadic as they are. Warburton's (Chapter 5) study of relations between Egypt and the Hittites makes extensive and innovative use of textual sources to this end.

Moorey (2001) has stressed the role of Late Bronze Age royal courts, and their interactions, as vehicles and stimuli for the transmission of technology. Through the later second millennium a broadening of international contacts between states such as New Kingdom Egypt, the Hittites of Anatolia, the Kassites of Babylonia, the Mitanni and the Assyrians of Upper Mesopotamia (Warburton and Matthews, Chapter 6), all of which were ruled by literate elites, encouraged the movement of crafts and artisans across large swathes of south-west Asia and beyond. Important technology transfers included the horse-drawn chariot, introduced from south-west Asia to Egypt at this time, and the relatively free movement of specialists such as physicians (ever-ready to pander to courtly hypochondria), musicians, architects, sculptors and builders. The stimulus to interaction provided by a second millennium arms race is indicated in the presence of specialist Hittite artisans at Piramesse in the eastern Nile Delta, attested by the use of stone moulds in the production of Hittite-type shields for the Egyptian army (Van Dijk 2000: 300). A key aspect identified by Moorey is the openness of Egypt to foreign contact subsequent to the Hyksos domination of the land earlier in the second millennium. Prior to the Hyksos, Egypt's imports had been restricted principally to tin, lapis lazuli, oils, resins, and timber. Following the Hyksos, Egypt participated much more intensively and profitably in the burgeoning international scene of the Late Bronze Age. As Moorey (2001: 12) puts it:

> Had it not been for the shock of the Hyksos, the Egyptians might well have gone on slowly developing traditional indigenous technologies without sudden, extremely significant infusions of foreign knowledge and skill.

In Chapter 4 Bevan examines interactions between Egypt and it neighbours across the sea to the north-west in the Aegean in the light of stone vessel exchanges. Egypt's borrowing of cultural traits from the Mesopotamian world in the later fourth millennium was conducted at a structural and functional level, rather than in terms of a random transfer of motifs and technology. Elite groups at Byblos in the Early Bronze Age structured their social dominance in life and death at least partly through the adoption of Egyptian cultural traits. There is good evidence that elite social structuring in the Late Bronze Age Aegean was also strongly influenced by the Egyptian model. In addition to the stone vessels discussed by Bevan, points of comparison include the practice of wall painting or frescoes. Egyptian frescoes of eighteenth Dynasty date at Tell ed-Dab'a in the eastern Delta attest connections with Cretan palace paintings, which they predate by more than a century, including bull-leaping scenes and the convention of portraying men with red/brown skin, women with white (Bourriau 2000: 216; Dickinson 1994: 89). Further structural connections may include the introduction to Minoan Crete of both sealing and writing as administrative acts, both perhaps learnt, as ideas only, from Egypt. Evidence from the Mari texts that merchants from Kaptara (Crete) were resident at the north Levantine port of Ugarit may indicate one potential locus of contact between Cretans, Egyptians, and others. Egyptian copies of the polychrome painted fine pottery of Crete, Kamares ware, as well as arguable Minoan influences on the metalwork buried under the Middle Kingdom temple of Montu at Tod in Upper Egypt, show that influences travelled both ways. Finally, wall paintings in tombs at Thebes in Egypt depict people described as coming from Keftiu, perhaps to be equated with Kaptara/Crete, "the Islands in the Midst of the Sea" (Cline and O'Connor 2003: 111), bearing tribute or gifts in the form of rhyta and bull figurines (Dickinson 1994: 248).

The international flavour of the Late Bronze Age is perhaps best encapsulated by a single extraordinary archaeological site, the shipwreck of Uluburun, located off the coast of south-west Turkey (Bass 1995). Complete excavation of the wreck, dated to the late 14th century BC, yielded a cargo of some 10 tons of copper, a ton of tin, 100 ingots of blue and turquoise glass, a ton of terebinth resin, and a vast range of exotic items such as ebony logs, ostrich shells, hippopotamus teeth, fruit and spices. One specifically Egyptian find in the wreck was a gold scarab bearing the name of Nefertiti, consort of Akhenaten, and items on the boat originate from areas as diverse as Africa, Babylonia, Syria, Palestine, Cyprus, the Aegean, and Europe. The total excavation of an intact site such as the Uluburun wreck gives some idea of the richness that is generally missing from the archaeological record, and at the same time lends some credence to what have been seen as grandiose pharaonic claims. From this single wreck, only some 16 m long, comes a vastly greater quantity of tin and copper than has been recovered from all excavated Late Bronze Age sites put together (Mark 1998: 125). The recovery of huge quantities of metal from one wreck puts into a new perspective claims such as those made by Amenophis II, of the eighteenth Dynasty, to have plundered 500,000 *deben* of copper from a single campaign in Syria (Bryan 2000: 252). On the basis of the Uluburun wreck, this apparently astonishing amount, about 54 tons, converts into a mere five and a half ship-loads.

Additionally, as Bass (1995: 1,429) puts it:

> The Uluburun ship points out the danger of basing archaeological theories on negative evidence, for none of its cargo would have been recognized as Near Eastern in origin had it reached its destination; the raw materials would have been quickly manufactured into products typical of the culture that imported them.

This cautionary note encourages us to stress that future archaeological investigations, perhaps especially of the numerous shipwrecks yet to be found and excavated in the eastern Mediterranean and beyond, are certain to amplify our understanding of how Egypt interacted with its neighbours through time.

## Textual (and archaeological) perspectives on Ancient Egypt

The notion of 'perspectives' involves a subject who views, and an object that is viewed. This book deals with Egypt as such an object. The perspectives change while the viewing subject and the viewed object change too. What is visible today is the result of this constant change on both sides. In this process, both partners can go through periods of taking no notice of each other or of close admiration, understanding, or aversion. The subject can have in mind a certain feature of the object and thus form a perspective on the object as a whole. There may be just a single class of people on the one side who form their view of just one class or one feature of the object on the other side. Perspectives in this sense are, by their nature, limited views. By following the changing perspectives, we learn about the object, but we learn even more about the subject, the one who views.

It is only from the time when we have written evidence of people's views on each other that we can recognize 'perspectives' in an articulated sense. The archaeological evidence of Egyptian ceramics in parts of the Mediterranean shows that people were open to that kind of product, maybe that they liked it, but does not necessarily imply a detailed knowledge of the country from which the pottery came beyond that it hosted potters who produced such a type of pottery. Thoughts of people are to some extent detached from archaelogical material, whereas in texts we trace their memories, fears and astonishment.

Greek and Roman viewers have left an enormous wealth of written evidence on what they thought about Egypt and the Egyptians (Tait 2003). Nevertheless, these texts are limited views; they were written by individuals who aimed at different audiences and served different purposes. There are the curious travellers, like Herodotus, who wanted to understand the world better, but still looked at the country with the eyes of the Greeks whose superiority was unquestioned, and there are poets like Horace who served a regime that was hostile to the Egyptian queen. Both authors are eclectic in their perspectives, but they both represent approaches to a foreign country that are typical for their times. With Herodotus, it is the political self-consciousness of the Greeks after the Persian wars that generated his views on a 'barbarian' country, but at the same time, he respected the superiority of Egyptian culture in terms of its old age and wisdom (Harrison, Chapter 8). For Horace, the Augustan propaganda formed the image of the seductive, barbarian queen who worships gods in animal shape; but at the same time there seems to be a more favourable view in his poem (Maehler, Chapter 12).

The literary sources reflect the views of an elite. They are written to inform, educate or entertain the elite. Archaeological finds from elite contexts correspond to these views inasmuch as they are the expression of the elite's *Lebensgefühl*. Such correlations can be detected between archaic Greek art and literature, and in the art and literature of the early Roman Empire. The stimulus for this correlation is dictated by the ruling class.

Written documents like the numerous papyri excavated in Egypt from the end of the 19th century are a different kind of evidence. They contain contracts, private letters, orders of arrest, love charms and curses, and concern the daily life of mostly ordinary people. The perspective that Greeks living in Egypt had on their Egyptian environment shows itself at random in these documents. They, nevertheless, are a unique source for understanding the life of people of all classes, and provide a counterpart to the archaeological finds from outside the kings' palaces and grand temples.

Herodotus and other Greeks of the fifth century BC recognized that Egypt was different from other 'barbarian' countries. All people who did not speak Greek were considered barbarians, with features that the Greeks despised. They were either loathsome tyrants, devious magicians, or dull and effeminate pleasure-seeking individuals. But Egypt had more to offer; like India, it was full of old and venerable wisdom. For the Romans, the negative side of the Greek image of the 'barbarians' prevailed, for this image served the ruling political class of the time. Thus, the perspective on Egypt mirrors the perspectives of the Greeks and Romans on themselves. For the Greeks, Egypt was, at least in some respects and for some time, a challenge to their self image, while for the Romans it was a country to be subdued.

In the long period of time before Alexandria was founded, Egypt was not an obvious counterpart for the people who dwelled on the shores of the Mediterranean. She must have seemed more like the 'Country behind the Seven Mountains' to those who sailed to the ports of Cyprus, Crete, Sidon or Byblos. Egypt did not have a harbour on her northern coast; Rhakote, where Alexander was to found his city, enjoyed the sleepy existence of a small fishing village. The capital of the country lay far inland, finding its place only in the latest period in the Delta, at Sais, closer to the northern shore than ever before (except for a short period under Seti I and Ramesses II). In the Saitic period (664–525 BC), Egypt started to look more intensively towards the Mediterranean and the Greek speaking world. The perspective on each other changed on both sides.

It may be assumed that the Egyptians were no great seafarers themselves. Their sea was the Nile, and goods were brought into the country to a large extent on the land routes or along the shores of the Red Sea and the Mediterranean (O'Connor and Reid 2003: 15; for the scarce evidence of ships built for the use on open water, see Casson 1995). That she had not been isolated, though, from her neighbours to the east is shown by the archaeological finds of Egyptian stone vessels and pottery in the Near East and Levant, and her relationships with Asian rulers over long periods of time (see above and Chapters 2–6).

Archaeological evidence indicates that by 660 BC Greek settlers had established the harbour of Naucratis for the exchange of commodities in the western Delta, not far from the capital Sais. The first of these settlers had not come as colonists as the Greeks colonized many other places, founding cities and giving them Greek laws and governments. The settlement of Naucratis was granted by the Egyptian pharaoh Psammetichos I, the first king of the Saitic Dynasty. The Greeks had to obey strict regulations about where to open their trading places and where to move around in the country, if at all (Möller 2000: 184–215; for the dating see Venit 1988).

Egypt must have been special for the first Greek settlers as she had been for Greek and Carian mercenaries who had come to the country to serve the pharaoh. Psammetichos I also established a camp of Greek mercenaries in the Delta, and the newcomers seem to have accepted willingly the conditions placed on them. The image of the country they came to may have prepared them for special conditions. Egypt was immensely rich, it had a powerful king, and it was full of marvels. Some graffiti show that the country's guests appreciated the marvellous buildings of the pharaohs as sites on which they wanted to leave a mark of their presence. The graffiti of Greek mercenaries at Abu Simbel and Abydos (Jeffery 1990: 354–359; Rutherford, Chapter 10) illustrate their awareness and curiosity for the marvels of Egypt well before Herodotus came to the Nile. What Herodotus (III.139) claims to be the reality of the time of Cambyses may well have been influenced by his own time, but rooted to some extent in the seventh and early sixth centuries as well: "They came to trade, to be soldiers, or just to see the country."

At the end of the eighth century, Egypt had reached the horizon of the Greek speaking world. When people were listening to the rhapsodes performing Homer's songs they heard of the Nile, of the king's power and hospitality, and of the immense richness of the country. But Egypt is, in Homer, still the 'Country behind the Seven Mountains'. It is reached by a "long and difficult way" (*Odyssey* IV.483). Even the island of Pharos is located wrongly, far distant from the Nile. Menelaus encounters here gods of the sea, not human beings. The sea god Proteus is just another fabulous creature who constantly changes his appearance. Menelaus has to disguise himself as a seal in order to catch him. Within the epic poem, the perspective changes: Odysseus' account of his visit to Egypt may have more of a real background (*Odyssey* XIV.257 ff; cf. Austin 1970: 12). It may reflect the raids of Cretan pirates on the northern part of the country in the eighth century. Odysseus claimed that his companions went to the villages in the Delta, killed men and abducted women and children, but that he himself enjoyed the protection of the king. As always in the Homeric poems, there is no problem of language or understanding. Egyptians communicate with Odysseus as all other people of foreign countries do (even the Cyclops on his isolated island speaks Greek). The Greeks had not yet begun to classify 'people' by their different languages (Dihle 1994: 16). The view of Egypt's people was generalized, while particularizing their enormous wealth and craftsmanship.

Already in the *Iliad*, the wealth of Thebes is notorious. For Achilles, the richness of that Egyptian city is topped by "gifts as many as the sand or the dust is" (*Iliad* IX.381–385; cf. *Odyssey* IV.126–127). The precious materials and the craftsmanship of Egyptian household articles that Menelaus received as gifts from his Theban friends add to Helen's god-like appearance in front of Telemachus (*Odyssey* IV.120–137).

This view seems to correspond with the archaeological evidence of the Greek archaic period. Egyptian craftsmanship was influential on the art and craftsmanship in the architecture, sculpture, and faience production of the time (Tanner, Chapter 7). The perspective on Egypt may be described as openness towards the skills of the people from the Nile Valley, admiration, maybe, for what they could do in handling stone and other materials, and for their ability to produce life-size or even larger sculpture and to assemble columns higher and bigger than any living tree. The fact that the result of this influence was a temple very different from the Egyptian temple in layout and outer appearance does not exclude the admiration that the Greek-speaking craftsmen had for their Egyptian colleagues. In the "widely shared culture of ideological materialization common to the eastern Mediterranean world" (Tanner, Chapter 7) that saw tyrants rising and looking for means to make their power visible to others, the transfer of technology may just be a small element that expresses itself more clearly than the ideology of the self that developed in different ways in different parts of the Mediterranean at that time. Greek sculptors have names that remained connected to their work, while Egyptian artists are anonymous. Greek sculptors never added a back pillar to their statues as Egyptians sculptors did. It seems that at one level technologies were borrowed, while at other levels the transfer did not occur. Two hundred years later, Herodotus will claim that the names and cults of the Greek gods derive from the Egyptian gods.

Solon is said to have travelled to Egypt in the 10 years after he had given new laws to the Athenians (between 594 and 584 BC). "To be away from the city, so that the

Athenians would not be able to force him to change any of the laws, and to see the world" as Herodotus (I.29–30) says. But King Amasis in Sais is just one station on the journey (*theoria*) that Solon continues to Sardes to see Kroisos. Solon does not go to Egypt to get inspiration for his laws. When Herodotus (II.177) later says that Solon had taken the idea of tax laws from Amasis, this second view may reflect the image Herodotus' own time had of Egypt. Two centuries later, Plato has Solon asking the priests at Sais about the "oldest stories" that were expected from the Egyptians (*Timaeus* XXIe–XXVd). Plato has a different perspective on Egypt. Before that, the first part of the "period of travellers" (Assmann 2000: 24) sees the Greeks more as recipients of skills and beholders of the marvels of the country.

This Egyptian discourse receives new dimensions the more the Greeks developed their curiosity about their own world and the worlds of others (cf. Hornung 2001). Saitic Egypt, with her turning back to the great pharaonic times and her consciousness of a great cultural past, the memory of which reaches back to a time long forgotten ("Saitic Renaissance": Assmann 2000: 15–16), is seen as the teacher of knowledge and wisdom, for she is recognized for her old age and for her wisdom that derives from that antiquity. It seems to be especially this "cultural memory" (Assmann 2000: 15–16) of Saitic Egypt that determines the image of Egypt in later Greek generations. When Solon stays with the priests in Sais, Plato says, he is teased by them "as the Greeks are always children", and "their souls are always young, because they do not have any old opinion about anything nor any knowledge which has grown old by time" (*Timaeus* XXIIb).

When Herodotus travels to Egypt (around 420 BC), the country is ruled by the Persians and is trying to keep her identity by looking back to the Saitic period and the 'cultural memory' of that time. Herodotus already knew a lot about the country he came to. The geographer Hekataios of Miletus had been here, and his narration of what he had seen was widely read (most of it is lost today). Athenian soldiers had sailed up the Nile to Memphis to support a revolt against the Persian occupation (Thucydides I.104). By this time, the horizons of the Greeks had further expanded. For centuries, they had founded colonies around the Mediterranean, and had started to ask new questions. Maps of the known world were drawn, they became interested in the origins of everything, and developed a curiosity for others. Odysseus' experience of having seen "many people's cities and having understood their way of life" (*Odyssey* I.3) becomes a thought pattern.

It seems that Egypt stimulated their interest more than other countries did. The enigma of the Nile flood had aroused first the fantasy and now the scientific curiosity of philosophers and travellers. The fact that the form of government in Egypt was considered as very stable (lasting through different dynasties) evoked curiosity about Egyptian laws and constitutions. But the religion remained an oddity with its animal cults and too many different gods (as it seemed) of whom only Isis and Osiris were recognized in every part of Egypt (Herodotus II.42).

Herodotus shows curiosity for all these different features. He also has an enormous admiration for the craftsmanship of the Egyptians, less for the preciousness of the materials and the finesse of their elaboration (as in Homer) than for the monumentality of the buildings. The pyramids and the labyrinth are admired especially for the countless workmen involved in the construction of the chambers they contain. But he also claims that Egyptian priests may be dishonest; the view that all Egyptians are cunning becomes a recurrent feature in the perspectives on the country (cf. Hyperides, *Against Athenogenes* III).

Thus, Herodotus' "account – far from representing an elite intellectual viewpoint opposed to popular prejudice – is, at least in its selection of themes and topics, in fact rooted in a broader, more popular milieu" (Harrison, Chapter 8). This more popular view is now, by Herodotus' time, characterized by the self esteem of the Greeks as special human beings who assembled against the Persians and were able to defeat them. The experience of the successful fight against Persia united the Greeks in drawing a clear line against the 'barbarians' who were beyond the lines of their own 'Greekness' (Hall 1989).

Herodotus knows the story of Helen whom Paris was forced to leave behind in Egypt under the guardianship of the just King Proteus (!). For him, there is no question that Helen stayed in Egypt. "Would the Trojans have been so stupid not to deliver Helena if she had been at Troy while the Greeks besieged the city?" (II.120), his enlightened mind asks. Egyptian priests confirm this version. Here, in contrast to the popular view of the craftiness of the Egyptians, the country with its old age and wisdom is credited with the knowledge of something that the Greeks would have considered genuinely theirs. This is a step yet further than admiring and crediting them for the invention of a good calendar or even claiming that the names and cults of Greek gods were inherited from the Egyptians who were so much older than the Greeks (Harrison, Chapter 8). But it is the distant past as well as the more recent past about which the Egyptians are believed to have the ultimate knowledge and in which they play a decisive role.

Stesichoros, who composed choral lyric songs about 600 BC, seems to have adjusted the Homeric story of Helen and her kidnapping by Paris to a narration about a phantom being brought to Troy. The real Helen never reached Asia Minor but stayed in Egypt with Proteus, where she was finally rescued by Menelaus (*Palinodia* I). Probably Stesichorus used this adjustment with regard to the sacredness of Helen's cult at Sparta, and Egypt would have offered herself as an appropriate place in the story, exotic and still somewhat removed. Herodotus does not mention the phantom. For him, Helen's stay in Egypt is not mentioned in Homer, but is at least made very plausible by the words of the epic. Herodotus finds an explanation in Homer; Stesichorus, as far as we know, had not asked for it (Davison 1968: 196–225; Kannicht 1969: 26–48).

Not very many years after Herodotus brought back his stories and observations from the Nile, Euripides put his *Helen* on the stage of the theatre of Dionysus at Athens (412 BC); the plot is situated in Egypt and the play ends with the flight of Helen and Menelaus from the country. The cleverness of the Greeks has overcome the awkwardness of the barbarian Egyptians and their ruler, a lewd tyrant. It is striking that there is no attempt by Euripides to give this play a genuine flavour of Egypt. In the first verses of the play, Helen indicates that "these are the Nile's fair virgin's dreams" (*Helen* vv. 1–2). Thus, the scene is set; no more about the river, the desert, palm trees, or crocodiles. All parts of the play have Greek names, the king goes out hunting wild boars, the king's palace is on the shore, etc. The country is just "wild" and "barbarian" and that is enough. The Athenian audience's perspective on Egypt was determined by their perspective on other non Greek speaking countries. Curiosity for all the other marvellous features did not have a place in the theatre. Here the political self assertion of the Athenians was more important (Hall 1989).

Such was not Alexander's frame of mind when he entered Egypt in December 332 BC. His knowledge of and openness towards the ideas of religion and kingship of the country on the Nile determined his successful arrival and first encounter with the Egyptians. He allowed (and wanted) the oracle at Siwa to make him the son of the sun god Amun, and most probably he was crowned in the pharaonic ritual in Memphis with the consent of the powerful Egyptian priesthood. Alexander seems to have looked on Egypt with respect for her ancient traditions. This view persisted into the age of the Ptolemies, whose dynasty was to run the country for the next 300 years. Egyptians had to suffer little discrimination, the Greek rulers adopted their religious ideas and allowed the Egyptian legal system to remain in place (La'da, Chapter 9). Despite some revolts in Upper Egypt, the cohabitation of Greeks and Egyptians in the Ptolemaic period seems not to have been too problematic. The little evidence of opposition literature does not encourage a national rebellion (Koenen 2002: 187).

The Ptolemies had understood, as Alexander had, that to handle the institutions of the country with respect would be not just appropriate; it would also be the most practical attitude. This understanding shows not only respect for the subdued 'barbarians' but also a certain admission of inferiority which seems to conflict with the self-assured attitudes towards all non Greek speaking people. The image Egypt had gained in the meantime had strengthened the elements that had been part of that image from the beginning. Her wealth now attracted hundreds of thousands of immigrants who saw the Ptolemaic kings as the successors of a monarchy that had been stable for thousands of years. Indeed, the Ptolemies adopted the ideology of pharaonic kingship (Koenen 1993).

But Egypt now did not just attract soldiers, merchants and travellers (Butler 2003). With the foundation of the museum and its library in Alexandria, the first Ptolemies built a centre for learning and research that was to become the "shrine of Greekness" in a foreign land, now ruled by Greeks. The library contained copies of all known Greek literature, and industrious scholars worked assiduously on Homer, the archaic lyric poets and other texts to establish the best text, or what they thought was the text which was closest to what the poet had written. Ships were detained in the harbour so that government officers could seize any valuable books on board. Famous doctors from Cos and Cnidos, the established centres of the time for medicine, worked in the museum, as did astronomers and geographers. The research programme of that 'university' included all areas of the visible world, thus following the path of Aristotle's *Peripatos* in which the understanding of the world was derived from its many different visible features. Did the Ptolemies just want to claim their place amongst the other hellenistic states as the real heirs of the Athenian cultural heritage, or was there also the idea of establishing a counterpart to the surrounding Egyptian culture that Herodotus and others had described? The Egyptian approach, however, to questions posed by the visible world, as for instance the enigma of the Nile flood, was different. It can be characterized as consultations of their holy books from which they deduced interpretations rather than explanations (Assmann 2000: 59), whereas the Greeks observed related phenomena and deduced explanations from their comparison. If the Ptolemies had understood the difference of approach in these terms, it seems reasonable to understand their plan of the museum and its library as a deliberate competition with the achievements of their new country. Their respect for Egypt did not lead, though, to an open-minded attitude towards those living in the chora, i.e. those living outside Alexandria. As far as the evidence goes, none of the Ptolemies before Cleopatra VII ever tried to learn Egyptian; the Greek poets working in Alexandria took little notice of the country and its marvels. Posidippus writes epigrams on all sorts of buildings at Alexandria, landmarks of the greatness of her rulers such as the Pharos, but not on the pyramids. The city on the sea was "*Alexandria ad Aegyptum*" as the Romans called her, not "*in Aegypto*".

Religion was another challenge. As far as the evidence goes, there are no cremations, not even in Alexandria, after the third century BC. The attraction of the idea that the unharmed body would be necessary for the afterlife of the individual had taken root in the minds of the Greeks. Mummification was widespread at all levels of the population, provided that people could afford it. The temples that the Ptolemies built looked like Egyptian temples and functioned as houses of the gods in the way temples had functioned in pharaonic times. Greeks living in the country had overcome the old aversion to animal-shaped gods. When, at the beginning of the first century BC, a priest in Upper Egypt, drawing up a Greek contract, presents himself as a "priest of Aphrodite and Souchos" (*P. Köln* I: 50) we can be sure that the statues in his temple bore the cow head of Hathor, and the crocodile head of Souchos.

But the rejection of the Egyptian gods remained a vigorous part of the perspective on the country of those abroad. Cicero (*De republica* III.9), in the first century BC, still denounces the cult of animal gods whom he calls monsters. The dog-like Anubis is a cheap object of attack for all those who in fact want to castigate the Egyptian queen, Cleopatra (Maehler, Chapter 12).

Nevertheless, from the second century BC onwards Egyptian religion became widespread around the Mediterranean. Isis and Serapis appealed also to non-Egyptians, the latter being a creation of the first Ptolemies, presenting an amalgam of Zeus and Osiris. Already at the end of the fourth century, Isis had been worshipped in Attica, but now she had sanctuaries in Italy and even further to the west (Takács 1995). Isis and Serapis usually appear in human form, which may have made them more acceptable, but the connection to animal worship remained a visible feature when Isiac priests marched in processions wearing the mask of the dog-shaped Anubis (Apuleius XI.11.1).

The spread of these cults gave a new turn to the Egyptian discourse of the peoples around the Mediterranean. Now, something which was recognizable as truly Egyptian had become part of their daily lives. Evidence for the cult of Isis includes remains of her official sanctuaries (e.g. at Pompeii) and texts that deal on a highly sophisticated level with the religion (Apuleius, Plutarch), as well as objects and wall decoration from private houses of the lower and upper classes.

The message to the followers of Isis and Serapis was easily understood and open to everybody: Isis ruled the underworld, she was the one who had rescued her brother and husband Osiris from death and had resurrected him. Isis was also the goddess of the sky, of fertility and of seafaring, thus incorporating Greek features that she had not held in the pharaonic period. In her, the power of all the other gods was united. Isis could be Demeter, Aphrodite, and any other goddess and fulfil the functions of all of them (Merkelbach 1995: 94–101). She promised individual protection in life, and help against the dangers of the underworld. Meeting with the philosophy of the Stoics in this nearly monotheistic concept, the cult of Isis can be seen as an expression of the same understanding of the world. But while the Stoic philosophy reflected the *Lebensgefühl* of the elite, Isis and Serapis were worshipped by the lower classes. Theirs was not a religion concerned with the affairs of the state; it spoke to the individual and promised everybody a chance in the afterlife. It was this individualistic concept of religion that prevented for a long time the founding of an Isis temple at Rome while urban centres all over Italy had already established temples and sanctuaries for her. Only at the end of the Roman Republic was the first temple of Isis opened in the heart of Rome when the insistence of her followers had become too disquieting for the ruling class (Cassius Dio XLVII.15.4; Maehler, Chapter 12).

From 30 BC onwards, Egypt is part of the Roman Empire. The defeat of the last Egyptian queen, Cleopatra VII, and her lover, the Roman general Marc Antony, moves Egypt closer to the Romans and alienates her at the same time. Augustus' propaganda against his rivals exploits the old prejudices against the country that had been common for centuries: the animal-shaped gods of the Egyptians and their sexual licentiousness, the latter being a connotation of all barbarians and now showing in the behaviour of the Egyptian queen. These two patterns of aversion recur in the works of poets who support Augustus, and determine Egypt's image in the poetry of the following centuries (Maehler, Chapter 12).

A different path is taken up in the decoration of Roman houses and gardens, making visible the strong dividing line which runs between official and private perspectives. Egyptian landscapes in miniature are created in the gardens of Pompeii's rich, showing that the cult had reached the upper classes (wall decorations in these houses disclose their inhabitants as followers of Isis).

But apart from the religious context, Egyptian motifs such as palm groves with exotic birds, hippopotamus and crocodiles, or even priestesses of Isis, seem to have been disconnected from their 'barbarian' background and now only serve the quest for the exotic (de Vos 1980: 75–76). Even the house of Augustus' wife Livia bore such decorations. In 10 BC, the Roman knight Caius Cestius Epulo had a tomb erected for him by his heirs in the shape of an Egyptian pyramid (Humbert 2003: 38).

Emperors like Claudius and Nero, and Caligula in particular, are attracted by the exotic, and above all by the exoticism of Egypt, looking back, it seems, to their 'Egyptian' ancestor Antony (Walker, Chapter 11). Their inclination towards the country on the Nile may have incited the caricatures showing black pygmies fighting with hippopotamus and making love to white women in boats floating between these exotic animals (Walker, Chapter 11; see cover illustration).

Whether as a source of religious inspiration or as the exotic country absolute, Egypt had become part of the Greco-Roman world around the Mediterranean. More intimate experience produced more refracted perspectives. Still the old age of Egypt and her marvels are considered a reason to visit the country (Tacitus, *Annales* II.59 on

Germanicus' journey to Egypt "*cognoscendae antiquitatis*"). The *topoi* of Augustan propaganda remain a fossil restricted to Roman poetry.

Apuleius, a lawyer from north African Madaura, who had enjoyed the typical education of the upper classes in Greece and had stayed in Rome for some time, writes a novel at the end of which he reveals his affiliation to the cult of Isis. *Metamorphoses*, or *The Golden Ass* as St Augustine called it, tells the story of a young man who, by reason of his curiosity, is transformed into a donkey, and regains his human shape having recognized the power of Isis. Written in Latin in the second century AD, this is the most extended description of the Isiac cult. Apuleius is trained in philosophy and rhetoric, and his first concern is not to recruit new followers. The novel seems to play with platonic concepts, cultic mysteries and pure entertainment on different levels, thus being a typical product of the 'Second Sophistic' (Harrison 2000a). What Apuleius (*Metamorphoses* II.28 ff) is interested in is not the exotic but rather the marvellous in the Egyptian priest who is able to resurrect a dead body and have him speak if only for a short time. The perspective in his book is not focused on Egypt as a country but on the religious experience that derives from Egypt but has become available all over the empire. The Nile only plays a part in ritual formulae, Isis is the goddess of "a thousand names" who is venerated in all parts of the world (*Metamorphoses* XI.5).

What the Greek polymath Plutarch (*De Iside et Osiride* 377F) writes about Isis and Osiris shortly before Apuleius could be taken as a commentary on the relationship of Greek and Egyptian gods as they were seen by this time:

> Nor do we regard the gods as different among different people nor as barbarian and Greek and as southern and northern. But just as the sun, moon, heaven, earth and sea are common to all, though they are given various names by the varying peoples, so it is with the one reason (*logos*) which orders these things and the one providentia which has charge of them, and the assistant powers which are assigned to everything: they are given different honours and modes of address among different peoples according to custom.
>
> (trans. J. Gwyn Griffiths)

In Greek narrative, on the other hand, Egypt remained the exotic land, still showing all the features that had given rise to the prejudices against it, but which were also the source for its admiration. In all Greek novels which have come down to us, Egypt plays a prominent part as a country where the heroes are bound to find themselves facing dangers that are less articulated in other countries: human sacrifices, pirates ready to kill everybody, and lecherous women, but they also encounter wise men here (Kalasiris in Heliodor's novel; for a general introduction see Holzberg 1995).

The dichotomy of perspectives between fascination and aversion that had determined Herodotus' view when he travelled to Egypt in the fifth century BC was still felt. But as Egyptian religion was increasingly accepted, and the country was absorbed into the Greco-Roman world, perspectives had shifted. Isis had become Venus, and the 'barbarian' had become the 'exotic', belittled and caricatured in the wall decorations of Roman houses.

## Modes of interaction, types of perspective

On the basis of these highly diverse strands of textual and archaeological evidence scattered over a period of several millennia and a geographical range of hundreds of thousands of square kilometres, it is clear that ancient perspectives on Egypt were generated, maintained, shaped and altered through the combined effects of a great range of highly variable factors. Perspectives on Egypt were substantially dependent upon the ways in which Egypt, as the most powerful regional polity for much of its existence, behaved towards others. The following table considers some of these possible interactions, several of which could naturally co-exist in time and space, and their associated perspectives on Egypt from outside.

| Mode of interaction | Perspective on Egypt from foreign party |
| --- | --- |
| Trade between equals | Opportunism, entrepreneurship, stimulus to arts and crafts, sharing of symbolic and/or structural traits |
| Diplomacy between equals | Gift exchange, movement of royal brides and dowries between courts, exchange of embassies, stimulus to trade and production, exchange of religious and cultic notions and practices |
| Warfare between equals | Fear, aggression, hatred, arms race, definition of borders, exchange of technology in peace intervals, movements of populations |
| Warfare by Egypt against weaker nations | Dread, terror, regional abandonment, collapse of complexity, cultural suppression |
| Economic exploitation by Egypt of weaker region | Terror, resentment, development of local polities involved in material acquisition, depredation of physical and cultural environment |
| Egypt as victim | Aggression, greed, exploitation, plundering, looting, romanticization of Egypt |

In looking at perspectives on Ancient Egypt, it is clear through the following chapters that approaches are at the same time constrained and empowered by the quality and quantity of available sources. These sources are themselves the product of specific interests and field programmes of researchers into Ancient Egypt. The next major step forward in the study of the Egyptian past will undoubtedly be an increased commitment to the development of research programmes that employ highly integrated, inter-disciplinary approaches to the contextual study of all available sources, textual and non-textual, for which Egypt is especially suited.

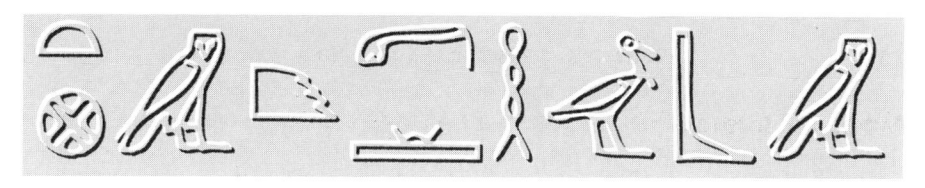

**CHAPTER 2**

# SOUTH LEVANTINE ENCOUNTERS WITH ANCIENT EGYPT AT THE BEGINNING OF THE THIRD MILLENNIUM

*Eliot Braun*

## Introduction

Recent excavations at sites in central Israel and in the Palestinian Autonomous Zone of Gaza have unearthed important new information on interconnections between Egypt and this part of the southern Levant that is revolutionizing perceptions of the archaeological record of the late fourth and early third millennia BC. These new discoveries are yielding hard evidence for what may be the key to understanding the nature of the relationship between the southern Levant and the Nile Valley within that time span. The relevant finds include large quantities of Egyptian-related material, Nile Valley imports and objects of local origin with definitively Egyptian associations that need to be explained. By considering this new information, and by re-interpreting earlier data from the archaeological record in Egypt and the southern Levant, I propose a model for understanding the nature of Egyptian-south Levantine encounters at the dawn of history (see Table, p. 37).

## Towards a model for evaluating Egyptian encounters in the southern Levant

Archaeological data presently available suggest that within the chronological parameters of a developed (i.e. late) EB I and early EB II (= 'Early Bronze Age'; i.e. ca. late fourth and early third millennia; Braun 2001) and a somewhat circumscribed locality or 'core area,' roughly encompassing the northern Negev and the southern Shephela (a piedmont between the coastal plain and the central, mountainous region) of Israel, and corresponding latitudes of the Mediterranean littoral (located within Israel and the Palestinian Autonomous Zone of the Gaza Strip; Figure 2:1), indigenous south Levantines encountered Egyptian influence on a scale that ranges from massive to virtually nil.

Examining the archaeological record of the relevant, major south Levantine sites within this core area allows us to quantify the magnitude and type of Egyptian influence; the evidence is found in the artefacts they have yielded. The results form a rather variegated and interesting patchwork of information offering a still somewhat sketchy, but nevertheless fascinating, picture of south Levantine EB I people's 'encounters with Ancient Egypt'. They suggest a history of progressive development over a time trajectory that mirrors changing political and social realities. While there is nothing new in this general observation, recent detailed increments in knowledge of the archaeological record help to draw a more accurate picture of this relationship than was possible just a few years ago.

Available evidence suggests that it is possible, within limitations, to grade the degree of Egyptian influence on EB I sites in the southern Levant in a roughly tripartite hierarchical system, the basics of which were set forth by E. C. M. van den Brink (1998). The hierarchy suggested here is based on three major parameters: (a) relative chronology; (b) the relative size of a site; and (c) the degree to which Egyptian influence is apparent in the material culture assemblage a site has yielded to date. It should be noted that in the first instance information is probably most reliable because it is based on known, quantifiable parameters. In the second instance site-size parameters

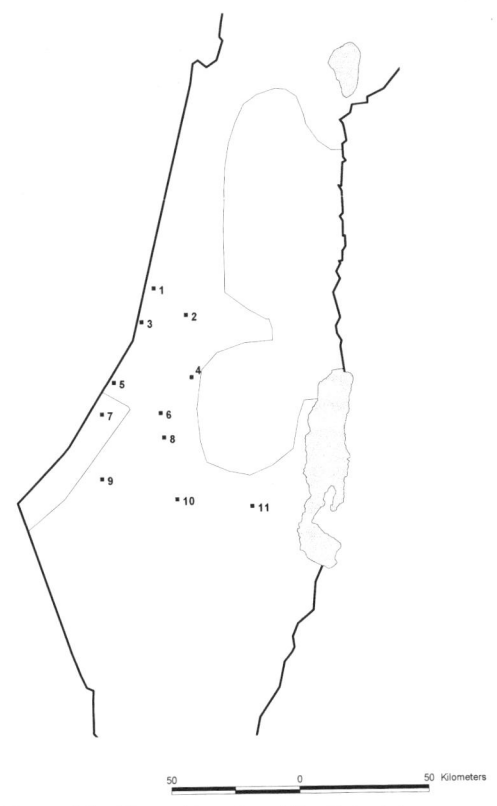

Figure 2:1  Map of Israel and the Palestinian Autonomous Zones with sites where Egyptian and Egyptianized artefacts have been found:
1 Azor; 2 Lod; 3 Palmahim Quarry; 4 Horvat 'Illin Tahtit; 5 Afridar (Ashqelon); 6 Tel Erani; 7 Tell es-Sakan; 8 Tel Ma'ahaz; 9 'En Besor; 10 Tel Halif; 11 Arad.

are often absent and poorly understood; in virtually every case they may be expressed only in vague or relative terms, such as large, medium and small. A corollary to this quantification lies in the concomitant difficulty faced in interpreting the level of social organization of the different communities at these sites.

The third parameter is both the most important for this discussion and the most problematic. It is measurable to the degree that relevant material has been recovered (dependent upon the vagaries of chance) and is available (i.e. published or accessible and citable) but it is also, to a great extent, a function of interpretation. It includes what is termed here 'Egyptian' (i.e. an import from that segment of the Nile Valley that is present day Egypt) and what is understood as 'Egyptianized'. 'Egyptianized' is a subjective evaluation used to indicate any artefact of local (i.e. south Levantine) origin that is perceived as having derived from, or been inspired by, a source in Egypt. Such a definition is fraught with problems because it involves a degree of subjectivity (Braun 2002a, forthcoming; see also below) in that perceptions of cultural identity tend to vary from individual to individual.

Identification of Egyptian imports in this sense is often visually straightforward and, especially in the case of pottery, which makes up the overwhelming bulk of imports, verifiable by petrographic examination (e.g. Porat 1992). Determining what is Egyptianized, however, is quite another story. Nevertheless, there is a solid base of agreement that much of the material under question can be placed within this category, and it is to the interpretation of it that I now turn to suggest the general outlines of a model for interaction between the southern Levant and Egypt in this time period.

## The sites

In order to discuss the question of the degree and kinds of encounters that the inhabitants of the southern Levant had with Egypt in this far off period, it is necessary to review the archaeological evidence from the core area. The discussion of sites is mostly in descending order that roughly approximates their relative sizes and importance as presently understood.

**Tel Erani:** This is a massive site of more than 24 hectares. It has an overlying EB III occupation, which has also yielded an important EB I sequence (Brandl 1989; Yeivin 1961) that probably represents one of the major population concentrations in the region for that time span. The size of the EB I occupation, however, remains obscure and is subject to controversy. Two major alternate, stratigraphic sequences have been suggested for the site, based on work in two contiguous areas by two expeditions (Brandl 1989: 360–361; Kempinski and Gilead 1991). Alphabetical stratigraphic designations derive from the excavations of Kempinski and Gilead, while numerical appellations refer to Yeivin's earlier work at the site.

The more recent excavations by Kempinski and Gilead suggest two distinct cultural phases within an EB I sequence. The earlier is associated with Strata D (without architecture) and C (a chrono-cultural phase sometimes identified as Erani C), possibly devoid of evidence for Egyptian influence (Y. Yekutieli, pers. comm., *contra* the excavators' opinion; Kempinski and Gilead 1991).

A post-Erani C, or Late EB I phase has been identified in adjacent, but limited precincts of the site by the earlier expedition directed by Y. Yeivin (Brandl 1989). Extant structures there include one large courtyard building, part of a street and portions of additional structures, possibly agglutinative houses, that suggest a hierarchical social development beyond the village level (Brandl 1989: 366; Ciasca 1962). A massive mudbrick defensive wall that apparently circumvallated the site has been partially excavated in different areas of the mound. Some scholars attribute it to EB I, while others (e.g. Kempinski and Gilead 1991: 189) suggest an EB III date for it (Brandl 1989: 379–383; Yeivin 1961). Either interpretation is feasible given our present understanding of the archaeological record of the EB period in the southern Levant.

The later EB I phase is associated with a great deal of Egyptian and Egyptianized material that probably dates to around the time of Narmer, whose name is found on a *serekh* from this site (Yeivin 1960). The symbol (incised before firing, apparently on an Egyptian wine jar) is complete, but all that was recovered of the vessel was a single sherd (ca. 14 x 10.5 x 4.5 cm) clearly not found *in situ*. Apparently no additional pieces of the vessel were recovered. The stratigraphic attribution of this object is to an occupation identified as Stratum V by the first excavator of the site, Yeivin (1960). Specifically, the *serekh*-bearing sherd is described as deriving from a mudbrick mass (a collapsed wall?), beyond the limits of a floor of this stratum. On the basis of the published evidence this precise attribution, as all proveniences of objects from Yeivin's excavation (Brandl 1989), is of dubious chronological value.

While convinced that there is a large and important element of Egyptian and Egyptianizing material at the site, especially in the ceramic assemblage, I disagree with Brandl's (1989, 1992) interpretation that suggests it was more important than the local element (Braun 2001: 79, 2002a). There is a good case to be made, especially in the light of new finds from Tell es-Sakan, that the material culture of this site (including architecture, ceramic, ground-stone, and chipped-stone industries) is primarily and typically local. Many of the objects that Brandl assumes to be Egyptianized (e.g. wheel-made bowls and vessels of south Levantine morphology fashioned of local, loess clay) are totally local phenomena. Egyptians apparently did not use the wheel for making pottery until sometime in the late Old Kingdom (Arnold 1993: 41) indicating that these bowls derive from the EB III occupation, while loess was traditionally used, and perhaps favoured, by local potters from at least chalcolithic times.

Noteworthy objects from Tel Erani include a modicum of Egyptian imports, and artefacts showing Nilotic influence, bread moulds, local hybrid types of ceramics, certain aspects of flint technology (Rosen 1988) and several bullae that unfortunately lack decoration but are reminiscent of Egyptianized examples from contemporary sites. While there is a likelihood of an Egyptian ethnic element residing at Tel Erani, it should be understood as limited in size within a primarily local, south Levantine population.

**Tell es-Sakan:** Situated on the north bank of the Wady Ghazzeh, only 0.5 km north of Tel el Ajjul is the large (8–12 hectares) EB site of Tell es-Sakan. The site was only recently discovered (de Miroschedji and Sadek 1999a, b, 2000a, b). The excavators note that the occupational sequence covers the entire EB Age (i.e. EB I to EB III) with four strata (A9–A6) attributed to EB I. Relative dating suggested by the excavators is according to Kaiser's (1957) Egyptian chronology because, despite the site's south Levantine location, apparently more than 90 per cent of recovered ceramic material in the soundings in these levels is Egyptian or Egyptianized. The time span suggested for these levels is between Naqada IIIa and the beginning of the first Dynasty. The current opinion of the excavators is that the Egyptian involvement with the site ceased at the end of EB I (ca. 3000 BC; Braun 2001); afterwards "Tell es-Sakan became a Canaanean city" (de Miroschedji and Sadek 1999a). Unless results of future excavation demand a reappraisal of these preliminary observations, Tell es-Sakan may be considered as a major Egyptian colony, most probably the centre for Egyptian activity in the region and period under discussion.

**Taur Ikhbeineh:** Further west along the Wady Ghazzeh, only a short distance from the Mediterranean coast, is the site of Taur Ikhbeineh. The size of the site remains uncertain, but it would seem to be no less than 2.5 acres (1 hectare) in area and perhaps as large as 7–8 acres (2.83–3.24 hectares). It has been subjected to very limited soundings (ca. 50 $m^2$) and surface investigations (Oren and Yekutieli 1992) that have yielded evidence of five successive occupational phases numbered respectively from late to early, I–V, the first four of which date to the EB Age. Phases V–III are notable for ceramic types dating to an early (but not the earliest EB I; Braun 2000) and a middle EB I horizon that roughly correlates with the Erani C Phase.

Apparently local ceramic production includes typical EB I and Egyptianized types; they and imports from the Nile Valley appear to be attributed to the four phases of this sequence. To the extent that the results of such a limited sample accurately reflect the entire site, there is evidence for a marked increase in the number of Egyptian imports in Phase II. This seems quite plausible in the light of the discovery of nearby Tell es-Sakan. Phase II should probably be dated to Late EB I, although the published material does not contain diagnostics that allow for a definitive affirmation of this dating. The present evidence suggests it was likely to have been primarily local EB I in character. If this is indeed the case, then here is one of the best examples of an encounter with ancient Egyptian neighbours domiciled a short distance away at Tell es-Sakan.

**The Halif Terrace:** This site, estimated alternately at 2 hectares (Alon 1972: 34), 4.8 hectares (Dessel 1991: 58) and 16 hectares (Levy *et al.* 1997: 3), is probably closer in size to Dessel's estimate, but could be as large as 8.8 hectares if the basal layers of Tel Halif are included (Dessel 1991), occupying the summit of the same hill, about which there is no information. In any event, it appears that the site is significantly smaller than the EB I occupation at Tel Erani.

The exposed structures at the Halif Terrace do not suggest that it attained any social development higher than village level, although further exploration could alter this impression. The known EB I site, a large sloping terrace on the east side of the tell, has been extensively excavated by two major expeditions (Levy *et al.* 1995, 1997; Seger 1990, 1996). It too exhibits a primarily south Levantine material culture, dated to Late EB I, with an important admixture of portable Egyptian and Egyptianizing artefacts. Underlying this stratum are very early EB I and chalcolithic deposits, possibly devoid of foreign imports (but see Dessel 1991: 421–425).

Assessments by Levy *et al.* (1995, 1997) of the quantity of this foreign element have been somewhat exaggerated because they failed to take into account results of earlier work at the same site in a contiguous precinct of the terrace that produced only a modicum of Egyptian and Egyptianized artefacts (Dessel 1991; Seger 1990, 1996). The rather heavy concentration of Egyptian-related objects in a different precinct of the site may also be informative; it suggests an area distinctly related to Egyptian associated activity. In addition, a lack of Egyptian traditions in the chipped stone technology of the site suggests that the level of Egyptian impact or involvement is considerably less than at Tel Erani (Braun 2002a; Seger 1996). Nevertheless, several (two or possibly three) *serekhs*, bullae showing Egyptian iconography, and other Egyptian and Egyptianized elements retrieved from this site, indicate a direct and important encounter with exponents of the contemporary culture of the Nile Valley.

**Afridar/Ashqelon:** This site, estimated minimally at 1 hectare in size, but possibly once much larger, is located almost on the beach, ca. 1.5 km north of Tel Ashqelon, in the Afridar Quarter of the modern town. It has been subjected to limited excavation that exposed evidence in Stratum 2 (Brandl and Gophna 1994) of a large structure of mudbrick with at least seven rooms. This stratum yielded a small quantity of material including typically Egyptian and Egyptianized pottery and local ceramic types associated with the Erani C horizon (Gophna, pers. comm.).

Brandl (1992) saw Egyptian influence in the all-brick structure, including foundations, as he does for all-brick architecture at Tel Erani, but such a conclusion is unwarranted. Notably, the bricks in this building are not of a size that conforms to Egyptian standards (Gophna and Gazit 1985), and since there is in any case a well-documented history of local mudbrick architecture at Ashqelon (Braun 2000) and in the region in general, the burden of proof falls on those claiming an Egyptian character. Certainly mudbrick construction without stone foundations should not, *ipso facto*, be associated with Egyptian influence.

**Small Tel Malhata:** This small village of no more than 2 acres (0.8 hectares) is notable for EB I and EB II settlements that have yielded what can be described as a considerable quantity of imported Egyptian wares, including three sherds, incised with *serekhs* before firing. Two of these, quite fragmentary and lacking identifying names, are attributed to the EB I occupation in an early report (Amiran *et al.* 1983: 78). The same publication indicates a third, attributed to Horus Narmer, to be a surface find.

A later publication (Amiran and Ilan 1993), by omission, appears to disavow the ascription of Egyptian pottery to the EB II occupation (Stratum 3). Part of the description for Strata 5–4 (EB I) is noteworthy: "The finds include both local and Egyptian pottery. Especially noteworthy are three sherds of Egyptian storage jars bearing an inscribed *serekh* with the name Narmer" (Amiran and Ilan 1993: 939). Thus, two interpretations remain concerning the chronological parameters for encounters between the ancient inhabitants of Small Tel Malhata and contemporary Egyptian material culture, although it appears to be confined to Late EB I.

**Tel Lod:** A massive salvage and rescue operation at Tel Lod in Israel has recently unearthed evidence of more than 2,100 m$^2$ of an EB site, estimated on the basis of poorly preserved, extant remains, to have been between 2 and 4 hectares in size. The occupations relevant to this discussion range from Late EB I into EB II (Yannai and Marder 2001). Between four and five superimposed architectural strata, mostly of mudbrick without stone foundations, belong to this time span. Virtually all the buildings are constructed of a type of large, rectangular mudbrick commonly associated with local building traditions. Notable exceptions are several poorly preserved wall fragments of much smaller rectangular mudbricks of a standard size found also at the En Besor residency, where they have a clear Egyptian association (Gophna and Gazit 1985).

While no buildings of clearly public function were encountered, some structures are large, multiple roomed affairs with very substantial walls. They are of the order of those found at Tel Erani and Ashqelon/Afridar (see above), suggesting, if not an urban level of societal development, one that may have attained a supra-village status. No signs of fortifications were encountered at the site, but the possibility of their having existed cannot be definitively ruled out as a result of the excavations to date.

While virtually every EB stratum at Tel Lod yielded quantities of Egyptian and Egyptianized finds, preliminary research suggests that most are likely to have been in non-primary deposition. Several concentrations of this material, found *in situ*, probably belong to the earliest EB level, apparently dating to Late EB I. Soundings in a somewhat more distant, northerly precinct of the site by van den Brink (forthcoming) suggest a somewhat different sequence, with Egyptian material associated with only one stratum, sandwiched between two occupations of local character.

Finds from Tel Lod include bullae (unfortunately without decoration) from the northern precinct and a wide range of Egyptian and Egyptianized pottery scattered throughout fills in most of the excavated precincts. In addition, there are three concentrations of Egyptian and Egyptianized pottery that apparently date to the earliest EB occupation encountered, Late EB I. A small quantity of flint objects exhibiting clear Egyptian technology and a fragment of an alabaster cylinder jar make up the complement of non-local artefacts for EB I. Included in the Egyptian imports that Tel Lod has yielded are nine *serekhs* incised before firing on ceramic vessels (Figure 2:2), the largest collection of such objects found to date at any one site in the southern Levant (van den Brink and Braun 2002).

All appear to be on Egyptian vessels, but only one has so far been examined petrographically (A. Cohen-Weinberg, pers. comm. 2001) and may be definitively labelled so; the others all appear to be fragments of typical Egyptian fabrics. Five bear the name of Horus Narmer, but three are fragmentary and lack the crucial portions of the sign that indicate the name. They could also have been incised with the name of Narmer. Another, also fragmentary, is nevertheless well enough preserved to allow the name of Horus Ka (King Narmer's immediate predecessor) to be read. Thus, the date of these objects corresponds to the end of Dynasty 0 and the beginning of the first Dynasty, corresponding well with the date for the Late EB I and EB II local material associated with these levels. None of these *serekh*-bearing objects, incised before firing in Egypt, was found *in situ*, and unfortunately all are on very small fragments of objects that became separated from the remains of complete vessels. All, recovered in non-primary deposition, are of indeterminate stratigraphic origin.

Also included in the ceramic repertoire of this site are quantities of bread mould fragments with distinctive, coarse fabrics and stippled or uneven bases associated with this type of Egyptian vessel (e.g. Petrie 1953: fig. II, 8e–9s). Some others are of similar wares, but have slightly rounded, smooth bases and flattened rims. They could be functionally similar to the bread moulds, but morphologically belong to a separate class. They may have been intended for another function, or may be a local imitation or translation of an Egyptian idea. Perhaps they represent a later development, a hybrid type in which some of the distinctly Egyptianized features no longer prevailed.

Although for the present no absolute quantification is possible concerning Egyptian and Egyptianized elements in the material culture of EB Lod, the massive number of sherds recovered, found in several thousands of excavated units of fill (i.e. baskets) removed from the site, is derived from pottery of local origin, types well documented at sites of this region within this chronological milieu. Egyptian imports and what appear to be Egyptianized vessels make up a statistically small but notable sample, far less than 1 per cent of the whole, probably representing scores or more of individual ceramic vessels.

Figure 2:2 Seven of the nine potsherds of Egyptian origin bearing *serekhs*, incised before firing, recovered from Tel Lod.
1   *Serekh* with whiskered catfish in name compartment, associated with King Narmer, first king of Dynasty 1.
2   *Serekh* with whiskered catfish in name compartment, associated with King Narmer.
3   *Serekh* of unknown king, probably end of whiskered catfish in name compartment associated with Narmer.
4   *Serekh* with whiskered catfish in name compartment, associated with King Narmer.
5   *Serekh* of unknown king, probably end of whiskered catfish in name compartment associated with Narmer.
6   *Serekh* with upraised hand (one of a pair) in name compartment, associated with King Ka, the predecessor of Narmer (last king of Dynasty 0).
7   *Serekh* and other incised lines.

Unquestionably the majority of EB denizens at Lod were local south Levantines. The cultural milieu encountered in the excavations is typical of the period and in general does not suggest much foreign influence. Whether the Egyptian and Egyptianized material from Lod, including a small quantity of flints, is indicative of a Nilotic ethnic element in residence within a primarily indigenous populace is unclear, although one interpretation favours such a hypothesis (van den Brink and Braun 2002). Perhaps van den Brink's excavations indicate a separation or isolation of Egyptians, or specific functions associated with Egyptian administrative paraphernalia, within a greater community. Notably a group of bullae derives from an occupational level in the northerly precinct excavated by van den Brink. Whatever the reality reflected in the archaeological record, the inhabitants of EB Lod certainly experienced important encounters with their contemporaries from the Nile Valley.

**Tel Dalit:** On the basis of the material culture it displays (Gophna 1996), this site of ca. 4 hectares is contemporary with at least part, if not all, of the EB I and EB II occupation of Tel Lod. It lies within the same valley, only 7 km away as the crow flies. There are no natural boundaries between the two sites and without doubt the denizens of these neighbouring communities must have been in direct communication. The most striking feature of Tel Dalit within this chrono-cultural context is that, with the exception of a single sherd of obvious Egyptian origin (R. Gophna, pers. comm.), the entire ceramic and artefact repertoire of the site (including the EB I and EB II occupations) so far recovered is typically local to the region.

EB II Tel Dalit is notable for a circumvallating wall, making it one of a number of small, fortified towns of this period. The existence or absence of a counterpart construction at Tel Lod in the same time span (*contra* Yannai and Marder 2001) could possibly indicate something of the political climate of the times. It would perhaps help us to understand what appears to be a notable lack of intercourse with Egyptians at Tel Dalit as compared with that experienced by their contemporary neighbours at nearby Tel Lod. One explanation for this could be associated with the stratigraphic origin of such material. If, as I suspect, the stratigraphic origin of the Egyptian material is in the earlier phases of EB at Tel Lod (i.e. in EB I), then it is likely to derive from a contemporary occupation at Tel Dalit. In fact, the EB I occupation was subjected to restricted soundings and produced limited quantities of artefacts. Thus, there remains the possibility that more Egyptian pottery could characterize the assemblage, although, considering the present sample, it would be unlikely to be considerable.

**Palmahim Quarry:** This site is a large, sprawling village on the Mediterranean littoral approximately 15 km south of Tel Aviv, near where the Soreq stream debouches into the sea (Braun 2002b). Its size is difficult to estimate as much of it was quarried away before it could be measured, but I suspect it was minimally 2 hectares in area and possibly larger. Excavations over 1200 $m^2$ of two strata (2 and 1, respectively earlier and later) represent successive Late EB I occupations, the material culture of both of which is overwhelmingly local in character.

Stratum 2 yielded part of an Egyptianized storage vessel bearing a *serekh* (without a name) incised into it before firing. The morphology of its distinctive thickened, rounded rim suggests that it may be vaguely imitative of one class of Egyptian wine jar. Notably, it is a unique example of this type amongst numerous storage jars of local morphology recovered at the site. Indeed, this type of rim has only limited parallels in the southern Levant, all derived from Horvat 'Illin Tahtit (see below) and Lod. The Egyptian association is further emphasized because the incised vessel from Palmahim Quarry is one of a pair (see below) that can be dated to early within Dynasty 0 (Braun and van den Brink 1998; Braun *et al*. 2001: figs. 4.2, 4.4).

Aside from this vessel, there are only one or two additional objects that may indicate Egyptian associations. They are a small palette of rose-coloured limestone (Braun and van den Brink 1998: fig. 4.7: 3), several piriform maceheads (one of a finely smoothed black stone) and half of a beautifully fashioned, large spherical bead of highly polished hematite. The palette is probably of local manufacture but its inspiration may result from Egyptian influence, as may one or more of the maceheads. The hematite bead, its surface finely worked and highly polished, is likely to be of Egyptian origin due to its craftsmanship. Notably lacking at the site is evidence of additional Egyptianized pottery in the considerable assemblage recovered. Of further interest is one Egyptianized, drop-shaped bottle of local manufacture from a nearby small site, Givat Ha-esev. It was uncovered in association with a typical, EB I hemispherical bowl (Braun *et al.* 2001: fig. 4.31) serendipitously by naturally shifting sands.

**Horvat 'Illin Tahtit:** Further to the east, on a small, dry water course, near where the Soreq stream leaves the Judean incline and enters the Shephela, is the site of Horvat 'Illin Tahtit (Braun *et al.* 2001: 60–61), estimated to be about 1 hectare in size. Two Late EB I occupation levels of this small, unfortified village have yielded a statistically minuscule assemblage of Egyptian objects. They number no more than 40 and are culled from a sizable quantity derived from more than 1,300 3-dimensional excavation units (i.e. baskets) containing scores of thousands of sherds, many thousands of flint objects and a small quantity of other stone artefacts. Egyptian or Egyptianized objects include one or two flint tools, a calcite macehead (probably an Egyptian import; Braun *et al.* 2001: 60–61, fig. 4.7: 2), and more than a score of sherds of obvious Egyptian origin (Braun and van den Brink 1998).

The most notable Egyptianized object (one of a handful of jar rims similar to those on Egyptian wine jars) recovered is a second storage jar incised with a *serekh* (Braun *et al.* 2001: fig. 4.2: 5, pl. 4.4A), of which only the corner of the name compartment is preserved. Recovered *in situ* in Stratum IV (the earlier of two Late EB I levels), it is the counterpart to the *serekh*-bearing jar from Palmahim Quarry and one of only four or five vessels from Horvat 'Illin Tahtit with this distinctive rim. By contrast, scores of additional storage jars, complete and fragmentary, have other rim forms, types well attested at other EB I sites.

**El-Maghar:** About midway between Horvat 'Illin Tahtit and Palmahim Quarry on the Soreq Brook is another site from which a quantity of Egyptian pottery is derived (Braun *et al.* 2001: 79–80). No estimate for the size of the EB Age settlement is available. There is some suggestion, based on Egyptian pottery types, that this site may be dated to very late EB I and have continued into EB II. Although the site was subjected to formal excavation, no information is published on the work done there and even an archival file (Levy n.d.) lacks pertinent information. All additional information available on the Egyptian and Egyptianized material is from surface finds made by R. Gophna in casual sherding of the site many years after the excavation. Presumably the bulk of material is of local manufacture; at least there is no mention in Levy's report of Egyptian material. Thus, available information suggests that el-Maghar is another typical EB I–II site, for which there is evidence of some contact with Egyptians.

**'En Besor:** The Egyptian nature of the small (0.16 hectare) settlement at 'En Besor (Stratum III) has long been documented (Gophna 1995). Sandwiched between an earlier, Late EB I occupation and a later, EB II settlement, it is most noteworthy for its overwhelmingly Egyptian character. Some of the most important features are the large corpus of Egyptianized bullae recovered from one building, the typically

Egyptian type mudbrick architecture (Gophna and Gazit 1985) and the Egyptian and Egyptianized pottery associated with this level.

A recent discovery suggests some interesting phenomena at this site. A large, coarse ware basin of Egyptian style sunk into the floor of one building, presumed to be for the processing of beer, was for many years assumed to be of local manufacture, but lately a sample was subjected to petrographic examination and the vessel turned out to be an import from the Nile Valley (Gophna and Buzaglo 2000). One may wonder why the inhabitants of this site felt the need to transport such a large, fragile, simple and utilitarian object all the way from Egypt when it could easily be produced locally, as were so many Egyptianized vessels. Perhaps the contents of this vessel were more significant that the vessel itself. Not all encounters between the Egyptians in the southern Levant were straightforward, and even simple types of objects were not always obtainable from local producers. The possible historical realities behind a find such as this Egyptian vat are intriguing.

**Tel Ma'ahaz:** Tel Ma'ahaz is a small (0.5 hectares) site in the northern Negev that had been looted of Egyptian material (Amiran and van den Brink 2001; Beit-Arieh and Gophna 1999) prior to two brief seasons in which limited archaeological investigations were undertaken. Amiran and Gophna (Amiran 1978a; Amiran and Gophna 1993) noted the presence of stone architecture in Stratum 1, including installations, but suggested that the site could have been a temporary settlement. Beit-Arieh and Gophna (1999) suggest, on the basis of a considerable quantity of looted Egyptian and possibly also Egyptianized pottery, that this was an 'Egyptian settlement', albeit of a character somewhat different from 'En Besor (see below). Notable differences are in the stone architectural remains, as opposed to mudbrick (see above). Of interest is the presence of several *serekhs* on Egyptian imported pottery (Schulman and Gophna 1981).

**Wady Ghazzeh ('En Besor) Site H:** Macdonald's (1932: 12–16) excavations at site H, roughly estimated to have been ca. 5 hectares in size (but of uncertain density), indicated settlement dated to early in EB I. Architecture and the bulk of artefacts are of local derivation. The site is also interesting for having yielded a small quantity of Egyptian imports (Gophna 1995: 46–58; Roshwalb 1981: 271–278, *passim*), suggesting that the route for their introduction into the southern Levant was opened early in EB I.

**Hartuv:** The relatively small (ca. 3 hectares) site of Hartuv on the Soreq Brook is located at the most easterly extent of the Shephela, near modern Beth Shemesh. Although not more than 1 km from Horvat 'Illin Tahtit, there is no overlapping sequence in the settlement. Hartuv was abandoned by the time the latter site was first settled in EB I. Most of the pottery of the earlier site is clearly identifiable with types of Erani C horizon. Several bowl types from Hartuv have been identified as having 'Egyptian affinities', but they are locally made (Mazar and de Miroschedji 1996: 21–22; Porat 1996). Some of these vessels do have an Egyptian flavour and their attribution to this early phase of EB I is plausible in the light of the appearance of Egyptian imports at Site H (see above) and Nizzanim (see below).

**Nizzanim:** The small (ca. 1 hectare) coastal site of Nizzanim, north of Ashqelon, has yielded from limited soundings a sequence of three successive occupations ascribed to EB IA (i.e. Early EB I; Yekutieli and Gophna 1994). It is noteworthy for its predominately local material culture with a slight degree of Egyptian influence. Once again there are indications of early encounters with Egypt.

**Azor Cemetery:** A number of EB I tombs have been excavated in the south Tel Aviv area of Azor and have yielded a small quantity of Egyptian and Egyptianized artefacts in primarily local EB I cultural assemblages (e.g. Amiran 1985; Ben-Tor 1975; Perrot 1961). They include ceramics, a flint knife and a slate palette. These objects are likely to have been prestige items, related to the status of the deceased.

**Arad:** Several Egyptian artefacts from Arad in the northern Negev are a minor complement to a primarily local material culture assemblage encountered in large-scale exposure of the site over numerous seasons (Amiran 1978b, 1992; Amiran and Ilan 1996). Stratum IV, the Late EB I pre-urban settlement, a sprawling settlement located below the ca. 9 hectares of the EB city, has yielded only one Egyptian object: portions of a sizable fragment of a large, imported jar with a *serekh* of Narmer incised into it before firing (Amiran 1974, 1976, 1978b). From later EB II levels there is evidence of a small quantity of Egyptian pottery, including sizeable fragments of large jars. Notably absent from the assemblage is any evidence for Egyptianized ceramics.

The local ceramic assemblage at Arad includes vessels of types sometimes identified by the misnomer of "Abydos Ware" (Amiran 1969: 59–66). This category includes a motley collection of imported, south Levantine, EB II jars, jugs and juglets, fashioned from an assortment of fabrics (i.e. 'wares') exhibiting different types of surface treatment and decoration (e.g. combing and painting in specific patterns). The name actually derives from their original find-spots in the first Dynasty royal cemetery at Abydos in ceramic assemblages of tombs from the time of Djer/Zer (e.g. Petrie 1902: VIII, erroneously labelled "Aegean Pottery") onwards.

**Tel Apheq/Rosh Ha-Ayin:** Little on the major (12 hectare) site of Tel Apheq at the headwaters of the Yarqon River has been published. A very sizable, urbanized, Late EB I occupation, to which are attributed a public building and a fortification wall, is identified by distinctive local ceramics (Beck 1985, 2000: 97, fig. 8.4, 8, 9; Beck and Kokhavi 1993). Very little Egyptian or Egyptianized pottery is associated with this occupation because the excavators indicate that imports from the Nile appear only in the succeeding, EB II stratum (G2). No further information on the nature and quantity of these artefacts is presently available.

**Lachish:** The north-west settlement of Lachish, primarily deposits from natural caves, has produced evidence for an EB occupation. Included in the published pottery are some types that suggest Egyptian affinities, perhaps dated to EB I–II. Brandl (1992: 456–464, figs. 4–6) has listed and illustrated numerous vessels which he attributes to this group, but it seems that only a few bowls, jars and perhaps a bottle (1992: 456–464, figs. 4:16, 20, 25, 28 and 74) may be labelled Egyptianized with even a modicum of confidence (Braun 2002a, forthcoming); the remainder are probably bowls of EB III date or vessels of a type of clay (loess) that he equates with Egyptian-inspired technology but which has a history of utilization by the indigenous population as far back as the chalcolithic period. It seems likely that he has made the same, erroneous chrono-cultural identification for many similar objects from Tel Erani (see above).

**Gezer:** Most of what is known about the EB I settlement at Gezer comes from caves. Published materials indicate that the prevailing material culture is local EB I. Brandl

(1992: 455–457) has suggested a number of Egyptian and Egyptianizing elements from the site, only two of which (both are cylinder seals) seem *bona fide* nilotic imports. A third, rare double vessel (1992: 455–457, fig. 3, 3) is of dubious inspiration that could derive either directly or ultimately from the Nile Valley, but could also be local. Alternately the vessel could belong to another period; it comes from Macalister's excavations at the beginning of the 20th century, which were accomplished with little precision.

## Summary: the significance of the evidence

The earliest penetration of Egyptian and Egyptianized material culture into the southern Levant appears to begin in the chalcolithic period (Kaplan 1959; Perrot 1959), probably as part of a two-way interaction (Faltings 1998). There is, as yet, no definitive evidence for it in the initial phases of EB I (Braun 2000) in the southern Levant, although recent analysis of mollusca from one of the earliest EB I sites, Afridar, area E, has identified a number of shells of *Aspatharia rubens*, generally considered to derive from the Nile Valley (Daniela Bar-Yosef, pers. comm. 2002). No artefactual evidence for imports is associated with it or a cluster of contemporary sites in the same region. In addition, there is some evidence for south Levantine influence at Ma'adi early in EB I (Rizkana and Seeher 1987: 73–77).

## Early Phases of EB I

It is in an advanced phase of the period, a post Initial EB I or later phase of Early EB I, and then only in the lowlands of south-western Israel and the Palestinian Autonomous Zone of Gaza, that we see the reappearance of small quantities of Egyptian and Egyptianized artefacts. These have been recognized at sites such as Wady Ghazzeh, site H, and the early levels of Taur Ikhbeineh, in the caves at Lachish and perhaps also at Nizzanim. The material culture from these sites does not as yet suggest anything more than a casual encounter with Egypt, although it is possible that site H, with its Egyptian element in the chipped stone industry (Roshwalb 1981: 333) might be indicative of something other than occasional trade. A few pieces of the published pottery of this site can be related to the succeeding, Erani C phase of EB I and it may be that the Egyptian element is related to the latest horizon there. Notably, Yekutieli (1991) has demonstrated that the Egyptian material from the site apparently comes from the upper level(s ?).

The significance of this material in determining the nature of encounters by local people with Egypt in the early phases of EB I is open to discussion. Possible modes of interaction between the peoples of the south Levant and Egypt in that period include groups of Egyptian potters permanently resident in the southern Levant, or the imitation of imports by local potters. Either way, the wares produced may have been intended for consumption by locals or by immigrant groups from Egypt. The contents of traded vessels may have been as important as the vessels themselves, or more so. Contacts may have been mediated through small group of traders, of Egyptian, south Levantine, or mixed ethnic identity, or through sizeable elements of the population engaged in communications at some level.

**The Erani C Phase:** By the time of the Erani C phase of EB I in the southern Levant there appears to be a slight increase in the quantity of artefacts associated with Egypt, although the question of their presence at the site itself is arguable. Brandl (1989) and Kempinski and Gilead (1991) assert the presence of Egyptian and Egyptianized artefacts in the early levels of the sequence, while Yekutieli (1991: 45–49, pers. comm.) suggests that these objects are more likely to derive from a later EB I occupation of the site.

Small quantities of imported and Egyptianized objects are known from Taur Ikhbeineh in the same period, but otherwise there is little hard evidence for the nature and scope of encounters by these EB I peoples with contemporary Egypt. Too few sites have been excavated, and those unearthed remain inadequately published for any serious attempt at assigning a hierarchical order for Egyptian impact on the cultural life of the southern Levant in this period. The same questions that help us to characterize the possible types of encounters of EB I people in the preceding period (see above: Early Phases of EB I) remain valid also for this phase.

**The Late EB I Phase:** By contrast with the Erani C period, there is a vast increase in the quantity of Egyptian related artefacts late in EB I, albeit only at specific sites. While the picture is still far from clear as to many details, there is available a great deal of information concerning a number of sites, so that it is now possible to classify them as to the scope of Egyptian activity during Late EB I as follows:

I    Sites with primarily Egyptian material culture:
    A    Large population centres
        1    Tell es-Sakan
    B    Small to minor population centres
        1    Tel Ma'ahaz I
        2    'En Besor III

II    Sites with primarily local EB I material culture exhibiting a substantial increment of Egyptian and Egyptianized material:
    A    Large population centres
        1    Tel Erani
        2    Tel Lod
    B    Medium to large-sized population centres
        1    Halif Terrace
        2    Small Tel Malhata
        3    Taur Ikhbeineh
        4    el-Maghar?

III    Sites with primarily local EB 1 material culture exhibiting only a modicum of Egyptian material culture (represented primarily or solely by imports) but with *serekhs* or other evidence of royal Egyptian involvement:
    A    Medium to large-sized population centres
        1    Arad IV
        2    Palmahim Quarry 2
        3    Horvat Illin Tahtit IV

IV    Sites with primarily local EB I material culture with only occasional or no evidence of imported Egyptian objects:

A    Large population centres
    1    Tel Apheq
B    Medium to large-sized population centres
    1    Tel Dalit
C    Small to minor population centres
    1    'En Besor IV

The hierarchy outlined above gives a rough picture of the scale of Egyptian influence, that is, the degree to which indigenous EB I peoples of the southern Levant, in the region under discussion, came into contact with Egyptians, either directly or indirectly. If the archaeological record as presently understood accurately reflects the temper of the times, then it seems that the 'Egyptian experience' runs virtually the full gamut of possibilities.

If, as seems likely, the excavators' present assessment of Tell es-Sakan is correct, then denizens of Taur Ikhbeineh and any neighbouring sites of which we are presently unaware are likely to have been confronted with a massive presence of presumably ethnic and culturally identifiable Egyptians who settled in for a lengthy stay in the south-western reaches of the southern Levant. They appear to have transported many of their traditions from their place of origin in the Nile Valley. Obviously such a large population as is postulated for EB I Tell es-Sakan could not live in total isolation and accordingly, the degree of influence the colony exerted would have been felt in different degrees, dependent upon physical proximity or distance and political and economic factors for which we have little information. Notably, Tell es-Sakan was apparently fortified throughout its existence as an Egyptian colony, which suggests that relations with the indigenous inhabitants may not have been entirely peaceful.

This same phenomenon of Egyptian settlement is probably responsible for the significantly smaller centres exhibiting similar aspects of material culture at 'En Besor and Tel Ma'ahaz. Indeed, communication between them and what we might dare to call a 'mother colony' at Tell es-Sakan, as supplier, would do much to explain the presence of administrative paraphernalia, bullae and perhaps even *serekhs*. That the Egyptian involvement in the southern Levant is related to official, Egyptian activity is clearly indicated by the widespread presence of so many of these royal symbols within the zone of their operation.

Large population centres of local EB I people were clearly in contact with their not so near Egyptian neighbours. Whether Nilotic peoples may have actually resided within these same communities, either as small, distinct entities or perhaps dispersed throughout the population, is not clear. The present evidence is scanty and capable of producing equivocal interpretations. What is certain is that at sites such as Tel Erani and Lod, there is a notable Egyptian impact on the material culture, obviously derived ultimately from exotic influences. Van den Brink and Braun (2002) even suspect special supplies of Nilotic origin to be directed towards small clusters of ethnic Egyptians at the site of Lod that would help to explain the presence of relatively copious quantities of imported material there.

Centres of Egyptian populations, albeit few, are understood to be sources – or at least inspirations for – production of what we call Egyptianized pottery; whether pure, borrowed forms made locally (i.e. bread moulds and bowls of typically Egyptian morphology), or hybrid types that combine features of the two disparate ceramic traditions. While we do not yet know enough of chrono-stratigraphic sequences and the associated Egyptianized finds to attempt to ascertain relative placement of particular objects, it is nevertheless clear that this interaction was a long-term process with a history of varying intensity.

Where once scholars were automatically wont to ascribe the occurrence of Egyptian 'kitchen ware' to the presence of ethnic Egyptians within a local population, new knowledge of a major settlement of Egyptians at Tell es-Sakan allows fresh interpretations. Formerly encounters with Egypt had to be understood as either direct from the Nile Valley, or from one or two minuscule south Levantine settlements of Egyptians. There is now a much closer and more significant source for Egyptian inspiration situated within the region. It can be understood as responsible for the transmission of Nilotic concepts, both directly and indirectly. At least in theory such a site is capable of trans-shipping and producing the large quantities of Egyptian imports, Egyptianizing pottery and other artefacts that seem to have flooded the southern reaches of the southern Levant in Late EB I.

Given this scenario, the very considerable lesser degree of Egyptian influence at such population centres as Tel Apheq, Tel Dalit, Palmahim Quarry and Horvat 'Illin Tahtit, contrasted with that of the above mentioned centres, seems highly significant. Certainly there are no natural boundaries between sites in this region and a lack of communication is unthinkable. Quite clearly the people of these communities did not have the same type of encounters with Egypt as did their contemporaries at sites such as Taur Ikhbeineh and Lod, where the interaction between ethnic groups must have been of a greater intensity.

It is clear that the archaeological record reflects some type of selective mechanism that regulated the degree of intercourse between two ethnic populations present within the region. Obviously there were economic and political factors that must have governed them, and it will take further research and fieldwork before more detailed explanatory scenarios can be generated. Suffice it to note for the present that these factors are reflected in a hierarchy of Egyptian contacts that change rather precipitously with the onset of EB II.

## Table

The table opposite gives approximate correlations of selected south Levantine (Southern Region) EB I phases with Egyptian chronology. The Egyptian chronology employed here is based on Braun and van den Brink 1998: table 2; Hendrickx 1996: table 9.

| S. Levant | Sites | Egypt | Dynasty | Kings |
|---|---|---|---|---|
| Initial EB II | Arad III | Naqada IIIC1 | first | Djer |
| Late Southern (latest phase) | HIT III Pal. Quarry 1 Halif Terrace IIb Arad IV | Naqada IIIB IIIC1 *Horizont A* | Late 0 Early first | Nameless kings, Irj-Hor, Ka-Narmer, Hor-Aha |
| Late Southern (late phase) | HIT III Pal. Quarry 2 | Naqada IIIA1-IIID *Horizont A* | Late 0 | King? Double Falcon |
| Erani C phase | Tel Erani D, C Hartuv II | Naqada IIIA1 | 0 | Scorpion I |
| Initial EB I/ Afridar Area G | – | Naqada IIC-IID2 | Predynastic | – |

## *Acknowledgments*

Thanks are due to a number of colleagues at the Israel Antiquities Authority. E. C. M. van den Brink for his help, once again, in understanding the intricacies of Egyptian protodynastic chronology. L. Barda kindly produced the map indicating sites with major Egyptian and Egyptianizing finds. M. Salzberger, as always, skilfully photographed the *serekhs*.

I am grateful to E. Yannai and O. Marder, the principal excavators of Lod, and S. Dorfman, director, for permission to reproduce photographs of the seven *serekhs*.

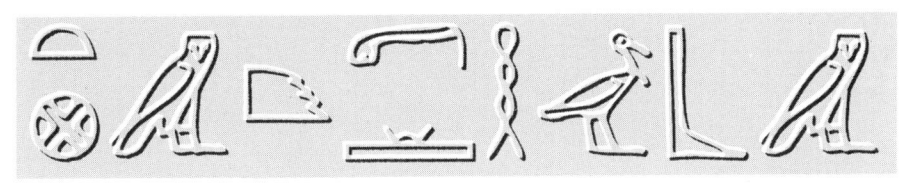

CHAPTER 3

# EGYPTIAN STONE VESSELS AND THE POLITICS OF EXCHANGE (2617–1070 BC)

*Rachael Thyrza Sparks*

## Introduction

Egyptian workshops had been manufacturing stone vessels since the predynastic period: for everyday use, for ritual purposes such as foundation deposits and temple votives, and as essential equipment accompanying the deceased on their journey to the afterlife (for corpora of Egyptian stone vessels, see Aston 1994; Kaplony 1968; el-Khouli 1978; Lilyquist 1995; Petrie 1937). A wide variety of different stone types was available either in Egypt itself or in its desert periphery, while growing involvement in long-distance trade networks increased the range of materials available for exploitation (Aston *et al.* 2000; Harrell 1989; Klemm and Klemm 1993). Despite great variability in stone use in the early periods of production, especially in the first and second Dynasties, Egyptian calcite came to dominate stone vessel assemblages from the Old Kingdom onwards (Aston 1994: fig. 21). This was probably due to a combination of ready availability, ease of manufacture and a visual appeal that satisfied consumer demands (Sparks 1998: 308, fig. 44). The more exotic stones tended to be reserved for social elites such as the royal family and high ranking officials.

High production output led to standardization of methods from an early period, the mechanics of which are illustrated by debris at production sites, and depictions of stone vessel workshops in numerous tombs (Caton-Thompson and Gardner 1934; Stocks 1988: 173–174). Several attempts have been made to determine the physical parameters of this technology through replication experiments (Gorelick and Gwinnett 1983; Stocks 1988, 1993). Methods changed little over the course of one and a half millennia, the main developments appearing to be the introduction of the tubular drill bit around the first Dynasty (Lucas and Harris 1962: 425), the handle-driven drill mechanism some time between the third and fifth Dynasties (Stocks 1988: 170), and a shift from using multiple weights to a single weight fitted onto the drill shaft by the New Kingdom (Stocks 1988: 176; 1993: 598).

Although most Egyptian stone vessels were uninscribed, a small percentage carried hieroglyphic inscriptions naming the Egyptian pharaoh or members of the royal family; these are found primarily in royal burials and temples (e.g. Leeds 1922: pls. I–II; Lilyquist 1995; Pinch 1993: 17). They were occasionally trimmed with precious metals, and many represent oversized versions of forms more commonly known from middle ranking burials (cf. Petrie and Brunton 1924: pl. XLI.30, ht. 48 mm, with el-Khouli 1993: cat. 2, ht. 399 mm). Smaller model versions of traditional forms such as the concave-sided cylindrical jar were also produced for use in foundation deposits outside tombs and in temples (e.g. Adams 1975: fig. 3; Hayes 1959: 128; Mond and Meyers 1940: pl. 23.40.17, 41). The significance of the inscription itself varies depending on the purpose for which a vessel was made. Some contain formulae and titles that indicate that the objects were designed for funerary use, such as the epithet "justified before Osiris" which treats the individual named as deceased (Lilyquist 1995: 4). Some are labels which inform of the vessel capacity and contents (e.g. Lilyquist 1995: 16–17), while others are less specific in intent. The use of inscriptions was not purely a royal phenomenon, and stone vessels with inscriptions naming private individuals are also known, often associated with funerary contexts (e.g. Jacobsson 1994: 20, cat. 80; Lilyquist 1995: 62, figs. 154–155). In general, the presence of a royal cartouche may be a means of indicating that these goods were made within a royal workshop, either for use by members of the royal family, or for distribution by them as rewards for loyalty and outstanding service (e.g. Lilyquist 1995: cat. 43; for a similar gift in silver, Breasted 1906–1907: 231).

## Egyptian stone vessels in the Levant

Egyptian stone vessels were popular elsewhere in the Near East, as recent catalogues of examples from Cyprus and the Levant indicate (Jacobsson 1994; Sparks 1998). These are usually distinguished as Egyptian through a consideration of their shape, decoration and the technology employed in their manufacture, although it has been suggested that Egyptianizing stone vessel workshops became active in the Levant at some stage in the Late Bronze Age (Lilyquist 1996). If this was the case, these must have operated using imported raw materials and under heavy Egyptian artistic influence, with close links being maintained with stylistic developments back in Egypt itself (Sparks 1998: 194–201). There is no evidence at present to suggest that this was the case for the stone vessels bearing Egyptian inscriptions.

Stone vessels naming private individuals are extremely rare (e.g. Edel 1983: cat. 98; Jacobsson 1994: cat. 80). Some may have been traded to the Levant as a by-product of tomb robbing.[1] Inscriptions naming pharaohs or members of the royal family are more frequent, although with only 69 provenanced and identifiable examples known from the Levant during the entire third and second millennia BC, they were never common (Appendix). At Ugarit (Figure 3:1), where Egyptian stone vessels were most popular, royal inscriptions are found on only 4.4 per cent of the total assemblage (Caubet 1991 – 19 out of the 427 fragments published). Royal name stone vessels are even scarcer elsewhere in the Near East, with four examples in Mesopotamia, two examples from Crete, and single examples known from Cyprus and Anatolia (von Bissing 1940: figs 1–4; Cline 1994: cat. 680, 742; Jacobsson 1994: cat. 79; Lilyquist 1995: cat. 1, 12, 95 and cat. A). It is this very scarcity that commands attention, and raises the question of how and why this kind of object found its way into foreign assemblages, and whether they had the same meaning there as back in Egypt.

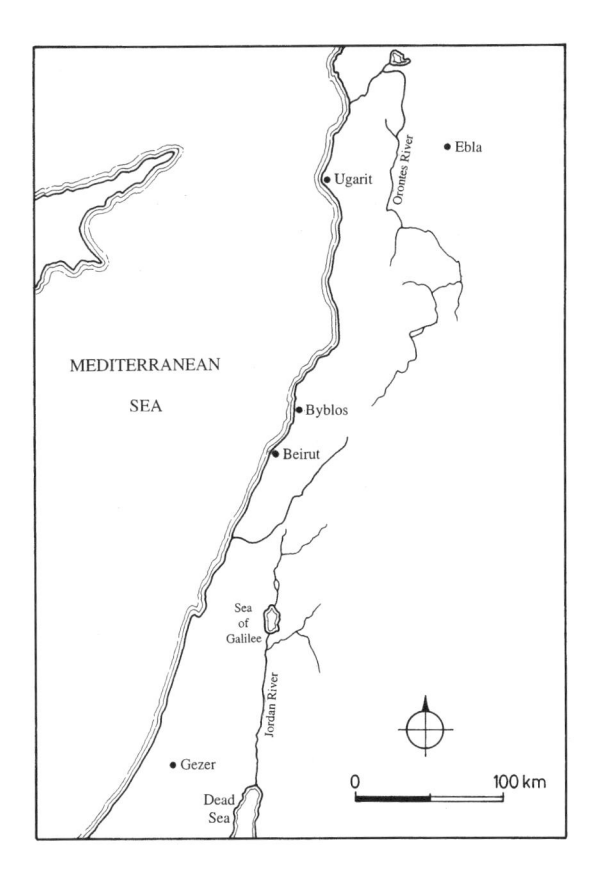

Figure 3:1 Map of sites mentioned in the text. Ugarit covers the area of modern Ras Shamra and Minet el-Beida.

## Mechanisms of distribution

There are many ways in which Egyptian inscribed stone vessels could have been distributed outside Egypt. This could have been through some kind of formal exchange, whether as gift exchange between royal courts, or as a more commercial form of trade. The vessels could have been transferred as valuable objects in their own right, or as containers for some other product. In either case, the transfer of the object from the Egyptian palace would be a deliberate act, and as such, would carry considerable meaning in terms of international diplomatic relations. Stone vessels could have been sent as parts of larger consignments designed to accompany diplomatic marriages, or as greeting gifts that were often directed at specific individuals within the court, such as the royal wife, chief sons, or high officials. The intent of this kind of exchange was to impress the recipient with the resources at the command of the sender, and in this context, marking the exchange with a royal cartouche would presumably have been particularly appropriate, as it would serve as a reminder of the origin of both gift and obligation.

An alternative mechanism would be through more aggressive activities such as the seizure of war booty, or the exaction of tribute or taxes from a conquered state. This may have become a factor in the secondary distribution of Egyptian goods once they had entered the Levant. It is only likely to have been a significant mechanism for the initial export of material outside Egypt itself in periods of civil unrest, such as during the First Intermediate Period or under Hyksos rule in the late Second Intermediate Period (Ryholt 1997: 143–148). It may be difficult to identify goods which have circulated through military activities, as opposed to traded or gifted items, except for those rare occasions where the seizure of booty has been commemorated by additional inscriptional evidence on the object itself, as illustrated by a series of stone vessels found in Mesopotamia which were inscribed "booty of Elam" and "booty of Magan" (Potts 1986, 1989).

Tomb robbers may also have had a role in disseminating luxury goods, some of which may have been lying dormant in the ground for many years (Phillips 1992). Some of the looted material would only have survived for a short time after being placed in the tomb, as was probably the case with precious oils stolen out of calcite jars in the tomb of Tutankhamun (Reeves 1990: 96–97). Yet stone vessels could equally have been a target: they survive burial well, and the raw material from which they were made seems to have maintained its value as a commodity throughout the pharaonic period, guaranteeing a market for this kind of object (see below). Vessels looted from tombs may be more noticeable in the archaeological record than those taken from temple or palace treasuries, as in Egypt this kind of material sometimes carried inscriptions testifying to its original function as a funerary offering. Even uninscribed vessels may be identifiable as coming from burials, if it can be demonstrated that their shapes predate their archaeological contexts by several hundred years. This is seen in several examples of predynastic or early dynastic type found in late bronze age deposits in the Levant (Sparks 1998: 128–130). It is perhaps more likely that these came back into circulation after this kind of looting, rather than surviving above ground as heirlooms (Jeffreys 2003c) over such a long period of time (Phillips 1992: 168–172, 173–181).

Stone vessels found in the Levant with royal name inscriptions are unlikely to have been derived from such sources for a number of reasons. First, they do not bear the types of funerary formulae that one would expect of objects taken from burial contexts. Second, the penalties for despoiling royal burials in the Bronze Age would have been severe, as suggested by papyri describing trials of tomb robbers during the late Ramesside period (Breasted 1906–1907: 245–273, sections 499–556; Phillips 1992: 160; Reeves 1990: 97). Therefore if such looting did take place, it seems logical that anyone attempting to trade in such risky material would take the precaution of obscuring its origins by removing incriminating inscriptions or converting the vessel into smaller objects such as amulets or inlays. In this case, the royal origin of the stone vessel would not be detected. The source of those jars which can be identified as royal was therefore probably quite different. It seems likely that they were selected from workshop or palace stock, or on rare occasions commissioned especially for particular individuals (e.g. Bordreuil and Pardee 1989: 97, fig. 26; Caubet 1991: 213; Desroches-Noblecourt 1956: 179–220; Schaeffer 1956: 40–42, figs. 118, 126).

If it is valid to associate such objects with Egyptian royal workshops, and if it can be demonstrated that they did not get exported through foreign or non-official channels, then it seems likely that their distribution abroad is somehow related to Egyptian foreign policy and diplomatic activities, particularly as they usually appear in palace or temple contexts abroad. This raises a number of questions, not the least being how to determine the intent behind sending such an object to a foreign court, let alone the manner in which it was received. If the gift was valued, was it because of its Egyptian origin or character, because of the status of the sender, or because it was inherently valuable? The question also remains as to what happened to the object in the period between arriving in the Levant and entering the archaeological record there, and whether there was any shift in the manner in which these vessels were used. Archaeology is quite capable of quantifying the physical attributes of an object; but to understand the significance of that object in its contemporary context is a more difficult task.

## The meaning behind the cartouche

Investigating the purpose behind inscribing royal cartouches on stone vessels leads on to a wider methodological problem: how should other objects with royal labels be interpreted? The addition of a royal name or insignia to an object could have a variety of meanings, depending on context and the nature of the object itself. It is important to consider the way in which different object classes would have functioned in their original setting to understand these differences. Some categories of object may reflect the making of a political statement, such as boundary stelae, inscriptions erected or displayed in a public place, or goods presented to a foreign ruler in diplomatic gift exchange. Others may reflect the process of government, with the royal name being used as a proof of authority or authenticity, such as when used to seal an official document on behalf of the pharaoh or the royal household. Royal seal impressions found on the handles of storage jars may have been a means of marking produce that belonged to the king or came from royal estates (Higginbotham 2000: 254). Use of the royal name could also be an official device for dating transactions, such as the collection of the grain tax by Egyptian officials in Ramesside Palestine (Goldwasser 1984). Cartouches on monumental architecture may have signified that the pharaoh had ownership of a building, or control of the activities that took place within it. The hieroglyphic inscriptions found in Iron I Beth Shan and Ashdod are good examples of this kind of material (Dothan and Porath 1993: 109–110; James 1966: 5–8). Finally, in a religious context, cartouches could be used to mark votive offerings made on behalf of the pharaoh, or which reflect the cult of the living or deceased king (e.g. Schulman 1988: 114–145).

The majority of these object classes share in common the presence of a royal cartouche which seems to act as an official statement, whether the aim of that statement be for propaganda, administrative or religious purposes. One type of object where the formal nature of this statement is less clear is that of royal name scarabs. In the past, these have often been interpreted as indicating some degree of royal influence or political authority, as in the case of the distribution of Hyksos royal scarabs in the southern Levant during the fifteenth Dynasty (Weinstein 1981: 8–10). Yet it has been argued on a number of occasions that this assumption is not justified (Ben-Tor *et al.* 1999: 53–55 and references). Unlike most other classes of objects with royal cartouches, in the Levant these scarabs appear to be distributed amongst the local population, rather than being confined to elite, temple or palatial contexts.

Actual impressions are extremely rare, as opposed to the scarabs themselves, suggesting that they were used mainly as amulets or items of jewellery. At Tell el-'Ajjul, for example, out of the 1,244 scarabs and seals recently republished by Keel, only one royal seal impression is recorded, compared to 103 royal name seals (Keel 1997: cat. 319). Moreover, while other types of scarab appear to be evenly spread between settlement and burial deposits, royal name scarabs appear primarily in tombs, with 70 being found in burials, compared to 14 from stratified deposits and 20 from unknown locations.

This association may argue for a specifically funerary role for many examples, which seem most likely to have had a protective function associated with royal cult, calling on the pharaoh in his role as a god, a power which could go well beyond his reign, as illustrated by the ubiquitous scarabs of Tuthmosis III (Ben-Tor *et al.* 1999: 54). Whatever the actual function of a royal name scarab, particularly in a Levantine setting, the evidence points to a somewhat different mechanism for distributing such objects across the region than for other classes of material, inscribed stone vessels in particular. This is illustrated by the different types of contexts in which the two groups appear at individual sites, as well as by the fact that royal name scarabs appear at a much larger number of settlements and are more evenly spread across the region. For all these reasons, it can be argued that this kind of object should be treated as distinct, when considering issues such as the extent of Egyptian influence or domination over the Levant during the Bronze Age.

Royal name stone vessels, on the other hand, appear to have functioned in a much more restricted setting within the Levant. Archaeological evidence shows a tendency for this kind of object to appear in elite contexts such as palaces, temples and royal tombs, and even then they are rare (see Appendix pp. 53–56). In cases where the size of the vessels can be determined, it would appear that inscriptions tend to be placed on large or monumental jars that represent a considerable investment of resources. This suggests that they were reserved for the highest grade of export, rather than being a common element in stone vessel production. This points to the addition of royal cartouches as a deliberate occurrence.

It is also evident from a variety of textual sources that even without a royal inscription, stone vessels were accorded a comparatively high status in bronze age society. The raw material had an intrinsic value of its own. Unworked blocks of stones such as calcite, malachite and lapis lazuli were often singled out in tribute and in offering scenes (e.g. Breasted 1906–1907: sections 30, 231, 234, 245, 446), while finished vessels from these and other materials such as *marhallu*-stone, *hiliba*-stone and *hulalu*-stone appear in booty lists and amongst the various precious objects provided as dowries accompanying diplomatic marriages of the eighteenth Dynasty (e.g. Moran 1992: EA 22 sections II.67–68, III.10). They appear in these lists not only as containers for a variety of precious oils and perfumes, but also without contents, indicating that the vessels were considered desirable in their own right (e.g. Moran 1992: EA 14, section III.47–73). This is also suggested by evidence that stone vessels frequently remained in circulation for long periods of time, sometimes necessitating repairs and modifications of damaged areas to allow the object to remain functional (e.g. el-Khouli 1993: cat. 19, 53, 55, from the Tomb of Tutankhamun, with mended rims, bearing inscriptions dating to the reigns of Tuthmosis III and Amenophis III). The materials involved may have had some role in determining the value of individual items, and considerations such as the rarity of the stone and how difficult it was to obtain, as well as its physical appearance and the amount of time and skill invested in crafting, it may have contributed to the inherent desirability of a particular object. Texts such as the Amarna Letters suggest that in the Late Bronze Age the values placed on stone vessels were shared across different cultural boundaries, as they were involved in exchanges both to and from the Egyptian court (Moran 1992: EA 22, EA 25, EA 14).

If it is accepted that stone vessels were highly valued by bronze age society, the question remains as to why some of these were marked with an Egyptian royal inscription. It seems probable that the message being conveyed by hieroglyphic inscriptions would be intelligible only to Near Eastern scribes trained in foreign languages, and yet it seems unlikely that they would have been intended as the main audience for this kind of artefact. More likely, the function of marking an object with an inscription, particularly one naming an Egyptian pharaoh, would be twofold. The visual appearance of the script, intelligible or not, would have conjured up associations with the culture and power behind it. It would be recognizable as Egyptian from its style alone, distinctive from contemporary scripts such as cuneiform. At the same time, the object beneath the 'message' bore its own cultural stamp, both in its physical shape, product of an Egyptian milieu, and in the high standard of craftsmanship that went into its creation. This visual 'signature' would have been especially powerful during the Old and Middle Kingdom periods, when Levantine contact with Egyptian artistic styles was more restricted, and such objects still a rarity. By the New Kingdom, Egyptian objects and motifs were more widely disseminated, as physical and diplomatic expansion of Egyptian borders into Syro-Palestine led to the Egyptianization of some aspects of Canaanite material culture and the development of a more hybrid style of art, often called the "intercultural style" (Higginbotham 1996, 2000; Kantor 1947). This occurred not only through direct exchange of goods, but through the movement of skilled craftsmen across the empire and between allies (Moorey 2001; Zaccagnini 1983). As a result, Egyptian-style objects, such as stone vessels and jewellery, may have become less powerful symbols than previously, as they became more widely available and produced in centres outside Egypt itself.

Nonetheless, the inclusion of a royal cartouche would have helped maintain the special character of an Egyptian gift. It would serve as a kind of validation, proof that the object came direct from one ruler to another. To display actively such a vessel in the palace of a Near Eastern ruler would be a statement in itself. It could be a visual symbol of an allegiance to Egypt and tacit support of Egyptian foreign policy or involvement in the region, a display intended to convey a message to Egyptian messengers or representatives visiting the court of an Asiatic king. This is the kind of support that some rulers felt the need to reiterate verbally in their written correspondence with the Egyptian pharaoh (e.g. Moran 1992: EA 45; 48; 49 from the king and queen of Ugarit; EA 119 from Rib-Hadda of Byblos). The importance of maintaining good relations between royal houses is emphasized in texts such as the Amarna Letters, where Asiatic rulers make a point of reminding the pharaoh of past treaties and ties, to elicit more favourable trade relations, or as a justification for present behaviour (Moran 1992: EA 9; EA 16: 19–31). Yet to an internal audience of subjects and family dependents, or visiting diplomats from other nations, the message conveyed could be quite different, showcasing their own power and influence through their success at obtaining such a strong ally as Egypt. In slightly different circumstances, such as when these objects were obtained through conquest, the message would be one of superiority over a vanquished enemy.

## Inscribed stone vessels and chronology

Much importance has been placed on the chronological value of Egyptian objects with royal inscriptions when found outside Egypt itself. These have been especially popular as means to anchor the relative chronology of other regions to the absolute chronology of Egypt. The calcite lid of the Hyksos ruler Khian found at Knossos is a case in point, being used to argue that the LMIA period had to postdate his reign (Betancourt 1987: 46; Manning 1999: 79; Warren 1995: 3; Warren and Hankey 1989: 56, 136–137). However, in order for this kind of link to be established, it must be demonstrated that object, inscription, and archaeological context are contemporary. This is by no means always the case. An inscription can be added to an object at any time after its manufacture, something that is particularly easy and cost-effective to do with stone vessels, which typically feature large undecorated surfaces. Appropriating an object can also be a simple matter of erasing and modifying existing names and titles, a practice familiar to many Egyptian pharaohs (e.g. el-Khouli 1993: 16 cat. 30, 40; Lilyquist 1995: cat. 49; Schneider 1996: pls. 24.262, 25.262, 71.262).

The first point that needs to be established is whether the inscription was contemporary with the object on which it appears, or whether it was added at a subsequent date. A study of inscribed stone vessels from royal burials in Egypt suggests that it was common practice for this kind of material to remain within the royal household for several generations (e.g. el-Khouli 1993: cat. 49; Lilyquist 1995: 3, cat. 81, 94, all from the tomb of Tutankhamun). In these circumstances, it seems quite probable that inscriptions of royal names may sometimes have been added to previously undecorated vessels from earlier periods. Lilyquist has suggested a similar reworking of a mottled stone vessel from Kamid el-Loz (e.g. Lilyquist 1993: 44; 1994: 217). It may be difficult to detect this kind of modification, unless both shape and inscription can be dated independently of one another, and with reasonable precision.

The contemporaneity of the archaeological context and of the inscription also needs to be established. Not only may objects of high value be kept in circulation for considerable periods of time, but they may also be brought back into circulation after their initial deposition, through processes such as tomb robbing and looting of temple storerooms. There needs to be some means of establishing an independent date for associated material. This is particularly important when studying the chronological distribution of stone vessels with royal names outside Egypt. The problem is illustrated by the contents of room 30 in the royal palace at Ugarit, which featured a mix of inscribed material including objects dating to the reigns of Amenophis II, Nefertiti and Ramesses II, covering a potential range of over 200 years (Caubet 1991: RS 15.201–203). These objects may have been retained because they were gifts reflecting a diplomatic relationship formed between Ugarit and Egypt in the past. As discussed earlier, texts such as the Amarna Letters show that traditional links of this kind were valued and often used as bargaining points in later diplomatic negotiations.

When an inscribed stone vessel antedates its archaeological context by a considerable period, this raises the issue of when and how it first reached the site in question. It is necessary to find some means of distinguishing between objects sent direct to a site, and material acquired through secondary channels, such as via looting. Failure to make this kind of distinction has led to errors in the past, such as the use of Egyptian statues of private officials found in the southern Levant as proof of some kind of Middle Kingdom Egyptian empire in Syro-Palestine (Ben-Tor 1997; Weinstein 1975; Wilson 1941). The Egyptian stone vessels found at Palace G at Ebla are also a case in point (see below). Understanding of Early Bronze Age international relations between Egypt and the Eblaite state varies, depending on whether objects were traded direct to Ebla, or whether Ebla obtained them from a third party. Where there is no additional textual evidence to fall back upon, and where no known local rulers are implicated in the inscriptions themselves, it may not be possible to discover the true state of affairs.

## The distribution of Egyptian stone vessels with royal name inscriptions in the Levant

### The Old Kingdom

Stone vessels with royal name inscriptions first appear in the Levant during the Early Bronze Age at Byblos, probably as a phenomenon resulting from the special relationship between Byblos and the Egyptian court. This relationship had developed out of Egypt's interest in a range of Lebanese products, including cedar wood, which was of sufficient size and strength to be used in architecture and for building seagoing vessels, and various associated resins and oils which were required for mummification and other ritual purposes (Prag 1986: 59; Wright 1988: 146). The majority of these stone vessels were recovered from around the temple complex of Baalat-Gebal; additional material purchased on the open market may also come from

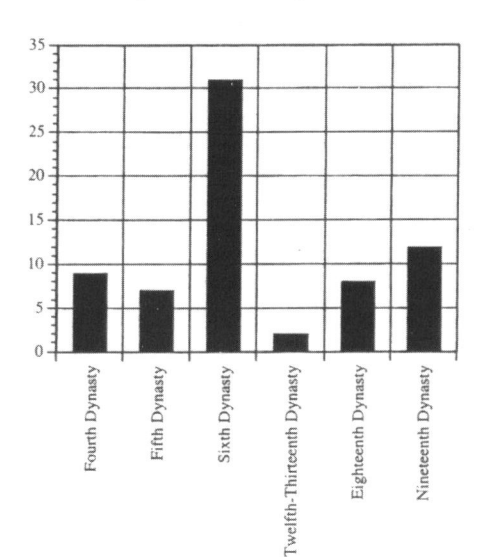

Figure 3:2 The chronological distribution of stone vessels with Egyptian royal name inscriptions found in the Levant.

Byblos, but has not been included here because of its lack of archaeologically derived provenance (Nelson 1934). The most notable characteristic of the provenanced group of material is its quantity, and the concentration of examples dating to the sixth Dynasty, especially to the reigns of Pepi I and Pepi II. This period represents a definite peak in terms of the distribution of stone vessels from Egyptian royal workshops abroad, unmatched in subsequent periods (Figure 3:2, Appendix, cat. nos. 18–47). The true number of actual examples is probably higher than represented here, as many inscriptions are incomplete and the cartouches have not survived.

Several theories have been offered to explain how, and indeed why, these inscribed stone vessels came to Byblos (see Wright 1988: 150–151). The concentration of material within the temple area suggests that most of these had been intended as votive offerings. If this was indeed the case, it is difficult to determine whether the offerings were being made by Egyptians, who had brought the items with them, or by Byblite rulers or officials who had obtained them from the Egyptian pharaoh or his representatives. The implications of these two scenarios are quite different. In the first instance, the actual gift of the stone vessel would have been to an Egyptian, and the circumstances behind the presentation need not have concerned the role of that individual in an international setting. The act of offering therefore would indicate only an Egyptian presence at Byblos, and their use of cult facilities there. In the alternative interpretation, the gift would have been from one ruler to a foreign court, and the transaction may well have had implications for international politics.

An additional, smaller group of stone vessels with royal name inscriptions was excavated at Ebla, in the Syrian interior (Appendix, cat. nos. 4, 31). These bore inscriptions of the pharaohs Khephren (2562–2537 BC), and Pepi I (2342–2292 BC). They were discovered on the floor of royal Palace G, in a destruction level that marked the end of this phase at the site and dating to around 2300/2280 BC (Astour 1992: 36–37). The lamp bearing the name of Khephren had therefore already been in circulation for well over 200 years before entering the archaeological record. It has been suggested that these vessels may have been obtained from Byblos rather than direct from Egypt, in which case they cannot be used to draw conclusions regarding Egyptian diplomatic involvement beyond the Lebanese coast (Scandone Matthiae 1982: 128, 1988). Two further inscribed vessels of archaic form were also found at Kamid el-Loz in Late Bronze Age contexts (Lilyquist 1996: pls. 28–29); however these may represent looted material rather than Early Bronze Age links with Egypt. In any case, neither features a royal inscription, and the date of the inscriptions themselves has also been questioned (Lilyquist 1993: 44, 1994: 217, 1996: 154–155).

## *The Middle Kingdom and Second Intermediate Period*

The association between Byblos and Egypt may have continued or have been re-established during the Middle Kingdom, as some inscribed stone vessels and objects dating to pharaohs of the twelfth and thirteenth Dynasties also appear at the site (Montet 1928: cat. 610–611, 614; Naville 1922; see also Albright 1964; Lilyquist 1993: 41–44; Appendix, cat. nos. 48–49; Tufnell 1969). A close relationship is attested from evidence such as the adoption of hieroglyphic characters for Byblite inscriptions, use of the Egyptian title of 'mayor' (*ḥȝty-ʿ*) by Byblite leaders, and even adaptation of Egyptian formulae for their own purposes (Kitchen 1969: 86; Redford 1992: 97). One calcite vessel fragment from tomb IV names a Byblite ruler, ḥȝty-ʿ Yantin, raising the question of whether this object was produced or inscribed locally, rather than in Egypt (Lilyquist 1993: 42; Montet 1928: pl. CXVII.787). The degree of Egyptianization evident in the ruling elite at Byblos may be a product of the long history of contact with Egypt. It has been suggested that some of the Egyptian objects with royal name inscriptions may have been sent as gifts to Byblite princes to celebrate their accession (Helck 1971: 63–64). There are no further stone vessels naming later kings of the Second Intermediate Period in the region, although examples bearing inscriptions of the Hyksos ruler Khian were excavated at Knossos and Boğazköy (Lilyquist 1995: cats. 1, A; Warren 1969: 113). If contemporary with their findspots, these may point to sporadic diplomatic activity abroad.

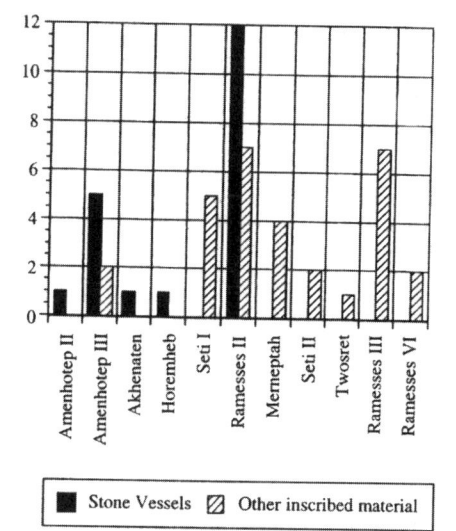

Figure 3:3  Frequency of objects (excepting scarabs) with New Kingdom royal inscriptions found in the Levant.

■ Stone Vessels   ▨ Other inscribed material

## The New Kingdom

With the rise of the eighteenth Dynasty and the expulsion of the Asiatic rulers from the Egyptian Delta, Egypt once again began to concern herself with international affairs. This is reflected in intensive military involvement abroad, primarily in Egypt and Syro-Palestine, and in a series of diplomatic ties that were enhanced through trade missions and royal marriages. Inscribed Egyptian stone vessels had their part to play in this process, although material of this kind is initially rare in the Levant, with solitary examples from the reigns of Ahmose and Tuthmosis III known from Cyprus and Crete respectively (Lilyquist 1995: cats. 12, 95; Warren 1969: 113). Although Schaeffer mentioned stone vessels with inscriptions of Tuthmosis III found at Ras Shamra he did not list registration numbers for these examples, and they do not appear in Caubet's inventory of stone vessels from the site (Caubet 1991; Schaeffer 1954: 41). The apparent absence of material relating to Tuthmosis III suggests that despite intensive military involvement in the Levant, this presence had little archaeological impact, at least where objects bearing royal inscriptions are concerned (Weinstein 1981: 11–12). It seems likely that any exchanges that occurred were one-sided, with material being taken back to Egypt as tribute and war booty rather than given out as diplomatic gifts.

The earliest confirmed royal name stone vessels found in the Levant date to the reign of Amenophis II, with sporadic occurrences continuing down to the time of Ramesses II (see Figure 3:3). This material was mostly recovered from Syria, focusing on large coastal entrepôts such as Ugarit and Byblos. At the former, finds were largely confined to the royal palace (courts II, IV, V, rooms 30, 31, 37, 68 and the archives; Caubet 1991: 214). Other examples were found in the 'South Palace', a building interpreted as a private residence attached to the court (Caubet 1991: 214), and in the *'maison aux albâtres'*, interpreted as the possible residence of an Egyptian, although Caubet (1991: 214) suggests that this example may have found its way there through a secondary deposit. The presence of inscribed stone vessels is therefore very much a 'royal' phenomenon within Ugarit. This contrasts with the more general distribution of non-inscribed Egyptian

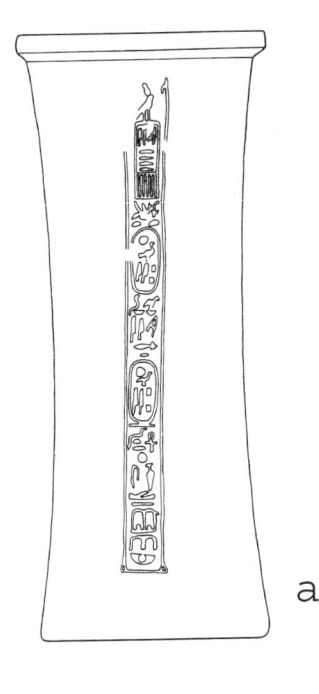

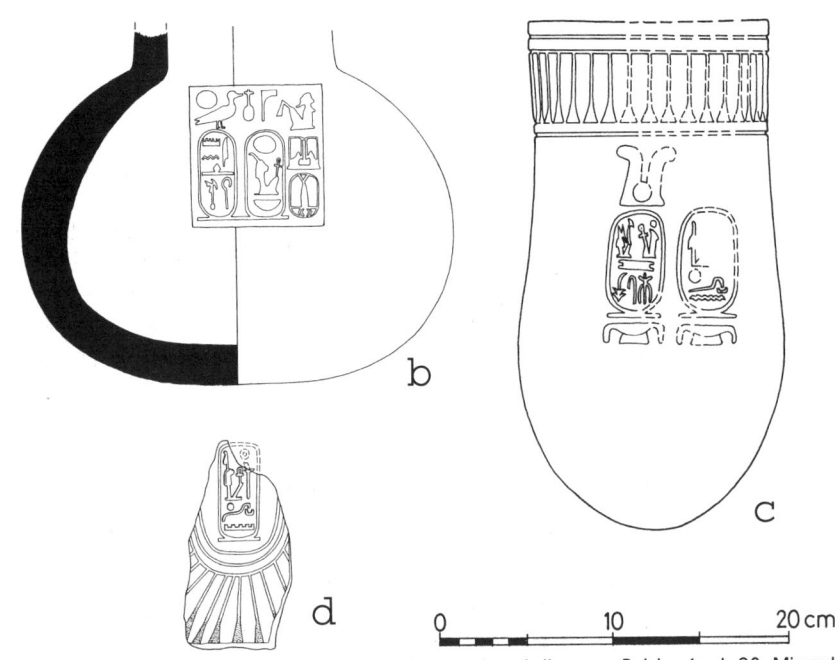

Figure 3:4 Stone vessels with Egyptian royal name inscriptions. a: Byblos (cat. 28, Minault-Gout 1997: fig. 3), b: Ras Shamra (cat. 51, after Caubet 1991: pl. XI.7), c: Beirut (cat. 58, after Saidah 1993-94: pl. 23.1.1), d: Gezer (cat. 69, after Macalister 1912: pl. XXIV.1).

stone vessels at the site (Sparks 1998: fig. 71, table 20). A similar pattern is seen at Byblos, where royal name vessels appeared primarily in the Royal Tombs (Tombs I, II, IV and V). At Beirut the situation is more ambiguous, with an inscribed stone vessel of Ramesses II appearing in a tomb whose owners were clearly wealthy, but not necessarily royal (Figure 3:4c; Appendix, cat. no. 58). Overall, the distribution focuses on sites of both commercial and strategic importance, perhaps pointing to Egyptian concerns with maintaining maritime access to the northern Levant for Egyptian troops and supplies, as well as for exploiting the rich trade potential of the region.

Stone vessels bearing cartouches of Amenophis III and Ramesses II are particularly common (Figure 3:3). One possible explanation could lie in the relative length of both reigns, 38 and 66 years respectively. It is possible that contact over a longer period resulted in a larger number of such objects being exchanged over time, and hence their greater visibility in the archaeological record. However, if reign length were the sole criterion, one might expect to find a greater representation of inscriptions belonging to other pharaohs who were in office for considerable periods, such as Amenophis II (27 years), Akhenaten (16 years) or Haremhab (28 years). As this is not the case, an alternative explanation could be that these peaks reflect periods of genuine intensification in diplomatic contact. Conversely, the limited amount of royal inscriptions from the time of Akhenaten down to the early nineteenth Dynasty may bear some relationship to the political climate of the period, particularly regarding the more limited involvement of Ugarit in Egyptian foreign affairs after it had become a vassal of the Hittite empire.

A comparison of these stone vessels with other objects bearing Egyptian pharaonic inscriptions also reveals interesting patterns (Figure 3:3). Although royal-name stone vessel imports appear to cease after Ramesses II, this was not the case with other inscribed classes of material such as faience vessels, plaques, sculpture, stelae and architectural elements (Weinstein 1981, 1992). These other classes of object could have reached the Levant by different means, and for different purposes. If stone vessels were used as political tools their absence may reflect a diminution in diplomatic traffic between the regions, particularly in the northern Levant. It has been suggested that Egyptian influence in this area was much reduced by the end of the nineteenth Dynasty (Weinstein 1992: 143). This suggestion is supported by what is known of Egyptian military campaigning during the reign of Merenptah which focused on the southern Levant (Singer 1988). This in turn may relate to a change in the nature of empire, and Egypt's growing focus on Syro-Palestine at the expense of her military aspirations in the north. The destruction of Ugarit in ca. 1190/1180 BC may also explain the apparent absence of later inscribed material in the region.

In contrast to the evidence from coastal Syria and Lebanon, stone vessels with royal name inscriptions were almost entirely lacking in the southern Levant. The only provenanced example bearing an Egyptian cartouche was a fragment dating to Ramesses II, found amongst cistern debris dug into an earlier cave tomb at Gezer (Macalister 1912: 94; Figure 3:4d; Appendix, cat. 69). While it is difficult to generalize on a single piece, this lacks any association with the local ruling class found in the material from further north, perhaps suggesting that this vessel reached the southern Levant by different means, or was accorded different status. It may have arrived there as the result of commercial or secondary trade rather than as a royal gift. The paucity of inscribed stone vessels in the southern Levant may also reflect the different relationship between Egypt and her Canaanite vassals. In this instance, Egypt was very much the superior partner in any exchange, and probably did not see the necessity of sealing communiqués with diplomatic gifts or bribes.

## Conclusions

This survey has demonstrated how the distribution of stone vessels with royal names illuminates aspects of Levantine foreign relations during the second millennium BC. It has been argued that such objects had a specific role to play in the various gift exchanges which often accompanied Egyptian diplomatic missions to foreign courts, whether as vessels in their own right, or as containers of other luxury materials. Egyptian artefacts with royal inscriptions have been linked to these kinds of missions elsewhere in the Mediterranean (Cline 1987, 1995; Warren 1995: 3). The distribution of such finds indicates that contact was focused on the sites of Byblos during the Egyptian Old and Middle Kingdoms, and at Ugarit from the time of Amenophis II down to Ramesses II, although with some discontinuities. This may reflect Egypt's interest in maintaining a presence at these two sites. Ensuring open trade links to the Syrian interior and cross-Mediterranean routes was economically advantageous. During the New Kingdom these sites also became strategically important as the Egyptians came into direct conflict with the expanding Mitannian and Hittite empires (Warburton Chapter 5, this volume), significant both as a point of entry for Egyptian military expeditions arriving by sea and as a supply centre for Egyptian vassals in the region. The loss of Ugarit to the Hittite empire must have come as a particular blow to Egyptian military aspirations there, and it is possible that objects such as these inscribed vessels are traces of diplomatic efforts to maintain contact and win back local support. The chronology of these objects would support this interpretation, with exports of inscribed stone vessels appearing to cease after the time of Ramesses II. Once a political and military *status quo* had been reached between Egypt and the Hittites, it is possible that these kinds of manoeuvrings took on a less vital aspect, and that diplomatic gifts of stone vessels to north Levantine rulers were no longer deemed necessary. In contrast, the scarcity of this kind of material in the southern Levant probably reflects the different relationship between Egypt and her Canaanite vassals, where the language of diplomacy was that of master to vassal, rather than to a potential ally. In this climate, relations were maintained through the threat of force, rather than by gifts or promises. The types of royal objects that are found in the south therefore reflect a different type of activity, revolving around an active Egyptian civil and military administration within the region.

# Appendix: catalogue of stone vessels with royal inscriptions found in the Levant

Dates in the following catalogue are according to Kitchen 2000.

| No. | Inscription Date | Provenance | Shape | References |
|---|---|---|---|---|
| **UP TO THE END OF THE OLD KINGDOM: Fourth Dynasty** | | | | |
| 1 | Queen Hetepheris | Byblos, level XXII, 3/7 | Diorite vessel fragment | Dunand 1958: fig. 1045.17538 |
| 2 | Kheops (2593–2570 BC) | Byblos, level XXII, court A | Calcite globular jar | Dunand 1939: pl. XXXIX.4506 |
| 3 | Queen Meritytis | Byblos, foundation deposit, temple of Baalat Gebal | Calcite vessel fragment | Montet 1928: fig. 23.64 |
| 4 | Khephren (2562–2537 BC) | Ebla, floor of Palace G | Diorite lamp | Scandone Matthiae 1988: pls. XI.3–4, XII.1 |
| 5 | Mykerinos (2537–2519 BC) | Byblos, foundation deposit, temple of Baalat Gebal | Diorite vessel fragment | Montet 1928: fig. 21, pl. XXXIX.45 |
| 6 | ,, | Byblos, level IV, room E | Calcite vessel fragment | Dunand 1939: pl. XXXIX.1794 |
| 7 | ,, | Byblos, level VII | Calcite vessel fragment | Dunand 1939: pl. XXXIX.2367 |
| 8 | ,, | Byblos, level VIII | Calcite vessel fragment | Dunand 1939: pl. XXXIX.2471 |
| 9 | ,, | Byblos, level XXVI, room B | Calcite vessel fragment | Dunand 1939: pl. XXXIX.5120 |
| **Fifth Dynasty** | | | | |
| 10 | Neferirkare Kakai (2494–2484 BC) | Byblos, level XXIII, room B | Calcite cylindrical jar | Dunand 1939: pl. XXXVI.4909 |
| 11 | Neuserre Ini (2470–2439 BC) | Byblos, wall removal, levels XI–XX | Calcite cylindrical jar | Dunand 1939: pl. XXXVII.4030 |
| 12 | Unis (2392–2362 BC) | Byblos, foundation deposit, temple of Baalat Gebal | Calcite jar fragment | Montet 1928: fig. 21.46, pl. XXXIX.46 |
| 13 | ,, | Byblos, level XIX | Calcite globular vase | Dunand 1939: pl. XXXVIII.3867 |
| 14 | ,, | Byblos, level XX | Calcite globular vase | Dunand 1939: pl. XXXVI.3980 |
| 15 | ,, | Byblos, level XX | Calcite vessel fragment | Dunand 1939: 278 cat. 3981 |
| 16 | ,, | Byblos, wall removal, levels XI–XX | Calcite vessel fragment | Dunand 1939: pl. XXXVI.4029 |
| **Sixth Dynasty** | | | | |
| 17 | Teti (2362–2350 BC) | Byblos, level XVIII, room F | Calcite offering plate | Dunand 1939: pl. XXXVII.3753 |

| No. | Inscription Date | Provenance | Shape | References |
|---|---|---|---|---|
| 18 | Pepi I (2342–2292 BC) | Byblos, foundation deposit, temple of Baalat Gebal | Stone vessel fragment | Montet 1928: pl. XXXIX.47 |
| 19 | " | Byblos, foundation deposit, temple of Baalat Gebal | Calcite cylindrical jar | Montet 1928: 71 cat. 48 |
| 20 | " | Byblos, foundation deposit, temple of Baalat Gebal | Calcite offering plate | Montet 1928: pl. XLV.49 |
| 21 | " | Byblos, foundation deposit, temple of Baalat Gebal | Calcite offering plate | Montet 1928: fig. 22.50 |
| 22 | " | Byblos, level I, room B | Calcite cylindrical jar | Dunand 1939: pl. XXXVII.1359 |
| 23 | " | Byblos, level VII | Calcite plate | Dunand 1939: 161 cat. 2359 |
| 24 | " | Byblos, level VIII | Calcite jar | Dunand 1939: 169 cat. 2466 |
| 25 | " | Byblos, level IX | Calcite vessel fragment | Dunand 1939: 183 cat. 2865 |
| 26 | " | Byblos, level XXI, room B | Calcite cylindrical jar | Dunand 1939: 309 cat. 4147 |
| 27 | " | Byblos, level XXI, room B | Calcite plate | Dunand 1939: pl. XXXVI.4149 |
| 28 | " | Byblos, level XXII, room C | Calcite cylindrical jar | Dunand 1939: pl. XXXVIII.4366; Figure 3:4a |
| 29 | " | Byblos, level XXVI, room F; level XXVII, room E | Breccia jar | Dunand 1939: 145 cat. 5141, 349 cat. 5191 |
| 30 | " | Byblos, trench 63, surface find | Calcite plate | Dunand 1939: pl. XXXVIII.6496 |
| 31 | " | Ebla, floor of Palace G | Calcite lid | Scandone Matthiae 1988: pl. XII.3 |
| 32 | Pepi I or II | Byblos, surface find, temple region | Calcite cylindrical jar | Dunand 1939: pl. XXXVI.1113 |
| 33 | " | Byblos, surface find, temple region | Calcite spherical jar | Dunand 1939: fig. 13.1114 |
| 34 | " | Byblos, surface find, temple region | Calcite vessel fragment | Dunand 1939: fig. 13.1116 |
| 35 | " | Byblos, level IV, east of room D | Calcite vessel fragment | Dunand 1939: 117 cat. 1742 |
| 36 | " | Byblos, level XV | Calcite vessel fragment | Dunand 1939: pl. XXXVII.3530 |
| 37 | " | Byblos, building XVIII, room B | Diorite vessel fragment | Dunand 1939: pl. XXXVII.3792 |

| No. | Inscription Date | Provenance | Shape | References |
|---|---|---|---|---|
| 38 | ,, | Byblos, level XXIII, east of room C | Calcite cylindrical jar | Dunand 1939: 231 cat. 4941 |
| 39 | ,, | Byblos, foundation deposit, temple of Baalat Gebal | Calcite vessel fragment | Montet 1928: pl. XLV.51 |
| 40 | ,, | Byblos, foundation deposit, temple of Baalat Gebal | Calcite zoomorphic jar | Montet 1928: pl. XL.57 |
| 41 | ,, | Byblos, level XXII, 3/7 | Calcite plate | Dunand 1958: fig. 1044.17540 |
| 42 | Merenra Nemtyemsaf I (2297–2287 BC) | Byblos, level VI | Calcite vessel fragment | Dunand 1939: 133 cat. 1940 |
| 43 | Pepi II (2287–2193 BC) | Byblos, level VI | Calcite vessel fragment | Dunand 1939: pl. XXXVI.1927 |
| 44 | ,, | Byblos, level VII | Calcite vessel fragment | Dunand 1939: pl. XXXVII.2365 |
| 45 | ,, | Byblos, level IX | Calcite vessel fragment | Dunand 1939: pl. XXXVI.2874 |
| 46 | ,, | Byblos, building XVIII, room B | Calcite lid | Dunand 1939: pl. XXXVIII.3800 |
| 47 | ,, | Byblos, foundation deposit, temple of Baalat Gebal | Stone zoomorphic jar | Montet 1928: pl. XL.56 |
| **MIDDLE KINGDOM AND SECOND INTERMEDIATE PERIOD** | | | | |
| 48 | Amenemhet III (1853–1808 BC) | Byblos, tomb I | Obsidian and gold cylindrical jar | Naville 1922: fig. 8.1; Montet 1928: cat. 610, pls. XXXVIII–LXXXIX |
| 49 | Twelfth to thirteenth Dynasties | Byblos, tomb II | Grey stone shouldered cylindrical jar | Montet 1928: fig. 70, pl. XCI614 |
| **NEW KINGDOM: Eighteenth Dynasty** | | | | |
| 50 | Amenophis II (1427–1401 BC) | Ras Shamra, palace room 30 | Calcite vessel fragment | Caubet 1991: 230, RS 15.202 |
| 51 | Amenophis III (1391–1353 BC) | Ras Shamra, lower city west | Calcite flask | Caubet 1991: pls VI.2, XI.7, RS 11.329; Figure 3:4b |
| 52 | ,, | Ras Shamra, palace room 68 | Calcite lid | Caubet 1991: 233, RS 17.476 |
| 53 | ,, | Ras Shamra, ridge NW tell? | Calcite lid | Caubet 1991: pl. VI.6, RS 1–11.116 |
| 54 | ,, | Ras Shamra, palace court IV | Calcite lid | Caubet 1991: 232, RS 16.340 |
| 55 | Amenophis III and Tiy | Ras Shamra, palace court V | Calcite lid | Caubet 1991: 232, RS 17.058 |

| No. | Inscription Date | Provenance | Shape | References |
|---|---|---|---|---|
| 56 | Nefertiti | Ras Shamra, palace room 30 | Calcite lid | Caubet 1991: 230, RS 15.203 |
| 57 | Haremhab (1323–1295 BC) | Ras Shamra, palace? | Calcite lid | Caubet 1991: 233, RS 17.477 |
| **Nineteenth Dynasty** | | | | |
| 58 | Ramesses II (1279–1213 BC) | Beirut, tomb 4 | Calcite drop jar | Saidah 1993–4: pl. 23.1.1; Ward 1993–4: pl. II.3–5; Figure 3:4c |
| 59 | ,, | Byblos, tomb V | Serpentine vessel fragment | Dunand 1939: 93 cat. 1360 |
| 60 | ,, | Byblos, tomb V | Calcite juglet | Montet 1928: pl. CXLII.883 |
| 61 | ,, | Byblos, trench 61, 1 m depth | Calcite vessel fragment | Dunand 1939: pl. XXXVIII.6031 |
| 62 | ,, | Byblos, tomb V | Calcite vessel fragment | Montet 1928: fig. 102.890 |
| 63 | ,, | Ras Shamra, ridge NW tell | Calcite footed jar | Caubet 1991: pls VI.3, XI.6, RS 11.848 and 869 |
| 64 | ,, | Ras Shamra, palace, west archives | Calcite vessel fragment | Caubet 1991: pl. VI.1, RS 11.261 |
| 65 | ,, | Ras Shamra, ridge NW tell | Calcite vessel fragment | Caubet 1991: pl. VI.5, RS 1–11.115 |
| 66 | ,, | Ras Shamra, tomb 4912 | Calcite vessel fragment | Caubet 1991: 241, RS 34.030 |
| 67 | ,, | Ras Shamra, ridge NW tell | Calcite vessel fragment | Caubet 1991: pl. VI.4, RS 11.869 |
| 68 | ,, | Ras Shamra, palace room 30 | Calcite vessel fragment | Caubet 1991: 230 RS 15.201 |
| 69 | ,, | Gezer, cave 15.II | Calcite vessel fragment | Macalister 1912: pl. XXIV.1; Figure 3:4d |

## Note

1   This is a calcite offering plate inscribed with the name Nefer-Seshem-Ra. It has been suggested (Dunand 1939: cat. 5366; Wright 1988: 150) that this official was a scribe who was posted to Byblos and who placed the offering plate in the temple himself. This is plausible, as the temple was full of Egyptianizing and Egyptian material, the plate seems to be contemporary with the use of the temple, and is a type of object that is appropriate for use as a votive offering; nor does it bear any funerary formulae/epithets to suggest that it had seen prior use in a tomb.

## Acknowledgments

The author thanks Graham Reed for providing the illustrations, and Christine Lilyquist and Peter Ucko for their comments and suggestions on an earlier form of this chapter.

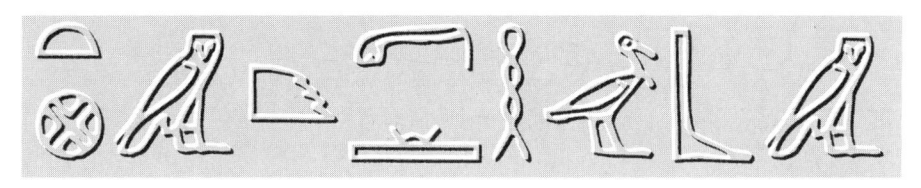

# CHAPTER 4

# RECONSTRUCTING THE ROLE OF EGYPTIAN CULTURE IN THE VALUE REGIMES OF THE BRONZE AGE AEGEAN: STONE VESSELS AND THEIR SOCIAL CONTEXTS

*Andrew Bevan*

## Introduction

Egyptian stone vessels are important evidence for early cultural contact in the Aegean. In the past they have been variously deployed by modern commentators not only as testimony of growing social complexity within certain Aegean communities and emergent elite consumption at a local level (Renfrew 1972), but also as tracers of a wider civilized package (including perhaps palaces and writing), spreading outwards to the Aegean from a Near Eastern core (e.g. Watrous 1987). Stone survives extremely well in archaeological contexts, especially in comparison to organic materials or metals (which often degrade, get re-cycled or otherwise vanish from the record) and this high durability offers both distinct analytical advantages (a larger dataset, less biased by gaps of differential preservation) and raises specific methodological problems (stone vessel curation and re-use). The following discussion considers the scale and significance of Egyptian influence through stone vessels in four different chronological episodes, corresponding to the third millennium, and the earlier, mid- and later second millennium respectively. It emphasizes (a) that the exchange and consumption of Egyptian goods in the Aegean is structured by very period-specific priorities and parameters, and (b) that Aegean patterns must be considered within a wider eastern Mediterranean response to Egyptian material culture.

## The third millennium (prepalatial Crete)

The third millennium is a period in which previously separate regions in the eastern Mediterranean gradually become incorporated into larger networks. In Egypt and the Levant, we see the emergence of a set of more direct and intensive interactions, but the degree to which this growing trade impacts on other areas such as Cyprus, western Anatolia and the Aegean remains difficult to pin down. Indeed, as Sherratt and Sherratt (1991) point out, it is possible that while interregional trade between the Aegean and the rest of the Near East in the third millennium was extremely limited in terms of the quantity of objects exchanged, its impact may have been disproportionately significant in social and political terms. This argument runs the risk of over-extrapolating from limited evidence but it nonetheless grapples with the fact that the value of exotic imports is often inversely correlated with frequency not least because such artefacts advertise rare access to (geographically) liminal knowledge and power (Helms 1988).

The single most important trading factor in the third millennium eastern Mediterranean was the advent and widespread adoption of the sailing ship. This technology is taken up unevenly across the whole region, and in the Aegean canoe-borne travel was probably the norm until quite late in the period (Broodbank 2000: 96–102). Elaborate longboats provided a high-risk, medium range, low carrying capacity method in which extra-local trade might be conducted and an EB2[1] 'international spirit' forged (e.g. Renfrew 1972: esp. 225 ff), but a crucial change seems to occur during EB3–MB1, when sail-driven vessels first appear in Aegean iconography (Basch 1991: 48–49; McGeehan-Liritzis 1996: 256, figs. 7.5.3a–b; Rutter 1993: 777–779, figs. 13–14; Yule 1980: 165–166, 28–29.52), pointing to a technological (and ideological) shift that is likely to have revolutionized not just the speed, but also the scale of regional interaction (Broodbank 2000: 341 ff). However, this new interaction followed preferred routes reflecting the fact that the eastern Mediterranean experiences winds and currents with critical effects on the organization of trading activities. The most important of these is a broad favouring of anti-clockwise eastern Mediterranean travel. Before the advent of brailed shipping (Casson 1995: 21, 273; Marcus 1998: 101; Roberts 1991: 55–56, 1995: 308–310), the Levant should be considered as a likely intermediary in trade, for example, from Egypt to Crete. More specifically, a chief filter was probably the site of Byblos which, from sometime in the first half of the third millennium, becomes pre-eminent in the range and quantity of its Egyptian imports and is also implicated in the early dissemination of sailing technologies (e.g. Breasted 1906–1907: passages 432–433; Simpson 1960).

It is with these parameters in mind that the evidence for the early arrival of Egyptian stone vessels in the Aegean must be assessed. In fact, before EMIIB–MMI or II on Crete, there is little evidence for imported stone vessels. Evans (1928: 16–17, fig. 7a–b) published three fragments from apparent late neolithic contexts under the Central Court at Knossos, but these are of doubtful Egyptian connection as regards both shape and material (see also Phillips 1991; Warren 1969: 109 n. 1).[2] Two of the three fragments were found in the highest levels of the neolithic deposits, which were subject to extensive later Minoan levelling operations, one being a body fragment of a large vessel in the type of polychrome stone sometimes used much later at Knossos during the Neopalatial period.

Another potential import of early date is a tiny fragment from a possible obsidian bowl from a secure EMIIA level on the 'Royal Road' (Warren 1981: 633–634, fig. 5; 1989: 634, fig. 5). The piece has no diagnostic features to identify it as a bowl, let alone as Egyptian. It has a slightly bevelled edge, which suggests it might be a rim fragment, and if Egyptian, would most likely come from a first Dynasty flaring cup (e.g. UC 36621, and therefore already an heirloom by EMIIA).[3] The evidence is equivocal, but if it is an import in EMIIA, it would represent an interesting example of an attenuated pattern of down-the-line trading.

These problematic pieces aside, there is nothing in terms of stone vessel finds to suggest strong contact between Egypt and the Aegean before the late Prepalatial period on Crete. Then the pattern changes, even if the details remain unclear. There are a handful of definite or likely Egyptian imports from EMII–MMI/II contexts (Warren 1969: 112, D327 P604; 1981: 633, fig. 4; 1989: 1 n. 1). Unfortunately, none of these can be closely dated either by context or style. It remains difficult to gauge when, within a period of four or five centuries, these pieces were arriving, and whether steadily or in a rush at the end of the time span.

Possibly more informative than the Egyptian imports at this time, however, is a series of local Cretan imitations. The latter range from exact matches for Egyptian shapes to less convincing partial borrowings, but this group contrasts with the pattern of the actual imports in two ways: (a) they have not so far been found at Knossos, but rather concentrate at Mochlos and in the Mesara tombs, and (b) they are a much more coherent group, copying a limited number of highly recognizable shapes of oil containers.

Broadly speaking, we can link the vessel styles imitated on Crete to prototypes produced in Egypt from the late Old Kingdom to early Middle Kingdom (Ward 1971: fig. 17; Phillips 1996). This agrees well with the rough EMII–MMII date range of their find contexts, but closer inspection suggests a tighter chronological and spatial pattern. Two imitative shapes (Figure 4:1) – the splayed cylindrical jars from Mochlos (Soles 1992: 84 fig. 33, pl. 30; Warren 1969: 76 D323 P423)[4] and several collared pots (e.g. Warren 1969: 72 D199 P360, D203 P365) – are more precisely identifiable as copies of late Old Kingdom (OK) products, sometimes surviving into First Intermediate Period (FIP) contexts, but characteristic of the sixth Dynasty (Aston 1994: types 35, 123–126; Petrie 1937: nos. 584–593, 650–652). These also seem to copy an OK material dichotomy which combined: (a) the dominance of the material travertine, and (b) the existence of a high-value alternative, usually anorthosite gneiss (Figure 4:1). Beginning at the end of the Early Dynastic period, but increasingly during the Old Kingdom, anorthosite gneiss (sometimes called Cephren diorite) gains prominence as a marker for royal and upper elite consumption.[5] The Cretan imitations arguably use a mottled dolomitic limestone to copy anorthosite gneiss and either a white dolomitic limestone or 'banded tufa'[6] to imitate travertine. The faithful transfer of the idea of this material double act to Crete is also made more plausible because both materials are represented in similar shapes at Byblos, whose probable role as a trading intermediary has already been mentioned.

These early imitations, the splayed cylindrical jar and the collared jar, can arguably be distinguished from slightly later imitations from the Mesara tombs (Figure 4:2). At least six examples of the latter are known and, in contrast to the Mochlos versions, they all exhibit shorter, more squared-off rims and bases and sloping sides, characteristic of FIP–early twelfth Dynasty prototypes. Likewise, another type of definite imitation is the closed jar with short everted rim, which copies a FIP–early Middle Kingdom (MK) form. A third shape, the squat alabastron, might, with less confidence, be linked to rare twelfth Dynasty versions. It seems likely therefore that the Mochlos and Mesara imitations represent early and late ends of a chronological spectrum of contact and influence spanning EMIIB–MMI or possibly MMII, while the interface between them is blurred by the relative archaeological obscurity of both EMIII in Crete and the FIP in Egypt.

Egypt　　　　Byblos　　　　Crete

a　　　　　　b　　　　　　c

d　　　　　　e　　　　　　f

g　　　　　　h　　　　　　i

Figure 4:1　Late Old Kingdom stone vessels from Egypt and Byblos and their Cretan imitations.
a　Sixth Dynasty (Pepi I) cylindrical jar in travertine from Egypt (UC 15791, ht. 147 mm).
b　Sixth Dynasty-style cylindrical jar in travertine from Byblos (ht. 80 mm; Dunand 1939: no. 1744, pl. cl).
c　Cretan imitation cylindrical jar in dolomitic limestone from Mochlos (Ag. Nikolaos M. 10364, ht. 42 mm; Soles 1992: pl. 30).
d　Sixth Dynasty-style cylindrical jar in anorthosite gneiss from Egypt (UC 41053, ht. 103 mm).
e　Sixth Dynasty-style cylindrical jar in anorthosite gneiss from Byblos (ht. 58 mm; Dunand 1958: no. 13566, pl. ccv).
f　Cretan imitation cylindrical jar in dolomitic limestone from Mochlos (HM 1294, ht. 41 mm; Karetsou 2000: no. 25c).
g　Late Old Kingdom-style collared jar in travertine from Egypt (UC 41356, ht. 118 mm).
h　Late Old Kingdom-style collared jar in travertine from Byblos (ht. not given; Montet 1928: no. xliii.97).
i　Cretan imitation of collared jar in 'banded tufa' from Platanos (HM 1665, ht. 70 mm (Karetsou 2000: no. 14).

Egypt                    Crete

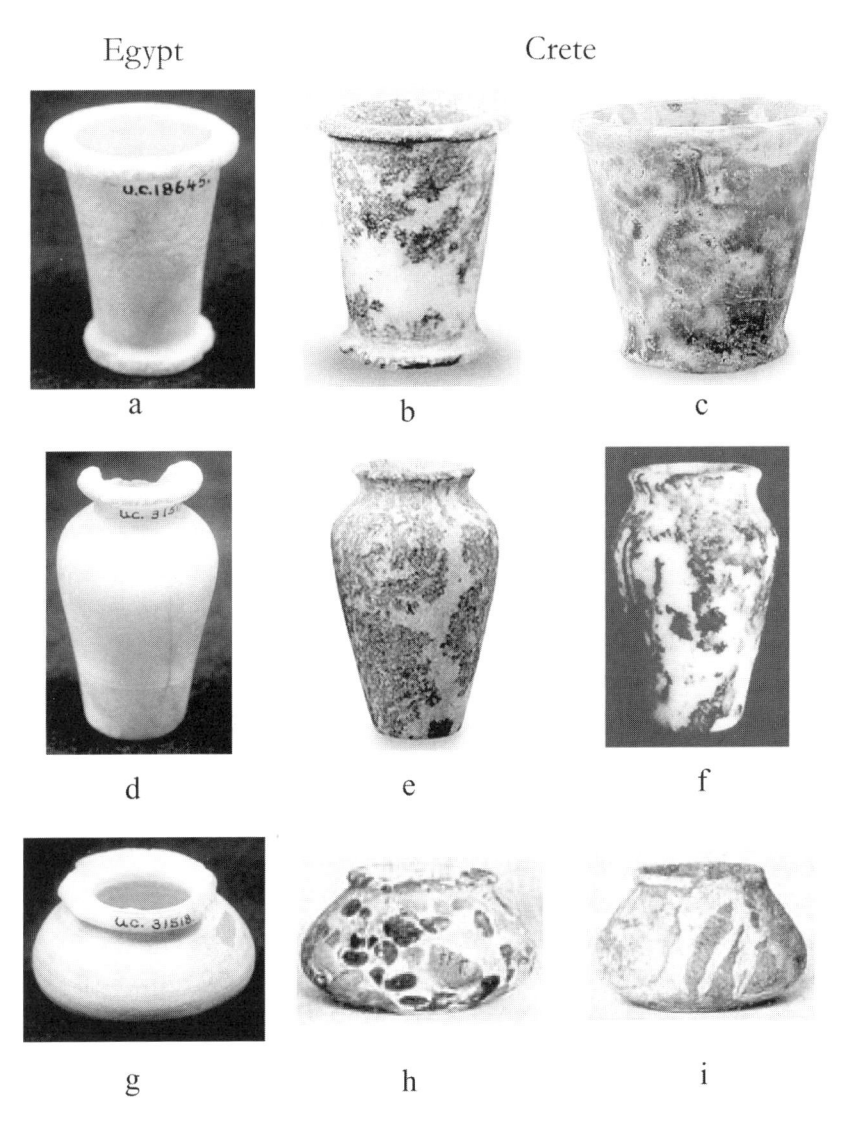

a     b     c

d     e     f

g     h     i

Figure 4:2  First Intermediate Period–early Middle Kingdom stone vessels from Egypt and their possible Cretan imitations from the Mesara.
a  Cylindrical jar in travertine from Haraga (UC 18645, ht. 58 mm).
b  Cretan imitation cylindrical jar in dolomitic marble/limestone from Agia Triada (HM 663, ht. 53 mm; Karetsou 2000: no. 25h).
c  Cretan imitation cylindrical jar in calcite from Platanos (HM 1637, ht. 54 mm; *ibid*: no. 25e).
d  Everted rim jar in travertine from Diospolis Parva (UC 31519, ht. 75 mm).
e  Cretan imitation everted rim jar in dolomitic marble/limestone from Agia Triada (HM 655, ht. 58 mm, Karetsou 2000: 38 no. 19a).
f  Cretan imitation everted rim jar in dolomitic marble/limestone from Kommos (HM 4271, ht. 57 mm; Schwab 1996: pl. 4.35).
g  Miniature alabastron in travertine from Diospolis Parva (UC 31518, ht. 32 mm).
h  Cretan miniature alabastron in conglomerate from Gournia (HM 554, ht. 36 mm; Warren 1969: P2).
i  Cretan miniature alabastron in breccia from Koumasa (HM 716, ht. 44 mm; Warren 1969: P4).

So far we have concentrated on the known imports and definite imitations from early contexts, but there is also some 'floating' material, in particular, a large number of vessels at Knossos, which are undeniably products of predynastic to Old Kingdom (PD–OK) times, but which come from unstratified deposits or are found as obvious antiques in much later, second millennium contexts. Significant debate has occurred over the degree to which these vessels represent recent arrivals to Crete in the later Bronze Age or had been locally curated, principally at Knossos, since an original exchange in later Prepalatial times. In favour of these being later arrivals, we can trace the appearance of such PD–OK antiques at a large number of MB–LB Aegean, Egyptian, Levantine, and Nubian sites (Figure 4:3), suggesting a phenomenon of eastern Mediterranean-wide proportions. Several commentators have suggested the possibility that such antiques were the traded proceeds of tomb-robbing in the Second Intermediate Period (SIP) and New Kingdom (NK), and the sheer numbers are excellent evidence that some recirculation was occurring. Moreover, some of these antique shapes were being imitated by Cretan artisans in this later period (see below).

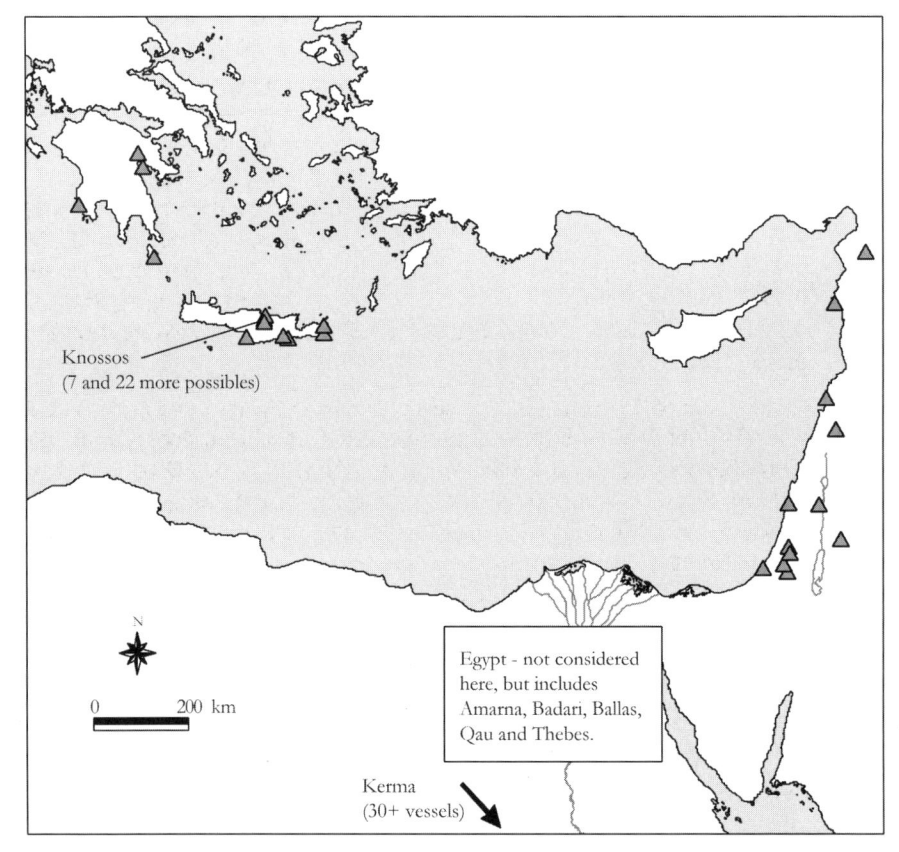

Figure 4:3 Sites with Predynastic–Old Kingdom stone vessels found in Middle–Late Bronze Age contexts (1–5 examples per site unless otherwise stated; for further information, see Phillips 1992; Sparks 1998; Warren 1969).

Two features of the problem are relatively certain: (a) that some degree of second millennium trade in such items was occurring, probably as the result of tomb-robbing, and (b) that if any of the 'floating' material is to be ascribed to earlier trade then it must have occurred in the EMIIB–MMI episode in which there is both definite evidence for real Egyptian imports in Crete and increased contact made possible by the sail. This weakens the possibility that some of the predynastic to early dynastic-style vessels found in Crete ever arrived contemporaneously with their floruit in Egypt, while at the same time posing the question: can we expect any of the Cretan 'floating' corpus to have been present in the traded assemblages of this late third millennium episode?

To pursue this point, it is worth examining a particular group of carinated bowls (Figure 4:4, top half; Aston 1994: shapes 112, 117). Fragments of at least five of these bowls are known from Knossos (Warren 1969: 111). In Egypt, this shape forms a tighter fourth–sixth Dynasty typological group than many of the floating Knossos finds. All the Cretan fragments are made of anorthosite gneiss, which by the late Old Kingdom was used mainly for bowls and lamps, essentially to mark out the household equipment and tableware of the royal family and upper elite. Good examples for such shapes, often in anorthosite gneiss, come from the tombs of Pepi II and Neit in Egypt (Jécquier 1934, 1935). Indeed, the proportion of this stone used for tomb equipment seems to correlate strongly with apparent social status.

Egyptian stone vessels are also found in the Levant at Byblos and Ebla in late third millennium contexts (Sparks Chapter 3, this volume). At Byblos, they are associated with two main areas: buildings XL (Dunand 1939: 288–308; Montet 1928; Saghieh 1983: 40–45, fig. 13) and XXV (Dunand 1958: 899–900; Saghieh 1983: 36–37, fig. 12a). The exact nature of the larger deposit from building XL is difficult to interpret, but is clearly a ritual deposit or temple store of some kind, associated with the Byblite divinity, Balaat Gebal. Here, there is a predominance of oil jars, offering tables and small collared pots, and although there are examples of earlier shapes, the vast majority of the assemblage can be ascribed to the fifth–sixth Dynasties on grounds of shape, material, and inscriptions.

A smaller group of Egyptian stone vessels comes from Byblos building XXV. This area was poorly published, but the vessels were found on a burnt floor within what seems to have been a large royal or elite residence (Dunand 1958: 899; Saghieh 1983: 37). Here, there is a greater emphasis on bowls and tables, suggesting that the use of these items related more to display and less to the manipulation of oils than those in the Balaat Gebal temple. It matches quite well the sorts of ostentatious stone tableware associated with the Egyptian royal family, as in the tombs of Pepi and Neit mentioned above, and the upper elite.

Another good parallel for the depositional context represented by building XXV comes from Ebla (Scandone Matthiae 1979, 1981, 1988), the only other north Levantine site to have produced stone vessels at this time. Here, over 200 travertine and anorthosite gneiss fragments were found in Palace G, close to the archive room. Bowls and lamps represent some 85 per cent of the identifiable pieces and again the link with consumption in a royal or upper elite domestic context is striking. Both assemblages, from Byblos building XXV and Ebla Palace G make good candidates for high-level transfers between royal households. Most important is the proportion of anorthosite gneiss, clearly present (but unquantifiable) at Byblos and ca. 35 per cent at Ebla: in

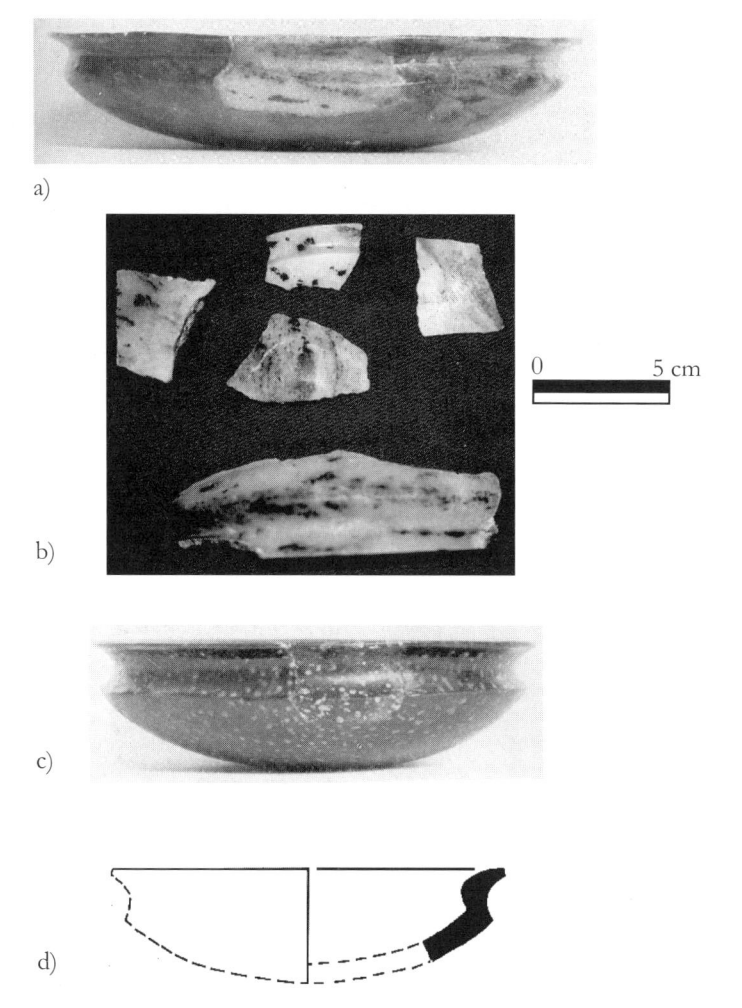

Figure 4:4  Egyptian anorthosite gneiss bowls and Cretan imitations.
a   Rim fragment (reconstructed as a whole vessel) of an actual Egyptian import in anorthosite gneiss from Knossos, Crete (HM 590, Warren 1969: P599).
b   Other fragments of Egyptian imports in anorthosite gneiss from Knossos, Crete (AM AE 2301; 1910.283; 1938.409a, 583).
c   Cretan imitation in Giali obsidian of Egyptian carinated bowl (HM 591, Warren 1969: P409).
d   Cretan imitation in quartz crystal of Egyptian carinated bowl (KSM Unexplored Mansion).

Egypt, a definite signature for the royal family or one of a very few powerful individuals around it.

If the Knossos carinated bowls were indeed early arrivals, they would fit well into such a series of official transfers, even gift exchange, in the late third millennium, characterizing the new long-range, maritime link-ups enabled by the adoption of the sail.

The main points concerning the third millennium can now be summarized. All possible Egyptian or Egyptianizing material comes from Crete and may be understood as a phenomenon associated with elite display on this island rather than extrapolated to the Aegean as a whole. There is little clear evidence for pre-EMIIB trade and this fits well with the view of EBA maritime voyaging technologies as limited in range and carrying capacity prior to the adoption of sailing. A few objects may have made it to Crete on the back of down-the-line networks, along with other possible early imports such as ivory or carnelian, but such objects were both rare and probably deracinated of original Egyptian meaning or social context. In contrast, by EMII–MMI there is clear evidence for Egyptian imports and their local Cretan imitations, and the challenge is to assess when these objects arrived (within this rather broad time period), in what numbers, and with what degree of cultural impact. On the basis of the limited contextual information from Crete itself, we can point to highly-constrained, royal or upper elite consumption of similar Egyptian imports in the contemporary Levant. It is possible that the trade in actual Egyptian imports was mutually directed, involving exchanges at a major centre such as Knossos, and that the phenomenon of imitations is testimony to a regional desire, first at Mochlos (perhaps contemporary with sixth Dynasty–FIP) and then later in the Mesara (probably contemporary with FIP–early twelfth Dynasty) to emulate import consumption patterns that were being played out elsewhere. Moreover, there is no sign in Egypt or the Levant of a return trade from Crete in the third millennium BC and we must consider the possibility that the contact was all one-way, perhaps not involving actual Cretan shipping until quite late. A likely intermediary in such trade is Byblos, which was both the main focus for Egyptian activity in the third and early second millennium Levant and a coastal centre closely associated with ships and sailing (Matthews and Roemer Chapter 1, this volume).

## The earlier second millennium (Protopalatial Crete)

The earlier second millennium sees the emergence of a more integrated system of exchange in the eastern Mediterranean, with greater interaction between different regions. It is therefore curious that, at first glance, imported Egyptian stone vessels are rarely if ever present in Aegean contexts of this date, particularly in Protopalatial Crete, where we might expect them after the signs of earlier imports described above. Part of the reason for this absence may be the fact that the kohl pot becomes the dominant shape in the Egyptian MK stone vessel assemblage, but does not appear to have been popular with Cretan elites at any stage in the Bronze Age. Even so, the invisibility of Protopalatial Egyptian vessel imports is probably misleading for at least two reasons. First, certain forms contemporary with this period, such as the MK ridge-neck alabastron, are found in later contexts in Crete and may have arrived in the Protopalatial and been curated locally. Second, as we have seen, there are a range of EMII–MMI/II imports and imitations that are often considered in relation to the Prepalatial period and aspects of Cretan state formation, but which may often be better seen as MM phenomena.

For example, the Mesara cylindrical jar imitations mentioned above are found in contexts mixed with MM material or tombs that begin in MMI such as at Kamilari and Kommos (Warren 1969: 76 P421). As we have seen, the shape is different from the Mochlos versions with a shorter rim and base. It is one of several imitations, including everted rim jars and possibly also alabastra, that begin in MMI, may still be in use in MMII (Phillips 1991: 36) and have direct contemporary parallels in FIP–early MK assemblages (Figure 4:2 above). The Mesara's involvement is probably due both to the emergence of Phaistos as a major island centre at this time and to the increased extent of interaction made possible by the regular use of sailing ships, which would have broadened the impact of Egyptian objects and ideas.

There is hardly any evidence for trade in Cretan vessels in the opposite direction. One exception is probably a serpentinite lid, noted by Petrie at Kahun where real and locally-imitated Kamares ware was also found (Fitton *et al.* 1998). In any event, as in the EBA, an important feature that has been neglected is the role of the Levant as a filter for this trade. The early stages of the MK saw the re-establishment of intensive exchange with Byblos, an apparent direct trading relationship that bypassed much of the southern Levant. In this sense the fairly exclusive, bilateral relations between these two had not really changed since the EBA. The two chief Egyptian shapes being imitated in Crete (cylindrical and everted rim jars) are ones that are also found in possibly earlier contexts (those including MBIIA material) in the Levant (Sparks 1998: 128–130).

## The mid-second millennium (Neopalatial Crete)

A large range of objects and imitative styles can be identified which point to the influence of Egyptian material culture and thought on Crete during the Neopalatial period (Warren 1995). One of the most clearly visible signs of this interaction in the archaeological record are stone vessels. Lilyquist and others have suggested that some of these apparently Egyptian vessels were made in the Levant (Lilyquist 1996, 1997; see also Sparks 1998, Chapter 3, this volume). Given the excellent evidence for raw stone, scraps, and finished vessels moving about the eastern Mediterranean in the LBA, possibly along with craft specialists as well, it is not possible to resolve this issue at this time. There are indeed a number of imported vessels from the Aegean that fall into a putative, Egypto-Levantine category and that may just as well have been products of a centre such as Tel el-Ajjul, as from Egypt itself (Bevan 2001: 193–197). The difficulty encountered in making such distinctions may fit into a picture of elite social identities that were becoming increasingly entangled during a period known for the high level of Levantine involvement in Egyptian political affairs.

In MMIII–LMI, significant numbers of SIP–early eighteenth Dynasty stone vessels are found at sites on the north and east coasts of Crete, particularly at Knossos (Warren 1989). Unfortunately, a large number of the fragments come from secondary deposits or unclear stratigraphical contexts.[7] Despite this, there is a sense in which the LMI period stands out, with a large number of datable fragments from contexts with significant LMI material and the occasional imitation of Egyptian stone vessels in contemporary ceramics (e.g. Boyd Hawes *et al.* 1908: pl.vii.15).

A large proportion (over 40 per cent) of the foreign stone vessel fragments from Crete are probably from Egyptian or Egyptian-style baggy alabastra. Although popular in contemporary Egypt and also in the Levant, the extent of this shape's dominance in Crete is noteworthy. Cretan elites were arguably being selective about those elements of Egyptian culture that they considered relevant to their own purposes. In Egypt, the alabastron was an all-purpose oil container, for a variety of products. In this respect, Cretan preference for this form was probably not the result of a predilection for a specific oil, but may rather reflect self-reinforcing, local ideas of what an exotic Egyptian container should look like. In contrast, kohl pots continue to be completely absent from Crete. This might be due to a lack of local demand and/or because intermediary Levantine sites were not interested in this vessel shape either.

Most of the Egyptian imports are made of travertine (often misnamed 'alabaster'). But this Egyptian stone[8] was also used as a raw material to make Cretan-style vessels. A small lump and several bore cores from hollowing out vessel interiors are known from Knossos (Warren 1969: 125–126, KSM Evans boxes 1427, 1894, MUM/67/895). Widespread trading in raw stone is an undeniable element of east Mediterranean exchange at this time, but the available supply does not always seem to have been adequate for the needs of local Cretan workshops. At Knossos, there are several scrapped, sawn up Egyptian vessels that were in the process of being re-used for the material out of which they were made. Travertine was being harnessed to add value to a specific range of elaborate, often experimental and/or ritual, palatial products, such as rhyta, footed goblets and elaborate pouring shapes (Figure 4:5). Consumption of such vessels appears to have occurred almost exclusively in and around the Cretan palaces and upper elite dwellings, contributing an important ideological component (e.g. evidence for contact with a geographically distant and diplomatically influential place) to ceremonial expressions of Cretan elite power.

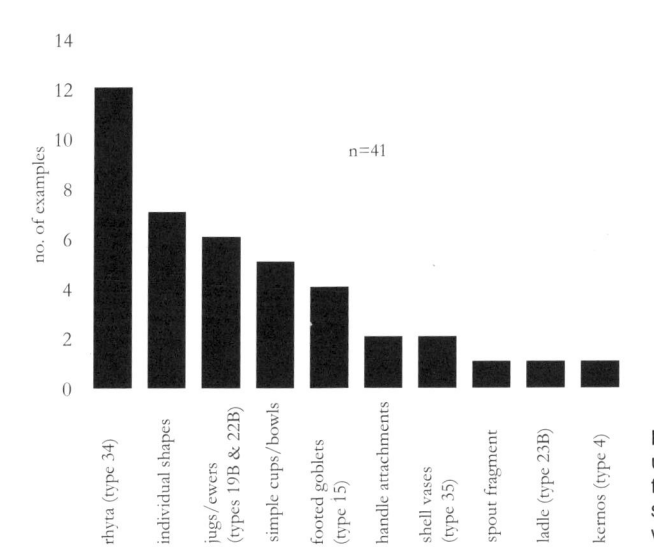

Figure 4:5 Chart of the use of imported travertine for Cretan stone vessel shapes (from Warren 1969 with a few additions).

Cretan imitations of Egyptian stone vessels occur also in the Neopalatial, but in contrast to early acts of copying, what distinguishes this period is the fact that it was not contemporary Egyptian shapes that were being imitated locally but predynastic–Old Kingdom (PD–OK) Egyptian vessels. This exclusive emphasis on imitating only antique shapes is a new and unique phenomenon in the eastern Mediterranean at this time. The main models seem to have been the spheroid bowl, the 'heart-shaped' jar, the squat collared bowl, and the carinated bowl (Warren 1969: 74–75). For the first three, harder local stones of limited availability were always chosen, but the dominant local material is a variety of bluish-black gabbro with massed white phenocrysts that was presumably meant as a close substitute for the porphyritic/dioritic stones used in the Egyptian originals.

The carinated bowls highlighted earlier as possible candidates for early high level exchange are also imitated in the later period (Figure 4:4 bottom half). Two examples are known from Knossos. These are made of quartz crystal and Giali obsidian, which are the two hardest stones (Moh's scale 6–7) worked by Cretan artisans; as with the use of gabbro, their deployment here probably reflects the fact that the Egyptian originals (including those found at Knossos) were themselves made of very hard anorthosite gneiss. However, the deployment of these specific stones may also have served a more complex ideological purpose. In Egypt, there is excellent evidence for the way that the mythological associations of different stones in general and the visual opposition of black and white stones in particular might be used to construct elaborate ritual ideologies, for instance between light and dark or good and evil.[9] The potential 'oppositional' properties of these identically-shaped obsidian and quartz crystal imitations may also reflect the existence of such priorities in Crete as well. Likewise, the potential use of white-spotted, black Giali obsidian copies alongside black-spotted, white anorthosite gneiss originals may have equally significant symbolic possibilities.

The actual Egyptian antique prototypes are found, often alongside contemporary Egyptian vessels, in MMIII–LMIII deposits. Unless we assume a considerable level of trade in EMI–II, completely unsupported by existing evidence from early contexts, then the vast majority of the other PD–OK antiquities found in Crete were produced in Egypt too early to be contemporary trade items in any quantity. The most likely scenario that can account for the circulation of these antique Egyptian objects in later periods is tomb-robbing (Phillips 1992: 170, 175–176; Pomerance 1973, 1984). Regular looting is attested in Egypt by the frequent evidence for the re-use of earlier grave goods in tombs of all periods. Re-excavation of antiquities was occasionally officially sanctioned: the most striking example is Amenophis III's search for the tomb of Osiris at Abydos, which probably emptied out (and recirculated?) items from the first Dynasty mastaba of Djer. However, periods of political instability presumably provided good opportunities for illicit looting and the activities of tomb-robbers is documented in written records from the Third Intermediate Period (Phillips 1992). Likewise, the mid-second millennium was arguably another period of heightened looting activity, especially since Egyptian stone vessel assemblages of this period are characterized by the frequent re-use of older vessels, both in provincial middle class tombs and apparently also in royal workshops (Bevan 2001: 188 ff).

Views have tended to polarize between the two options of curation and tomb-robbing, but even we accept that recirculation was occurring it is quite possible that a combination of the two processes was at work. As we have seen, if the carinated anorthosite gneiss bowls and perhaps a few other vessels were early arrivals then they would fit into a pattern of high-level third millennium gift exchange also visible at Byblos and Ebla. If so, then one reason for the Neopalatial imitation of antique vessels in Crete may have been that there existed an important interaction between curated trade items from an earlier time, already incorporated into the ideology of the palace centre (e.g. as evidence of early legitimacy), and the increased prominence of similar vessels looted from Egyptian tombs later on and exchanged around the eastern Mediterranean. If tangible links to the past were being made by a favoured few, using locally-curated heirlooms, it would be understandable if there was a broader Cretan elite who sought to claim similar ancient or hereditary connections using the looted antiquities available through eastern Mediterranean trade. In other words, heirlooms and looted vessels may have been playing off each other and distinguishing between them may have been as important, and as difficult, for LBA Aegean consumers as it is today.

The earliest dated Cretan imitation is a possible PD–OK spheroid bowl from MMIIB–III Knossos (Warren 1969: 75). This is approximately the period to which a series of Knossian bridge-spouted jars in gabbro can be stylistically dated (Warren 1969: 33–34) and there may be a connection between the arrival of the earliest antiquities and local aspiration to produce more elaborate vessels in harder stones. Not least we should remember how gabbro was also being used as local simulacrum for Egyptian hard stones. This imitative link becomes visible in a series of Cretan conversions of imported vessels (Warren 1996). Such conversions make use of imported PD–OK jars and SIP/early eighteenth Dynasty alabastra and generally take one of two forms. In one, only simple modifications are made, for example by carving grooves in them or piercing the bases to make rhyta. In the other, a limited number of local shapes are made into amphorae, ewers and bridge-spouted jars, reworking the imports as body segments and adding additional handles and spouts. The most impressive examples are perhaps those from the Zakros Shrine Treasury (Warren 1969: 109 P593) and from Mycenae Shaft Grave V (Sakellarakis 1976: 177, pl. ii.4). There is a temptation to see these as rare or one-off efforts, but fragmentary examples from Knossos suggest that they may have been relatively common, at least in the workshops around the palace.[10]

The connection with the gabbro bridge-spouted jars, the Egyptian antiquities, the Cretan imitations, and the Cretan conversions comes full circle with an example from Mavro Spelio (Warren 1969: P403). This is a Cretan gabbro imitation of an antique Egyptian spheroid bowl, and a drilling has begun, but is not finished, in the shoulder. The other examples make it clear that this represents a half-way point in the production of a multiple assembly bridge-spouted jar that, for example, could have taken new loop handles and a spout. This inversion, an imitation made to look like a foreign antiquity so that it could then be incorporated into a seemingly reworked Cretan piece, is a rich example of how complicated and nested the value regimes involved could become. The Mavro Spelio vessel makes it clear that, at least on occasion, the producer was at pains (to the point of feigning Egyptianness) to make this transformative process explicit, implying that it was recognized and understood by the consumer as well. Such conversions were not just physical alterations, but also involved the transformation of a prime symbol of (past) Egyptian culture into a strongly Cretan symbol.

## The later second millennium (the post-Neopalatial Aegean)

The trading regimes of the later second millennium are transformed by major sociopolitical developments, including Tuthmosis III's extensive campaigns in the Levant, the increasing power of Hittite Anatolia, the growth of Cypriot urbanism, the end of Cretan Neopalatial society, and the rise of Mycenaean palaces. More generally, LBA trade reflects the workings of an integrated system with relatively large numbers of goods, people and ideas regularly travelling over long distances. The degree of interaction gave rise to elites that shared similar social identities and overlapping cultural inventories.

Despite this overall pattern, there are both similarities and contrasts with the rest of the eastern Mediterranean in the way that the Aegean was consuming Egyptian stone vessels at this time. Over 60 Egyptian examples are known from post-Neopalatial Aegean deposits. These occur on Crete, particularly in the Knossos valley, but are also found in some numbers from mainland contexts (Warren 1969: 114–115; Dickers 1995). Despite this broadening geographical range, the reference to a 'post-Neopalatial' world is apt because we cannot always be sure how many of the imported stone vessels from these later contexts are heirlooms originally procured in MMIII–LMI Cretan trading activities. For example, the baggy alabastron remains the most commonly found shape, even as late as LHIIIB, despite the fact that it occurs much more rarely in Egyptian tombs after Tuthmosis III. In fact, it is difficult to identify many stylistically 'late' Egyptian stone vessels: a two-handled jar from Katsamba has a cartouche of Tuthmosis III (and would have been readily identifiable as a later form anyway; Alexiou 1967: 46, fig. 33, pl. 10) and two base-ring style jugs from Isopata (Figure 4:6 col. pl.) and Mycenae (Bosanquet 1904: pl.14) are likely to have been made during or, more probably, after the reign of Tuthmosis III. However, no clearly diagnostic Amarna period or Ramesside vessels have been found in the Aegean at all, which is surprising, (a) because distinctive vessel styles do exist in Egypt at this time (Aston 1994); (b) given the continued importance of the mainland palaces until at least the end of LHIIIB; (c) in view of the apparently large volumes in which interregional trade was occurring; and (d) because it contrasts strongly with the Ramesside stone vessels found at contemporary Ugarit (Sparks Chapter 3, this volume). One explanation might be that a more drawn-out decline in Egyptian stone vessel acquisition and consumption throughout LB3A–B was being obscured by the continued deployment in tombs of Egyptian vessels (notably baggy alabastra) curated from earlier Neopalatial trading or looted from Neopalatial deposits.

The largest assemblage of Egyptian vessels from a single context in this period is from an LMII deposit in the large monumental tomb at Isopata, north of Knossos (Figure 4:6 col. pl.) and this offers a special insight into how foreign exotica were occasionally being used. It includes 10 travertine vessels (Figure 4:6a col. pl.): two plain bowls from a disturbed deposit within the fore-hall, and a base-ring style jug, a footed jar, a flask and five assorted baggy alabastra which were all found together in the main tomb chamber. We can identify the latter – by the shapes involved and their deployment in a discrete group of seven or eight – as a possible Egyptian sacred oil set, comparable, for example, to one from the roughly contemporary tomb of the architect Kha at Thebes (Bisset et al. 1996: fig. 1). In Egypt, one of the functions of such sets was to aid the buried individual in their passage through each of the seven gates of the underworld (Gee 1998: table 7.5; Robinson 2003: 146–149).[11]

Two hard stone vessels also come from the tomb (Figure 4:6b–c col. pl.): the smaller fragmentary example is a PD–OK antiquity similar in shape to ones found at Archanes, Katsamba and Agia Triada (Warren 1969: 110–111, P596–598). The larger, more complete bowl appears to be in the same sort of black and white andesite porphyry as many other Egyptian vessels finding their way to the Aegean (e.g. AM AE 2303, KSM Evans 1894; Warren 1969: P591, P593). One possibility is that this was a worked-down version of a PD–OK spheroid bowl modified in Crete (Warren 1996: no. 8, pl. lxxxi), but set against the rest of the corpus of such conversions, in which vessels of instantly recognizable Cretan style such as bridge-spouted jars were created, this unique form seems curious. Its best parallels for shape are with north Levantine bowls, especially two serpentinite examples from Alalakh (BM 1951.1–3.42; Woolley 1955: 296) and a silver bowl from Byblos (Montet 1928: 125 no. 605, pl. lxxi). Indeed, Levantine workshops produced a range of prestige stone vessels in high-value materials (Bevan 2001: 199–202), including imported stones such as obsidian and possibly travertine, so the use of porphyritic stones for similar purposes, derived from imported raw material via Mesopotamia or from Egypt, is quite plausible.

The Isopata tomb stone vessel assemblage is therefore a relatively complex amalgam of local Cretan vessels, one or more PD–OK antiquities, bowls, and an oil set. The sheer numbers suggest that the owner was at pains to advertise an ability, real or not, to acquire foreign trade goods, but the fuller meaning of the assemblage can be better assessed from a broader comparative perspective. For instance, chamber tomb 102 at Mycenae is a good example of a similar set of claims being made through grave goods on the mainland (Bosanquet 1904). As a square rock-cut chamber between the Atreus and Clytemnaestra tholoi, it lacked the monumentality, but perhaps shared the social standing of the Isopata burial. It contained two Cretan lamps with whorl decoration and an Egyptian base-ring style jug, which are direct matches for vessels at Isopata (Figure 4:6a left centre, 4:6e col. pl.). Another jug-shape is a well-known Cretan ritual form, but made in imported Egyptian travertine. Likewise two gabbro bridge-spouted jars are similar in shape to an example in 'banded tufa' from Isopata (Figure 4:6d col. pl.). These links, along with several others, add to the impression that the nexus of values is identical in both graves, expressing Aegean elite ideals and an awareness of the appropriate roles of foreign exotica.

In fact, it is quite possible that such a nexus was evoking a pan-Aegean and Levantine trading persona. Within the Knossos valley, the Isopata tomb is unique for its monumental design. However, the ashlar masonry and niched recesses have striking parallels in the intramural tombs at Ugarit (Schaeffer 1949: 90–92, figs. 78–89, pls. xvii–xvix).[12] In addition, Ugarit and its port town provide good comparanda for footed travertine jars, antique Egyptian stone bowls, and travertine base-ring style jugs, as well as the same type of Cretan lamps with whorl decoration (Caubet 1991: pls. vii. 2, xii. 10, probably also RS 16.022). So we should imagine certain individuals, perhaps traders, at places such as Knossos, Mycenae and Ugarit, but also at Enkomi in Cyprus and Ura in Cilicia, who shared similar values and valued objects (see Bevan 2001: 257 ff).

## Conclusion

Egyptian stone vessels were status objects whose acquisition and consumption was limited to a few privileged contexts. Until quite late in the Bronze Age, most if not all examples, both definite and disputed, come from Crete, suggesting that these objects tell a particular story about the island's path towards greater social complexity. As such it would be inappropriate to build such observations into an explanation of cultural change in the wider Aegean context. In any case, when appropriate attention is paid to the different spatial and temporal scales at which they must be explained, or to the multilateral cultural interactions they might represent, imported Egyptian stone vessels represent an excellent example of the methodological challenges and interpretive opportunities offered by the study of interregional contact in the bronze age eastern Mediterranean.

### Notes

1. Bronze age period sub-divisions with Arabic numerals are used in this chapter to refer to broad pan-Aegean chronological patterns. Where greater precision is required, local ceramic (e.g. LMI=Late Minoan I) or cultural (e.g. Neopalatial) labels are preferred. See Table.
2. The following abbreviations are used for museum accession details: AM (Ashmolean Museum); HM (Herakleion Museum); KSM (Knossos Stratigraphical Museum); and UC (Petrie Museum, University College London). Only one of the three Knossos fragments can now be located (AM 1938.653).
3. By the Old Kingdom, obsidian was only being used for rather crude, thick-walled, model vessels (Aston 1994: 24 ff, types 137–138).
4. One of two splayed cylindrical jars from Mochlos comes from an EMIIB–III context and the presence of these two early-style jars at Mochlos might suggest that this area was an important landing place or point of contact for early trading ventures.
5. The stone comes from quarries at Gebel el-Asr near the Wadi Toshka in the Western Desert (Shaw et al. 2001). There are two varieties but the lighter anorthosite version is more commonly used for stone vessels. The stone becomes very popular in royal and private tombs in the third-sixth Dynasties (Aston 1994: 63–64; Reisner 1931: 140, 180).
6. Warren (1969: 124–156) uses this term as a working label for a particular variety of banded pink, grey, brown and orange (probably travertine) calcite to distinguish it from other local Cretan calcites and Egyptian travertine ('Egyptian alabaster').
7. The earliest two fragments, a lid inscribed with the name of the Hyksos pharaoh Khian and a baggy alabastron, are probably MMIII (perhaps early and late in the period respectively, Warren 1969: 112–113). The dating of the Khian lid deposit (North Lustral Basin; Pomerance 1984; Warren 1969: 33; Warren and Hankey 1989: 56, 136) is disputed.
8. Geologically confirmed sources are known chiefly from Egypt (Aston et al. 2000). Poorly investigated sources of the stone have also been suggested in other areas of the eastern Mediterranean (Lilyquist 1996: 140–141; Sparks 1998: 271).
9. Perhaps the best archaeologically and textually attested example is the use of model obsidian and quartz crystal vessels during the opening of the mouth ceremony (Mercer 1952: utterances 47–55; Roth 1992). Obsidian and quartz crystal are seen as dark and light colours of the same generic stone in both Egyptian and Mesopotamian classifications (André-Salvini 1995: 79; Aston 1994: 24).
10. Evans identified badly damaged stone vessel fragments from the Central Treasury as a lioness rhyton, but they are actually parts of a converted oval-plan alabastron similar to the one from Mycenae Shaft Grave V (Evans 1935: 827; AM AE 1181 and unregistered fragments). Many separate handles and spout pieces in suitably Egyptianizing local materials (e.g. 'banded tufa', beccia, chlorite with inlay pieces) have also been found at Knossos (Evans 1935: 976, suppl. pl. lxvi.ai2; Warren 1969: 105; KSM Evans unprovenanced box 1891).
11. Baggy alabastra have also been found in the stomion area, on the threshold of the burial space, in both the Atreus tholos, where fragments of at least four were found, and the Clytemnaestra tholos at Mycenae (Wace 1921–1923: 356, 367). This area is better lit than

the chamber where later looters, more interested in possible gold leaf caps to the alabastra than the stone itself, could have discarded fragments. It is also possible that such oil flasks were being deployed here specifically as a way of facilitating the transition into an afterlife.

12  The chronology of these connections is difficult, because many of the Ugaritic tombs are at least 50 years later in date (Preston 1999: 137, also n. 39). Moreover, the dromos is much longer in the Isopata version and the tomb itself is extramural. Even so, earlier tombs at Ugarit are similar but not identical – it is certainly possible that an unexcavated prototype for both the known Ugaritic tombs and Isopata exists at the former site.

| B.C. | Dyn. | Egypt | Crete | Mainland Greece | Aegean | |
|---|---|---|---|---|---|---|
| 3000 | 0-1 | Early Dynastic (ED) | EMI | EHI | EB1 | |
|  | 2 |  |  |  |  | |
|  | 3 |  | EMIIA | EHII | EB2 | longboat imagery |
|  | 4 |  |  |  |  | |
| 2500 | 5 | Old Kingdom (OK) | EMIIB | early Prepalatial |  |  |
|  | 6 |  |  | EHIII | EB3 | advent of sailing |
|  | 7-8 |  |  |  |  | |
|  | 9-10 | FIP | EMIII | late Prepalatial |  |  |
| 2000 | 11 |  | MMIA |  | MB1 | |
|  | 12 | Middle Kingdom (MK) | MMIB | MH |  | |
|  | 13 |  | MMIIA-B |  | MB | |
|  | 14 |  | MMIIIA |  |  | |
|  | 15-17 | SIP | MMIIIB | LHI |  | |
|  |  |  | LMIA | Shaft Graves |  | |
| 1500 | 18 |  | LMIB Protopalatial Neopalatial | LHIIA | LB1 | Thera eruption |
|  |  |  | LMII | LHIIB | LB2 | |
|  |  |  | LMIIIA1 | LHIIIA1 | LB3A | |
|  |  | New Kingdom (NK) | LMIIIA2 | LHIIIA2 |  | |
|  | 19 |  |  | LHIIIB1 | LB3B | |
|  |  |  | LMIIIB | LHIIIB2 |  | |
|  | 20 |  | LMIIIC | LHIIIC | LB3C | |
| 1000 | 21 |  |  |  |  | |

Table: Chronology for Egypt and the Aegean
(FIP = First Intermediate Period; SIP = Second Intermediate Period;
the prefixes E, M, L = Early, Middle and Late respectively;
these are found with M = Minoan, H = Helladic, B = Bronze)

## Acknowledgments

Permission to reproduce relevant photographs was kindly supplied by the Herakleion Museum, Joseph Shaw, Jeffrey Soles and Peter Warren. Many thanks also to Cyprian Broodbank, Jacke Phillips, Sue Sherratt, Rachael Sparks, Peter Warren and Todd Whitelaw for discussions about this topic.

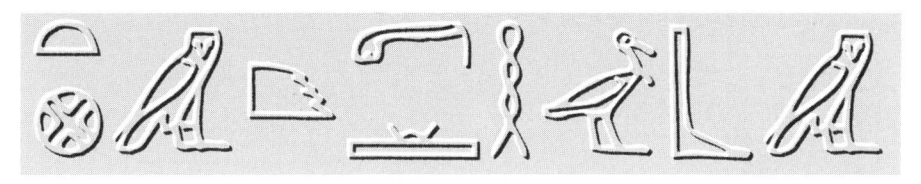

## CHAPTER 5

## LOVE AND WAR IN THE LATE BRONZE AGE: EGYPT AND HATTI

*David Warburton*

### Introduction (Figure 5:1)

In the early spring of 1274 BC, Ramesses II (1279–1213) of Egypt and Muwatalli of Hatti were with their respective armies in the first famous battle in world history: the battle beneath the walls of Kadesh in the Orontes valley in Syria. Whatever happened, it must have been momentous and terrifying, at least for Ramesses II, whose accounts of the battle have defined the age for us. Before he died in ca. 1213 BC, the war had been ended with a peace treaty and Ramesses II was married to at least one Hittite princess and had fathered at least one Egyptian princess who was half-Hittite (Kitchen 1982, 1995: 763–774).

For the modern world (like the ancient), battles, treaties and dynastic marriage alliances would appear to be the ordinary stuff of politics. After all, the Akkadian kings had conquered Syria and Iran, just as the Babylonians had been conquered by the Hittites and the Assyrians. Treaties likewise assured that relations between the major kingdoms were put on a legal footing when wars ended. Marriage was the easiest way of sealing such a deal, and thus foreign princesses adorned the courts of the ancient world.

For Egypt, however, these events were quite unique. Kadesh is the only major battle the Egyptians claimed to have fought with any of the important powers of antiquity, and the treaties with the Hittites are the only known treaties connecting Egypt with a foreign power. The battle was a set piece matter where the Hittites took the initiative and the Egyptians reacted. The treaty corresponded to Hittite usage. The Hittites were late-comers to the world of the ancient Near East, whereas the rest of the ancient world could barely recall any civilization older than the Egyptian. The fact that the Egyptians fought the battle and signed the treaties would appear to confirm the extent to which relations between Hatti and Egypt were determined more by Hittite policy than pharaonic whim. It is difficult to grasp just how the upstart Hittites had such an effect on the Egyptians and how the Hittites managed to communicate with the Egyptians so successfully.

The earliest treaties between these two powers belong to an era when it was unlikely that the two empires would come into conflict. The final treaty reflected the

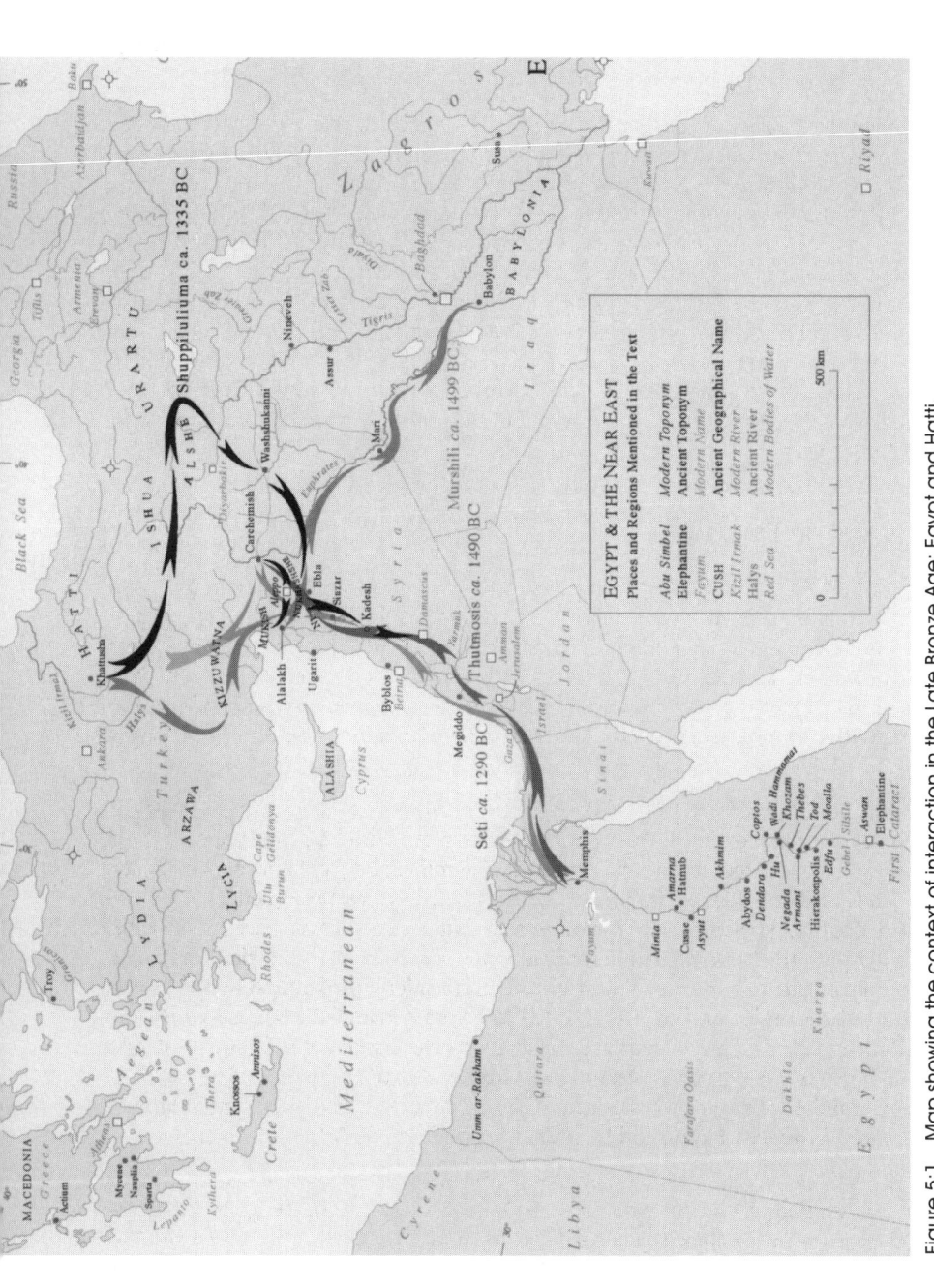

Figure 5:1   Map showing the context of interaction in the Late Bronze Age: Egypt and Hatti.

implicit recognition that both parties viewed further conflict as futile. By the time Merenptah (1213–1203) sent the Hittites the earliest known shipment of surplus grain in the form of famine aid, relations between the two had been transformed. Egyptian contact with the Hittites thus moved through four stages, with the reign of Ramesses II forming the period of decisive transition.

During the earliest stage (before 1550 BC), Hatti and Egypt were not in conflict with each other, nor did they share a common border with a common neighbour. The second stage followed from the late 16th century as Hittite advances into Syria were matched by Egyptian efforts to move north. By the middle of the 15th century, the Hurrian state of Mitanni lay between the Egyptians and the Hittites. The third period began when the Hittites destroyed Mitanni in the 14th century, creating a common border highly contested until the middle of the 13th century. Up until that time, the Egyptians had been moving gradually north and east, and the Hittites more rapidly west, south, and east. With the standoff at Kadesh, Egyptian and Hittite military expansion came to an abrupt halt. Relations were cordial during the final period, from the middle of the 13th century until the end of the Hittite Kingdom at the start of the 12th century BC.[1]

## The Egyptian Empire

Warburton (2001) claims that the Egyptians did not have a major empire in Asia, and that their military activity was largely conditioned by the Mitanni and Hittite empires, which did have significant holdings in northern Syria. Neither Mitanni nor Hatti were alone, however, as they too had other neighbours, and their neighbours had neighbours, so that Elam influenced Babylon, which affected Assyria, which was in contact with Mitanni. Hatti lay on the other side of Mitanni, and the Mycenaeans beyond the Hittites.

Many earlier interpreters (e.g. Redford 1992; Weinstein 1981) assumed that the Egyptians were successful in their military encounters with Mitanni, and that these successes were related to the existence of a significant Egyptian empire, which included Ugarit and Aleppo, before the decline of the Hittites. Both Klengel (1992: 92–93) and Redford (1992: 158–161) assume that Tuthmosis III was victorious in his encounter with the Mitanni army in the campaign ca. 1445. The Egyptian army may indeed have reached the Euphrates and did considerable damage as far as the Euphrates bend at Emar, but it is difficult to contend that Tuthmosis defeated the armed forces, as some authorities aver. This interpretation was largely borne out of a comparison of the various texts and archaeological sources rather than a consideration of the possible context. This Egyptian-oriented interpretation has influenced historians of Syria and the Hittites (e.g. Klengel 1992).

The lack of any Mitanni archives is a major problem. However, all further Egyptian campaigning took place in the Orontes valley, which suggests that the Egyptians were not militarily successful in pushing Mitanni back, but rather that Mitanni influence increased. Many view the struggle between Egypt and Mitanni as a titanic conflict, ascribing ambition and power to both. This neglects the possibility that the destruction of Aleppo and Alalakh should not be ascribed to Mitanni (as e.g.

Klengel 1992: 87 suggests), but rather to the Hittites (von Soldt 2000: 110–112). Attributing great power to both Mitanni and Egypt neglects the fact that their mutual contest ended in a draw, whereas the Hittites were ultimately able to extinguish Mitanni.[2]

## Aleppo, Carchemish, and the Euphrates

The events leading to contact between the Hittites and the Egyptians did not take place in isolation, nor did they take place in the homelands of these two nations. Relations between the two can only be understood in the context of the international situation in the second half of the second millennium BC.

The Hittites were not natives to Anatolia, but were already settled there when they emerged from prehistory. The contact zone between Egypt and Hatti lay in northern Syria, and not in Anatolia. To some extent the city of Aleppo in northern Syria played an important role in the national ethos of Hittite expansion. A Hittite temple dedicated to the weather god stood on the citadel of Aleppo. This temple does not antedate the Hittite expansion into Syria, but there was a major cult of a local weather god at Aleppo from the first half of the second millennium, long before the appearance of the Hittites. Certainly neither Aleppo nor northern Syria could ever be counted part of their homeland and yet the possession of Aleppo is a recurrent theme in Hittite history. The region was a breadbasket, and Aleppo lies halfway between the Euphrates, which flows towards Babylonia, and the Mediterranean with its links to the Aegean.

Egyptian interest in western Asia is more difficult to understand, as it appears not to have appreciated either the people or the weather, and had no need for grain from Syria, let alone its access to the Mediterranean. Egypt merely found the Euphrates to be a "peculiar river which flows downstream by flowing upstream", which was the way it was described because it flowed in the opposite direction to the Nile. Nevertheless, the Egyptians had a peculiar fascination with the Euphrates, a fascination that took a purely military form, unrelated to weather gods and transport. Both the Egyptians and the Hittites had an interest in the city of Carchemish, on the Euphrates. Unfortunately for the ancient inhabitants of Aleppo, their city lay between Egypt and the Euphrates and between the Hittites and Carchemish (when crossing from Cilicia, as the Hittites did before Shuppiluliuma). The city's significance in this regard begins, however, at a time when Egypt was not remotely interested in the Euphrates, and the Hittite state did not exist. Carchemish was then under the control of Aleppo, the independent capital of an urban kingdom in northern Syria and more powerful than Babylon at its second-millennium greatest. Whatever the reasons for the conflict, it was not merely an issue of a power vacuum.

## The Old Babylonian period and the appearance of Mitanni (ca. 18th century–15th century)

Initially, the Hittites must have begun to form states in Anatolia at a time when Assyrian and Babylonian power was on the rise, after recovering from the collapse of the Akkadian empire (and therefore during the twelfth Dynasty, but Egypt was irrelevant in Anatolia at the time). Between Naram-Sin (ca. 2119–2082) of Agade and Tiglath-Pileser I (1114–1076) of Assyria, no great Mesopotamian ruler could claim the Mediterranean coast. When Naram-Sin invaded Anatolia, the Hittites had not yet arrived or coalesced, and when Tiglath-Pileser I struck the coast, the Hittites were no more. Their greatest day was in the second half of the second millennium BC when Syria was the scene of mighty contests as the powers of the day converged with their armies on the fields of northern Syria.

During the Middle Kingdom (ca. 2000–1700), Egyptian influence spread along the Levant coast as far as Ugarit, but even at its zenith, its power was restricted to the Nile Valley. Egypt therefore had no role to play when the drama started. Before the middle of the second millennium BC, Egypt had no political competitors in its dealings with the Levant: Levantine and Aegean traders and potentates were in touch with both Mesopotamia and Egypt. Mesopotamian influence stopped in the plains of northern Syria, while Egyptian influence did not extend significantly inland beyond the Levant coast.

Neither the Mesopotamian empire of the Third Dynasty of Ur (2018–1911 BC), nor the north Syrian kingdoms of Urkish and Nawar had any significant political impact in western Syria. It was only in the aftermath of the collapse of Ur III, around 1900 BC, that competing powers emerged in northern Syria. Initially, Assyrian interests were commercial, as their caravans passed through Syria into Anatolia. The significant Assyrian colonies (such as Kanesh) lay in Anatolia, and Syria was a necessary part of their transit route. The Assyrian presence in Syria changed dramatically with Shamshi-Adad's conquest of Assur, which permitted him briefly to change the power structures, and to establish Assyria as a major power in Syria. The effort was short-lived, as his sons quickly lost all. Although the death of Shamshi-Adad (1680?) ended the Assyrian domination of northern Mesopotamia, it opened the way to Babylonian influence. Hammurabi (1696–1654 BC) of the first Dynasty of Babylon was able to expand Babylonian influence, but neither he nor his successors approached the bend of the Euphrates where Shamshi-Adad had held court.

During Ur III, the contemporary city of Ebla was the most powerful in western Syria. Thereafter, Aleppo was generally the dominant power. During this entire period, however, the Assyrians continued to trade in Anatolia, as they had for generations. And it is with level Ib of the Assyrian colony of Kanesh (Veenhof 1995: 859–871), which can be dated to the reign of Shamshi-Adad, that the Hittites appear on the stage of world history. Their entry thus coincided with, rather than caused, the end of Mesopotamian power in northern Syria and Anatolia. Their arrival in Anatolia can be linked to the simultaneous appearance of the Indo-Europeans in Greece and India. It was also a nadir in Egyptian history.

The Hittites were able to expand almost at will. But their capacity and desire for expansion had its limits, and their foes may have been the least of their problems. Their propensity for adventurism is well illustrated by the fate of Murshili, who led his armies as far as Babylon. For reasons that remain obscure, he plundered the city and ended the rule of the first Dynasty of Babylon. After this phenomenal success he was murdered upon his return home, an act typical of Hittite dynastic feuding.

This unfortunate episode would probably have been of no great significance to history, were it not accompanied by two other factors. One of these was the gradual appearance of Egyptian armies in western Asia, and the other was the sudden expansion of the Mitanni kingdom. The political configuration of northern Syria was extremely complicated by the time Tuthmosis III passed Aleppo and crossed the Euphrates at Carchemish (ca. 1445 BC). In principle, it can be assumed that the Egyptians were pursuing the Hyksos out of Egypt, which provided the momentum to break out of Palestine and into Syria. The expansion of Mitanni can be associated with the power vacuum in Syria after the end of the first Dynasty of Babylon (Sasson 1995: 901–915; Whiting 1995: 1,231–1,254). The Hittite kings Hattushili and Murshili had destroyed Aleppo on the way to Babylon, and thus opened the conflict when the power of the Hittites crumbled in the dynastic feuding following the conquest of Babylon.

With Aleppo and Babylon eliminated, the Kassites moved into Babylonia and Mitanni assumed control over northern Mesopotamia. Upper Mesopotamia was left without a central power, as Assur was not yet prepared to reassume a leading role, and Aleppo was temporarily eclipsed. The Mitanni kingdom thus spread across northern Mesopotamia, linking a number of local kingdoms under a single political system. Although fragile, Mitanni was sufficiently powerful that Egyptian efforts to penetrate the Mitanni heartland failed. The Hittites therefore applauded the efforts of Tuthmosis III, while the Hittite kings Tudkhaliya and Arnuwanda continued their expansion in western Anatolia.

By this time, Carchemish was deep in the Mitanni kingdom that ruled the entire region from the Zagros to the Mediterranean. To the east, however, the Assyrians were gradually recovering confidence, building their city walls and asserting their independence. To the south-east, Babylonia contested both Mitanni and Assyrian aspirations, attempting to claim sovereignty over most of what is now the state of Iraq. Apparently heedless of the Assyrian threat, the Mitanni empire expanded south-west into Syria, and north into Anatolia. Mitanni thus came up against both the Hittites and the Egyptians, who were both slowly increasing their power. It is not surprising, therefore, that Egypt and Hatti were not opposed in the late 15th century BC, for both were separated by and jointly opposed to Mitanni. Under the circumstances, it is perhaps remarkable, but readily understandable, that the Egyptians and Hittites may have appreciated the importance of each other in these decades when both felt threatened by Mitanni expansion.

It was in this period that the Hittites and the Egyptians seem to have agreed to some form of non-aggression pact for the first time. It was customary for the Hittites to define all relations in terms of treaty arrangements, and thus it is natural that they sought such an agreement with Egypt. Assyrian commercial activity in Anatolia had been conducted according to codes of inter-state conduct, and thus the Hittites' first contact with the Near East was with a world organized by law. They will have readily appreciated the advantages of employing military means to conquer their new neighbours and then ratifying the new state of affairs with a treaty. It soon became a Hittite custom, even more common than fratricide (see Beckman 1996; Roth 1997). It may be assumed, therefore, that for the Hittite court a non-aggression pact with Egypt represented the mere ratification of an existing state of affairs. Given the presence of

Mitanni, it was unlikely that Egypt and Hatti would come into contact. For the Hittites, therefore, it is logical that they sought to ratify the relationship in treaty form. It is remarkable that the Egyptians agreed to sign such a document since the Egyptians rarely viewed their neighbours as anything other than rebels and troublemakers. There are passing references in the Egyptian documentation to declarations of friendship, but treaties are virtually unknown, except with the Hittites.

The Kurushtama treaty is thus a bit of an anomaly. This is the first recorded treaty between Egypt and Hatti (early 14th century?). The treaty itself and its clauses are unknown, and thus the subject-matter is open to speculation (O'Connor and Cline 1998: 243–244). This status is enhanced when it is appreciated that the treaty seems to have dealt with some kind of population exchange whereby the Hittite weather god apparently caused some Hittite subjects to be settled on Egyptian land in Syria or Palestine. One could associate this with a move caused by Mitanni expansion, pushing Hittite subjects south into Egyptian possessions rather than north, back into Hatti. Modern interest in the affair can hardly have matched that of the Hittites, but they will nevertheless have felt that something needed to be done, if only to satisfy their legalistic inclinations. The presence of these foreigners seems to have been ratified by inter-state agreement, but it is not known who signed the treaty, let alone why and when.

Nevertheless, this first vaguely documented example seems to indicate that the Egyptians and the Hittites understood one another remarkably well. The Hittites will have felt that the situation required a satisfactory resolution. The Egyptians will doubtless hardly have been perturbed about finding some Hittite subjects in a region under their hegemony. The Egyptians will simply have made sure that they paid their taxes and considered the affair closed. They seem also to have realized, however, that the Hittites desired a treaty and acquiesced to it.

This capacity for mutual understanding must be understood in the cultural context. Egypt was one of the most ancient nations in the Near East, Hatti one of the youngest. The two had little in common, perhaps best illustrated by the approach to brotherly love in the two royal houses. Whereas the Egyptian royals of the eighteenth Dynasty tended to marry their half-sisters or daughters, as e.g. Tuthmosis II, Amenhotep II, and Amenophis III (Redford 1965: 115 n. 3), normal procedure in the Hittite royal family was to kill one's brothers. The two practices are by no means mutually exclusive, but it would not appear that the Egyptians and the Hittites shared the same habits, and thus the assumption of a contrast is admissible. Given their distinctive customs it is readily understandable that both houses displayed an unusual interest in ritual; otherwise, these two parties had little in common, and yet seemed to have understood one another remarkably well. For most of history, the two will hardly have been concerned about each other, and thus it is hardly surprising that the Kurushtama treaty reveals a pragmatic and legal solution to an inconvenient problem.

## Conflict

This rather auspicious beginning preceded Shuppiluliuma's advances towards the Egyptian borders in Syria in the third quarter of the 14th century. Ironically, the

Kurushtama treaty would become a bone of contention for the Hittites rather than the Egyptians, as we shall see. The initial conflict was due not to Egyptian advances, but rather to the unexpected successes of Shuppiluliuma, one of the greatest field commanders and statesmen in history. Shuppiluliuma's immediate predecessors had begun a gradual process of reasserting Hittite hegemony beyond the walls of Hattusha, their capital. Their progress in central Anatolia was accompanied by gradual pressure on their southern flank as Mitanni pressed into Hittite territory. Under the circumstances, the Hittite rulers became accustomed to solving local Anatolian problems with force, and it is well known that they had no hesitation in using force against larger powers as well, even if the violence was accompanied by ritual and treaty-making.

Shuppiluliuma spent much of his life on the battlefield (Macqueen 1995: 1,085–1,105; Pritchard 1969: 318–339). Already before inheriting (or acquiring) the throne, he was fighting in Anatolia. His successes ultimately established a new hegemony in Anatolia, allowing him to progress into northern Syria. While the earlier Hittite kings had faced local rulers in Syria, Shuppiluliuma faced the new Mitanni kingdom that had emerged in northern Syria after Murshili's destruction of Babylon. For a century, the Egyptians had been attacking Mitanni, and thus the appearance of the Hittites was greeted with enthusiasm by the Egyptians. It was the Hittite pressure on their northern flank that pushed the Mitanni rulers into negotiations with the Egyptians.

Shuppiluliuma also maintained contact with the Egyptian court, but half-heartedly. He and his predecessors wrote several letters to Amenophis III, Akhenaten, Tutankhamun, and Aya (and possibly Smenkhara; Moran 1992: EA 41–44). The two courts seemed to have greeted each other on a formally correct basis and exchanged gifts. The contact must have been conducted through the city of Ugarit on the Syrian coast, for Mitanni controlled Alalakh and the Orontes, and there was thus no direct overland route between Egypt and Hatti. The city of Ugarit would benefit from the conflicts around it throughout the remainder of the Bronze Age, changing sides and taking tolls, until the great powers proved unable to save the city.

Although superficially conciliatory and not exactly hostile, the preserved letters from the Hittites to the Egyptians nevertheless imply an arrogant attitude (Beckman 1996: 122–132). A Hittite prince wrote requesting gold from the Egyptian king, a bid usually restricted to the highest kings of major states in antiquity. On the other hand, however, such a letter betrays the ambivalence of the relationship, as will become clear later. Whether in a state of near war or ratified peace, members of the royal houses corresponded with one another freely, whereas neither in the Amarna correspondence nor later does one find a similar degree of familiarity in relations between Egypt and major powers. In the Egyptian archives, letters were usually exchanged from king to king, queen to queen, official to official. Between the Hittites and the Egyptians it was quite different. Eventually Ramesses II would have his whole family writing letters to the Hittite court, aside from the letters of the highest officials. The request for gold is thus common and anomalous. Equally peculiar is Shuppiluliuma's request for lapis lazuli. All the lapis lazuli in antiquity came from Central Asia. The courts of western Asia (the Kassite Babylonians, the Assyrians, and the Mitanni rulers) all dispatched pieces of lapis lazuli to Egypt. Shuppiluliuma alone requests that the Egyptian king send lapis lazuli to him (Moran 1992: EA 41).

It could be assumed that Shuppiluliuma had only a vague understanding of international affairs and geography, which induced him to make the request. Such an outlook might also account for the fact that he received a bride from Babylon. According to diplomatic etiquette in the marriage market, brides generally travelled from the lesser power to the greater. By general agreement, Egypt was viewed as the greatest power of the age and Egyptian royal daughters stayed at home (albeit consorting with their brothers and fathers). Our modern appreciation of the ancient Near East suggests that Babylon was a greater power than Hatti and thus we would expect the bride to travel from Hattusha to Dur Kurigalzu, rather than the reverse. The possibility that the Kassite rulers of Babylonia were so uncivilized that they did not appreciate the rules can be excluded. When the Babylonian king Burnaburiash wrote to the Egyptian king requesting a bride, he realistically and humbly suggested "Send me a beauty as if she were your daughter. Who is going to say, 'She is not a royal daughter'?" (Moran 1992: EA4).

The nuances of the contemporary world are half hidden from us, but the various states cannot be assumed to have been ignorant of diplomatic etiquette and oblivious to political developments beyond their borders. It is difficult to imagine that a statesman as successful as Shuppiluliuma was not familiar with both diplomatic etiquette in the marriage market and the geographical distribution of lapis lazuli. The fact that Shuppiluliuma obtained a Babylonian bride is thus curious and interesting, but hardly accidental. His request for lapis lazuli will have betrayed a great deal of confidence, which can hardly have been very appealing to the Egyptian court, but they had become accustomed to the less civilized ways of the Kassites and other foreign rebels. That was the difficulty of being a great power in an international and cosmopolitan age. More difficulties were in store.

Shuppiluliuma knew what he was doing, and so did others. During his reign, Akhenaten received some Assyrian officials (ca. 1339 BC?). Assuming that Babylonia alone had the right to represent Mesopotamia on the world stage, the Babylonian Kassite king Burnaburiash objected to the presence of Assyrian envoys in Egypt (Moran 1992: EA 9). The actual messengers would probably have appreciated the Babylonian king's concern, for Akhenaten had the Assyrian envoys stand in the sun for hours (Moran 1992: EA16; Warburton and Matthews Chapter 6, this volume). One may assume that this reflected Akhenaten's particular form of solar worship. We have no record of similar complaints from other courts. It may be that other diplomatic missions were aware of Akhenaten's idiosyncrasies and saw no reason to discuss the matter. Being new on the world scene, Assur-Uballit may not have been so familiar with revolutionary religious thought in a distant land, and thus might have been taken unawares. It may also be the case that the Assyrians were consciously selected for such treatment, and that Akhenaten was simultaneously informing the Babylonians that he recognized Assyrian independence while making the Assyrian king conscious that his willingness to do so was indulgence and not a recognition of equality.

Shuppiluliuma's behaviour should be understood in this context. The fact that he expected to receive a bride from Babylon and a piece of lapis lazuli from Egypt would imply that he expected recognition as a major power and an equal. Shuppiluliuma's conquests were not restricted to the peripheral regions of Anatolia, and Egyptian attitudes will have changed as Shuppiluliuma's armies gradually approached the frontiers of Egyptian influence.

The coldness of the Egyptian response must be understood in this context. Egyptian armies had been unable to penetrate Mitanni territory for a century before the Amarna period. Ever since the latter part of the reign of Tuthmosis III, Mitanni had continued to expand into Egyptian zones of influence along the coast and in the Orontes valley. Militarily, little had changed since the defeats of Amenophis II in Syria. There had nevertheless been a substantial improvement during the reigns of Tuthmosis IV (Bryan 1991) and Amenophis III, as independent centres such as Ugarit bound themselves to the Egyptians. The impact of the simultaneous growth of Hittite and Mitanni military strength in the north-eastern corner of the Mediterranean contributed to a rise in the popularity of alliance arrangements with Egypt, which in turn bolstered the Egyptian military presence throughout the region. Working from a position of strength with armies in the field, Akhenaten presumably relied on Mitanni to hold off the Hittites, and Assyria to hold off Babylonia, keeping both Mitanni and Hatti occupied. Recognition of Assyrian independence would thus form part of a nuanced policy on the part of the Egyptian court. Akhenaten apparently failed to appreciate that the Assyrians could make common cause with the Hittites and finish off Mitanni.

Akhenaten's aloofness may not have influenced Assyrian policy with regard to Mitanni, but Shuppiluliuma's cunning is thrown into bold relief. Conscious that Assyria would be more concerned with its southern neighbour, and confident that Assyria would not threaten Hittite rule in Syria, Shuppiluliuma could prepare himself for the coming confrontation with Egypt. He appreciated that his expansion was placing him on a collision course in Syria. His great fortune was that the Egyptians were oblivious to the boldness of his plans and the true character of their own power. Unaware that their successes had not been the result of victory in the field, the Egyptians were unprepared for the shift in the balance of power that would follow the elimination of Mitanni.

The Egyptians may have been misled by the behaviour of Amurru in particular. Abdi-Ashirta and Aziru, the kings of Amurru during the Amarna period, both maintained relations with Egypt while the latter did not conceal his links with the Hittite court as well (Izre'el and Singer 1990). The Hittite military advance into Syria was thus accompanied by careful political preparations intended to ensure that the Hittite border with the Egyptian zone of influence would be established as a *fait accompli* before any response could be anticipated.

The initial result was the *volte-face* in Amurru and Ugarit, which Shuppiluliuma had not only foreseen, but brought about through crafty negotiations carried out parallel to his campaigns against the Mitanni cities. Shuppiluliuma had grasped the weakness of the Egyptian hold on Syria, while recognizing the importance of Egyptian power. He endeavoured to avoid a direct conflict with Egypt, dealing with allies and vassals rather than assaulting the Egyptian forces directly.

It was noted above that the correspondence between the court at Amarna and the external world included a letter to the Egyptian king from a Hittite prince who requested gold. This peculiar request has its counterpart in a letter from

Tutankhamun's queen, written to Shuppiluliuma while he was besieging Carchemish. The whole matter has gone down in history as the '*dakhamunzu*-affair', because the word *dakhamunzu* appeared in the Hittite version of events intended for their own consumption and not for others, and yet the word appeared foreign. Initially, it was assumed that the form concealed the name of an Egyptian queen. Yet such a name could not be recognized in the Egyptian records until it was realized that the word *dakhamunzu* was a cuneiform transcription of the Egyptian *ta hemet nesu*, or "queen". The search for a queen's name as a chronological peg would thus prove futile, but the fact that the Hittites were familiar with Egyptian-language royal titulary is culturally instructive, and demonstrates their external awareness (Pritchard 1969: 318).

The siege of Carchemish represented the final stage of Shuppiluliuma's destruction of independent power in Syria, and Egyptian policy had been dedicated to supporting Mitanni precisely in order to hold off the Hittites. At this moment, the Egyptian pharaoh died without male issue (ca. 1322 BC, see Kitchen 1998: 253 n. 137). The royal widow sent a letter to Shuppiluliuma requesting that he send her a son whom she could marry and make king of Egypt. "My husband has just died and I have no son. People say that you have many sons. If you were to send me one of your sons, he might become my husband. I am loathe to take a servant of mine and make him my husband" (Pritchard 1969: 318). The queen was thus trying to appease a dangerous foe abroad while holding off the officials at home. It is clear that the court officials were opposed to this course, and they ultimately defeated the queen's intentions. However, the queen's behaviour reveals that some at court considered Hatti as a great power. This group would contend that Egypt could, indeed had to, live in peace with Hatti, as later proved to be the case. At the time, however, the intentions and responses of both the queen and Shuppiluliuma are hard to deduce.

Shuppiluliuma did not believe the message, and with due reason: "Such a thing has never happened before!" he exclaimed. He sent messengers to Egypt and it took a while for them to move to and fro, and thus a considerable time elapsed before he found out that the Egyptian queen was acting in what appeared to be good faith. Despite his profoundly distrustful attitude towards the whole affair, Shuppiluliuma did eventually dispatch a son to the Egyptian court. By the time the Hittite prince arrived, the Egyptian official Aya seems to have been able to marry the royal widow, and thus become the rightful king of Egypt. The Hittite prince's arrival was thus too late. He died in Egypt, without becoming king and before being able to return to his father. Apparently, the Egyptians sent a note to inform Shuppiluliuma of what had happened, letting him know that his son had died. Shuppiluliuma obviously concluded that his son had been mistreated in Egypt, and told Aya so. Aya denied this, claiming that he "had done nothing" to him. Then Shuppiluliuma wrote an angry letter to the Egyptian king, complaining that Aya had not told him that he had ascended the throne, pointing out that he had only been carrying out the widow's wishes when he sent his son, and pointedly stating that Aya could simply have let his son go home. "What have you done with my son?" he cries. Regardless of Aya's claims to the contrary, Shuppiluliuma must have been convinced that Aya had done away with his son, and perhaps also that he had not only been humiliated, but that the whole affair had been a plot, as he originally suspected. In his anger, he threw his forces directly against the Egyptians in Syria, and thus transformed the neighbours into foes at war (Hout 1994).

The most curious questions to arise out of this matter remain unanswerable. Did the Egyptians really create the whole *dakhamunzu* incident? Was there a party that hoped that peace could be secured through a marriage alliance? Was there another party that co-operated with the plotters but had the object of killing a Hittite prince or of trying to keep one as a hostage? Did Shuppiluliuma fall into a trap, as he thought? Or should we see the young widow as one of the great women of the eighteenth Dynasty? Others before her, such as Ahhotep who may have created the links with the Aegean and thus ultimately contributed to her son's victory over the Hyksos, may have tried to play international politics. Both solutions can be argued. Or are we victims of the Hittite version of events? Was the story yet more complicated than the Hittite version implies? Regardless of the actual nuances, the events cannot have been very different from those implied, i.e. Shuppiluliuma was convinced that his son could become king of Egypt by marrying pharaoh's widow.

It cannot be imagined that the queen was acting alone, nor that Shuppiluliuma did not fail to realize that the affair presented a fine opportunity. Both during and after the reign of Akhenaten, Shuppiluliuma's letters to the Egyptian court betray a haughty distance. Had his confidence and success led some to conclude that he had to be assuaged at any price? Had his arrogance led others to believe that they could deceive him? Was he himself partially author of the plot? Certainly his response to the request demonstrates the confidence with which he was willing to exploit every possibility, and assume that it was possible.

## War

Even if it can all be traced back to the miserable state of a spoilt and broken-hearted teenager, the age of super-power confrontation reached an early pinnacle. With his son dead and an elderly general in the queen's bed, and therefore on the Egyptian throne, Shuppiluliuma set about getting revenge. For the first time in recorded human history, two of the greatest empires would find themselves in armed conflict for more than half a century.

Shuppiluliuma left the Egyptians under no illusions about his intentions. He wrote Aya to the effect that the Egyptians and the Hittites had previously avoided bloodshed, and that if the Egyptians had not actually started a war against his land, they had killed his son. He made it clear that he had not known that there was a king in Egypt when he dispatched his son: he sent his son to assume the role of ruler. Presumably, he argued that otherwise he would not have sent his son. He alleged that the queen had written to him repeatedly requesting his son, and that he had sent his son in good faith because the queen wanted him. Now, he suggested that the new pharaoh might well have killed his son, though the latter claimed that he had done nothing to him. This was too much for Shuppiluliuma.

He told Aya that he, Shuppiluliuma, did not take either the Egyptian chariotry or the Egyptian infantry seriously. Shuppiluliuma repeated his confidence in his army, and promised that the affair would be settled by the sun goddess of Arinna and the

Hittite weather god. Virtually all the other documentation indicates that the two sides would generally invoke the gods of both parties, whereas Shuppiluliuma simply ignored Amun-Ra and the gods of Egypt. It is clear that he viewed the gods of Egypt as even less relevant than the Egyptian armed forces. Dismissing any possibility of brotherhood and peace, he seems to have come as close to declaring war as one can imagine from the documents available to us. The text of the letter is fragmentary, but Shuppiluliuma may well have informed the pharaoh that his own rule might be threatened. Shuppiluliuma had sent his son to rule Egypt and may have hinted that he might not stop at less himself. Shuppiluliuma reminded pharaoh of what he had done to the Kashkeans in Anatolia and Mitanni in Syria. One wonders if he was himself thinking about Murshili and Babylon. Shuppiluliuma was serious and angry. The Egyptians should have been prepared.

Shuppiluliuma crossed the regions that had been the scene of his recent victories and moved into the Lebanese Beqa'a, where the Egyptians had been firmly in control for more than a century. There, he struck the Egyptian cavalry and infantry. His cavalry and infantry performed as he had anticipated, while the Egyptians failed to match the Hittites, as Shuppliluliuma had also anticipated. For the Egyptians, the result was a tactical defeat in the field, right at the start of the reign of Aya. There were casualties, but many prisoners were also rounded up, and they brought a plague to Hatti. Many succumbed, including Shuppiluliuma himself, whose hopes of ascending the throne of the pharaohs were thus quashed. The Hittites concluded that their weather god was punishing Shuppiluliuma for having violated a treaty of non-aggression that had been ratified by the gods of both the Egyptians and the Hittites. The Egyptians themselves may have been relieved by the death of Shuppiluliuma. Nevertheless, it may be assumed that the Hittite response to Shuppiluliuma's death cannot have been pleasing to the Egyptians. The Hittites sought only to assuage their god, rather than to make peace (Pritchard 1969: 394–396).

Throughout the reigns of Haremhab and Seti I (ca. 1320–1279), the Egyptians and Hittites faced each other in the Orontes and Beqa'a valleys and along the coast. Diplomatic negotiations accompanied the skirmishes and battles, but the lines did not change significantly. After ascending the throne (1290?), Seti I was able to set off to the Levant coast and re-establish an Egyptian royal presence, which had been absent from the field for decades. Although he put the route to Palestine across the Sinai into order, his campaigns were intended to secure more distant borders.

One initial effort was devoted to exploring the Hittite presence along the coast, probably as far north as the Nahr al-Kabir. Although he had demonstrated his presence in regions north of Byblos, Seti was less ambitious in establishing his lines of defence. Tyre provided a strong point just south of the mouth of the Litani. This coastal strip was protected by two parallel lines into the hinterland. One salient followed the Litani into the Beqa'a and then the Orontes, beyond Kadesh. Another followed the Yarmuk into Jordan, at least as far as Tell el-Shihab. From here, a route was established directly north to Damascus. A garrison was established on the Jordan at Beth-Shan, guarding the only possible entrance into Palestine from Jordan. The Yarmuk was a weak point, allowing forward defence, beyond the Jordan. Both Ramesses II and Seti campaigned across the Jordan to secure their positions in Palestine. The Hittites were the opponents further north, while local potentates will have posed the same problems as Abdi-Ashirta and Aziru in Amurru a generation earlier. River boundaries would thus secure the fortresses behind the rivers. Seti was conscious that Kadesh, Tyre and Beth-Shan were the essential posts along his proposed borders. These secure defences allowed him to pass beyond his borders with near impunity. Even if he should be obliged to return behind them, they provided a secure line which the Hittites were likewise obliged to observe.

Nevertheless, the Hittites extended their control along the coast, and slowly pushed back even the most cautious Egyptian advances. Seti was vindicated in seeking a line at Tyre rather than further north, regardless of how pessimistic this must have seemed. Less than half a century before, Ugarit had declared itself loyal to Egypt. Recognizing that the lands south of Tyre lacked any value, the Hittites turned to Seti's other lines. Appreciating that Kadesh would serve as an ideal staging post for a further advance into Syria, Hittite attention turned to the Orontes, where they penetrated as far as Kadesh, and were able to turn the allegiance of the local cities. The rulers of Kadesh saw no reason to announce their policies until the dust had settled, and the Hittites likewise felt no overwhelming desire to betray their designs. The cagey princes of Kadesh and the other states in the region will have discreetly hidden their Egyptian memorabilia, waiting for yet another change of days. In the meantime, however, everyone in the region was aware that the Egyptian sun was setting along the coast and in the Orontes valley.

Everyone, that is, except for the brash young son of Seti I. Ramesses II set out along the coast and passed north of Beirut. It is clear that the princes of Amurru were causing concern. While the coastal cities may have received him, Egyptian influence ended somewhere south of Byblos, which Seti had realized would be the reasonable line of defence. Ramesses had, however, failed to understand his father's elaborate system of defences, since these cautious lines had been combined with daring and successful offensives. By 1274 BC an unsuspecting Ramesses was confident that the basis he had inherited from his father could be maintained and used for expansion, into Jordan and Syria. While the Hittites could view his intentions in Jordan as benign, his plans in Syria were bound to result in conflict. Relying on Egyptian confidence and luck, the Hittite king Muwatalli led Ramesses into a trap at Kadesh. The presence of the Hittite army would assure that their might was respected, and their plan adopted.

Spies treacherously (according to the Egyptian version) informed Ramesses that the Hittites were far off, and thus reassured he moved on. It is revealing that Ramesses mentions this incident for it betrays at once that he had every reason to fear the Hittite army and also that his intelligence services failed to inform him of the change in political climate beyond the mountains. Either the Hittites were remarkably resourceful or the Egyptians over-confident, as it seems improbable that the trap could have been laid by Hittite artifice alone. In any case, the four divisions of the army marched north towards Kadesh. At the head of his army, Ramesses was in camp awaiting the other divisions when the Hittites struck. The blow was such that Ramesses was barely able to tear himself out of the fray. He was saved only because some remnants of his divisions were so far from the Hittite blow that he could seek safety out of range.

Thence Ramesses fled with his army as far as he could go. The smashed Egyptian armies could not cross to the coast, as the cities there were falling away from Egypt.

The crushed force had to flee through Hittite territory to the south, with the Hittite army in hot pursuit. The headlong flight of the Egyptians eventually brought them through Palestine, to their homes in the Nile Valley and Ramesses to his residence in the Delta. He probably did not even take the time to look back and notice that the Hittites had stopped north of the Yarmuk. The Hittites simply secured the region around Damascus and watched the backs of the last Egyptian soldiers disappear into the wastes of Jordan and Palestine.

## Peace

Although Ramesses was utterly defeated, the outcome of the battle between Ramesses II and Muwatalli is widely viewed today as a draw. The ensuing treaty is frequently designated the 'Kadesh treaty' although Kadesh does not figure in it. The name simply reflects the impression that the treaty was signed because of the battle, underscoring the perceived importance of the battle. After the treaty, Ramesses II married a Hittite princess, and the two courts exchanged letters dealing with all matters in the name of Ra of Heliopolis and the sun goddess of Arinna. When relations were settled, the Hittite queen Padukhep heaped scorn on Ramesses when she took advantage of the Hittite king Hattushili's absence to answer a letter before her husband returned from a business trip. She tried to admonish the brash pharaoh about his behaviour, referring to the presence of a certain Hittite prince at the Egyptian court: "Since Urkhi-Teshup is there, ask him ..." (after Beckman 1996: 126).

This particular 'prince' was known as Urkhi-Teshup, but had earlier been known as Murshili II, since he was actually the former king who had been deposed by his uncle, Hattushili, Queen Padukhep's husband, and thus potentially a source of trouble for all concerned. The idea of royal exiles is hardly new, and the Hittites were familiar with it. Another prince, one Shattiwaza of Mitanni, had fled to Babylon, only to be exiled from there as well, before ending his adventures by having Shuppiluliuma return him to his throne. The Hittite royal family cannot, therefore, have felt much comfort at the notion of a Hittite prince at Ramesses' court. They could only suspect the worst. Even if they were convinced of his incompetence, he could still be a nuisance.

Urkhi-Teshup had equal reason to distrust both his family and his benefactors. He was after all the son of Muwatalli, the Hittite king who had defeated Ramesses at Kadesh, and could not count on any affection. On the other hand, it was his uncle Hattushili who had deprived him of his throne, but somehow allowed him to flee with his life. That he fled to Egypt is another illustration of the ambivalence that governed relations between the two royal courts. Initially, Hattushili had incautiously let him go to the Orontes region on the edge of the empire, after defeating him in battle and dethroning him. From there, Urkhi-Teshup began to negotiate with Babylon, and was exiled yet further abroad while Hattushili hastened to improve relations with both Babylonia and Assyria in order to avoid further unpleasantries. At this, Urkhi-Teshup decided to head for Egypt, and thus the son of the victor at Kadesh turned up as an asylum-seeker at the court of the defeated Ramesses. Urkhi-Teshup had timed things well, and it may not have been entirely accidental. His advances had been rebuffed in Babylon before he headed for Egypt, and when Hattushili announced that

Urkhi-Teshup's presence in Egypt was *casus belli* for him, the Babylonians agreed to join him. Hattushili probably dismissed the Babylonian offer as absurd, but the Babylonians had reason to be concerned about international developments. It was at this moment that the Assyrians finally eliminated what was left of Mitanni.

While struggling with Babylonia, the Assyrians had also begun and sustained an expansion to the west. In a series of campaigns during the first years of Ramesses' reign, Adad-Nerari I and Shalmaneser I of Assyria conquered all of northern Syria as far as the Euphrates. Initially, there was some confusion as the Mitanni king was nominally left in place as a vassal loyal to Assyria. He confused the recognition of independent status with independence and briefly endeavoured to return to Hittite hegemony. The Assyrians sprang again, and Mitanni was eliminated, being incorporated into the Assyrian empire, to become a stepping stone on the way to the coast. This dashed Hittite hopes for further interventions in Syria, and it also meant that the frontiers of Hatti, Assyria and Egypt now met along the Euphrates and the Litani in Syria-Lebanon.

As Adad-Nerari moved further west, the Hittites appreciated that the difficulties of maintaining the conflict with Egypt diminished their capacity to deal with Assyria. At the same time, Hittite control in Anatolia itself was coming under increasing strain. Hattushili was not only concerned about Assyria and Egypt. The Mycenaeans were causing trouble along the Aegean coast and even inland. The death of the ambitious Shuppiluliuma may have been one reason why the Hittites did not press deep into Egyptian territory in Syria. The Mycenaeans may have been another. Murshili II had completely destroyed the Mycenaean presence at Miletus, and followed through with the conquest of neighbouring Ephesus the following year. Hittite control of the Aegean coast should have been secure with the Mycenaeans and their Arzawan neighbours thrown out of the game. But, while Seti I gradually built up secure frontiers for the Egyptian holdings in Syria, the Mycenaeans resumed their activities in coastal Anatolia. One way or another, women from the Aegean were ending up in the cities of the Mycenaean world, on the Greek mainland, and in Crete. They may have been captured in warlike missions or been caught by pirates who sold them to the Mycenaeans. The Hittites' prestige was suffering from the impunity with which their defences were breached.

Hattushili went against one of these pirates, a certain Piyamaradu, who was able to slip past the Hittites and escape into regions under Mycenaean control. Hattushili realized that pursuing him into mainland Greece would lead to war, and would have been conscious of the fact that the Hittites lacked a navy. Negotiating with the king of Ugarit to equip a navy to invade mainland Greece in order to protect the coastal cities was a thought that Hattushili dismissed, unwisely. Realizing that he was better off pretending that Piyamaradu was acting on his own, Hattushili was obliged to negotiate with the Mycenaean king. Hattushili thus turned to the Mycenaean king, asking him to restrain marauders along the coast. Just as Urkhi-Teshup had sought asylum in Egypt, Piyamaradu belonged to a family that had fled from Hittite influence in Arzawa, and received asylum among the Mycenaeans when Murshili II had destroyed the Arzawan capital at Ephesus before Ramesses II's time. With the Hittites distracted in Syria, the Mycenaeans had re-established themselves at Miletus where Piyamaradu was a welcome guest in a city just outside Hittite control. From here, he enjoyed sufficient protection to threaten cities along the coast from Miletus to Troy.

Long before the days when Mycenae was a political power, Mycenaean mercenaries wandered around the eastern Mediterranean, offering their services to other crowns, as well as following their own leaders. They may have provided decisive aid to the Thebans at the expulsion of the Hyksos. This was before the Mycenaeans had conquered Knossos and before the Hittites had conquered Babylon, so that the Egyptians may not have viewed them as politically valuable, even if their martial prowess was of use. Eventually, their political power was gradually consolidated, but primarily as a military force rather than as a political entity. This weakness would ultimately prove to be useful for the Egyptians once again, even if it was the Achilles' heel of Mycenaean power. The days of the Sea Peoples and the end of the Late Bronze Age were yet far off, however, and thus the danger imperceptible. In the middle of the second millennium and the start of the Late Bronze Age, these warlike passions served as the catalyst for the Mycenaean expansion into the Minoan realm, and the Aegean, for the conquest of Knossos was just a stepping stone. Therefore, while the Hittites were expanding under Shuppiluliuma, the Mycenaeans were moving east. While Shuppiluliuma was concentrating on northern Syria during the reigns at the end of the eighteenth Dynasty, the kingdom of Arzawa in western Anatolia sought to establish independent relations with Egypt. Appreciating any aid that would permit Mitanni to maintain itself against Hatti, the Egyptian court moved with alacrity.

A marriage was arranged, but the affair must have seemed bizarre to the Egyptians. Most of the diplomatic correspondence of the day was written in locally influenced versions of Babylonian Akkadian, and thus pharaoh kept a group of scribes skilled in cuneiform to carry out this correspondence. Pharaoh dictated his letters in Egyptian and the scribes wrote them in Akkadian, sometimes translating quite literally. Other courts proceeded in identical fashion. How anyone understood these stilted versions of Akkadian is not clear, but it testifies to the ingenuity of the ancient scribes. This problem was compounded by the fact that messengers took quite a while, several months on occasion, to take the clay tablets abroad. In the case of Arzawa, the communications proved even more difficult, for the kings of Arzawa wished that the letters written to them be in Hittite (Moran 1992: EA 32). This request may have whetted pharaoh's appetite, since it implied inroads against a distant foe. That he got another wife out of it will probably not have been significant. How long it took for pharaoh to find scribes able to write in Hittite, and finally get the letters to their destination, is not known.

These difficulties were compounded since the end of Mitanni removed the distractions of Syria from the Hittite programme, and the attentions of the Hittites were directed elsewhere. They were doubtless displeased at the idea of pharaoh corresponding directly with rulers in the middle of Anatolia. The initial result of the Egyptian efforts was, therefore, unsuccessful since Murshili II conquered Arzawa. Here the matter should have ended, except that Piyamaradu did not intend to leave the Hittites in peace. A scion of the royal family of Arzawa who had failed in his match with the Hittites, Piyamaradu enjoyed the protection of the Mycenaeans. The Mycenaeans were therefore able to establish themselves in Miletus, just south of

Ephesus, and Piyamaradu could sail into safe waters virtually anywhere in the Aegean. Unable to deal with this menace himself, Hattushili was obliged to turn to the Mycenaeans, and here he assumed that he could expect their agreement by saying that "a war would not be good", which is what he suggested the Mycenaeans say to Piyamaradu.

Hattushili may have felt that having the Mycenaeans, the Egyptians and the Assyrians as neighbours was quite enough. He therefore had to deal with the Mycenaeans gingerly, and to strengthen his neighbours at Troy and hold on to Ephesus, so as to keep the Mycenaeans in Miletus at bay. The last thing he wanted was to start an unnecessary war with Egypt. The Mycenaeans were thus requested to write a letter to Piyaramadu, advising him that he should leave Hittite territories and those of their allies in peace. Hattushili may have been relieved at the idea. He would probably have been less optimistic had he realized that he had betrayed his weakness to the Mycenaeans who were thus preparing to enter the fray themselves in a serious fashion.

Ramesses himself was doubtless well informed about the commotion along the Aegean coast, and must have realized that the local princes in the Orontes valley might be cajoled into changing sides once again. Ramesses may thus have dreamt of returning to Syria, with the hope of using recent changes to his own advantage. However, even Ramesses realized that Hattushili would be concerned about the Assyrians, and that both would be highly motivated to work with Egypt. Urkhi-Teshup could be guaranteed a friendly welcome as his presence alone would be valuable, even if his aspirations and designs were useless. Ramesses was probably weighing the advantages and dangers of trying to co-operate with his new neighbours, the Great Powers, as opposed to the old and unreliable princes of the Orontes valley who had betrayed Egypt so often in the past. Any reservations or goals he may have considered were smashed with a new offer.

Hattushili had no choice but to approach Egypt, and thus secret negotiations eventually ended in a treaty. A delegation arrived from the Hittite capital, and proclamation followed proclamation. Several copies of the treaty were kept, both on cuneiform clay tablets and on more elaborate ceremonial media. The actual document preserved in Egypt was a silver tablet written in Akkadian and sealed with the Hittite royal seal in the centre (the original tablet has been lost and thus we only have a description of it). The parties were Hattushili and Ramesses, and they agreed to settle their differences and abide by their agreement.

All the family fell into letter writing, as Ramesses' queen consort and mother were both encouraged to write to their counterparts at the Hittite court, as well as his son the Crown Prince. Following the pattern established under Tuthmosis III, gifts were exchanged at Ugarit, where the Hittite envoys met the Egyptians and each returned home laden with the gifts presented by the other. Ugarit benefited from the diplomatic niceties as it was thus acceptable to both Hatti and Egypt as partners in increasing the city's wealth. The benefits of this peaceful state were enjoyed all the way from the harbour district in Ugarit to the commercial centres of Cyprus and the Aegean. Mycenaean merchants would have listened and returned home with their news.

Ramesses dispatched a request for another wife, and the Hittites obliged. In honour of the events, Ramesses had an Egyptian translation of the Akkadian text of the treaty chiselled into the walls at the temple of Amun-Ra at Karnak (Kitchen 1982: 76; Figure 5:2). He also had a modest stela erected at Abu Simbel, recording his

Figure 5:2  Egyptian version of Egyptian-Hittite peace treaty, temple of Karnak (Kitchen 1982: fig. 24).

marriage, including notes about the dowry and the guest list. Although the dowry was probably adequate by international standards and accurately recorded, the same cannot be said of the guest list, which alleges that the Hittite king also condescended to come to the wedding. The stela recording the event begins with a quote in traditional rhetorical Egyptian style: "Words said by the great king of Hatti: I will come to you" (Kitchen 1979: 234). This can be viewed as a rhetorical flourish, but a much later text includes a quote from the king of Hatti encouraging a lowly prince to proceed to Egypt. Existing texts confirm that an invitation was issued, but there is no real evidence of such a meeting (Kitchen 1982: 90–91). Had it taken place, it would have been the only 'summit conference' in the Bronze Age.

Such a summit would be unheard of, but there were other reasons why Hattushili may have preferred to stay away. The treaty and the marriage stela were not the only contemporary inscriptions added to the walls of existing temples in Egypt, and not the most prominent of those relating to Egypt and Hatti. Ramesses may have been conscious that his aspirations in Syria were at an end, but he understood that regardless of his own inactivity, the Hittites were not in a position to dictate terms anywhere.

Realizing, therefore, that the Hittites were no longer a threat, Ramesses II covered public surfaces in Egypt with accounts of his victory at Kadesh (Figure 5:3; O'Connor 2003: Figure 9:4). The battle of Kadesh appeared on temple walls that had been standing empty, and also adorned the walls of new temples. The inscriptions chiselled into stone were supplemented with a poem written on papyrus. Ramesses devoted considerable funds to his propaganda effort. Indeed, he seems to have treated this defeat as the greatest accomplishment of his long life. The battle was treated not as a strategic and tactical catastrophe, but rather as a deed of personal valour by the king himself, alone and unaided.

In political terms it can be appreciated that the Hittites understood that it was in their interests to pursue a peaceful policy in their relations with Egypt, and that they behaved to that end. They were doubtless concerned, however, to hear that Ramesses II had court poets portray his crushing defeat as a victory over the Hittites, and even more so at his depiction as the sole victor against great odds. One can imagine that Hattushili regretted that Muwatalli had not permitted him to send his infantry across the river to finish off the brash youth and his routed troops. At the very least, he may have sent a letter to the Egyptian king stating that his Hittite troops had ceased to pursue the fleeing Egyptians somewhere near Damascus, merely because they were fatigued and not because they had any reservations about going further. He may also have complained about Ramesses' lack of respect in describing the performance of the various armies. Ramesses claimed in the Egyptian reliefs and even in a letter to Hattushili that he had been quite alone in repulsing the Hittite army. In his letter, Ramesses apparently said that he had faced the Hittite forces alone, without even his charioteers, and even that he had carried off prisoners. Hattushili knew full well that the Hittite thrust had been successfully executed, and that Ramesses was wildly exaggerating. He wrote a long letter back, with some very precise data about the position of the Egyptian forces, asking "Were there really no armies?" (after Edel 1949: 208–209). As far as Hattushili was concerned, the story was simple. In his own records of his life he noted laconically that his father "had defeated the king of the land of Egypt and the country of Amurru" (Pritchard 1969: 319).

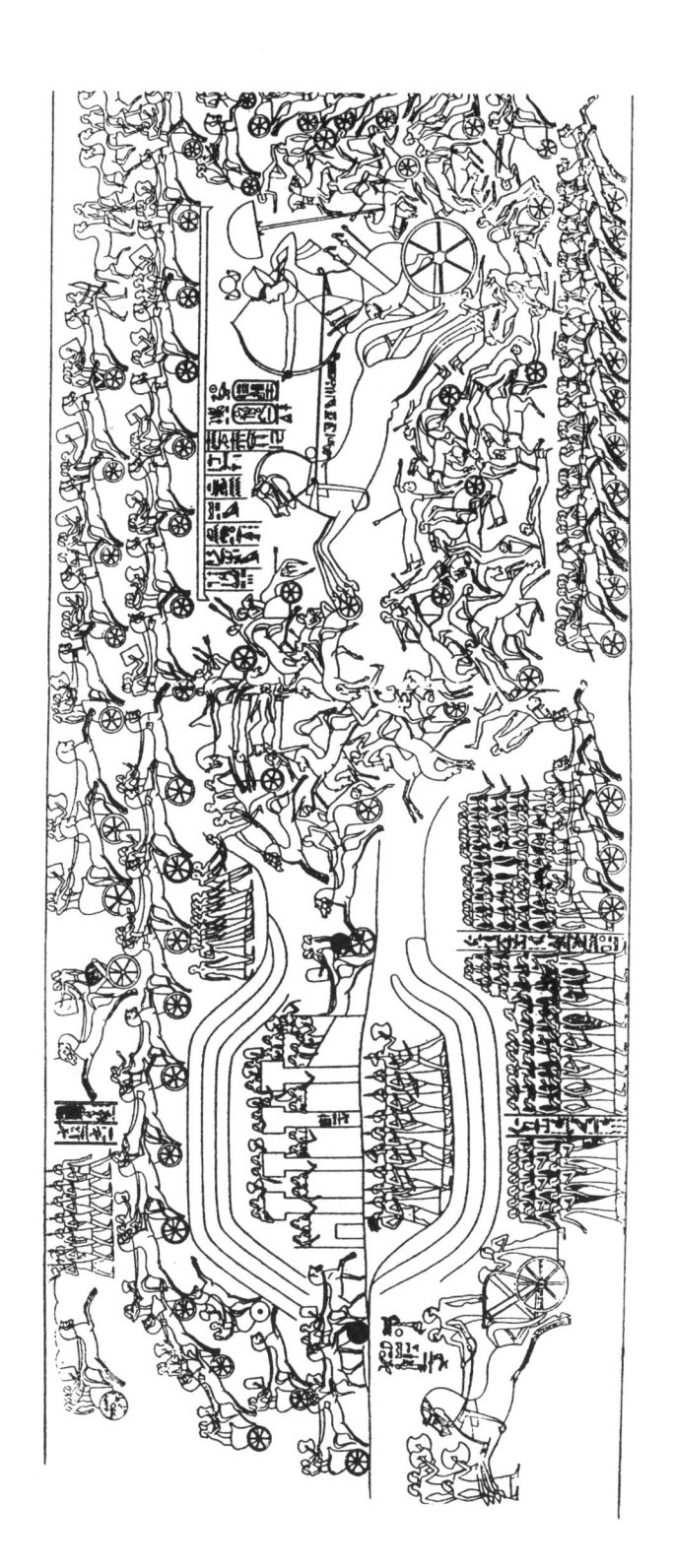

Figure 5:3   Relief scene of battle of Kadesh, Luxor temple (after Kitchen 1982: fig. 19).

Indeed, the tone of Hattushilli's letter recalls Assur-Uballit's remarks about the harsh treatment of his envoys. Foreigners were simply dumbfounded when faced with Egyptian behaviour and generally kept their critical remarks brief. Neither letter can be compared with Shuppiluliuma's reaction to the treacherous murder of his son, and certainly Assur-Uballit could not have threatened Egypt with a violent retaliation even had he felt moved to do so. The insolence with which the Egyptian rulers behaved must be weighed against their confidence that they would be able to weather any blows. The Egyptians may have understood that Shuppiluliuma desired to go down the Nile as Murshili had gone down the Euphrates. Perhaps the leaders of external lands failed to appreciate the Egyptian pharaohs' image of themselves and their role as the sole representative of the sole civilization in a world governed by chaos.

Hattushili's responses must have been quite caustic. The Hittites did make peace, but the king can hardly have been satisfied with Ramesses' self-laudatory inscriptions any more than Queen Padukhep of Hatti could bear the thought of Urkhi-Teshup plotting away in peace at the court of Ramesses: "… As you, my brother, know the magazines of Hatti, do I not know that it is burned down? And Urkhi-Teshup gave what remained to the great god. Since Urkhi-Teshup is there, ask him if this is so, or not so …" (after Beckman 1996: 126).

She not only emphasized that Urkhi-Teshup had burnt down the royal palace in the Hittite capital before receiving asylum in Egypt, but also regaled the pharaoh with tales relating to his behaviour as told in foreign courts. Unfortunately, Ramesses was not open to such criticism and the efforts were wasted. Ramesses wrote back, and added details about the flight of the Hittite king and the capture of prisoners that bore no resemblance to any Hittite version of reality. Ramesses still maintained that he had been quite alone, and perhaps he believed it himself. In reality the Hittites were bound to tolerate the arrogance, as they had no alternative. A Hittite prince who saw Ramesses' reliefs first hand in Egypt returned home and, later as King Tudkhaliya, added large-scale art to the accomplishments of the Hittites. Had Ramesses heard of this, he would doubtless have been flattered at the idea of the wretched defeated Hittites copying his new art.

The letter-writing and bride-collecting was accompanied by the dispatch of medical teams to the Hittite court. Hattushili developed a foot infection that served as a convenient excuse to postpone his departure for Egypt. Several of Ramesses' letters concern treatments for Hattushili's eyes. Some female members of the Hittite family were suffering from infertility, and Ramesses may have hoped that his efforts to heal them would be rewarded with an additional princess. Ramesses also made certain that the Babylonian princesses at the Hittite court were in good care. The Babylonian king will hardly have been displeased at the efforts of the Egyptians. One of the Babylonian physicians had died at the Hittite court, and that king was probably loath to send more.

With the Assyrians encroaching on Hittite and Egyptian territory, Ramesses' attentions were hardly unwise and selfless gestures. Conscious that under Tukulti-Ninurta I the Assyrians were moving into the Hittite breadbasket in northern Syria, the Egyptians also dispatched grain to the Hittites. The grain was sent through Ugarit, but the Egyptian medical team remained in the Hittite capital. The Hittites also dispatched Egyptian physicians to the courts of their vassals, provided the medics attended in their palace at Hattusha to await orders for displacement to another court. The various doctors no doubt reported back to Ramesses about the situation in Anatolia and, much as the Hittite court might desire to conceal the matter, things were not in the best possible state (Edel 1976). Ramesses may have appreciated that the Assyrians were not the only difficulty. Ramesses and his son Merenptah therefore pursued a diplomatic route with the foes of Hatti to the west. The pressure on the coast had not eased, as the Mycenaeans strengthened their foothold along the Anatolian coast of the Aegean. The Egyptians intensified their relations with the Mycenaeans by establishing an outpost at Umm ar-Rakhkham (Mersa Matruh) where goods could be delivered directly from Crete to Libya and sent along the coast to the Delta, and thence down the Nile.

The concentration of Mycenaean pottery at Gurob near the Fayum may reflect one of the final destinations of the imports from Crete and the mainland. It is also possible that some of these women kidnapped from Aegean regions may have ended up weaving textiles at the harem at Gurob. It was also here that Ramesses' Hittite bride ended her days. She was at least formally partly responsible for affairs, yet one can imagine how she felt, surrounded by other women kidnapped from Anatolia. These Egyptian links with the Aegean were intensified throughout the eighteenth and nineteenth Dynasties, and may be viewed as a prelude to the invasions of the 'Peoples of the Sea' as much as an effort to stay in touch with the neighbours of the Hittites to the west.

The Egyptians were thus in the position of supporting both the Hittites and their opponents in the Aegean, a position more complicated than in Syria and Palestine, where the Assyrians were a menace to both Egypt and Hatti. Initially, the Assyrians were more of a direct threat to the Hittites, an attitude which can be read in the correspondence. While the Assyrians protested with assurances of friendship, the Hittite court was aware of the danger, and did not conceal their irritation. Tukulti-Ninurta maintained his steady pressure. While trying to treat with the Mycenaeans, the Hittite rulers could not view the Assyrian progress with complacency. Even so, the Assyrian move also meant the end of any remaining Egyptian influence, especially as the allies of the Mycenaeans began to extend their raiding from the Aegean coast to the Levant and Egypt itself.

Making common cause against these various foes was beyond the power of Hatti and Egypt. At the time, the Egyptians and the Hittites doubtless presented their treaty to the outside world as a reasonable solution to a futile conflict. In reality, the Hittites had no motive for penetrating into Palestine and thus the abandonment of their forward thrusting meant that they were relinquishing little. Ramesses, for his part, had to acknowledge that there was little prospect of the Egyptians gaining hold of the Orontes valley, which had eluded them since their first incursions into Syria. Egyptian influence in this region had increased only due to Hittite pressure on Mitanni and not as a result of direct success on the field of battle.

In the wide context, it is appropriate to observe that the Hittite effort to cease hostilities was at least partially the result of similar pressures on Hatti. Akhenaten had recognized that Assur would represent a threat to Babylonia. Akhenaten may have appreciated the Assyrian threat to Mitanni, but knew that it was not Egyptian recognition that propelled Assyria to success on the world stage. It was, however, at least partly Assyrian activity that induced the Hittites to seek a peaceful accommodation with Egypt less than a century after Akhenaten's death. It was thus in the interests of Hatti to make peace with Egypt, as was confirmed when Tukulti-Ninurta I continued to push further west.

At the end of the nineteenth Dynasty, the powers were at a stalemate, unable to move forwards, and likewise both unwilling and unable to move back. Letters between the Assyrians and the Hittites were full of tension, but elsewhere there was not the same sensation, as can be seen in the letters exchanged between the Hittite and Egyptian courts. Most of these epistolary exchanges reveal little more than a close connection during the period after peace was made. Ramesses II's mother writes to the Hittite king and queen. His son writes to the Hittite king, as do various high officials, and the content of the letters is quite banal:

> Thus, Seth-her-khepesh-ef, the son of the great king, king of the land of Egypt, to Khattushili, the great king, king of the land of Hatti, my father. Say: You, great king, king of the land of Hatti, my father. May you be well, may your lands be well. Behold, I, your son, am well. The lands of the king of Egypt, your brother, are well. Behold, the great king, the king of the land of Hatti, my father, has written to me to enquire about the welfare of his son, and I was very, very happy that my father had written to enquire about my welfare. The Sun-god and the Weather-god will now enquire about the great king, the king of the land of Hatti, and they will make the peace and the fraternity of the king of the land of Egypt with the great king, the king of the land of Hatti last forever, and they (the gods) will cause the years of the great king, the king of Egypt, and the years of the king of the land of Hatti, his brother, to be extended since they (the kings) are content on beautiful peace since they have become brothers for eternity.
>
> Now I have sent a gift to my father, as a greeting present for my father, through the hand of Pa-Re-her-wenem-ef: a drinking vessel of fine gold inlaid with the face of a bull whose horns are white stone and eyes are black stone, weighing 750 [grammes] of fine gold; a fine linen garment, and a fine new two-sided linen bedspread.
>
> (after Edel 1978: 130–133; see Beckman 1996: 122)

It is difficult to grasp the extent to which the Egyptians and the Hittites adjusted to one another. The number of Egyptian words used in the Akkadian correspondence between the Hittite and Egyptian courts suggests that the connection was quite close. Entire grammatical constructions in the diplomatic correspondence were written by Egyptian scribes translating literally from Egyptian into Akkadian. This need not mean that the Hittites actually understood it. In fact, the sheer difficulty of understanding a complicated letter may have rendered it preferable to send vacuous ones that were at least easy to understand. Certainly, Egyptian practice does not mean that the Egyptian scribes realized what they were doing. One could argue that the letters were the essential feature and that the content was secondary, as the presence of Egyptian words seems to confirm. The Hittite royal family are unlikely to have been conversant in Egyptian. Nevertheless, this usage long preceded amicable relations, since the Egyptian word for "queen" (*ta hemt nesu*) appeared as *dakhamunzu* in the Hittite text dating to the reign of Shuppiluliuma when the powers were certainly in conflict, and the text was not meant for international audiences.

## The End

The Hittites must have been concerned by Egyptian protection of political dissidents and boasting about victory where shame over defeat would have been more appropriate. They can hardly have been amused at pharaoh having his letters written in Egyptianizing Akkadian, and even less so at the destinations of those written in Hittite, to the foes of Hatti. The Egyptians were confident that they could withstand criticism or assault.

The Mycenaean pottery at Amarna, Gurob and Umm ar-Rakhkham illustrates an unusual case, since Mycenaean pottery was not common in Egypt. On the other hand, the distribution of Mycenaean pottery outside the Aegean corresponds to those regions heavily influenced by Egyptian activity, whereas Mycenaean wares are rare in regions under Hittite influence. Similarly, the destructions wrought by the Peoples of the Sea at the end of the Bronze Age meant the end for most of those states closely allied to Hatti (e.g. Ugarit, Emar, Carchemish, Troy), whereas those states working with Egypt (e.g. Byblos, Ashqelon) survived the impact, albeit with transformed political structures. It is thus evident that while making peace with Hatti, the Egyptians may have understood the inevitable course of Mycenaean activity, which ultimately contributed to the demise of the Hittites. Since both the Hittites and the Mycenaeans disappeared, Egypt's survival under foreign rule can be viewed as more than a mere humiliation.

Hatti had sought Egyptian recognition throughout the Late Bronze Age. In general, Hittite policy was based on the exploitation of force, which enabled the destruction of Arzawa, Aleppo, Babylon and Mitanni. Hatti was the only second millennium power to destroy two major neighbours (aside from the neighbours in Anatolia). Facing Egypt, Hatti was unable to pursue such a policy, as the expansion was accompanied by the simultaneous growth of competing powers to the west and east. For Hatti, making peace with Egypt was the only alternative until the Assyrians and the Mycenaeans could be dealt with. The Egyptians responded by shifting alliances without breaking them. By making peace with Hatti while responding in measured tones to the Assyrians and the Mycenaeans, the Egyptians kept their options open. Admittedly, the Egyptian policy of supporting the Assyrians and the Mycenaeans in the second millennium ultimately resulted in the Assyrian and Macedonian conquests of the first millennium BC. During the Bronze Age, however, Egypt and Hatti pursued two very different policies with equal degrees of success.

Well, almost equal. Troy, Hattusha, Ugarit, and Carchemish fell in rapid succession. Ramesses III will hardly have viewed it as accidental when he gloated that Hatti had been destroyed whereas Egypt had survived the onslaughts of the Peoples of the Sea. And he would doubtless have been pleased at the fate of Pylos and Mycenae, which were also eliminated from the roster of the civilized world. Mycenae and Hatti were no more. Egypt had prevailed.

### Notes

1   The author accepts the new 'Ultra-Low Chronology', presented in Gasche *et al.* 1998a, which proposes that Babylon fell to the Hittites in 1499 BC, rather than 1595 BC as in the familiar 'Middle Chronology', and that Tuthmosis I reached the Euphrates a few years

later (ca. 1490 BC). The issue is still unresolved, however, as both the Egyptian and Mesopotamian chronologies continue to be debated. Many Assyriologists employ the Middle or Low Chronology for Mesopotamia, and thus there are several potential correlations for the beginning of the story. This aspect is significant, as the correlations used here are those developed by the author, and are not widely used in the literature as hitherto published, although they are based upon chronological frameworks developed by others.

According to this scheme, the Mitanni empire emerged virtually simultaneously with the Egyptian empire, whereas a correlation employing an earlier date for the fall of Babylon would allow the Mitanni empire to form at an earlier date. For the chronology used here see Gasche *et al.* 1998a, b; Kitchen 2000; Warburton 2000b, 2002.

2   The Hittites and the Egyptians were not isolated entities. There were neighbours in the Aegean as well as Mesopotamia and Syria. Aside from Beckman (1996), Klengel (1992), Moran (1992), O'Connor and Cline (1998), and Redford (1992), more evidence, interpretation and references to past commentaries of the relations between the various parties discussed here will be found in Özgüç (2002; particularly sections by Niemeier, Canik-Kirschbaum), Latacz *et al.* (2001; particularly Stark, Neumann, and Latacz), and Cline and O'Connor (2003). The philological sources can be complemented with archaeological material. It is striking that the distribution of Mycenaean pottery (cf. map in Latacz *et al.* 2001: 54) is largely restricted to regions in the Aegean, and to Levantine regions under Egyptian control or influence. During the Late Bronze Age, Mycenaean material barely encroaches into Hittite regions; Assyrian material does not move into regions under Babylonian, Mitanni or Egyptian influence. While many authors have pieced together the evidence for the connections between the Hittites and the Mycenaeans or Egypt and the Aegean, or the Hittites and the Assyrians, the current, speculative reconstruction of the links between Hatti and all these contemporaries is the author's own, based on the same evidence, but viewed globally (Warburton 2001).

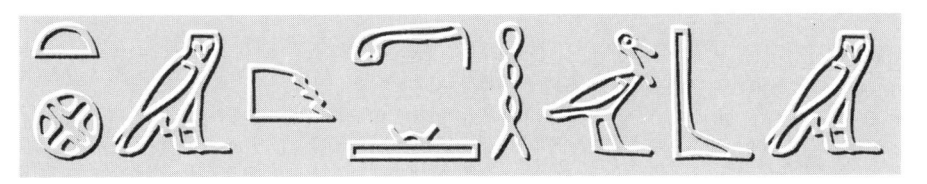

# CHAPTER 6

# EGYPT AND MESOPOTAMIA IN THE LATE BRONZE AND IRON AGES

*David Warburton and Roger Matthews*

## Introduction (Figure 6:1)

From the start of the Late Bronze Age ca. 1500 BC, political interactions between Upper Mesopotamia (Assyria) and Lower Mesopotamia (Babylonia) regularly involved Egypt. The significance of these interactions can be apprehended only on the basis of an appreciation of political and cultural factors within Mesopotamia. For the Assyrians and the Babylonians of the Bronze and Iron Ages, Egypt played a range of roles and was viewed from a variety of shifting perspectives dependent upon the specific conditions that pertained within Mesopotamia at any given time. In this chapter we survey the nature of the evidence for Mesopotamia-Egypt connections through the Late Bronze and Iron Ages, before examining particular episodes of regional interaction.

Although in sporadic contact with Egypt through the Late Bronze and Iron Ages, the Assyrians and Babylonians did not enter into a sustained long-term engagement with the Egyptians to the same extent as the Hittites (Warburton Chapter 5, this volume). There was never a comparable degree of interaction and mutual understanding, as far as the sources reveal. However, partly because of the long distances involved, relations between Egypt and Mesopotamia had a special flavour. In a letter to the Egyptian pharaoh, a Babylonian king of the 14th century BC described how he overcame his disappointment that the Egyptian king had not expressed concern for his health:

> Akhenaten, Great King of Egypt, my brother! Thus Burnaburiash, Great King of Babylonia! [...] I asked my brother's messenger if there was really a far-away country and a close-by one. He said, "Ask your own messenger whether [Egypt] is far away [from Babylonia]". Now, since I asked my own messenger and he said to me that the journey is far, I was not angry.
>
> (Moran 1992: EA 7)

Although Burnaburiash was not a native Babylonian, being of the foreign Kassite dynasty, nor as cosmopolitan as previous rulers, there undoubtedly was a great divide, spatial and cultural, between Egypt and Mesopotamia. Initial cultural connections can be detected at the end of the fourth millennium BC but the two regions appear to have grown apart through the third millennium and the first

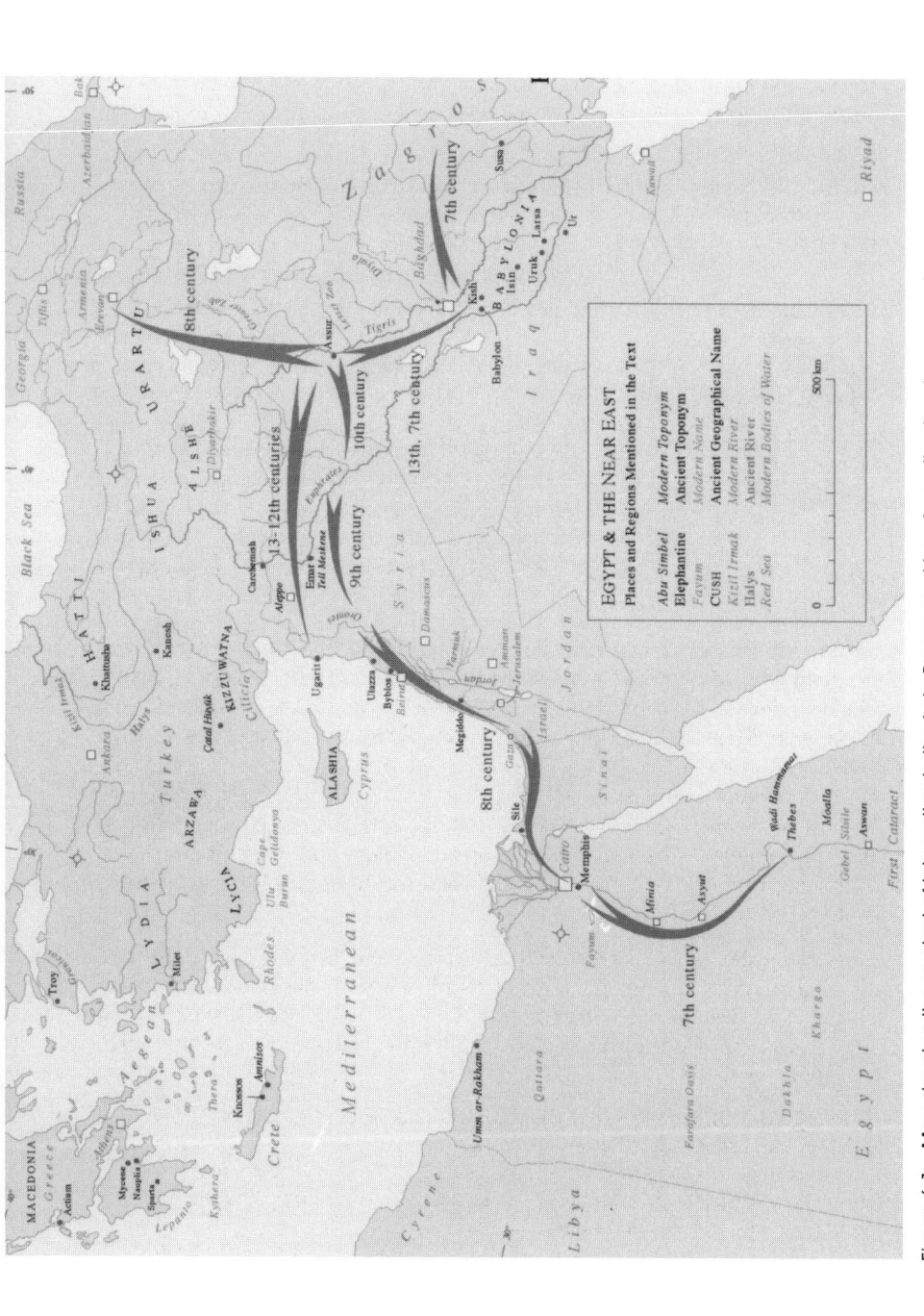

Figure 6:1 Map showing the context of interaction in the Late Bronze and Iron Ages: the Assyrian expansion.

quarter of the second millennium BC. During this long period, it is hard to detect in the archaeological and historical records any evidence for significant contact between the two regions. It was during the latter part of this period that Assyria rose to become a major, independent power.

From the early second millennium onwards, Babylonia and Assyria were at loggerheads, and relations between them were complicated by their individual histories.

> Babylonia and Assyria were united by the same language, the same script, the same religion, and the same art. They were divided by differences in the language, the script, the pantheon, and iconographic style.
>
> (Seidl 2000: 89)

To a considerable degree, Assyrian culture was a modified copy of the Babylonian, with the borrowing direct, one way, and conscious. The Assyrians altered the architecture, the myths and the kingship, but their Babylonian origin is indisputable. Many today have come to view Assyria as an independent region of Mesopotamia, sharing a common body of tradition, expressed in an idiosyncratic fashion. This approach fails to appreciate the degree to which Assyria was, culturally, a peripheral imitation of traditions in the southern alluvium, to which other traditions were added. The copying in Assyria was more successful and reliable than in distant regions, partially because of the proximity, but also due to the Assyrian elite's passion for detail and an appreciation of the foreign and exotic. Divided by a common culture, Assyria and Babylonia were too close for comfort.

From ca. 1500 BC onwards, local Mesopotamian conflicts between Assyria and Babylonia also involved Egypt, initially indirectly and later directly. At varying times, Egypt sided in inter-state conflicts with the Hittites (Warburton Chapter 5, this volume), Babylon, Mitanni and Assyria, and these powers were themselves often in conflict with one another or with other powers of the day. The states of south-west Asia had to deal with, and thereby develop perspectives on, the Egyptian superpower because of its pre-eminent position and because of their desire to engage Egypt within their own regional struggles. Mesopotamian relations with Egypt thus always stood in the shadow of Assyrian relations with Babylonia, and can only be understood in this context.

The Assyrians, the Babylonians and the Egyptians were thus in contact with each other, although cultural misunderstandings clearly underpinned at least some of these relationships. The Babylonian king had little idea of the long distance from Babylon to Egypt (see above), and an Assyrian king expressed concern about the treatment meted out to diplomatic envoys in Egypt:

> [Akhenaten], Great King of Egypt, my brother! Thus Assur-uballit, King of Assyria, Great King, your brother! […] Why should messengers stand in the sun and so die in the sun? If staying out in the sun means profit for the king, then let [the messenger] stay out and let him die right there in the sun, (but) there must be a profit for the king himself. Otherwise, why should he die in the sun?
>
> (Moran 1992: EA 16)

At first glance, then, the textual sources hint at a relationship between Mesopotamia and Egypt that was complex, tetchy, self-interested, and founded on basic misapprehensions by all parties concerning differing cultural and political values and codes of conduct. In this light, it is perhaps inevitable that such interactions culminated in the Assyrian sacking of Thebes in Egypt after its conquest by Assurbanipal in 663 BC.

## Evidence and interpretations

The sources for our appreciation of Egypt-Mesopotamia interactions comprise principally palace or elite records from both Egypt (Tell el-Amarna) and Assyria, which focus on elite politics, military engagements, and inter-polity alliances. In examining relationships between Babylonia and Egypt in the Late Bronze Age, the sources come principally from Egypt, in the form of the famous Amarna Letters, dating to the reigns of Amenophis III and Akhenaten in the 14th century BC (Moran 1992). These documents shed a sudden and brilliant light on the international scene of the Late Bronze Age over a period of some 30 years. The texts take the form of clay tablets written in the Semitic Akkadian language in the cuneiform script that had evolved in Mesopotamia over a period of some two millennia by that time. Diplomatic texts from Hattusha, the capital of the Hittites (see Warburton Chapter 5, this volume), confirm the significance of Akkadian as the *lingua franca* of its day, used by rulers of Mesopotamia, Egypt, Anatolia, the Levant, and even Cyprus. Royal courts of each of the states of the time would certainly have employed bilingual scribes who could operate in Akkadian plus the language of the local court, at least (Wente 1995: 2,217). Most of these texts betray the influence of local syntax and many include both local words and loan words. Some of the letters received at Tell al-Amarna were in Hurrian, but these are exceptions: the Mitanni court generally observed diplomatic practice and wrote in Akkadian. Only in Anatolia was the Indo-European influence such that the kings of Arzawa demanded that the tablets sent to Arzawa "always be written in Hittite" (Moran 1992: EA 31, 32, 103). Otherwise, Babylonian literary texts found at Tell el-Amarna suggest the presence there of native Babylonian scribes, probably imported in order to teach Akkadian to local Egyptian officials (Moran 1992: EA 358).

On the Babylonian side there is very little direct textual evidence relating to international relations at this time. The Kassites had arrived in Babylonia in the 16th century BC, probably from the mountains to the north-east, but they rapidly adopted traditional Babylonian social, cultic and cultural practices, including language, to the extent that apart from their unusual names there is little to distinguish a specifically Kassite culture. All we know of their language is that it was regarded as strange by Babylonian scribes and must have differed substantially from Akkadian (Sommerfeld 1995: 917).

As to Assyrian records relating to contact with Egypt, the major sources in the Late Bronze Age, the so-called Middle Assyrian period, come principally from the great city of Assur on the Tigris, as well as from other contemporary sites in Upper Mesopotamia. The Amarna Letters once more are a key resource for approaching relations between Egypt and Assyria in the 14th century BC. From the time of King Tiglath-Pileser I (1114–1076 BC), Assyrian royal inscriptions take the form of 'royal annals'. These texts were inscriptions in Akkadian cuneiform cut into royal buildings, palaces and temples, of the Assyrian capital cities, and they provided a systematic, if naturally biased, account or *res gestae* of successive Assyrian kings from the late 12th to the late seventh centuries BC. Their emphasis was very much on the military achievements of the king, the lands conquered, peoples subjugated, and temples built to the glory of the state gods. The very form of these texts, cut into monumental buildings, as well as their militaristic content reify a fundamental element of the Assyrian state, which has an important bearing on its relations with Egypt, and that is its apparently incessant military expansionism.

Larsen (1979: 90) has argued that for the Assyrian king expansion appears to have been regarded as a religious duty owed to the national god Assur. There is no doubt that each Assyrian king strove to outdo his predecessors in battle and conquest, and that he committed this intention and its execution to writing on important public buildings. The desire for material wealth appears to have been a significant motivating factor for such Assyrian expansion, wealth that could be employed to enhance the status of the king, his palace, his gods, and his capital city; "a symbol-laden statement of awesome power" as the Nineveh of Sennacherib's time has been called (Lumsden 2000: 820). Contacts between Assyria and Egypt need to be appreciated in this light, as potential opportunities for Assyrian kings to strengthen their strategic position with regard to hostile neighbours, real or imagined, and significantly to enhance their material wealth.

For the later Assyrian periods, through the Iron Age, the sources increase in quantity and type (Kuhrt 1995: 501–505). In addition to royal annals, major forms of text include letters, many between kings and officials, legal, cultic and oracle texts, all written in Akkadian cuneiform on clay tablets, as well as inscriptions cut into stone as an integral element of large-scale palace wall relief scenes (Reade 1998).

Our perspectives are inevitably shaped, and restricted, by the form and content of such sources. While we gain often highly detailed insights into exchanges of royal correspondence and regal neuroses, for example, we have much less understanding of interactions and connections at less elevated social levels. We are obliged to consider, even if we examine the sources with an appropriately sceptical eye, what Van de Mieroop (1999: 39) has called "history from above", the boasts and rants of kings and ambassadors about battles, treaties and achievements. From the available sources we gain little direct idea of how elite-level interactions affected the bulk of the population. But we should nevertheless encourage the non-elite onto the stage and into the wavering spotlight of history.

Some of the texts do refer to non-elite elements engaged in regional interactions, such as merchants. A Kassite Babylonian envoy to Egypt travelled with a merchant caravan, which was plundered en route through Canaan, prompting the Babylonian king to write to the pharaoh:

> Now my merchants who came up with Ahutabu [the Babylonian envoy to Egypt] stayed behind in Canaan in order to carry on their business ... Canaan is your land, and its kings. I have been robbed in your land. Bring them to account, and the money that they took, replace it! And the people who killed my servants – kill them and thus avenge their blood. If you do not execute them, they will kill again, whether it be one of my caravans or your own messengers, so that our exchange of envoys will be cut off.

(Moran 1992: EA 8)

From this text it is clear that significant commercial intercourse was taking place in conjunction with diplomatic exchanges. Almost certainly involved in these exchanges with Egypt, at both diplomatic and commercial levels, was lapis lazuli, reaching Babylon via the jealously guarded and by now most ancient trade routes from Afghanistan to Mesopotamia (see Matthews and Roemer Chapter 1, this volume).

Other non-elite social elements involved in Egypt-Mesopotamia interactions were the soldiers who fought in the battles between them, and every Assyrian male was obliged to serve in the army (Grayson 1995: 959). Another element was the people of the cities, towns and villages conquered by traversing armies. Towards the peoples of towns that had resisted and the soldiers of defeated armies, the Assyrians appear to have shown extreme harshness, as depicted and narrated in royal relief scenes and annals, which relate the killing, burning, mutilation and dismemberment of defeated peoples (Grayson 1995: 961). Part of the purpose of these scenes and texts, their depiction and propagation, was doubtless to terrify potential rebels into long-term quietude, and we should not assume that every act of oppression depicted or related was necessarily carried out.

Enforced long-distance movement of entire urban populations across the reaches of the empire was another tactic employed by the Assyrians as a means of quashing resistance and securing labour for specific projects in the home territories (Grayson 1995: 961). For these peoples at such times, whose voices have not directly reached us in written documents, the only meaningful perspective was on how to stay alive and on how to eat from day to day.

Due to the wide range of divergent written sources covering the world of Egypt in the Iron Age, including Herodotus, the Old Testament, the Egyptian, Assyrian and Babylonian records, our interpretations are to some extent shaped by academic specialization as well as by individual interest (from the point of view of Assyrian expansion and perspectives, see Lamprichs 1995; Mayer 1995. For Egyptian perspectives, see Grayson 1981; Onasch 1994; Redford 1992; and Spalinger 1974, 1977, 1978). This study represents one particular understanding of the relevant political entities, their interactions, and the relevant chronology (Warburton Chapter 5, this volume; Gasche *et al.* 1998a, b; Kitchen 2000; Warburton 2000b, 2001).

An example of potentially differing interpretations concerns the battle of Qarqar on the Orontes in 853 BC. There, the Assyrian king Shalmaneser III defeated a local lord and his allies. It is not clear whether the Egyptians were present at this battle: Lamprichs (1995: 85) and Redford (1992: 339) assume they were, while Mayer (1995: 284–285) and the present authors assume they were not at the battle. The text names "Musri", but it is uncertain that this refers to Egypt, and it is difficult to imagine the proud Egyptians forming one contingent in a coalition of statelets. If the Egyptians did in fact participate in this *ad hoc* coalition, we may appreciate why the Assyrians viewed Egypt as little more than an inconvenience two centuries later. How such a participation could serve Egyptian interests is highly problematic, for the Egyptians could not hope to stop the Assyrian advance without a more serious effort. Our interpretation of the texts is naturally influenced by our understanding of the history, and thus the issue cannot be definitively resolved. Comparable difficulties affect interpretation of contact at the end of the eighth century BC. Were the Egyptians pursuing an aggressive policy that the Assyrians failed to appreciate, or were the

Egyptians acquiescing to Assyrian rule in Palestine? Assyriologists and Egyptologists may not view the same evidence in the same light.

Turning to the archaeological evidence, it is striking that there are no recovered and identified physical traces of the Assyrian presence in Egypt:

> The conquests of Egypt by the Assyrian kings Esarhaddon and Assurbanipal in the first half of the seventh century BC have left neither traces nor records of any kind in Egypt. All of the important sources for the history of this period do not come from Egypt itself.
>
> (Onasch 1994: 1)

To what extent this apparent absence is a factor of research programmes that have failed to formulate suitable strategies for distinguishing and recovering the nuanced niceties of an Assyrian presence in Egypt is arguable. At the same time, it is notable that during the Middle Bronze Age, when Assyrian merchants engaged in intimate and wide-ranging trade with local polities in central and northern Anatolia (Veenhof 1995), enclaves of Assyrian merchants living in the Anatolian city of Kanesh are attested solely by their written texts and associated seal impressions. In material culture terms they appear to blend seamlessly into the local scene, perhaps assimilated into local culture (as with later Greeks in Egypt: see La'da Chapter 9, this volume). We cannot therefore discount the possibility of a significant Assyrian presence in Egypt that has yet to be located, recovered, and identified.

Egyptian material, by contrast, is found throughout the Mediterranean in the Late Bronze and Iron Ages, not only in the Levant but also in Carthage and even the Iberian peninsula (Gamer-Wallert 1978; Niemeyer 1982; Vercoutter 1945). Many of these items represent material distributed during the decline of Egyptian power in the first millennium BC, underscoring the degree to which Egypt played a significant role in widespread commercial interactions. This distribution of Egyptian material in the Levant and Aegean can be traced back to the second and third millennia (Karetsou *et al.* 2000; Matthews and Roemer Chapter 1, this volume), and thus antedates the Assyrian expansion as well as the interventionist naval policies of the Saites and Ptolemies. Egyptian influence throughout the Mediterranean is a tenacious feature of Mediterranean history (see Bevan Chapter 4 and Sparks Chapter 3, both this volume).

Assyrian culture expressed itself in a fashion fundamentally different from that of Egypt, Assyrian culture being highly receptive to foreign influence. The Assyrians acquired many of the fundamentals of their civilization, including writing, myths and architecture, from Babylonia, and incorporated both the Syrian *bit khilani* design and the Elamite *salle à quatre saillants* (Roaf 1973) into their palace architecture, as well as filling their palaces with Egyptianizing ivories, and possibly even decorating the walls with Egyptian-influenced frescoes (Kaelin 1999). In sum, few material traces of Assyrian culture are found outside Assyria but many traces of foreign culture, including Egyptian, are found inside Assyria.

## Motives, policies, and modes of interaction

During their westward expansion, the Assyrians developed a policy of 'divide and rule', based upon local vassals whose independence was recognized. Overland trade routes and historical ties linked both the vassals and the foes of Assyria. Lamprichs (1995: 213–215) has argued that Assyrian rule depended upon a network in which vassals were offered sufficient independence so as to remove the incentive to form anti-Assyrian coalitions while simultaneously applying sufficient power that the idea of a revolt was unappealing. When Egypt was added to the Assyrian empire, overland connections were lacking, so that the network imposed by the Assyrians did not match the organic counterparts in western Asia. This difficulty was compounded by the fact that Egypt was a central power, able to call upon distant allies, and thus oppose Assyrian rule in the manner of a 'great power' rather than a 'rebellious vassal'.

The Assyrian network system functioned according to several principles, but in one respect the Egyptian and Assyrian systems were fundamentally at odds: this was over the importance of commerce. The commercial importance of networks had been a fundamental feature of Assyrian foreign dealings long before the appearance of a strong state (in the early second millennium BC, cf. Larsen 1976; Veenhof 1995). This commercial importance was still a fundamental feature of the Assyrian empire in the first millennium BC. When expanding into the Mediterranean, the Assyrians likewise perceived the commercial import of the Phoenician network, and they thus developed it according to their political and military appreciation.

This approach was incompatible with the presence of Egypt for several reasons. One was the fact that the Egyptians had not perceived themselves as major commercial actors, and they had never viewed their empire as primarily a source of revenue. The Egyptians were major political players, and accustomed to interacting as such with their contemporaries. Assyrian inability to view the Egyptians as a major political entity would ultimately contribute to the Assyrian failure. It also prevented them from understanding that their military expansion was into commercial domains that had hitherto served Egyptian interests without being politically controlled. Esarhaddon of Assyria had been conscious of the difficulties. His intention had been to quash the Egyptian capacity to interfere in Asia, a logical outcome of Egyptian interference in Assyrian rule along the Levantine coast. The resulting intervention in Egyptian territory was well executed, but ill-conceived. The Egyptians had earlier ended their overt hostility and proved amenable to peaceful relations. Then Sennacherib's more menacing strategy had provoked Egypt, leading to the tensions that ultimately induced Esarhaddon to invade. The capacity to project force, even as far as Thebes, was not, however, integrated into a policy that could deal on equal terms with an independent state.

The Egyptian empire in Asia had collapsed with the appearance of the small states of western Asia at the end of the Bronze Age. It was these small states that eventually formed the backbone of the Iron Age Assyrian empire, since that empire was constructed by connecting the states into a network based upon independent loyalty to Assyria. The Egyptian empire of the Bronze Age had been assembled on the basis of alliances between small states, an empire that indulged in political manoeuvring amongst its various contemporaries (Hatti, Mitanni, Assyria). The Egyptian empire was thus dependent upon the existence of the other empires. The Iron Age Assyrians were unaccustomed to dealing with separate competing empires.

Ultimately, the Assyrians did learn how to deal with competing empires. Upon settling the civil war brought about by his brother, Assurbanipal faced both Elam and

Urartu. Eventually able to defeat Elam in battle, Assurbanipal could turn to Urartu. Assurbanipal depicted these events in a giant mural in his palace (Figure 6:2). The scene is dominated by the battle of Til-Tuba, but a Urartian peace delegation appears in the corner, although neither spatially nor temporally related, since the delegation appeared some nine years after the battle, and certainly not on the Elamite river. Assurbanipal had mastered the art of defeating rivals in Asia where he had failed in Egypt. The lesson appears to have been learnt.

Kaelin (1999) has argued that the artistic representation of the Til-Tuba battle drew upon the inspiration of Egyptian reliefs dating to the reign of Ramesses II, depicting the battle of Kadesh (see Warburton Chapter 5, this volume). He suggests that the similarity of the two cycles in detail, composition and character are too similar to allow for coincidence. He further argues that Assurbanipal chose this form as most suitable to present a coherent interpretation of events, and that the appearance of the stylistic form after Assurbanipal's Egyptian campaign may explain why this form did not appear earlier. It was inspired by the sight of the Egyptian originals. Kaelin does not, however, pose the question of why Assurbanipal made this particular choice for the representation of the defeat of two rival empires. It may be that Assurbanipal deliberately drew upon the Egyptian reliefs as a warning to Egypt. The use of a characteristically Egyptian narrative form depicting an Assyrian victory to express a message of imperial dominance amongst competing rivals would have been both subtle and powerful.

Ultimately the Assyrian experiment failed, as it proved unable to resist the Medes and their allies. The Medes and the Babylonians made common cause, and thus the Egyptians found themselves fighting an Assyrian war, trying to fend off the heirs to Assurbanipal's conquests. During this period, Egypt was successively opposed to and allied with Judah. From Judah's standpoint, this wavering was unwise as it led ultimately to defeat by both Egypt and Babylonia. The Egyptian policy hearkened back to that of the Bronze Age where the brunt of the conflict was intended to be borne by the vassals and not by Egypt. The Babylonian policy proved to be a continuation of the successful Assyrian policy under Tiglath-Pileser III and Sargon, recognizing the Egyptian state, but claiming control of Philistia and regions to the east. Sennacherib and his successors had pursued a more aggressive policy that provoked an Egyptian response, and thereby obliged Assyria to pursue a policy of expansion. Even if its end was nigh, Assyria was at the peak of its power when Psammetichos assumed the kingship as an Assyrian vassal.

Babylonian perspectives on Egypt were different. Babylon had rarely been an expansionary power. Egypt may have been expansionary, but the Egyptians were reluctant to expend the efforts needed repeatedly to quell rebellious vassals. A Babylonian king could spar with an Egyptian pharaoh by suggesting that Egyptian vassals in Palestine had turned to Babylonia in an effort to gain support for independence from Egypt. Naturally, the Babylonian king claimed that support had been denied. Equally naturally, however, the pharaoh realized that no matter how tempting Babylonian support for the rebellious vassal may have been, it may not have served the interests of Babylon, for their foe was Assyria, not Egypt or Mitanni. The pharaoh did not hesitate to upbraid his Babylonian counterpart as a merchant who retailed his daughters for profit (Kitchen 1998: 254; Moran 1992: 1).

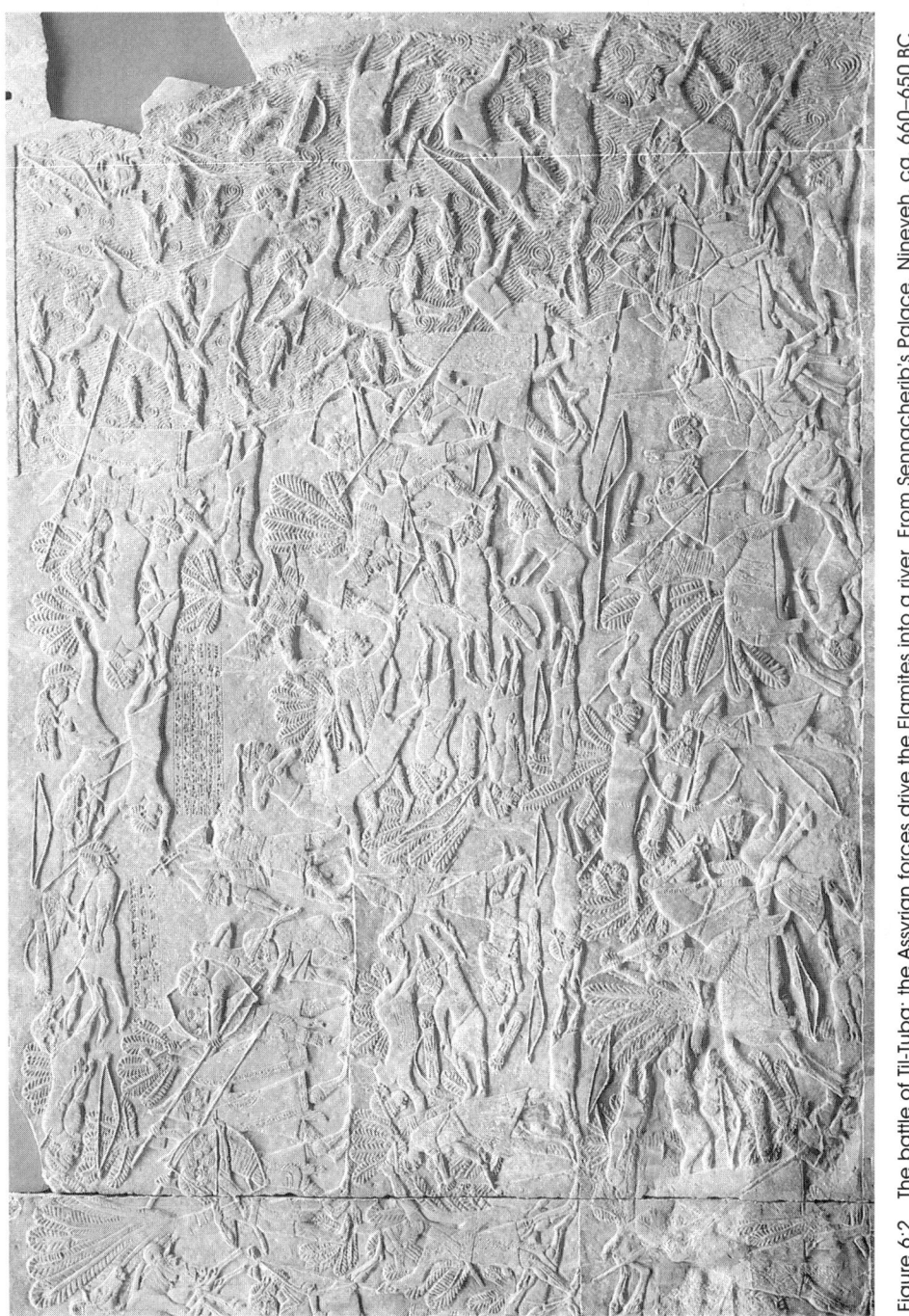

Figure 6:2 The battle of Til-Tuba: the Assyrian forces drive the Elamites into a river. From Sennacherib's Palace, Nineveh, ca. 660–650 BC (Reade 1998: fig. 91).

Babylon and Egypt were not destined to clash over fundamental interests, in the fashion that the Assyrians were destined to clash with both Egypt and Babylon, even if in different ways. It is a striking artefact of history that although Persians and Macedonians from the peripheral regions to the east and west of the ancient Near East would both conquer both Egypt and Babylonia, neither Egypt nor Babylon ever conquered and occupied the other. In fact, they only briefly came into direct conflict, when the Babylonians inherited the Assyrian empire towards the end of the Iron Age. Relations between Egypt and Babylonia were generally conducted in an unabrasive, but competitive fashion.

The three powers of Egypt, Assyria and Babylonia thus interacted with each other in very different ways, while to some extent sharing common attitudes. Egyptian expansion was pushed by an ideology based on pharaonic grandeur, and restrained by the appreciation that a generous distribution of gold and competition among enemies would serve the national interest. Babylonian policy was not expansionist, and the commercial character of its culture discouraged unnecessary conflict. By contrast, Assyrian policy was based on expansion for its own sake. Their ideological competition was primarily with Babylon, and Egypt was viewed in the same fashion as rebellious vassals. Given its heritage, Egypt was incapable of viewing powers such as Assyria and Babylon as either equals or competitors. The result was an Egyptian tendency to underestimate Assyrian power. This perspective was balanced by the fact that the Assyrians could not view the Egyptians as a true power, since the Assyrians understood power primarily in military, not cultural, terms. This failure led to repeated Assyrian destruction of Babylon, their cultural ancestor, and to the occupation of Egypt. It also contributed to the demise of the Assyrian empire and the virtual extinction of its memory. The Assyrians contributed significantly to the flourishing era of the Egyptian 'Late Period' by the expulsion of the Nubians, yet this same Assyrian expansion into Egypt was perhaps the over-extension that was ultimately decisive for the collapse of the Assyrian empire. Both the cultural giants, Babylon and Egypt, who avoided conflict, survived Assyria, which viewed power and conquest in purely military terms.

## Persian ending

The Persian king Cyrus (559–530 BC) entered Babylon in 539 BC and, by the end of the reign of Cambyses (530–522 BC), the Persians had conquered the entire Near East, ruling the vast regions from Elam to Egypt and Anatolia. The defeat at Pelusium (525 BC, von Beckerath 2002) was a bad omen for the Egyptians, for both Esarhaddon and Nebuchadrezzar had been halted there, Essarhaddon temporarily, and Nebuchadrezzar permanently. The invasion that followed the defeat at Pelusium marked the end of Egyptian independence.

Although unsuccessful as a Mediterranean naval power, the Persians were familiar with the importance of sea lanes. During the first millennium BC, Iranian influence is clear in the pottery and ritual practices of the Persian Gulf. Darius (522–486 BC) appreciated that the Egyptians were willing to serve a ruler who observed their customs, and thus adopted the Egyptian style, easing the weight of foreign domination and discouraging an uprising. The approach differed significantly from that of the Assyrians. At the same time that Persian influence swept into Greece, during the 'Orientalizing Era', Greek influence began to appear in the Levant and even in the Gulf itself, long before the conquests of Alexander.

At the end of the Peloponnesian War in 404 BC, the united Greeks managed to aid the Egyptians in their resistance against Persian opposition. While Xenophon's 10,000 conducted their campaign deep in the Persian empire, Egypt was freed. The 'Murashu Archive', the records of a businessman in Babylonian Nippur, came to an end at the beginning of the reign of Artaxerxes II (Stolper 1985: 108), but more importantly, when his major employer, the Persian Governor of Egypt, lost his job. Even the ensuing decades of Greek civil war were insufficient to allow the Persians to recover Egypt. It was only when Philip of Macedonia made peace with the Persians that they were able to march unimpeded back into Egypt, which they did in 343 BC. The Persian victory was short-lived, however, for Alexander soon drove them out of Egypt, and then eliminated their power over the entire empire. Alexander thus inherited the empire created by Esarhaddon, and the Macedonian conquest can be understood as an Assyrian legacy.

The Assyrian conquest had broken the spirit of Egypt, and opened the way for Macedonian rule, in a fashion injurious to Egyptian independence. It was the legacy of the Assyrian conquest that likewise eased the way for the Romans centuries later. The irony of the legacy was that it had been the Mycenaean Greeks who had aided the Egyptians in expelling the western Asian Hyksos rulers from the Delta more than a millennium earlier, yet now the Greeks ruled the entirety of Egypt, at least the Nile Valley and the Delta. The history of Egypt's subjugation to foreign rule can also be traced in its moments of independence during the Iron Age. In 663 BC, the Assyrians drove out the Nubians, and the Assyrians in their turn departed due to distractions further abroad. The brief *floruit* after 404 BC occurred when the end of the Peloponnesian War allowed the Greeks to intervene in Persian politics again. The liberation of Egypt in 654 BC and again in 404 BC had taken place with minimal effort on the part of the Egyptians: it was just a matter of international politics.

## Conclusion

Relations between Egypt, Babylonia and Assyria were determined by a range of factors, all of them historically contingent. Our appreciation of Mesopotamian perspectives on Egypt is constrained by the nature of the sources, as we have seen, but in the end it is perhaps surprising how little we can say about Assyrian or Babylonian perspectives on Egypt. Underlying differing Assyrian and Babylonian perspectives it is possible to discern a fundamental divergence in religious conviction, the Assyrians apparently believing in the right of their state god, Assur, to conquer and rule the entire world, through the person of the king, while the more polytheistic and less militaristic nature of Babylonian ruling elites, as so far attested, did not generate a head-on conflict at an ideological level with Egypt. Despite this distinction, there is no evidence to suggest that Assyrian rulers and their officials attempted to impose an ideological, cultic or religious unity across the territories of their empire, once political supremacy had been achieved (Grayson 1995: 968). To the contrary, there is good evidence for Assyrian respect for the gods of foreign peoples, including the Judaean

Yahweh (Kuhrt 1995: 512). Previously conquered peoples were on occasion allowed to transport the effigies of their gods back from the Assyrian capital to their home towns once the threat had been removed, under the sanction of the Assyrian king and the god Assur. In pragmatic terms, the main concern for the Assyrian elite appears to have been the smooth operation of a tax and tribute garnering system that could feed into the glorification of the king, the state, and the supreme god Assur in his home city. Egypt impinged on Assyria solely insofar as it obstructed or facilitated this one end.

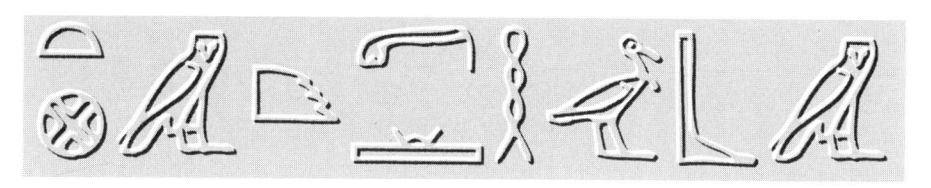

# CHAPTER 7

## FINDING THE EGYPTIAN IN EARLY GREEK ART

*Jeremy Tanner*

The relationship between early Greek art and Egyptian art has been a subject of learned debate since classical antiquity itself (Pliny *Naturalis historia* VII.205; XXXV.15–16). Each year brings forth fresh studies in which adherents of Greek originality and Egyptian influence cross swords. The purpose of this chapter is not to resolve those debates, which are probably not as such capable of solution in the terms they are generally set up: in Bietak's (2001) recent edited volume addressing the Egyptian influences on the development of Greek monumental architecture, some contributors (e.g. Gebhard) argue there are no grounds for seeing an Egyptian contribution, whilst others (e.g. Sinn) argue that the developments are inconceivable without just such influences. Still less do I intend to offer a synthetic survey of the relevant data: one recent collection of *aegyptiaka* in archaic Greece ran to some 3,000 pages and included more than 5,000 items (Skon-Jedele 1994). Instead, I explore the way the question of the relationship between Greek and Egyptian art has been framed in modern art history writing, and how different frames might allow us to write different stories about the development of art in the eastern Mediterranean world from ca. 800–500 BC. I examine how ethnic models of art, and orientalist epistemologies, have shaped and continue to shape the writing of the history of early Greek art, and in particular the role attributed to Egyptian 'influences' in such development. I suggest, as an alternative frame, exploring the relationship between Greece and Egypt in the archaic period in terms of recent archaeological theories of world systems and materialization strategies. I consider four key categories of art production in early Greece: bronze sculpture, faience, marble sculpture and monumental temple architecture. The highly variable articulation of these media with technical, stylistic and iconographic traditions in Greece and Egypt call into question the meaningfulness of a unified category of 'Greek art' in the archaic period. 'Greek' art, like 'Greece' itself, was very much in the making (cf. Osborne 1996) in the period from 800–500 BC. Its characteristic features are perhaps best understood in terms of the adaptation of transnational models of monumental self-assertion, and the tools of ideological materialization associated with them, to the particular political contexts of a network of Greek states increasingly closely incorporated into a wider eastern Mediterranean state system.

## Ethnic identities and historical models in 'classical' art history

No field of classical studies better illustrates Martin Bernal's *Black Athena* thesis than that of art history. Bernal (1987, 2003) argued that a recognition of profound indebtedness to oriental, and specifically Egyptian, culture on the part of both the ancient Greeks and early modern Europeans was replaced in the 18th century by an Aryan model which denied any racial admixture between Greeks and Egyptians, and minimized the importance of oriental – Egyptian and Phoenician – contributions to the development of Greek culture. This radical shift in attitudes towards the Greeks, beginning with the Enlightenment and developed further in Romantic thought, was rooted in changes in class structure and political organization, associated with the development of capitalism, in particular the industrial revolution, and the formation of modern national states. It was also shaped by changing geopolitical relationships, notably the relative decline of the Ottoman empire in relationship to western European nation states and the increasing colonial intervention of such states in North Africa, the Near East and Egypt (Bernal 1987; Held 1997). Various forms of cultural classicism provided a unifying ideology for the new more differentiated elites – intellectual, political, business – which displaced the church and aristocracy as ruling classes, under the watchwords of reason and liberty, inherited from the Greeks (Bowen 1989; Held 1997).

Art and art history played a central role in these developments. Enlightenment philosophers such as Turgot and Diderot had already located the origins of the fine arts in ancient Greece, and identified Greece as the sole tributary to the modern national traditions (Held 1997: 260). The core values of emerging western political and national cultures were encoded in narrative form in Winckelmann's *History of Ancient Art* (1764). Winckelmann attributed the flowering of Greek art to the Greek discovery of freedom and rationality. He contrasted the dynamic character of Greek art with the stagnation of Egyptian art, the natural growth of which was stunted by repressive monarchic political culture (Bernal 1987: 212; Potts 1982). These concepts received physical embodiment in national art museums founded in the late 18th and early 19th centuries. Where Egyptian artefacts were not excluded from such museums – as they were from Humboldt's plan for the national museum in Berlin, on the grounds that they were merely of intellectual interest, whereas Greek (and Renaissance etc.) *Kunst* was publicly improving (Bernal 1987: 254) – the role of Egypt was merely to set the stage for Greece. Greek art represented the linchpin of art history, and distinctive national traditions were displayed as the heirs to and continuators of the Greek tradition (Duncan and Wallach 1980; Jenkins 1992).

All narratives, whether written in texts or embodied in museum displays, select and omit facts, shape them according to a certain point of view, in order to constitute them as "components of comprehensible stories" (White 1978: 44). Recent work in archaeological and art historical theory has shown how the "boundedness, homogeneity and continuity" of national traditions of material culture (Jones 1997: 103), and in particular art traditions, was constructed as past reality by highly selective national histories of art, and culturally realized through national art academies of the 19th century, sponsored by states (Fyfe 1996). Far from emerging 'spontaneously', art styles which are ethnically distinctive and self-consciously signal ethnic identity may be historically relatively unusual, and dependent on very specific conditions

(Pasztory 1989: 17). The institutions of the art world and practices of art history writing in the 19th century were constitutive factors in the creation of distinctive national traditions, and the projection of such national distinctiveness into the past (Brown 1998: 1–5; Tomlinson 1997: 1–4).

The tendency to construct the history of past art in ethnic terms is conspicuous in the case of early Greece. Moreover, the ethnic paradigm takes a particularly striking and strident form since it is overlaid by orientalist tropes which serve to create a radical distinction between oriental and occidental culture, consonant with the role of ancient Greece in the foundation myths of western cultural distinctiveness and superiority (cf. Said 1978). The distinction between Greek and oriental is taken as axiomatic, representing both the starting point and the goal of research. John Boardman, for example, having asserted that Greek art is uniquely characterized by "monumentality, tectonic composition and narrative" (Boardman 1967: 64), suggests that the archaic period was one in which "the Greeks became more and more aware of what distinguished them from barbarians" (Boardman 1967: 81). Consequently, any study of the relationship between Greek and oriental art, he argues, should focus less on how or from whom forms were borrowed, how the orient influences Greece, but more on the processes by which such influences were assimilated, for these "reveal … those qualities which are essentially Greek … and which make even the most exotic product of Greek craftsmen in these years readily distinguishable from those of their overseas colleagues" (Boardman 1967: 108).

The artistic culture of archaic Greece's eastern neighbours, the countries of the Near East and Egypt, are represented in classical art history with the same ambivalence as the countries and cultures of the orient in 19th century orientalism – at once both decadent and ripe for domination, intrinsically subordinate cultures, and at the same time a grave peril to the integrity of western civilization (Gunter 1990; cf. Said 1978: 250). On the one hand, oriental art is seen as corrupting and dangerous, embodying formal qualities that were the antithesis of the Greek artistic instinct, and delaying the natural trajectory of development in Greek art towards naturalism, monumentality and constant change. If the orientalizing period in Greek art was "one of marking time, if not of positive retrogression in some fields", it is clear where we should point the finger of blame in halting the natural "development of Greek art as a bold imaginative progress, ever forward" (Boardman 1967: 108). Black figure technique, emulating incision in Near Eastern metalware, was "so restricted and conventionalized" as to impede progress in vase-painting skills for a century (Boardman 1967: 107). When the "sterile frontal conventions" of Daidalic sculpture, based on Near Eastern models, were overcome, it was only to run the "danger of falling into the even more sterile and conventional manners of Egyptian sculpture" (Boardman 1967: 107), "a danger that the new marble statuary would be bound by quasi-mathematical conventions … a danger that this almost mechanical method of composition would be copied by the Greeks" (Boardman 1967: 98). On the other hand, and with no apparent sense of contradiction, oriental influences, whilst acknowledged, are minimized, being seen as – by definition – not essential to the development of what was specifically Greek about Greek art. Oriental influences are characterized as "largely superficial" (Boardman 1967: 74). The process of cultural exchange is represented as one dominated by the Greeks, since it is held that "the decision to be influenced is a mark of cultural strength" (Hurwit 1985: 135), and whilst

Greek culture, already strong, was in a process of growth, the arts of the orient "were already in decline" (Boardman 1967: 74). The story is one of ethnic purification: how, despite the oriental menace, Greek and with it western art emerges in distilled form by the end of the sixth century, "purged of all that seems foreign" (Boardman 1967: 109) as it takes up the role of leadership in the development of world civilization.

Such an account of art in early Greece would have made no sense to its inhabitants either conceptually or materially. The very categories in which such narratives seek to embed and emplot the story of early Greek art, polarizing the Greek against the oriental and barbarian, either did not exist or had very different content and structure in the archaic Greek world. The word *barbaros*, for example, distinguished Greeks from non-Greeks solely on the basis of language. The boundary between Greek and non-Greek was extremely diffuse, constructed on an aggregative basis through myths of shared descent from the eponymous Hellen. Not only were the Greeks' eastern neighbours included as (distant) relatives on such family trees but exchanges of gifts, wives and names between Greek aristocrats and their Near Eastern and Egyptian counterparts created horizontal linkages across linguistic and political boundaries which militated against ethnic difference playing a highly salient role in individual's social identities (J. Hall 1997: 46-47; La'da Chapter 9, this volume). The construction of Greek identity on an oppositional basis of difference from a stereotypical barbarian 'other' developed only in the fifth century, created on the basis of the experience of the great conflicts of the Persian wars, and massively promoted as part of a pan-hellenic ideal which legitimated the expansion of the Athenian empire as a defence against the Persian threat in the eastern Mediterranean (E. Hall 1989: 60). Even in the classical period, as the Greeks became aware of and reflective about the character of their own art production, they do not seem to have been overly interested in its ethnically distinctive character. Both the origins of monumental sculpture and architecture (statues, altars and temples to gods – Herodotus II.4) and those of painting (Pliny *Naturalis historia* VII.205, XXXV.15–16, citing Aristotle) were attributed to Egypt.

Such an ethnic paradigm selects out of the story of art in Greece works which, whilst they were not made by Greeks, were perhaps for Greek users and viewers of art the most prestigious and significant items in the repertoire of contemporary Greek visual culture. The boundary between Greek art and Egyptian art is, in certain periods and media in archaic Greece, soft to the point of vanishing. And insofar as Egyptian art was different from Greek, that difference seems to have entailed superiority, not inferiority, as far as Greek consumers of art were concerned. Two categories of early Greek visual culture illustrate this: bronze sculpture and faience.

Far from being a period of decline, the Kushite and Saite periods of Egyptian art have been characterized as something of a "renaissance" (Edwards and James 1984: 125), seeing important innovations in both stone and bronze sculpture which conditioned developments in those media in Greece in quite fundamental ways (Bianchi 1991; Palagia and Bianchi 1994). By the end of the Third Intermediate Period (1070–656 BC), Egyptian artists were using the lost-wax process to hollow-cast life-size bronze figures, sometimes assembled out of several parts using tenons and sockets and elaborately cold-worked with gilding and inlays (Bianchi 1991; Guralnick 2000: 36). Unlike much Egyptian sculpture, these statues were not used as grave goods but dedicated by private individuals in sanctuaries and temples, where they would have been visible to visitors (Bianchi 1991: 72). Some 200 Egyptian bronzes from the end of the Third Intermediate Period and the beginning of the Saite Dynasty have been found in contexts of the late eighth and early seventh century in the sanctuary of Hera on Samos (Jantzen 1972: 1–39; Skon-Jedele 1994: 1,401 ff). These range from mirrors and animal figures (falcons, Apis Bull, cats, ibis) to dozens of solid and hollow-cast statuettes of human figures (and gods – Ptah and Osiris as mummies), some as large as half life size. Greek bronze figures of this period are generally somewhat rough in their finish, and rather small – seldom over 20–25 cm in height. One of the best preserved of the Egyptian statues from Samos – a bronze statue of a man, one arm forward holding perhaps a staff, dressed in a kilt, with a panther skin over his shoulder, and added gilding on his necklace (Figure 7:1) – originally stood some 68 cm, almost three times the height of contemporary Greek bronze statuettes.

Figure 7:1   Egyptian bronze statue of a man clothed in a panther skin, from the Heraion, Samos. Late eighth, early seventh centuries BC (© German Archaeological Institute, Athens). Height 26.6 cm.

An extraordinarily elegant solid-cast statuette of Neith (Figure 7:2), the Egyptian counterpart of Athena and a goddess much cultivated by the Saite pharaohs, is beautifully finished. The crown, her flesh parts, the fine lines of the folds of her clinging drapery are each given distinctive textures that indicate an extremely high level of competence in the initial casting. Cold work included attachment of the arms, gold inlay for her necklace and a falcon's head on her back, and copper inlay for her nipples (Jantzen 1972: 27) – all of which will have contributed to the *poikilia*, or variegatedness, so prized as an aesthetic value of precious objects by early Greeks (Fowler 1983). Greek artists could not have competed with work of such technical expertise and aesthetic refinement during this period. Almost certainly, these superb Egyptian bronzes will have been amongst the most admired objects dedicated to Hera at this time. The prestige of Egyptian metalwork in early Greece is reflected in contemporary poetry. In the *Odyssey*, for example, the poet's description of the palace

Figure 7:2 Egyptian bronze statuette of Neith, from the Heraion, Samos. Late eighth, early seventh centuries BC (© German Archaeological Institute, Athens). Height 22.5 cm.

of Menalaus includes finely worked objects in gold and silver, which Menelaus himself had received as gifts from his own guest-friends, Alcandre and Polybus in Egyptian Thebes (*Odyssey* IV.120–137). Not only were such Egyptian works of art amongst the most prestigious items of contemporary Greek visual culture, but it is also all but certain that they provided the stimulus for the development of Greek hollow-cast bronze sculpture. The first Greek hollow-cast bronzes, griffin-heads for cauldron attachments, were from Samos, and the literary tradition suggests that Samian artists took the lead in the development of large-scale bronze hollow-cast statuary in the early sixth century, capitalizing on their early acquaintance with the technique from Egyptian sources, and the long tradition of bronze work since then (Kyrieleis 1990).

It was not only the extremely wealthy who had access to and favoured Egyptian-style material culture. Egyptian scarabs and amulets and little statuettes of deities are found in sanctuaries, and also in tombs, in eighth–sixth century Greece, in regionally varying frequency, and are particularly associated with burials of women and children (De Salvia 1983, 1991). One class of comparably 'demotic' material which particularly strikingly calls into question any radical distinction between Greek and Egyptian art are the faiences produced on the island of Rhodes, between the first half of the seventh century and the mid-sixth century. Faience, like bronze, became a particularly important medium of artistic production in Egypt during the Third Intermediate Period (Webb 1978: 3). From ca. 660–550 BC large quantities of faience objects were produced on Rhodes, from where they were distributed throughout the Greek world, though with a particular concentration in eastern and western Greece, where they are found in tombs and sanctuaries (Webb 1978). Whilst some objects copy Greek vessel types, for example Corinthian *aryballoi*, in their form at least (their decoration is Egyptian style), others closely copy Egyptian prototypes in their form, style, iconography and decoration. A double-vase, from a tomb in Kamiros on Rhodes (Figure 7:3 col. pl.), consists of a cosmetic pot moulded in one piece with a figure kneeling in the conventional pose of a presenting servant, a characteristically Egyptian typological and iconographic concept, as is the little frog seated atop the jar. The servant figure is represented as a Nubian, according to standard Egyptian conventions – thick nose, protruding lips – and also betrays archaizing features characteristic of Saite art, such as the marked curve to the upper eye lid juxtaposed with a straight lower lid (Webb 1978: 11–13, no. 1). Figures of kneeling women with babies on their back and an ibex in their lap also draw upon the Egyptian iconography of the presenting servant. A figure from a well in Kamiros, in a deposit closed by ca. 650 BC, is a particularly good example, and again shows distinctively Egyptian features in the slender, slightly elongated upper body with small breasts placed high on the chest in the characteristic style of the Third Intermediate Period (Figure 7:4; Webb 1978: 29–34, no. 121). So close are some figures, particularly those of Bes, in both form and scale to their Egyptian prototypes that it seems likely that the moulds were made by Egyptian artists and imported, along with the prime material constituent of faience, natron, which comes from Egypt (Hölbl 1979, 1: 197–199; Skon-Jedele 1994: 382, 1,981). Conceivably the artists of the first generation were in fact Egyptians (Webb 1980: 88). This may be confirmed by the exceptionally assured technical quality of the earlier pieces. The incised decoration on low relief figured vessels, for example, is filled with black glaze, without any overlapping of the incised lines. This suggests a

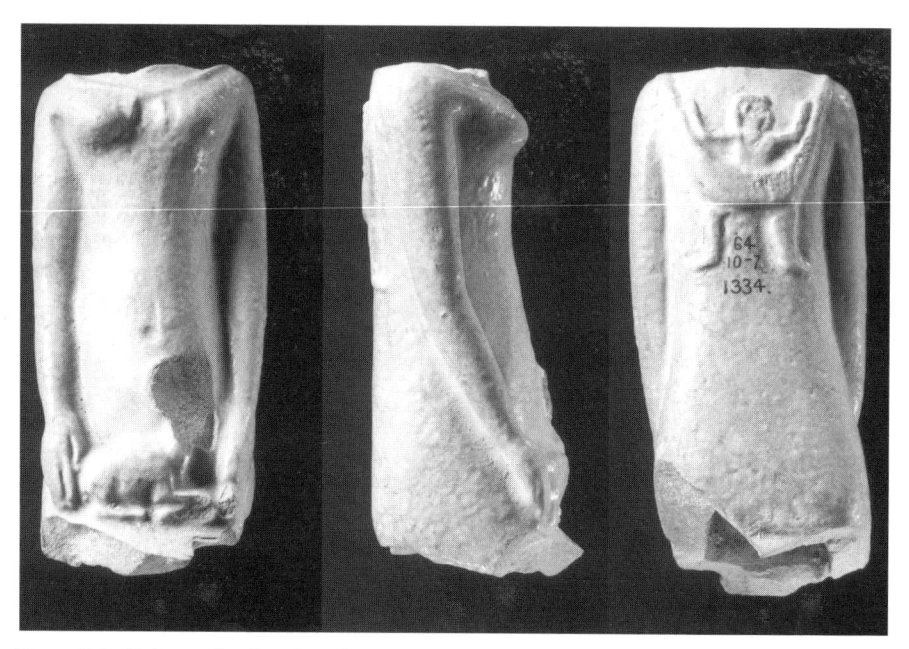

Figure 7:4 Faience figurine, female servant, from Kamiros, Rhodes. Mid-seventh century BC (© British Museum 64.10-7.1334). Height 9 cm.

surprisingly high level of technical and practical experience, in an industry which is born to all appearances fully fledged in early seventh century Rhodes (Webb 1978: 61; 1980: 88). In the second generation, this quality falls somewhat, and gratuitous and (in Egyptian terms) senseless iconographic features are introduced, for example 'Hathor locks' on the neck, largely to simplify production procedures by strengthening fragile features which required particularly sensitive modelling (Webb 1980: 88).

Notwithstanding their virtual invisibility in standard histories of Greek art, Egyptian bronzes, especially statues, were probably amongst the most prized and esteemed objects in the visual culture of late eighth and early seventh century Greece.[1] In the case of faience production, the boundary between Greek and Egyptian art is to all intents and purposes indiscernible, but for a slightly paler fabric (Guralnick 1997: 129). Representing the story of early Greek art as a struggle to realize ethnic identity through art, to discover an ethnically authentic and original mode of aesthetic expression, tells us much about the purposes and processes which shaped artistic development in the 18th and 19th centuries, and the role played by art in the construction of modern national and cultural identities. It tells us little about the purposes and processes shaping the development of visual culture in Greece in the archaic period.

## Greece and Egypt 800–500 BC: representations and relations

Recent work has been more accepting of the cultural hybridity of early Greek art, but it has not wholly escaped the limiting perspectives of ethnic paradigms of art history.

Sarah Morris (1992: 124) has argued that the early Greek world was part of an east Mediterranean cultural *koine* from the mid-second millennium to 480 BC, and that the culture of early Greece was no more Greek than oriental. "Orientalization", she suggests, is a dimension of classical antique culture from the Bronze Age through late antiquity, flourishing as much in the fifth and fourth centuries as earlier, and comparable to the hellenization of Roman culture in the last centuries of the millennium (Morris 1992: 130, 369). Although a valuable corrective to orientalist histories of Greek art, Morris' perspective runs the danger of simply inverting them, largely as a result of underplaying the structural properties of the societies concerned, their interrelationships, and the cultural systems in question (in particular their varying boundary maintaining properties). Thus, whilst many eastern, in particular Persian, motifs and artefact types are incorporated into Greek, more particularly Athenian, artistic culture during the course of the fifth and fourth centuries BC (Miller 1997), they do not enduringly transform the structural bases of Greek art in the way in which either hellenization does Roman art, in later periods, or interaction with the Near East and Egypt does art in Greece during the archaic period.

It is in part because she places the origins of the polis in the Late Bronze Age that Morris is unable to adduce any significant political or social-structural change in the Greek world with which to explain the changing structure of its interaction with the Near East. Ian Morris (1997b; 2000), by contrast, lays emphasis on the uses of orientalizing art in the context of social conflicts generated largely internally to the Greek world by processes of state formation which began in the eighth century BC and were elaborated during the following centuries. These conflicts took place between 'elitists', who wished to turn the clock back to the aristocratic world of the Homeric poems, and the adherents of a 'middling' ideology, which decisively shaped the development of the characteristically egalitarian social and political institutions of the Greek polis. Ian Morris accepts the cultural hybridity of early Greek culture, but he is more interested in what the Greeks do with borrowed cultural patterns, not, as in earlier work like that of Boardman, as the expression of some inner Greek essence, but rather as components in locally varying social and cultural strategies which give rise to varying patterns of deposition of 'orientalia', in sanctuaries, burials and public spaces, in different regions and times in early iron age Greece. The uses of oriental art internal to social struggles between 'elitists' and adherents of 'middling' ideology is emphasized at the expense of exploring the changing nature of the structural relationship between Greece and the East, and in particular how processes of cultural exchange, conditioned by those structures, causally shape and determine internal processes of development in the Greek world, in particular transforming fundamental structures of art production. Sarah Morris places Greece in a larger Mediterranean world, but both social structure within Greece, and Greek relations with eastern neighbours, are seen in a relatively unstructured way, thus resulting in a largely diffusionist account of early Greek art. Moreover she strongly discounts the importance of Egyptian influence on Greek art, largely because she does not recognize the structural transformation in Greek sculptural practice effected by the encounter with Egypt (Morris 1992: 240–241, with comments of Bernal 1995: 125–133). Ian Morris has a very clear view of changing social structure within the early Greek world, and how that predisposes Greek consumers to make use of oriental and orientalizing art in very specific ways, relevant to internal social and political goals and purposes.

However, he to some degree brackets from his consideration the structure of the interrelations through which oriental art and culture are mediated to the Greek world and become available for use in indigenous conflicts. Furthermore, his emphasis on the new exotic motifs and ideological contents which contacts with the eastern Mediterranean afforded, underplays the technologies also transmitted through such exchanges. Such technological transfers structurally transformed the capacity of Greek artists and their patrons to materialize ideology and thereby significantly affect social relations, independently of the specific motifs or cultural contents on which Morris concentrates.

Two current strands of archaeological theory may help to integrate the complementary strengths of Sarah Morris' and Ian Morris' approaches, and offer a different frame in which to understand the role of Egypt in the development of early Greek art. Braudel's (1972, 2001) studies of both the early-modern and the ancient Mediterranean and Sherratt's (1993; Sherratt and Sherratt 1993) development of world-system perspectives have sought to transcend the opposition between internalist and diffusionist models of civilizational development. Both Sherratt and Braudel emphasize interregional relationships in the Mediterranean as crucial structural settings in explaining particular local patterns of development. Imbalances in the development of different regions in the Mediterranean set limits on and create opportunities for interrelationships between regions through compensatory exchanges of goods, information, services and people (Braudel 2001: 33; Sherratt 1993). The expansion of world systems has not only economic dimensions, but also ideological ones. Integration into a world system is associated with flows of information as well as materials, sometimes creating "ideological turmoil in peripheral areas" (Hannerz 1992: 225), whether by expanding repertoires of cultural expression or introducing new communicative technologies which permit new ways of materializing meaning and mobilizing it in the context of social and political relations (Sherratt 1993: 12; Woolf 1990: 54–55). An interest in the cultural technologies by which ideologies are materialized, and power symbolized, as opposed to the particular meanings encoded and transmitted within specific traditions through the use of those technologies, is also characteristic of recent archaeological work on states and civilizations (Baines and Yoffee 2000; Blanton *et al.* 1996; De Marrais *et al.* 1996). Rather than seeking to decode the specific meanings of works of art, according to iconographic protocols often heavily dependent on the availability of texts, archaeologists have pointed towards more general shared characteristics of ideological materialization processes in early states and civilizations: the role played by artistic technologies in embodying and communicating the ideologies of order that legitimate the new social relations involved in creating the more tightly structured social worlds associated with the development of states (Baines and Yoffee 2000: 14); the characteristic materialization strategies employed by relatively inclusive, broad based 'corporate' elites (monumental settings for group ritual activity for example), versus those characteristic of more exclusionary elites (participating in prestige goods systems and commissioning monuments celebrating the high status of a small number of specific individuals; Blanton *et al.* 1996: 4–6). The attraction of such a perspective is that it allows one to focus on the aspects of ideological systems that are relatively easily shared between different societies and cultures within a larger interregional or world system (De Marrais *et al.* 1996: 20). This brings out very different dimensions of how interregional relationships may have played a constitutive role in the development of Greek art than traditional (though still important) debates as to whether specific motifs borrowed by Greeks from their eastern neighbours retained their original meanings, or whether they acquired new specifically Greek meanings by virtue of the new Greek contexts in which they were used (cf. for example Carter 1987 versus de Polignac 1992). Abstracting from the cultural specifics of meaning at either end of the transfer facilitates a focus on the process of cultural transfer itself, and the communication and interaction networks through which such transfer is accomplished.

A more interesting story of the development of art in Greece can be told by focusing less on the issue of the relative priority of the Greek or Egyptian elements in early Greek art or the specific meanings which Egyptian styles or motifs take on in Greek contexts, than on the structural role played by relationships with Egypt in reconstruction of artistic agency in archaic Greece and the technologies of power which such agency makes possible. Art in the archaic Greek world acquires its specific character not by virtue of signalling Greekness or totally transforming inherited motifs to pre-existing purely Greek cultural ideologies and aesthetic predispositions, but rather by adapting transnational modes for the aesthetic materialization of ideology to contexts of meaning and structures of social relations specific to the developing Greek polis. Greek art develops its own specific regional character and becomes more integrated into a broader eastern Mediterranean artistic culture as part and parcel of the same cultural process.

But before focusing on selected artistic materials, the changing structures of interrelationship between Greece and Egypt in the Early Iron Age must be understood, to provide a frame within which the specifically artistic exchanges can be analyzed. Although Egyptian objects are found in protogeometric contexts at Lefkandi on Euboia, associated finds suggest that such objects were mediated by Phoenician traders rather than transmitted directly (Skon-Jedele 1994: 1,093). By the late eighth and early seventh century, however, with Greek colonies established in Sicily and Cyrene, Greeks seem to have been sailing all over the Mediterranean, and the lack of associated Phoenician finds with the Egyptian bronzes from eighth and seventh century contexts in Samos suggest direct contacts (Guralnick 1997: 141). These developing contacts are reflected in the narratives of the *Odyssey* which recount both piratical raids on Egypt by Cretans, and stories of guest friendship between heroes of the Trojan War and their aristocratic Egyptian counterparts (Murray 1980: 215). Egypt is characterized in early Greek literature as a land of extraordinary wealth and fertility, and its people as well-ordered, just, and hospitable towards strangers (Froidefond 1971: 30, 46). Greek mercenaries were employed by the Egyptian pharaoh Psammetichos I (663–609), in his usurpation of the Egyptian throne as early as 664 BC, roughly the same date as the earliest Greek pottery at Naucratis, and he may well not have been the first of the quarrelling petty dynasts in early seventh century Egypt to make use of foreign mercenaries (Froidefond 1971: 50). Psammetichos gave his Ionian and Carian mercenaries land for settlement in the Delta, so there was a significant Greek presence in Egypt by ca. 650 (Austin 1970: 15–16). By the middle of the seventh century voyages to Egypt seem to have been routine (Herodotus IV.52).

Relationships intensified during the later seventh and the sixth centuries, through various interrelated media of exchange and communication: commerce, mercenaries, and elite level guest friendship and gift exchange. The increasingly contested character of rulership in Saite Egypt, as well as the pressures Egyptian pharaohs faced from their Assyrian, Babylonian and Persian neighbours, made them increasingly reliant on the use of Greek mercenaries and, eventually, naval power (Austin 1970: 37). Necho (610–595) made use of Greek mercenaries in campaigns in Syria. Carian and Ionian mercenaries fought for Psammetichos II (595–589 BC) in Nubia, leaving graffiti on the massive statues of Ramesses at Abu Simbel (Fornara 1983: 24–25). Apries (589–570 BC) used a force of 30,000 Ionian and Carian mercenaries in his war against the rebel Amasis who overthrew him with the support of a revolt by Egyptian soldiers. Amasis himself also preferred to trust mercenaries over native Egyptians to form his bodyguard (Murray 1980: 221). Increasing external threats to security drove the Egyptians, never great seafarers, to seek to develop naval power, and for this also they relied heavily on Greeks. Relationships of guest friendship with Periander tyrant of Corinth (625–585 BC) – whose nephew and short-lived successor was named Psammeticho, presumably after the pharaoh (Aristotle *Politics* I.315B) – may be linked with Necho's use of Corinthian naval architects to design ships for a fleet capable of countering the Phoenician navy at the disposal of the Babylonians (Herodotus I.33–38; Skon-Jedele 1994: 210–211).

Recruiting such large numbers of mercenaries can by no means have been straightforward. Conspicuous dedications in Greek sanctuaries (also centres for the recruitment of mercenaries) and gift exchanges in the context of guest friendships with particularly prominent Greeks – most notably the autocratic 'tyrants' who were a characteristic feature of seventh and sixth century Greek politics – facilitated access on the part of Egyptian rulers to Greek military resources (Murray 1980, 218). In 608 BC, following a campaign in Syria in which Greek mercenaries had participated, Necho dedicated his armour in the sanctuary of Apollo at Didyma, in the territory of Miletus (Herodotus II.149). In addition to gifts in money and materials to Sparta and Delphi, Amasis (570–526 BC) sent two wooden portrait statues to Polycrates, tyrant of Samos, to be dedicated in the sanctuary of Hera, in the context of a relationship of guest friendship, cultivated by Amasis in the hope of support from Polycrates' considerable naval power against the growing threat of Persia (Herodotus II.180–182; III.39). Amasis also dedicated two statues of Athena in the sanctuary of Athena Lindia on Rhodes, a gift to the tyrant of Lindos, Kleoboulos. This stressed the (somewhat equivocal) mythical links of kinship between the Egyptians and the Greeks, since the sanctuary at Lindos had supposedly been founded by the daughters of Danaos, ancestor of the Greeks, fleeing the sons of Danaos' brother, the eponymous Aigyptos, who had expelled them and their father from North Africa (Herodotus II.182; Francis and Vickers 1984a, b; Overbeck 1868: no. 327). In addition, Amasis may have contracted a connection by marriage with the ruling family of the Greek city of Cyrene, and there dedicated both a portrait of himself and a statue of Athena (Herodotus II.182). Exports, primarily of corn, through Naucratis, and the taxes paid on all exchanges taking place there, earned the Greek silver with which the pharaohs were able to pay their mercenaries (Murray 1980: 221).

## Egypt and the development of Greek architecture

The debate concerning how important these contacts with Egypt were to the development of Greek monumental architecture hinges on three issues: the dates of the earliest temples which can be counted as exempla of the conventional form of a monumental Greek temple; what counts as sufficient similarity in formal architectural detail to point to a genetic relationship between Greek temples and their putative prototypes; and how monumentalization is motivated and realized (Bietak 2001: 12–15 and Osborne 1996: 211 ff for good recent discussions). Many of the formal details of the monumental Doric temple can be argued either way in terms of indigenous Greek or external Egyptian sources. Doric columns, like Egyptian columns, have 16 flutes, and they share similar proportions (Figure 7:5), but Egyptian column-capitals have only a square element (the abacus), not an additional curved one (the echinus), characteristic of the Doric column (Figure 7:6). Columns in Mycenaean architecture and iconography – for example on the Atreus tholos and the Lion Gate at Mycenae – have both an abacus and an element like an echinus, but the columns themselves are unfluted, of quite different proportions than their Doric counterparts and taper downwards (Figure 7:7; Coulton 1977: 39–41; Lawrence 1983: 123–138). The 10th century 'heroon' at Lefkandi has a peripteral colonnade, but since it is curvilinear and built entirely in wood it is held to represent a wholly different concept from the rectilinear stone building with colonnade for which the best parallels are Egyptian temple-courts (Bammer 2001). Egyptian temples, however, have a directional character which is quite unlike a Greek temple, whose simple rectangular cella bears

Figure 7:5 Temple of Apollo, Corinth, with detail of Doric capitals. Sixth century BC (© Bildarchiv Foto Marburg).

Figure 7:6   Deir el-Bahri, Egypt. Portico of shrine of Anubis (15th century BC) (Coulton 1977: pl. 4).

Figure 7:7   'Treasury of Atreus', Mycenae, ca. 1300 BC. Restored elevation of façade (British School at Athens).

closer relationship to Mycenaean megara (Ostby 2001). The specific character of the monumentalization of the Greek temple is equally equivocal for endogenous and diffusionist arguments. On the one hand, the petrification of what perhaps were originally wooden elements may have been necessitated by the use of heavy mould-made clay-tiles to roof the earliest monumental temples: the temple of Apollo in the city and the temple of Poseidon at Isthmia, both in the territory of Corinth (Gebhard 2001: 59; Lawrence 1983: 123). On the other, the quarrying techniques used by the Greeks are the same as those of the Egyptians (although these could have been transmitted via the Near East – Gebhard 2001: 45–46; Waelkens *et al.* 1990). So also were the means used by archaic Greek architects to bind adjacent blocks together (very fine jointing of dressed stone and dovetail clamps) and the techniques used in the finishing to ensure an absolutely smooth surface to the dressed masonry, which presumably can only have been learnt in Egypt (Coulton 1977: 49). The most securely dated of the two early Corinthian temples is that at Isthmia, where pottery beneath the peripteros suggests that this part of the temple was begun by at the latest 650, implying preparation of the building area, and planning of the temple in the first half of the seventh century (Gebhard 2001). The participation of mercenaries in Psammetichos' usurpation of the Egyptian throne, ca. 660 BC, is usually taken as the earliest date for the beginning of any kind of intense direct interaction between Greeks and Egyptians, such as could have been the stimulus to monumentalization or the means of transmission of specific techniques. But the earliest Greek pottery at Naucratis has been shifted back in date – now to about 660 BC (Venit 1988), Egyptian bronzes at Samos suggest earlier direct connections (Guralnick 1997: 142–143), and it is by no means certain that Psammetichos' Greek mercenaries were the earliest to be active in Egypt (Froidefond 1971: 50). The dates are too close to rule in or rule out Egyptian contacts as a decisive factor in the development of these first monumental temples.

Although the exact relationship between indigenous and external factors in the genesis of Greek monumental architecture in the seventh century remains obscure, the change from wood and rough cut stone to ashlar masonry and stone columns significantly transformed the whole practice of temple construction. Careful specification of measurements, both of the stylobate, and of many of the temple's constituent parts (stone column sizes, standard blocks for cella walls) had to precede construction; such conceptualization of design transformed building into architecture (Coulton 1977: 43–46; Gebhard 2001: 61). Standardized parts needed to be prepared by a range of specialized technicians. Quarrying and the transportation to the building of blocks cut to specific shapes and measures required new levels of organization, as did the placing of the elements in their position on the building.

Once architectural design in Greece had started down this track, it is demonstrable that the further elaboration of these features by Greek architects and their patrons, to make the kinds of architectural and political statements represented by monumental building, drew heavily on Egyptian techniques and models, and how such transfer might have occurred can be traced with some precision. Both the two sixth century Heraia on Samos (ca. 575 and 530 BC) and the sixth century temple of Artemis at Ephesos (ca. 550 BC) are massively larger than any earlier Greek temples. The earlier temple at Samos was 25 times as large as its predecessor in plan, 100 times in volume (Kienast 2001: 35). Both it and the sixth century Artemision at Ephesos

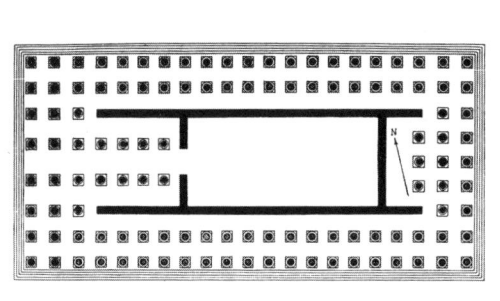

Figure 7:8 Temple of Artemis, Ephesus. Commenced mid-sixth century BC; completed fifth century. Plan and reconstruction view (after Boardman *et al.* 1967; © Hirmer Verlag).

(Figure 7:8) have eight columns along the main façades, and are 'dipteral', with a double colonnade running all round the cella. In both cases the entrance to the cella was given added monumental emphasis by widening the distance between the axes of the centremost columns, and proportionately reducing the outer interaxial distances – unprecedented in Greek temple architecture, but a common feature of Egyptian temple halls, which may also have provided the model for the innovative massing of forests of columns (Lawrence 1983: 162). These temples also attest the massive growth in the size of the blocks being quarried, transported and lifted into place by Greek architects, from about half a ton at Isthmia to regularly as much as 20–40 tons, reaching even 70 tons in the late seventh and sixth centuries (Coulton 1977: 45; Snodgrass 1980: 149). Working on this scale required new techniques and technologies, and new patterns of social organization of the building process. Blocks must have been lifted into place using the Egyptian techniques of ramps and rollers; when the Greeks began routinely to use cranes (attested by rope-slings and cutting for lifting tongs) at the end of the sixth century the highest weights conventionally used drop back below 20 tons (Coulton 1977: 45; Snodgrass 1980: 149). The use of multiple drums for the huge columns and iron dovetail clamps to join the massive blocks were also Egyptian techniques. When the first Samian Dipteron had to be replaced (it was sinking due to inadequate foundations), its successor utilized the Egyptian practice of a sand bed foundation (Kienast 2001: 38).[2] On one level, this process of monumentalization is clearly explained by mechanisms internal to the Greek world: peer polity interaction between neighbouring poleis, seeking to outdo each other in the monumentality of their temples, even if only by a carefully calculated few inches (Snodgrass 1986). On another level, the extraordinary leap in scale and monumentality is difficult to imagine without the stimulus of Egyptian models, and specific features of architectural design and the technical means used to achieve that monumentalization were clearly derived from Egypt: even the basic unit of measurement used in the Samian temples, the Samian cubit, is perhaps not coincidentally the same as an Egyptian royal ell, as Herodotus was aware (Kienast 2001: 38).

Where and how did the architects of these temples encounter the Egyptian features and techniques they utilized? One Rhoikos is named by Herodotus (III.60) as the first architect of the second Samian Dipteros, and may well have been responsible also for the first (Davis 1981: 74). He wrote a treatise on one or other of the temples, co-authored with a younger relative, Theodoros, who was also involved in the building of the Artemision at Ephesos (see Pollitt 1990: 27 for a brief discussion of the complex genealogy of these artists, and the contradictory sources; Hoffmann 1953: 194). Both were also connected with the transfer of aspects of Egyptian sculptural technique to Greece (see below). The building of the first dipteral temple was accompanied by a major reorganization of the sanctuary of Hera, including the creation of a monumental altar for the first time axially oriented to the front of the temple. Earlier altars had employed cut stone, with a stone base and antae walls forming a bracket shape to protect ashes from the wind. But Rhoikos and Theodoros built a monumental altar with 14 steps. Stepped altars had been a feature of Egyptian sacred architecture since the third Dynasty, and Greeks resident in Egypt at Naucratis or Memphis could have seen examples at sites such as Deir el-Bahri or Saqqarah. The Samian altar was the first in the Aegean, but not in the Greek world: the sanctuary of Aphrodite in Naucratis has an altar, dated to the very beginning of the sixth century, with five steps and two wings possibly derived from the lateral ramps of its Egyptian prototypes. An eye bowl was found at Naucratis with the inscribed dedication "Rhoikos to Aphrodite", dated by the letter forms to the first half of the sixth century BC. Rhoikos is an unusual name, and in the light of other ancient testimony to the effect that Theodoros visited Egypt to learn the Egyptian sculptural canon, the identification of the dedicator of the eye bowl with the Samian architect is generally accepted (Diodorus Siculus I.98; Boardman 1980: 132 for an illustration of the cup; Davis 1981: 73; Hoffmann 1953; Skon-Jedele 1994: 1,414–1,415).

The specific features of design or architectural motifs which Greek builders acquired from Egypt were less important than the idea and the capacity to design, to make an architectural statement, and to make it on such a scale and with such controlled precision. Such an architectural statement was intrinsically a political statement – of a capacity to order men, materials and social relations, such as was presupposed by monumental architecture – on the part of both the community who sponsored a temple and any individual who played a particularly dominant role in the realization of such a project (cf. Fehr 1996; Onians 1999: 26–30 for the political iconography of temples). It is striking, in this regard, that the threshold phenomena in the monumentalization of Greek architecture are quite closely linked to 'tyrants', autocrats who achieved sole power over cities, in the contexts of the social struggles which arose out of the social dislocation consequent on the major processes of the elaboration of state institutions (the hoplite reform etc.) and the integration of the Greek world into the larger political and economic worlds of the eastern Mediterranean (Andrews 1956; Osborne 1996: 192–197). The crystallization of monumental architecture in Greece occurs in Corinth during a period when it was dominated by the tyrant Kypselos (ca. 657–625 BC), who also built the first treasury at Delphi (Hurwit 1985: 185; Murray 1980: 145–146). Kroisos, the king of Lydia, paid for a considerable number of the columns of the Artemision in Ephesos, which was effectively controlled by him during the period when the temple was being built (Lawrence 1983: 162). If the first Samian Dipteros was too early to have been sponsored by Polycrates himself (Osborne 1996: 276) – he was certainly responsible for the second – there is a very good chance that it was built by one of the three earlier members of his family who were, on and off, tyrants of Samos from the late seventh century onwards, most probably Syloson I (Shipley 1987: 71–73), conceivably an earlier Polycrates (Davis 1981: 74). The transfer and appropriation of such technology, and the restructuring of architectural agency which it entailed, was, in short, a political act as much as an aesthetic or purely technological one, and it is not surprising that in the case where we can trace the details, the artist who mediates the transfer is so closely connected with a political figure of the order of Polyrates.

## Finding the Egyptian in early Greek sculpture

Like Greek architecture, Greek stone sculpture was fundamentally, and quite rapidly, transformed in the second half of the seventh century BC, and the exact significance of Egyptian 'influences' in that transformation has been fiercely contested. The issue is most sharply crystallized by the invention of a new statue type, the 'kouros', in the third quarter of the seventh century BC (Figure 7:9; Ridgway 1977: 22–35 for summary of the evidence and debate; Stewart 1986: 56–57). Earlier Greek free standing sculpture, up to the middle of the seventh century, was on a relatively small scale, generally considerably less than 1 m tall, and carved in limestone. The new statue type, generally carved in marble, soon reaches heights of more than 3–5 m, and the largest example of which fragments survive, a statue on Delos, was more than four times life size.[3] There are important formal similarities between kouroi and Egyptian statues of pharaohs: both have the left foot forward, hands down at the side with some kind of baton or roll grasped in the hand. But there are also important differences: kouroi are nude whereas most Egyptian stone statues of pharaohs wear kilts; the Egyptian counterparts of kouroi normally have a back rest and a screen between the legs, whereas the kouros is fully free standing. There are significant differences in surface finish and style, particularly in the earlier examples of kouroi, which are carved in a rather abstract linear style in contrast to the careful modelling of facial features and musculature in their Egyptian counterparts (Cook 1967: 24; Osborne 1998: 75–77).

Richter saw important Egyptian contributions to the techniques, formal type and monumentality of the kouros, and includes in her early Sounion group a statuette from Kamiros in Rhodes (Figure 7:10) which bears especially close relationship to Egyptian prototypes by virtue of the treatment of the hair which, lacking any differentiation into strands, is very reminiscent of an Egyptian headdress (Richter 1960, 2–3; 57, no. 27). Adam (1966: 8–12) argued that the formal and technical similarities between Greek kouroi and Egyptian statuary could only be explained on the assumption that Greek sculptors had learned their craft in Egyptian workshops. Other scholars, most trenchantly Cook (1967; but see also Anthes 1963), have wholly excluded such influence, arguing that the kouros type, namely the male nude, existed before any possible contact with Egypt, and the drive to monumentalization in Greek

Figure 7:9   Kouros, ca. 590 BC (© Metropolitan Museum of Art, New York). Height 193 cm.

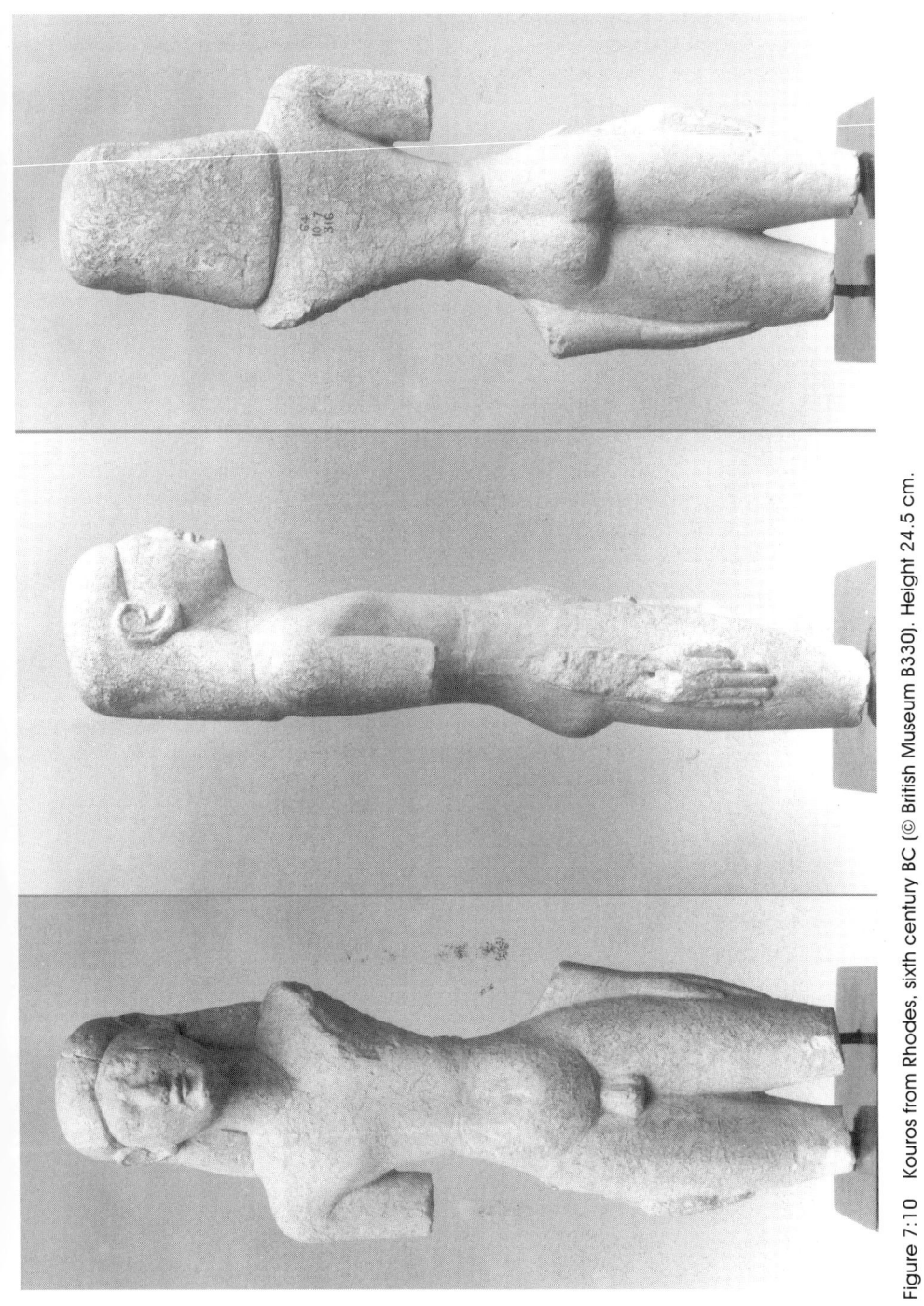

Figure 7:10 Kouros from Rhodes, sixth century BC (© British Museum B330). Height 24.5 cm.

sculpture is seen earliest in statues of the so-called Daidalic style, most notably female statues like Nikandre from Delos (650–625 BC; Figure 7:11), formally related to Syrian prototypes, small terracottas, rather than Egyptian (Cook 1967). Cook (1967: 25) goes so far as to doubt whether any Greek sculptor to the end of the seventh century had even seen an Egyptian stone statue.

Figure 7:11 'Nikandre'. Statue of a woman from Delos, ca. 640 BC (© German Archaeological Institute, Athens). Height 175 cm.

The Greeks themselves, in later periods, recognized major similarities between archaic Greek and Egyptian sculpture. According to Diodorus, the sculptures of Daidalos (in practice archaic statues attributed to the mythical artisan) had the same "rhythmos" or compositional pattern as ancient Egyptian statues (Diodorus Siculus I.97; Morris 1992: 238–242). Diodorus (I.98) also discusses a statue of Apollo on Samos, by the sculptors Telekles and Theodoros, the sons of Rhoikos, describing it as "for the most part rather similar to those of Egypt, as having the arms stretched stiffly down the sides and the legs separated in a stride" (see Davis 1981: 74–75 for a full discussion of the text and the issues of interpretation it raises). Diodorus attributes this similarity to the brothers having learned the procedures of the Egyptian canon, which he is able to describe with passable accuracy (Iversen 1957, 1968), whilst living amongst the Egyptians. Although some scholars still dismiss Diodorus' text as nothing more than a story betraying "antiquarian interest", with no historical value (Morris 1992: 240–241), the ancient Greek view has now been largely vindicated, in substance if not in every detail, by the work of Guralnick (1978, 1981, 1982, 1985). The second Egyptian canon, produced as a revision of the first canon during the twenty-sixth Dynasty (663–525 BC) ensured consistency in the proportions between statues by designing them on the basis of a grid, consisting of 21¼ elements, in which each key body part has consistent proportion and placement in relation to others: for example, the navel on the line between 13th and 14th square, the eyes in the 21st square, the knees taking up most of the 7th square (Iversen 1968; Osborne 1998: 76–77). Guralnick (1978, 1985), rather than relying solely on superficial visual similarities, took measurements of the distances between key body points – chest width, waist width, height knee to navel, height knee to sternum, height knee to nipples, height of head etc. – and compared these with the corresponding proportions of the second Egyptian canon. The New York kouros comes out as to all intents and purposes identical in its proportion and structure to the second Egyptian canon (Figure 7:12), whilst several further kouroi (Thera, Tenea, Athens NM 12, and Melos) are closer to each other and the Egyptian second canon than they are to other kouroi or a statistically perfectly average adult modern Greek male, used as a control measure of naturalism (Davis 1981: 63, 74; Guralnick 1978, 1985). At the time of Guralnick's original investigations none of the larger statues from Samos was sufficiently well preserved to be included in the sample, notwithstanding that their immense scale was highly suggestive of Egyptian models. The recent discovery of a kouros of 15'8" in height, roughly three times life size, dedicated in the Samian Heraion by one Isches in ca. 580 BC, has confirmed Guralnick's initial picture, and lends some credence to Diodorus' story (Guralnick 1996; Kyrieleies 1993: 150). When the statue is divided up according to the canonical grid,

> key anatomical heights – the top of the knee, navel, eyes and top of the head – may all be described in whole numbers of canonic grid modules. There is only one observable difference between the canon and Isches' kouros for these heights. The navel is placed one module higher than the conventional Egyptian II canon grid would place it, increasing the knee top to navel height from 6 to 7 modules and reducing the navel to eye height from 8 to 7 modules.

(Guralnick 1996: 519)

This seems to have been a "conscious reorganization" of the canon, so that each of the key measuring points – knee, navel, eyes – is exactly equidistant (Guralnick 1996: 519).

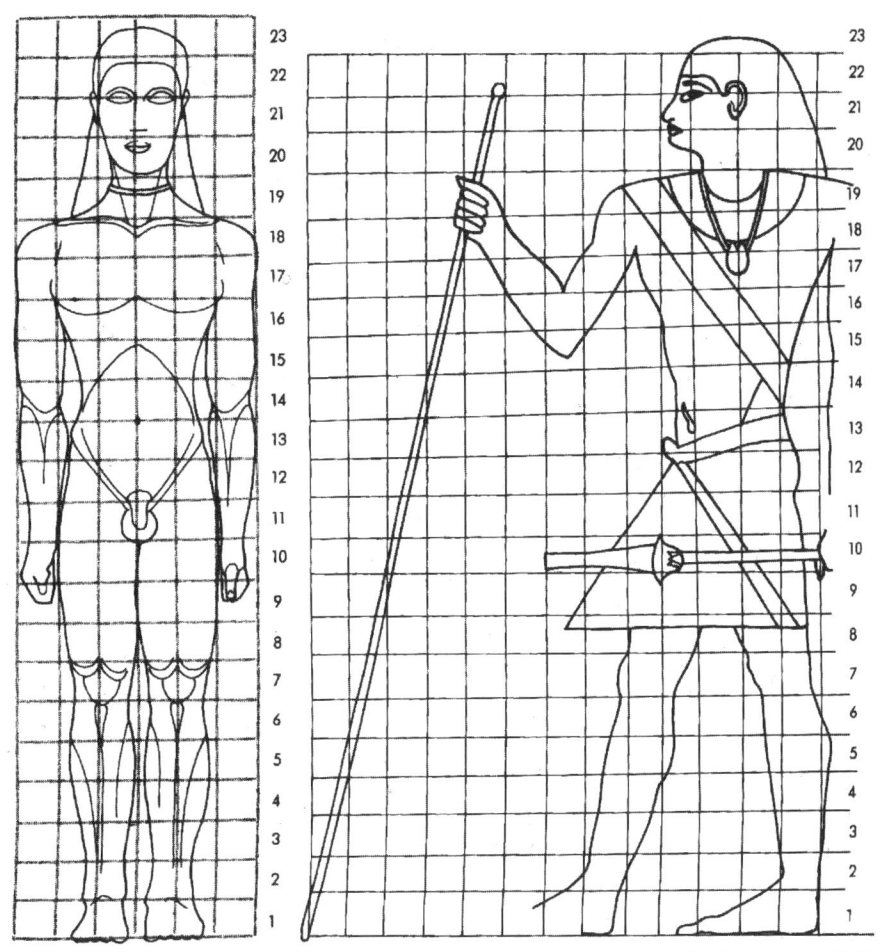

Figure 7:12 Reconstruction of the grid system used to plan archaic kouroi (after Stewart 1997; © Candace Smith and A. F. Stewart).

Furthermore, the unit of measurement used for the modules seems to have been based on a standard Egyptian palm of 7.5 cm, a common denominator of both the Samian foot and the Egyptian royal cubit, so the standard of measure as well as the technique of design seem to have been borrowed, with minor modifications, from Egypt. In the historical context, this is by no means surprising. We have already seen how close the contacts were between Samos and Egypt in exploring bronze sculpture and monumental architecture. Samos played an active role in the foundation of Naucratis, establishing a temple of Hera there. Mercenaries based near Memphis could have seen under production the colossal statues (4.50 m high) which were part of Psammetichos' building programme in the Apis Court, whilst the craftsmen and merchants living in or passing through Naucratis could easily have seen the construction projects of Amasis at nearby Sais, including the colossal statues at the temple of Neith/Athene – indeed many probably had no choice but to see them, since import and sales taxes exacted from Greek traders were paid to officials of Neith at

Sais who also acted as superintendents of the Greeks at Naucratis (Herodotus II.153, 175–176; Diodorus Siculus I.68; Davis 1981: 71, 79).

Perhaps surprisingly, this still leaves considerable room for debate about the importance which should be attributed to the model of the Egyptian canon in the formation and cultural significance of archaic Greek sculpture, and surprisingly few scholars see the relationship with Egypt as absolutely fundamental to the history of early Greek sculpture. In some cases this stems from ideological axiom. Having demonstrated that the claw-chisel – often thought to be a Greek invention and one of the technical preconditions of the distinctiveness of Greek sculpture – was in fact an Egyptian invention of early twenty-sixth Dynasty Egypt, Palagia and Bianchi (1994: 194) suggest that the relationship between Greek and Egyptian sculpture should be re-examined from a technological point of view, but only so long as the conclusions be decided before the research begins: "such an examination must stress that what the Greeks created in response to Egyptian stimuli remained characteristically hellenic, not oriental." In other cases it owes more to a theoretical stance concerning what counts as a satisfactory accounting for a work of art. Most recent work on kouroi has regarded the issue of origins secondary to interpreting the social and cultural meaning of them in their Greek setting (Hurwit 1985: 191–202; Osborne 1998: 77–82; Stewart 1986). Such studies emphasize what makes Greek kouroi different from their Egyptian counterparts both in the contexts in which they were used (votives in sanctuaries, tomb-markers in cemeteries) and in specific features of iconographic and stylistic patterning. They thus show how such statues communicated meanings specific to Greek culture and society. In particular, kouroi embodied an aristocratic ideology of *kalok'agathia*, in which youth, beauty and autonomy represented divine ideals participated in by the elite (Stewart 1986).

Whilst such iconographic and contextual studies are obviously indispensable to a full understanding of early Greek sculpture, an exclusive emphasis on the specifics of the meaning of kouroi in their Greek cultural context runs the danger of underplaying the degree to which the very capacity to materially encode and mobilize those meanings in sculptural form was so heavily dependent on the transfer of techniques of artistic design and sculptural production from Egypt. Indeed, part of the social meaning of the statues was to index that social and material capacity at the disposal of the sponsor of the statue. On a very general level, the new technology of canonical design lent archaic Greek sculpture "finish, elegance and precision; it took on a standard of order; it displayed a new and measured harmony" (Davis 1981: 66). Such precision and order was crucial to the social and cultural effects marble statuary was intended to achieve. The material encoding of some of the key iconographic meanings identified by modern interpreters was also dependent on the new technologies imported from Egypt. Only sculpture in hard stone – like marble rather than the soft limestone in which Greek statuaries had worked prior to their encounter with Egypt – could permit the stressful unsupported walking pose characteristic of the kouros, and conventionally held to signify exceptional strength and vigour characteristic of the aristocratic elite as warriors (Ridgway 1977: 26, 45; Steuernagel 1991).

Before the kouros, early Greek 'Daidalic' limestone sculpture required "no skill beyond that of the mason" (Cook 1967: 31). The small scale of most such figures, and the relative formal simplicity of draped female figures (as most Daidalic sculptures like their Syrian terracotta prototypes were), required relatively little planning in plotting out their design on the stone; much could doubtless be done by eye, with practical adjustments as the work proceeded, relatively swiftly in the soft medium of limestone. Such rough and ready techniques could not be applied when figures were scaled up over life size, particularly in the case of nude male figures; the only guarantee that a statue would bear some resemblance to a human being in its structure and proportions was careful measurement and preplanning objectified in the use of the canonical grid (Davis 1981). These techniques of canonical design served to guide work taking place at any part of the statue when – as was the case with a more than life-size image, and in contrast to the situation with small 60–100 cm Daidalic statues – it was by no means as easy to imagine the relationship between the part one was working on and the rest of the statue. The length of time required in the production of such a statue also militated against traditional techniques relying on a good eye and a design stored only in the artist's memory. When scaled up, as in the case of Nikandre (Figure 7:11), the monumentality of the Daidalic figures was very much undercut by their lack of depth in profile, probably inherited from their mould-made terracotta prototypes. This created an effect of slightness and fragility, perhaps considered appropriate for women but not for men. Canonical design allowed the creation of a more convincing monumental effect, facilitating the creation of sculptures in the round, with fully worked out and co-ordinated (if distinct) frontal and profile views. This was the material precondition of the four-square image of kouroi, used as a metaphor of the noble man in a poem by Simonides, dedicated to the theme of *arete*, manly virtue – "hand and foot alike four-square/an ashlar cut without a flaw" (fr. 452, 1–3 Page; Hurwit 1985: 199; Stewart 1986: 61).

In short, it was Egyptian techniques of design which permitted archaic Greek sculptors to materially encode the culturally specific 'Greek' iconographic meanings which those statues embodied, and also to mobilize those meanings to greatest effect through the impressive monumentality of the images in which they were instantiated. Both the detailed, specifically Greek meanings, and the overall 'power effect' achieved through successful monumentalization were fundamentally dependent on skills of sculptural design and production learnt from Egypt.

## Conclusions: connectivity and incorporation – Egypt and the formation of Greek art in an eastern Mediterranean world

Traditionally the debate over the role of Egyptian influence in the development of Greek art has been conceptualized in terms of an opposition between internalist and externalist explanations. Thus far I have argued that Egyptian architectural and artistic technologies were absolutely fundamental to the development of sophisticated architectural and sculptural design in archaic Greece. The internal development of Greek art, and Greek social and political structures, co-evolved with growing interconnectivity between the Greek world and the broader economic, political and cultural systems of the eastern Mediterranean, into which the Greek world was increasingly integrated (Murray 1980: 223–228; Osborne 1996: 225). Whilst the Greek developments cannot be reduced to an epiphenomenon of relationships with the east – the diffusionist position – they were (contrary to largely internalist histories of Greece and Greek art) structurally dependent on them.

The expansion of world systems often causes both social and ideological turmoil in peripheral areas which are incorporated, creating both constraints and horizons of opportunity within which social, political and ideological innovation can take place (Hannerz 1992: 225). Access to prestige goods from the orient seems to have been paid for by, in addition to silver for the few cities with access to mines, exports of agricultural produce, wine and olive oil, encouraging the wealthy to maximize these forms of saleable production and place pressure on the poorest subsistence producers (Osborne 1996: 225; Shipley 1987: 44–46). Increasing wealth and increasing inequalities in wealth created social frictions, both between rich and poor, and between the established aristocratic elites and the developing hoplite class whose augmented wealth and military importance were not recognized by corresponding political inclusion. This was fertile ground for "increasingly ambitious personal politics" in the Greek world, of which tyranny, autocratic rule by a single man, was the extreme manifestation (Gunter 1990: 143; Osborne 1996: 192–197, 244). The very concept of tyrant, a Lydian word not a Greek one, shows how, as they became connected with the eastern Mediterranean, Greeks looked to the east for ways of conceptualizing and organizing power (Fadinger 1993; Murray 1980: 132–144). The first autocrat to use the title or be referred to as tyrant seems to have been Gyges of Lydia, who violently usurped the throne of Candaules in 685 BC. He was emulated by Psammetichos, king of Sais, who successfully achieved sole rulership in Egypt, against Assyrian suzerainty and 11 other city dynasts, with the assistance of Ionian mercenaries. Kypselos of Corinth, who forced out the ruling Bacchiad aristocracy in 655 BC, was the first of a series of autocrats who followed the example of Gyges and Psammetichos in using mercenary support of some kind to seize and hold sole power (Fadinger 1993: 270, 278). He was followed by Orthagoras in Sikyon (ca. 650 BC), Theagenes of Megara (ca. 640 BC), Kylon's failed attempt at Athens (632 BC) in mainland Greece, in the east Pittakos at Mytilene, Thrasyboulos at Miletus, Polycrates and his relatives at Samos, and so on. "For a century or more after about 650 BC, tyranny was one of the prevalent forms of government in the Greek world" (Murray 1980: 133). Similarly, Psammetichos' nephew and successor Apries (589–570 BC) was overthrown by Amasis (570–526 BC), who, although rising to power through a revolt of Egyptian soldiers, consolidated his rule with foreign bodyguards (Fadinger 1993: 281).

As seen above, there were intensive interconnections between aristocrats, tyrants and other eastern Mediterranean rulers, motivated by complementary interests in prestige and in military security, whether against potential usurpers or the more grave threat of the great powers of the Near East, first Assyria and then Persia. These interconnections involved relationships of guest friendship, and exchange of names and of gifts which included works of art, like the statues dedicated by Amasis on Samos and Rhodes (Francis and Vickers 1984a). They extended to forms of artistic display and artistic patronage which crossed 'national' boundaries. Kroisos of Lydia was one of the primary sponsors of the massive temple of Artemis at Ephesus, as well as making spectacular dedications in the sanctuaries of mainland Greece, as did his predecessors (Herodotus I.15, 50–52). Theodoros of Samos worked not only for Polycrates, but also for Kroisos (Herodotus I.51). He also was responsible for possibly cutting and certainly setting the seal-stone of the famous ring of Polycrates. The stone itself seems to have been a hard green stone (smaragdos), possibly from Egypt and a guest friendship gift from Amasis (Francis and Vickers 1984b: 123). Some of the portraits dedicated by Amasis were probably made by Egyptian artists, to judge from the way they were displayed in the Heraion at Samos, which followed the Egyptian convention of placing paired statues either side of the doorway into a temple (Skon-Jedele 1994: 1,426). The statue of Athena dedicated by Amasis at Lindos, however, seems to have been commissioned from two Greek sculptors, Dipoinos and Skyllis, although the stone used was Egyptian (smaragdos again – green stone, symbolically appropriate to Athena as Neith), and the inscription was in hieroglyphs (Francis and Vickers 1984b: 119–120). Significantly Dipoinos and Scyllis are said by Pliny to have been the first Greek sculptors to become famous through working marble, a rather harder stone than the limestone used in Daedalic Greek sculpture. They were also well known for working in ivory and ebony, which must have been supplied from Egypt (Francis and Vickers 1984b: 125; Pliny *Naturalis historia* XXXVI.9, 14). In the political contexts I have outlined, the character of these more specifically artistic interconnections lent themselves strongly to transfer of the artistic technologies already discussed, as well as to the integration of the Greek city-states into a broader eastern Mediterranean culture of monumentality.[4] Notwithstanding the specifics of form and meaning, what Greek patrons of artists and architects like Isches and Polycrates were doing in drawing on the new technologies of ideological materialization bore a family resemblance of the genetic kind to the sorts of social and political purposes to which art and architecture was being put in Egypt, where both Psammetichos and Amasis sponsored major programmes of monumental building and sculpture as a means to legitimate their assumption of power (Diodorus Siculus I.68; Herodotus II.153, 175–176).

In this light, it is perhaps a mistake to see the kouros in particular, and even the temple, as symbols of communal development (*pace* Osborne 1996: 214, cf. 269–270), or to take too much for granted the ultimate triumph of a dominant middling ideology represented by the invention of Athenian democracy (Morris 2000: 185). Many tyrants were able to pass on their position to their descendants, over two or more generations. Autocratic domination must have seemed a viable long term possibility, within the broader Near Eastern context: the Phoenician model of a division of powers between an autocratic ruler and representative citizen assemblies (Blanton *et al.* 1996: 67) may even really have been a possible outcome for the development of Greek city-states until the radically egalitarian political revolutions of the last quarter of the sixth century (Morris 2000: 186–188) and the reinforcement of democratic norms and a hostility to hierarchy and autocracy as constitutive components of Greek identity which developed out of the Persian wars (Hall 1989). The criticism of excessive elite luxury which constitutes such a large component of the manifestation of 'middling' ideology in the archaic period is, after all, by no means peculiar to Greece, but is on the contrary characteristic of all hierarchically differentiated societies, particularly the class societies which emerged in Eurasia after the Bronze Age (Goody 1997: 263–266).

Both monumental architecture and monumental sculpture were technologies of power which could be subject to appropriation as part of 'exclusionary' elitist strategies, and as elements in more 'corporate' 'middling' or relatively egalitarian communal strategies (see Blanton *et al.* 1996 for exclusionary versus corporate; Morris

2000 for elitist versus middling). Kouroi could be dedicated by communities (e.g. Richter 1960: no. 15), but more generally seem to have been erected by individuals. Isches' kouros, at almost five metres, will – at least until the building of the Rhoikos temple – have dominated the Samian Heraion, standing higher than the by then ageing second temple of Hera. So massive a statue – a representation of a god, Isches himself or a heroic ancestor, all possibilities within the visual language of archaic Greek kouroi (cf. Tanner 2001: 263–265) – will have 'collapsed the difference' between this particular aristocrat and the gods in a parallel way to symposiastic ritual practices and paraphernalia modelled on Lydian court culture (cf. I. Morris 2000: 163–185 esp. 178). But it will have collapsed that distance in a way which, unlike symposiastic ritual and orientalizing pottery, was almost incapable of meaningfully competitive appropriation and emulation further down the social scale (S. P. Morris 1997: 64 for doubts about the exclusive character of orientalizing pottery). Temple building was primarily a communal project, but lent itself to appropriation to the credit of particular individuals or their families. This could occur through the direct control of autocrats like Polycrates and Kroisos, or the more moderate strategy of individuals like the Alkmaionids under Kleisthenes. They took on responsibility for the co-ordination and realization of the new temple of Apollo at Delphi, largely funded by public subscription, but secured special credit when they completed the temple to superior specifications than had originally been agreed, by executing the façade in marble (Herodotus V.62).[5] The individual asserted himself by riding on, and to some degree appropriating, a project which was ultimately dependent on the kinds of resources only a whole community could afford. Tyrants represent an extreme instance of this, occupying a position where they could effectively monopolize communal resources, largely control their expenditure, and augment their personal prestige though enhancing corporate identity of the state, normally at the political expense of other aristocrats (Snodgrass 1980: 115).

The borrowed technologies by which architecture and sculpture were monumentalized did not as such determine the precise political uses to which they were put – although perhaps kouroi lent themselves more to exclusionary elitist strategies, temple architecture to corporate collectivist strategies. But they did create within the Greek world qualitatively new ways of materializing ideology and mobilizing it in the support of individual, sectional or communal power, and thus contributed to the transformation of the social order itself.

Structural interconnection between the developing social and political structures of the Greek world, and the larger political and economic systems of the eastern Mediterranean, both motivated and provided the material means for the restructuring of the artistic culture of archaic Greek states which is represented by the development of monumental Greek architecture and sculpture. Moreover, those technologies should not simply be seen as foreign means to Greek ends, for means and ends are internally related through the materialization of power. As such, these cultural technologies are a part of a widely shared culture of ideological materialization common to the eastern Mediterranean world, but variably realized according to the different social and political structures of the different states and societies that composed the elements of that larger system. Greek art became both more like Egyptian art and more specifically Greek as part and parcel of the same process of political and cultural integration and differentiation within an expanding east Mediterranean world system.

## Notes

1. Samos, like other islands in the eastern Aegean, may well have been exceptionally well connected with Egypt. The exceptional quantity and quality of Egyptian bronzes found there certainly in part reflects this, but probably also is a result of the unusual building history of the sanctuary, extremely active during the archaic period, particularly in the seventh and sixth centuries, which gave rise to the preservation of the old votives in the deposits where they were found, but with rather little building activity thereafter. Osborne (1998: 47) is exceptional amongst standard histories of Greek art in illustrating one of the Egyptian bronzes from Samos, but primarily in order to contrast it with a wooden statuette from the Heraion by a Greek sculptor.
2. One of the characteristic rhetorical moves of anti-diffusionist theories, promoting a focus on the receiving culture, is to suggest that cultures only borrow from their neighbours what they are internally ready for. In this light, it is perhaps significant of the power of Egyptian models of monumentality that they were pursued by Greek patrons and architects beyond their ability to realize them. The first Samian Dipteros had to be taken down, within a generation of its initial completion, before it collapsed due to inadequate foundations. The second Samian Dipteros was never finished and the giant Peisistratid temple of Zeus in Athens only by the Roman emperor Hadrian (Murray 1980: 228–229).
3. Monumental statues: Richter 1960: nos. 2–5, 18, 24–25, 50, 78–79, 127 – all between 8 and more than 20 ft; with Stewart 1986: 64 for further examples.
4. This shared culture of monumental materialization of ideology of course extends beyond kouroi and temple architecture to other features of the monumentalization of sanctuaries – particularly noteworthy are the two rows of lions flanking the processional way in the sanctuary of Apollo on Delos, and the statues of local rulers, possibly placed alongside the processional way at Didyma – Boardman 1980: 173.
5. Under the classical democracy, the balance between individual and community in public building projects was shifted definitively in favour of the latter, by refusing private funding of communal buildings, and entrusting supervision and execution of projects to democratically constituted committees.

## Acknowledgments

I am grateful to the editors and to Cyprian Broodbank and Peter Ucko for comments which materially improved this chapter.

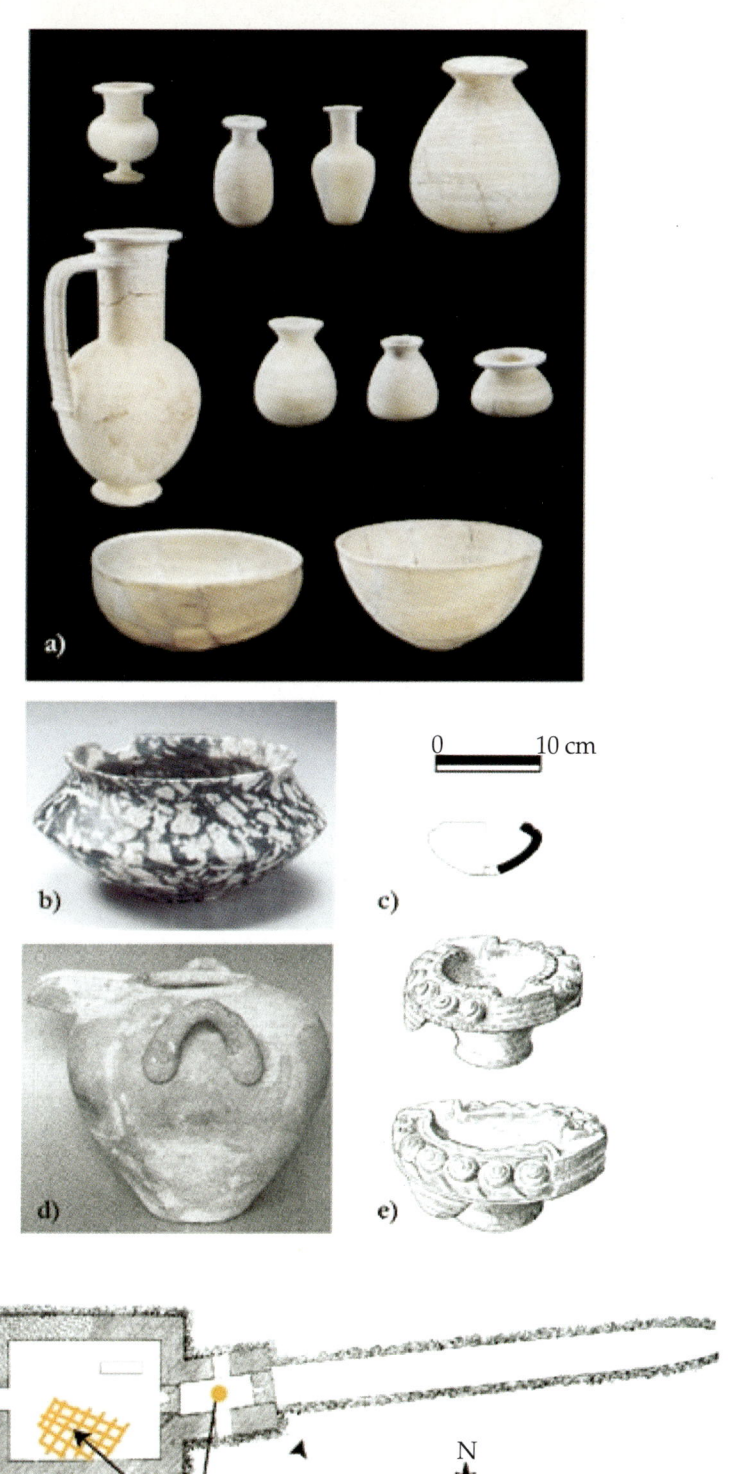

Figure 4:6 Stone vessels from the Isopata 'Royal Tomb' (the tomb plan is after Evans 1905: pl. xciii). Apart from the stone vessels shown here the tomb group also included one small bowl in local calcite and several serpentine lids.
(a) Egyptian vessels in travertine, including a possible oil set (after Keretsou 2000: nos. 232–237, 239a–b).
(b) Black and white porphyry bowl (Keretsou 2000: no. 238).
(c) Egyptian Early Dynastic collared bowl in diorite (after Evans 1905: fig. 128).
(d) Cretan bridge-sprouted jar in 'banded tufa' (Warren 1969: pl. 89).
(e) Two Cretan lamps with whorl decoration (after Evans 1905: figs. 126–127).

Figure 11:2  Painted panel from a colonnade: a parody of an Egyptian festival (Museo Archeologico Nazionale di Napoli I.N. 113195).

Figure 7:3  Faience double unguent vase of presenting servant, from Kamiros, Rhodes. Second-half seventh century BC; ht. 9.5 cm (British Museum 60.4-4.75).

Figure 11:3  Painted panel from a colonnade: a parody of a festive Egyptian symposium (Museo Archeologico Nazionale di Napoli I.N. 113196).

Figure 11:5 Details of the Nilotic mosaic of Palestrina: the festival of the inundations of the Nile (© Stuto/Archeomedia).

Figure 11:6  Symposium at the festival of the inundations of the Nile. Staatliche Museen zu Berlin, Preussischer Kulturbesitz, Antiken Sammlung Mosaic 3 (© Christa Begall).

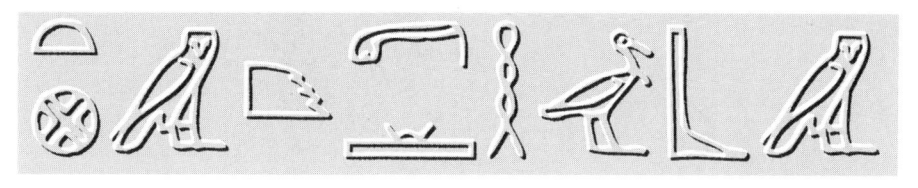

## CHAPTER 8

# UPSIDE DOWN AND BACK TO FRONT: HERODOTUS AND THE GREEK ENCOUNTER WITH EGYPT

*Thomas Harrison*

Of all the places and peoples with whom the Greeks came into contact, it was with Egypt and the Egyptians that they had the most complex relationship. Unlike their relationship with Achaemenid Persia, one which centred on the single fact of the Greek-Persian wars (490–479 BC) long after those wars were concluded, their relationship with Egypt was not at heart antagonistic, and was based on much longer and deeper memory of contact (e.g. Austin 1970; Lloyd 1975–1989: I.1–60; Möller 2000).[1] Egypt was indeed seen as the source of many of the most fundamental features of Greek culture, an essential detour for Greek writers. The historian Herodotus, the Athenian reformer Solon, Plato, Pythagoras, and Eudoxus are all reputed – with varying plausibility – to have visited Egypt and tapped its ancient wisdom. In doing so, they were joining a long list of more hazily historical figures: Homer, Lycurgus, Orpheus, Musaeus, Melampus and Daedalus (e.g. Herodotus I.30; Diodorus Siculus I.69.4, 96–98; Strabo XVII.1.29).[2] But at the same time as Egypt was elevated above other foreign lands as a source of Greek practice and ideals, it was also distanced, seen as representing – in its climate or its customs – the reverse of the normative (i.e. Greek) world, or subsumed into the collective cliché of the 'barbarian'.

The image of Egypt also changed over time (Froidefond 1971; Smelik and Hemelrijk 1984; Vasunia 2001). In part, this was in response to the course of events. Most strikingly, Alexander's conquest of the Persian empire (including Egypt) and the subsequent rule of the Greco-Macedonian Ptolemies led to a very different configuration of 'Greek' and 'barbarian', one in which a Sidonian prince with a Greek name, for example, could boast, in entirely Greek terms, of his Phoenician ancestry after winning the chariot race at the Nemean Games (Moretti 1953: no. 41 = Austin 1981: no. 121). But the polarity of 'Greek' and 'barbarian', that was (to an extent) destabilized in the light of Alexander's conquests, itself had only a limited history (Cartledge 1993; Harrison 2002a). Though many of the elements of the Greek portrayal of foreign peoples – the association with incomprehensible speech, with monarchy or excessive wealth – originate in the archaic period, such stereotypes are only organized and brought into sharper focus in the light of the Greek-Persian wars. And no sooner are they organized, and marshalled as a justification of empire by the Athenians, than they are problematized and refracted, with the tag of the barbarian being turned, for example, by the Athenian Euripides against the Greeks themselves

(Hall 1989; Saïd 2002).[3] The Egyptians played their part militarily in the Persian campaigns against Greece. This fact, however, by no means drowned out others. Greeks had been settled in the *emporion* of Naucratis from the last quarter of the seventh century (Möller 2000). Greeks had long served as mercenaries for the Egyptian kings, and in one case – the Nubian campaign of Psammetichos II – commemorated the fact with graffiti (Lloyd 1975–1989: I.21–3; Meiggs and Lewis 1988: no. 7; Yoyotte and Sauneron 1952). It was from this time, Herodotus claims, of Psammetichos' settlement of Greeks in Egypt that regular contact, and so a more accurate knowledge of Egyptian history, began (II.154). The mid-fifth century saw sustained (and ultimately failed) Athenian intervention in Egypt, but in support of the revolt of Inarus *against* Persian rule (Thucydides I.104–112; Diodorus Siculus XI.71–77). What impact this episode might have had on Greek perceptions of Egypt as distinct from Persia is impossible to assess,[4] but it is perhaps more likely to have confounded any simplistic identification of Egyptians with other barbarian peoples, providing food for more specific preconceptions.

It would be wrong, however, to expect the history of representations of Egypt to follow too closely the history of events. The representation of foreign peoples is driven by a number of factors other than experience or the desire for accurate knowledge. It may respond to events internal to the Greek world (the Athenians' need, for example, to advertize their role as a bulwark against barbarism), or to intellectual agendas quite divorced from the world of politics: the need to better or correct a previous ethnographic account, or to find a quasi-historical (but safely distant) precedent for a philosophical utopia (Hartog 2002: 217 on Plato's appropriation of Egyptian material; Livingstone 2001 on Isocrates' *Busiris*; O'Connor 2003: 159).

The autonomy of the history of representations can be seen clearly by examining the case of Herodotus' account of Egypt and its reception by later writers. Written half a century after the Persian wars, Herodotus' is the fullest account of Egyptian history and society by any Greek writer (Lloyd 1988, 1990, 2002). It also provides a point of reference for all subsequent accounts, to the extent that the focus of later writers appears at times to be directed more at the tradition of previous writing on Egypt than at their ostensible subject. Herodotus writes much nonsense, the geographer Strabo asserts (XVII.1.52), only to give his approval, shortly after, to his predecessor's story that the Egyptians knead mud with their hands, and dough with their feet (Strabo XVII.2.5; cf. Herodotus II.36).[5]

Herodotus' relationship with an earlier tradition – and the sources of his account of Egypt – are more difficult to establish. His dependence on predecessors, most notably on the early fifth century Hecataeus of Miletus, has often been exaggerated, as if his account were simply transcribed from an earlier written version (Fowler 1996). It is clear, however, that Herodotus' interest in, and knowledge of, Egypt emerged in the context of a much broader Greek milieu of fascination with foreign peoples (Thomas 2000), one which gave rise, for example, to Phrynichus' play *Egyptians*, the *Aigyptiaka* of Herodotus' near-contemporary Hellanicus of Lesbos, as well as to the wealth of ethnographic material on Egypt contained in Aeschylus' *Suppliants*. Whether Herodotus' knowledge of Egypt (Tait 2003: 29, 31) was also derived from personal observation, and from the interviews he conducted with Egyptian priests – as he repeatedly claims – is one of the most hotly disputed questions in ancient history (e.g.

Armayor 1978; Fehling 1989; West 1991, expressing varying degrees of scepticism; Lloyd 1995; Pritchett 1993; Rhodes 1994, reasserting Herodotus' veracity). Did Herodotus really see the buildings he claims to have seen? (Or did he really fail to see, or recall those – such as the Sphinx – of which he makes no mention?) Can the errors and distortions of his text be satisfactorily explained by difficulties of translation – by his interpreters converting what they heard into terms that their Greek-speaking visitor would understand – or by his and others' preconceived understanding of Egypt? And could the information he retells – his knowledge of the Egyptian word for crocodile, for example, *champsa*[6] – plausibly have derived from other sources?

What emerges clearly, however, is that Herodotus' account preserves material, often valuable, that originates, by whatever route and however distorted, in Egyptian sources: his account of the process of mummification (II.85–90), for example, of animal worship (II.65 ff), of Egyptian medicine (II.84 ff) – all themes that fascinated other Greek authors[7] – or his observation that the Egyptians term all those of another language barbarian (II.158), borne out by other evidence.[8] Herodotus is also aware of the regional diversity of Egypt, noting the difference of attitudes held towards the crocodile, for example, revered and dressed in earrings and bangles in one place, eaten in another (II.69; cf. II.92). What is also clear is that – regardless of whether he visited Egypt, and regardless also of the truth of the material he relates – Herodotus' curiosity was mediated and distorted by a whole body of preconceptions, that he travelled, as Gikandi (1996) has argued of 19th century English travellers to the Caribbean, to find out what he already knew.

Herodotus' account of Egypt cannot be divorced from its context in his *Histories*. It is presented as one of a series of ethnographic digressions incorporated within his narrative of the expansion of the Persian empire. The 'Egyptian digression' takes its start from Herodotus' report of the Persian king Cambyses' conquest of Egypt (II.1) – a pattern of "narrative framing ethnography" which occurs repeatedly,[9] and which, far from being simply a convenient device for including material that Herodotus could not bear to leave on the cutting floor, has the effect of building up the stakes for the Persians' clash with Greece by emphasizing their relentless accumulation of power.[10] Leaving aside this rhetoric of accumulation, however, Book II clearly contains abundant material that bears little direct relationship to Herodotus' overarching theme of Persian expansion. The unity of any literary work is relative, as Fornara (1971: 6) has written. Herodotus' Egyptian 'digression' is so lengthy as to strain the term to breaking point. His account of Egypt, then, must be motivated as much or more by the intrinsic value of its contents as by its role in the narrative (cf. Lloyd 2002: 418).

Herodotus indeed makes this explicit. He justifies the length of his Egyptian *logos* – he was evidently aware of its apparently disproportionate size – by the number of wonders and works (*thômasia ... kai erga*) that Egypt contains (II.35).[11] This criterion for inclusion is one which he applies elsewhere in his *Histories*, in his account of the island of Samos – on which he dwelled at excessive length on the grounds of its three great *erga*, buildings or "works", III.60 – and in commenting that a Lydian monument (*ergon pollôn megiston*), the tomb of the king Alyattes, was greater than all others apart from Egyptian and Babylonian (I.93). In Book II likewise, it is buildings that appear to rank highest in his hierarchy of wonders.

Herodotus' admiration of Egyptian buildings is not unremarkable (see Tanner Chapter 7, this volume). There was, already by the time of his writing, a Greek tradition of belittling (in some instances quite literally) such Egyptian achievements: this can be seen, for example, in the original meaning of a number of Greek terms for unfamiliar Egyptian phenomena, the obelisk (a roasting spit or skewer), pyramid (a variety of cake), or crocodile (a lizard; cf. Herodotus II.69.3), or in the various traditions (scorned by Herodotus II.134) that gave the credit for the smallest of the pyramids of Giza to a Greek courtesan, Rhodopis (cf. Strabo XVII.1.33; Diodorus Siculus I.64.14; Vasunia 2001: 82–84). Such Greek responses to Egypt are almost certainly humorous. They may even arguably be self-directed, reflecting the Greeks' acknowledgment of their own status as peripheral to an older and greater culture. By contrast, however, Herodotus' wonder is uninhibited. Though his account of the building of the great pyramid of Kheops lays heavy emphasis on the numbers of forced labourers required to build it (Herodotus II.124–128) – making the pyramid into a symbol of unaccountable monarchy – his lovingly detailed, virtuosic descriptions of the buildings themselves are nothing but admiring: "To build the pyramid itself took twenty years; it is square at the base, its height (800 feet) equal to the length of each side; it is of polished stones beautifully fitted, none of the blocks being less than thirty feet long" (II.124; cf. II.101, 108, 111–112, 136, 141, 175–176). In another context – that of the Labyrinth, a building whose very existence has been challenged (Armayor 1985; cf. Lloyd 1995) – Herodotus even compares Egyptian buildings favourably with Greek:

> I have seen this building; and it is beyond my power to describe; it must have cost more in labour and money than all the walls and public works of the Greeks put together – though no one would deny that the temples at Ephesus and Samos are remarkable buildings. The pyramids too are astonishing structures, each one of them equal to many of the most ambitious works of Greece; but the Labyrinth surpasses them.
>
> (Herodotus II.148)

Herodotus certainly indulges in none of the patronizing asides perpetrated, for example, by Strabo – who sneers at the absence in a Heliopolitan temple of any statue in human form (there is only a statue of some irrational (*alogos*) animal, XVII.1.28), or who comments on the barbaric manner of the columns, large and numerous and in many rows, contributing to a hall with "nothing pleasing or picturesque, but ... a display of vain toil".

Egypt presents many more objects of wonder than its buildings – none less than the land of Egypt itself. What actually is Egypt (Herodotus II.15–19)? Is Egypt properly only the Delta, as the Ionians claim (Thomas 2000), dividing the rest between Libya and Arabia? But if so, given that the Delta was the 'gift of the river', and a recent gift at that, how could the Egyptians have ever entertained ideas of their own antiquity? If this were true, moreover, the Ionians would be convicted of inability to count: for if the Delta was part of neither Asia nor Libya nor Europe, it must constitute a fourth continent on its own. Herodotus counters with a bluff common sense: "the whole country inhabited by Egyptians is Egypt, just as that inhabited by Cilicians is Cilicia, and by Assyrians Assyria"; the only boundary between Asia and Libya is the frontier of Egypt (cf. Herodotus IV.42–43). Just as in its buildings, moreover, so in its geography Egypt is on a different scale and of a different quality (Harrison forthcoming). In many instances, Herodotus sees distances in foreign lands and in the Greek world as comparable. So, for example, the distance from Heliopolis to the sea is the same as that from Athens to Pisa (Herodotus II.7; cf. IV.99); the cities of Egypt, during the inundation, take on the appearance of Aegean islands (Herodotus II.97; cf. Diodorus Siculus I.36.8);[12] the Nile Delta is compared with the alluvial plain of the Maeander or of the Achelous in Acarnania (II.10). But as that final example demonstrates, comparison can break down: "if," Herodotus qualifies, "I may be allowed to compare small thing with great, for of the rivers that have thrown up the soil that forms these countries, not one can justly be brought into comparison, as to size, with any one of the five mouths of the Nile." Indeed it appears that different countries require different scales of measurement – as Herodotus' (II.6; cf. III.89) calculation of the length of the coast of Egypt shows: "Now, all men who are short of land measure their territory by fathoms (*orguiêsi*); but those who are less short of land by *stades*; and those who have much by *parasangs*; and such as have a very great extent by *schoeni*. Now a *parasang* is equal to 30 *stades*, and each *schoenus*, which is an Egyptian measure, is equal to 60 *stades*."

Egypt was also a source of wonder in the extent and depth of its history.[13] Herodotus presents a number of vivid demonstrations of the length of Egyptian history. He records the primitive experiment – waiting to see which language was first spoken by two new-born children – by which Psammetichos 'proved' that Phrygian was the oldest language, and (with no evidence whatsoever) that Egyptian was the second oldest (II.2).[14] He claims to have been shown, by the Egyptian priests, a list of 330 rulers, each of whom (implausibly) ruled for a generation, of whom 18 were Ethiopian, and one a woman (Herodotus II.100). And he (Herodotus II.142–143) tells the story of the priests of Zeus' refutation of Hecataeus' claim to be descended from a god in the sixteenth generation: they refused to believe him, pointing to the 341 statues of priests dating from the first king of Egypt to Seti (Sethos), each of whom again represented a generation. The long line of kings, moreover, includes a number of individuals whose deeds Herodotus (II.100) deems worthy of description: Nitocris, who avenged her brother's killers by drowning them in an underground chamber, and who then died by flinging herself into a room full of ashes; Sesostris, the mythical conqueror of Asia and Ethiopia (Herodotus II.102 ff); or Rhampsanitus, who married his daughter to a man who had stolen from his treasury as a reward for his cleverness, or who descended into Hades to play dice with Demeter (Herodotus II.121–122).

Egypt, however, is more than just a gallery of exotic rulers. At times indeed it appears to be an archive of the 'dos and don'ts' of kingship. Stories such as those of Mykerinos, the son of Kheops, fated to die early on grounds of his just behaviour (Herodotus II.129–133), of Apries, suspected by his troops of leading them on a disastrous campaign to Cyrene so as to ensure his own survival (Herodotus II.161) or of Psammenitus, the son of Amasis, who displays great fortitude in dealing with the reversal of Persian conquest, only then foolishly to rebel against Persian rule (Herodotus II.14–15; Lloyd 1988: 51), all exemplify and explore the proper role and behaviour of kings in ways that anticipate later, more theoretical treatises concerned with monarchy such as Isocrates' *Busiris*. Perhaps the clearest instances of this pattern are two episodes from the account of Amasis (Herodotus II.172–174). Unable to gain the respect of some of his subjects, as a result of his humble origins, he had a gold footbath recast as an image of a god. When they automatically showed it reverence, he pointed out that they had formerly washed their feet, urinated and vomited in it. So, implicitly, with him: he deserved respect not for his origins but for the function he fulfilled. In similarly pragmatic fashion, he spent his mornings on royal business and his afternoons in drinking and amusement – and defended his insufficiently royal lifestyle on the basis that he would otherwise go mad. Like Herodotus' (I.96–100) version of the rise to power of the Median king Deioces – his establishment *ex nihilo* of all the characteristic features of oriental monarchy (spies, a fortified palace, elaborate court protocol, etc., all designed to make his former friends feel that he was now a different man from the one they had known before) – the anecdotal traditions of the kings of Egypt do far more than simply reflect and reinforce Greek prejudice; they explore and theorize the nature of monarchy.

Monarchy, moreover, does not cripple the Egyptians – as it is imagined to paralyze the Persians during the Greek-Persian wars.[15] Sesostris' extensive conquests in the Near East constitute a mythical analogue for potential Egyptian strength (Herodotus II.102 ff).[16] Though the narrative of the Egyptian rebellion against Persian rule is abbreviated into a prelude to the Persian expedition against Greece (Herodotus VII.1–7),[17] though in one context when Greeks and Egyptians are head to head the Egyptians complacently underestimate their Cyrenean opposition (Herodotus IV.159), and though finally the Egyptians may be rhetorically rolled together with other peoples by the king's advisers, as useless allies or as scapegoats for defeat (Herodotus VIII.68, 100), at the same time Herodotus' post-mortem of the battle of Artemisium ranks them as the best of the Persian fleet, crediting them with the capture of five ships and their crews (Herodotus VIII.17). The Egyptian warrior caste is given especial prominence (Herodotus IX.32; cf. II.47, 89–90, 141, 164 ff). Indeed, Herodotus' (II.100, 142–143) emphasis on the largely uninterrupted line of Egyptian kings seems, like the account of Diodorus Siculus (I.69.6) that depends upon it, to carry the clear implication that their customs must be good.

Unlike his successor, Herodotus does not build up Sesostris into a great lawgiver on the pattern of the Spartan Lycurgus: responsible for military training, a constitutionally limited kingship, the establishment of nomes, as well as for the building of canals (Diodorus Siculus I.53, 70–72, 54, 57; cf. I.94). Sesostris, in Herodotus' account (II.108, 137), did indeed build canals; he also distributed the land of Egypt into allotments (Herodotus II.109; cf. Diodorus Siculus I.54). However, the creation of Egyptian landscape and customs is more gradual: the Ethiopian king Sabacus, for example, punished criminals by ordering them to raise the ground to a level which reflected their offence (Herodotus II.137). The Greeks' borrowing of Egyptian customs, correspondingly, does not, for the most part,[18] fit the narrow template of constitutional innovations taken by one lawgiver from another (Herodotus I.65; Aristotle, *Politics* 1271b20 ff, 1274a22 ff), but seems again to be a more complex and a more piecemeal process.

The extent of the Greeks' debt to Egypt he leaves in no doubt, however. It was the Egyptians, for example, from whom the Greeks learnt the names of the gods (II.4, 50; Harrison 2000a: Appendix 2 with Thomas 2000: ch. 9), who gave images, altars or temples to the gods (II.54), who taught them to sacrifice to Dionysus and to perform the phallic procession (II.49), or to celebrate festivals (II.58–63). It was from Egypt that Greek shields and helmets are said to originate (IV.180), from where some Greeks (the

Orphics and Pythagoreans) plagiarized the doctrine of the transmigration of the soul (Herodotus II.123), or from where Solon took the law to Athens that each man should declare the source of his income (II.177, cf. II.160).[19] In this last case, the means by which an Egyptian custom reached Egypt are quite clear. In the case of the cult of Dionysus, similarly, Herodotus (II.49) ascribes responsibility for the Greeks' debt to Melampus, and speculates that Melampus' knowledge originated from Cadmus of Tyre and his fellow Phoenician settlers in Boeotia. In other contexts, he offers no such speculation, referring (VI.53–55) on one occasion to earlier writers for "how it happened that Egyptians came to the Peloponnese, and what they did to make themselves kings". Strikingly, however, that the Egyptians gave their customs to other peoples, rather than the other way around, is something that Herodotus (e.g. II.49) insists upon. He 'proves', for example, that the Egyptians could not have taken the name of Heracles from Greece by the argument (II.43) that, if so – as a seafaring nation – they would have borrowed the names of Poseidon and the Dioscuri – and yet these were unknown in Egypt. He (see II.104; cf. II.30) presented a similar 'proof' of the Egyptian origin of circumcision.

This presumption in favour of Egyptian origins might tempt one, with Plutarch in his essay 'On the malignity of Herodotus', to claim Herodotus as a barbarian-lover (*philobarbaros*), predisposed to see a foreign culture as exemplary. "Enthusiasm for a foreign culture," Lloyd (1975–1989: I.154–155) has written, "may easily lead to a generally derogatory attitude towards one's own and it is difficult to escape the suspicion that Herodotus, like many since, has fallen into this trap." Such a claim is apparently borne out by a number of passages in the *Histories*. The story, ascribed to "the Greeks", that Heracles, on the verge of being sacrificed to Zeus, broke free and killed tens of thousands of Egyptians, Herodotus (II.45) dismisses as typical of the foolish stories of the Greeks. How, he counters, could the Egyptians, so squeamish in their choice of sacrificial victims, think to sacrifice a man?[20] And how could one man kill so many others? His version of the Helen myth (originating in the *Palinode* of Stesichorus (frr. 192.2–3, 193.14–16 *PMG*) and reworked by Euripides in his *Helen*), with its relocation of Helen to Egypt and its transformation of the Trojan War into a wild goose chase, sees the Egyptian king Proteus cast in the role of the guardian of Greek *xenia* or guest-friendship, denouncing the impiety of Paris and preserving Helen and Menelaus' other possessions intact (Herodotus II.114–115). Herodotus' insistence on the direction in which customs were diffused, or his passing remark (II.53) that it was the "day before yesterday" that the Greeks learnt the nature of the gods, combine to suggest almost an anti-Greek focus to his ethnography.

Herodotus' Egyptian borrowings are not all they seem, however. First, the model of diffusion – the assumption, that is, that a custom must have had a single origin – is by no means an exclusive one. The Egyptians also provide material for direct comparison between customs, without speculation as to origins or antiquity: the Babylonians indulge in laments for their dead which are very similar to the Egyptians' (Herodotus I.198); whereas the Egyptian priests kill no animal "except for sacrifice", the Magi kill everything apart from dogs and men with their own hands (Herodotus I.140); the Egyptians – in this example we see again the germ of the use of foreign peoples as a model of the just constitution (cf. Herodotus IV.26 for the "equal power" of Issedonian women) – are similar to the Spartans in the signs of respect which they offer to their elders (Herodotus II.80). At the same time there is evidence, as has been much discussed, of a whole set of polarities in Herodotus' representation of Egypt (see esp. Cartledge 1993: 55–59; Hartog 1988: 15–18, 2002; Redfield 1985; Romm 1989). The course of the Nile can be deduced from that of the Danube, presuming apparently that one should be the mirror image of the other (Herodotus II.26–27, 31–34).[21] Herodotus (II.35–36) then associates the reversal of natural conditions with the reversal in Egypt of human customs: "the Egyptians, besides having a climate peculiar to themselves, and a river different in its nature from all other rivers, have adopted customs and usages in almost all respects different from the rest of mankind"; women go to market, men stay at home and weave, women urinate standing up and men sitting down – and so on.

This model of polarity clearly does not operate in isolation from other models (of relativism, or of diffusion) (Thomas 2000: 78, 96, 112, 200–2001, criticizing the proponents of Herodotean schematism). The report (Herodotus IV.47), for example, that Scythia has almost as many rivers as Egypt has canals, though it clearly reflects polarized thinking (Egypt's rivers are man-made), does so in a fashion which is more than simply geometrical, which accommodates a certain disorderly verisimilitude. Such polarities, moreover, do not necessarily imply pejorative judgments. When Sophocles' Oedipus, for example, adopts the Herodotean *topos* of the Egyptian reversal of customs, it is in the context of a good-natured teasing of his daughters Antigone and Ismene: "These two," he (Sophocles, *Oedipus Coloneus* 337–343, tr. Lloyd-Jones) says, "conform altogether to the customs that prevail in Egypt ... For there the males sit in their houses working at the loom, and their consorts provide the necessities of life out of doors." The model of polarity, however, is one which tends by its nature to emphasize a small repertoire of features of any culture – and to ensure that such features are exotic and garish (Redfield 1985). Though Herodotus' account of Egypt may only on rare occasions display explicit chauvinism towards its subjects, in its selection of themes, at least, it tallies neatly with more overtly prejudiced sources (cp. Smelik and Hemelrijk 1984: 1,873: "The traditional prejudices against Egypt ... hardly appear in Herodotus' work").

Herodotus' (II.28) allusion to the possibility that Egyptian priests may have been deceiving him, albeit in jest, taps into a long tradition of the deceit and dishonesty of Egyptians.[22] His (II.65 ff) lengthy account of Egyptian religious scruples, and of animal worship, is paralleled by a whole body of comic jibes which portray reverence for animals as *at the expense* of traditional deities. "You do proskynesis to a cow; but I sacrifice to the gods. You think the eel the greatest daimon, we the biggest by far of fish" – and so on (Anaxandrides fr. 40 K.-A.; cf. Antiphanes fr. 145 K.-A. Lycon (the eel "equal to a god"), Archippus fr. 23 K.-A., Euripides, *Helen* 865–867; Aristophanes, *Birds* 507 with Dunbar 1995: 346–347; see Long 1986: 37–38.). The various anecdotes he records concerning the building of Egyptian monuments – of how Kheops prostituted his daughter to raise funds, or the amount of money spent on radishes for the labourers (Herodotus II.124–128) – give rise to, and probably reflect, a *topos* of the Egyptians as, in the phrase of Livingstone (2001: 76), "a nation of ant-like, comically superstitious menial workers".[23] Similarly, many of Herodotus' (II.147–152; cf. I.96–100) stories of the kings of Egypt – in their emphasis, for example, on the inevitability of kingship (the interregnum giving way to a restoration of monarchy), on the disproportionate influence and cool cruelty of queens (Herodotus II.100, 107), or on the tyrannical abuse of women (Herodotus II.111, 126, 130) – reflect and reinforce a set of clichéd assumptions about the non-Greek world: in the unaccountable climate of foreign monarchies, such tyrannical behaviour is predictable (cf. Herodotus III.80).[24] Last, but not least controversially, his description of (II.104) the Egyptians (in the context of the argument, on the basis of physical resemblance, that the Colchians were Egyptians left behind in Sesostris' campaigns) as "dark-skinned and curly haired" (*melanchroes ... kai oulotriches*) chimes with a consistent emphasis, in portrayals of Egyptians in art and literature, on differences in physiognomy: hair, lips, and noses (see esp. Laurens 1986: 152; cf. Herodotus II.22; Aeschylus, *Supplices* 154–155, 291 ff, *PV* 851–852; Hall 1989: 139–143; Snowden 1981; West 1984).

Though Herodotus may, in some of his explicit judgments, strike poses in contrast to other, more explicitly chauvinistic Greek sources, in general his account – far from representing an elite intellectual viewpoint opposed to popular prejudice – is, at least in its selection of themes and topics, in fact rooted in a broader, more popular milieu (cp. Laurens 1986). Even his outright rejection of the story of Heracles' escape from imminent death on the altar (Herodotus II.45) should be seen in the context of a long tradition of versions of the same story, on vases and in literature: the king responsible, Busiris, unnamed by Herodotus, is then whimsically transformed by Isocrates from a lawless violator of the bonds of friendship into a model of just kingship (Laurens 1986: 147–148; for Isocrates, see Livingstone 2001).[25]

Moreover, even in his rejection of a crude hellenocentric chauvinism, even in his elevation of Egypt as a more ancient and exemplary culture, there are further twists. Most of the names of the gods may have arrived in Greece from Egypt, but by Herodotus' own day, as a result of receiving gods from other peoples (Poseidon from the Libyans, other gods from the Pelasgians and so on), the Greeks have clearly overtaken the Egyptians in their knowledge of the gods, if they have not indeed discovered all the gods worth discovering (Harrison 2000b: ch. 8). It is hard to resist the conclusion that, by closing themselves off to all foreign customs (Herodotus II.97; cf. II.79, 91, IV.76; but see Strabo XVII.1.19, who asserts that the Egyptians are unfairly maligned on this charge), Egypt for Herodotus has become transformed into a kind of museum of an earlier stage of development (cf. Thucydides I.6). The Egyptians' own insularity, indeed their 'Egyptocentrism,' allows ironically for the reassertion of a hellenocentrism. His observation that the Egyptians call barbarians all those who do not speak their own language (Herodotus II.158; cf. I.134) not only indicates the relative or subjective status of the definition of the barbarian (Thomas 2000: 131) but validates the Greeks in their own viewpoint: "Insofar as this attitude is reasonable in the Egyptians, so also is it reasonable in the Greeks ... Thus cultural relativism becomes ethnocentric and serves to reinforce the tourist's own norms; since he is Greek it is proper that he continues to be Greek" (Redfield 1985: 100). Herodotus' (II.41) account of the Greeks' own ritual impurity in the eyes of the Egyptians may be intended simply to discomfit his own audience or readership, but it also falls into a greater pattern of the representation of foreign peoples in terms of religion: though a clear principle is enunciated (Herodotus III.38) that men should respect the gods revered by others, it is characteristically foreign peoples rather than Greeks who perform acts of sacrilege – thus paradoxically giving grounds for Greek intolerance (Harrison 2000b: ch. 8, esp. 216–218; cf. I.182 with Harrison 2000b: 88–90).[26]

A final twist, or set of twists, lurks behind the Egyptians' reputation for antiquity. The Egyptians may, in their cultivation of memory and through their use of written records, be the most learned of men (Herodotus II.77), but as Hartog (2002: 215; cf. 1988: 277–283) has written, "this undeniable knowledge implies ... neither the appreciation nor the value of writing as such ... nor the devaluation of orality". Herodotus indulges in no *coup de théâtre* of the type performed by Plato – with Athens suddenly upstaging all rivals in antiquity (Hartog 2002: 217–220; cp. Vasunia 2001: ch. 4). Instead he suggests delicately that the uninterrupted good fortune of Egypt is under threat. His account of the inundation of the Nile, for example, and of the effortless ease with which the Egyptians below Memphis gather their harvests draws a contrast between the Greeks' (apparently virtuous) dependence on Zeus for rain and the Egyptians' seemingly complacent reliance on the inundation.[27] The Egyptians, learning of this difference, claimed that the Greeks would "one day suffer terrible hunger after being disappointed of their great hope" (Herodotus II.13–14). Herodotus, however, opines that, if the level of the land were to continue to rise as a result of the alluvial deposits of the Nile, it would be the Egyptians who would be left in this predicament.

Another reversal is implicit in the position of the Egyptian digression in Herodotus' narrative. Egypt's long, untroubled history – a history so stable that the constant nature of their seasons ensures good health (Herodotus II.77), that on the four occasions (in all of 11,340 years) that the sun changed its course the harvest was unaffected, and there were no diseases or deaths (Herodotus II.142) – becomes complete, in Herodotus' account, in the reign of Amasis. Egyptian good fortune then reached a peak, with the Nile providing sustenance for as many as 20,000 cities (Herodotus II.177). It is at this juncture, however, that Egypt meets with its greatest reversal: the Persian invasion, and Cambyses' promised turning of Egypt "upside down" (Herodotus III.3). Amasis himself, so confident in his own good fortune that he had broken off his friendship with the Samian tyrant Polycrates on the grounds of Polycrates' uninterrupted run of success (Herodotus III.39–43), had been safely embalmed and interred – only to have his body removed from its resting place, lashed with whips and pricked with gourds, and then finally burnt (Herodotus III.16). One other reversal of nature stood as a sign of the Egyptians' impending cataclysm: for the first and last time in Thebes it rained (Herodotus III.10).

## Notes

1. All abbreviations agree with those listed in the third edition of *The Oxford Classical Dictionary*. For Greek borrowings from Persia which run against the grain of Greek anti-Persian ideology, see Miller 1997.
2. For a dispassionate analysis of these 'students' of Egypt that predates the *Black Athena* controversy see Lloyd 1975–1989: I.49–60.
3. For a contrast of Aeschylus' *Persians* (performed 472) and Herodotus' *Histories* (written ca. 420s), see Harrison 2000a: esp. ch. 10.
4. See here Miller 1997: 16–18 with speculative flashes ("Every squadron relieved must have taken back to Greece their share of booty and stories").
5. See also the echoes of Herodotus at e.g. Diodorus Siculus I.36.8 (cf. II.97), 37–41, 69.3, or Vidal-Naquet 1964: 427 for an echo of Herodotus' Proem at Plato *Timaeus* 20e.
6. The word, seemingly preserved accurately (Černý 1943; Lambdin 1953), was in Hecataeus, *FGrHist* 1 F 324a. Herodotus' knowledge of foreign vocabulary is generally limited to luxury items and exotica (Harrison 1998).

7   These themes were also mined by other authors: Sophocles fr. 395, 712 Radt (mummies); Aristophanes *Birds* 504–506 (with Dunbar 1995: 344–345), Anaxandrides fr. 40 K.-A., Antiphanes fr. 145 Lycon K.-A., Timocles fr. 1 K.-A., Archippus fr. 23 K.-A. (animal worship); Homer *Odyssey* IV.219–234 (medicine).

8   See Meiggs-Lewis 7a for the description of Greek soldiers at Abu Simbel as *alloglosos* (of another language); for Egyptian attitudes to foreign languages more broadly, see Donadoni 1980. Now see Moyer 2002, emphasizing the agency of Herodotus' non-Greek sources.

9   And which is perhaps most clearly illustrated through an exception: after describing the peoples of Libya, Herodotus comments that most of these Libyan tribes had taken little notice of the Persian king, IV.197.

10  For the structure of the *Histories* as preparing for the Persian wars, see further Harrison 2002b. For ethnographic digressions as integral to Herodotus' narrative, see Lattimore 1958: 14.

11  See here Lloyd I.141–147 for the category of *to thômasion* (the marvellous) as central to Book II.

12  Cf. I.202.1 (the river Araxes has "many islands in it, some nearly equal in size to Lesbos", I.203.1 (the Caucasus the largest and tallest of mountains, containing "many and varied peoples of men").

13  Contrast the slightly churlish attitude of Diodorus Siculus I.9.5–6, denying the Egyptians' greater antiquity against Ephorus. See Vasunia 2001: ch. 3.

14  See esp. Vannicelli 1997; for parallels, see Sulek 1989; for Herodotus' conception of foreign languages, Harrison 1998.

15  For the tension in Herodotus' account of the Persian wars between a pragmatic acceptance of the military strength of Persia and a more stereotyped portrayal, see Harrison 2002b (with further bibliography). Contrast Herodotus V.3, where potential Thracian strength depends on either common purpose or a single ruler.

16  Cf. Strabo XVII.1.46 (Theban inscriptions reflecting past dominion over Scythians, Bactrians, Indians, Ionia), Diodorus Siculus I.53 ff (Sesostris), I.47.6 (Theban reliefs depicting Bactrian war). For the stelae from Asia Minor (possibly Hittite) that Herodotus attributes to Sesostris as proof of his conquests, see West 1992.

17  Contrast Isocrates, *Panegyricus* 140 in the context of a later Egyptian rebellion.

18  Cf. II.177 (Solon's borrowing of the law that every man should declare his source of income).

19  This sits uncomfortably perhaps with the remark, I.30, that Solon travelled to Egypt after implementing his reforms.

20  Contrast the version of Panyassis, Matthews 1974: 126–127.

21  For a similar schematism perhaps, see Strabo XVII.1.2 citing Eratosthenes on the shape of the Nile resembling the letter N reversed.

22  E.g. Aeschylus fr. 373 (Egyptians "terribly good at weaving wiles", with Hall 1989: 123), Aristophanes *Thesmophoriazusae* 922, Cratinus fr. 406 K.-A., Strabo XVII.1.29, Hyperides III.3, 26 (with Whitehead 2000: 266, 269–270, 287–288).

23  See e.g. Aristophanes, *Frogs* 1406 (not even a hundred Egyptians could lift the two chariots envisaged as being introduced on stage by Aeschylus), *Birds* 1133–1137 (birds need no Egyptians to build their city but 30,000 cranes from Egypt).

24  See here Hartog 2002: 216, emphasizing political above other factors; cf. Aeschylus, *Supplices* 370–375, with Hall 1989: 193. For the role of women in Greek representations of foreign monarchies, see e.g. Harrison 2000a: chs. 3, 8.

25  The image of Egyptians as lawless is common: cf. Aeschylus, *Supplices* 387–391, 914, 916–920, 934–937, with Hall 1989: 197, 199. For the contrasting image of Egypt in Homer, cf. *Odyssey* IV.125–135, XIV.285–286, though as Livingstone (2001: 74) comments, "there is still a sense that Egypt, like fairyland, is perilous as well as magical, dangerous to enter and difficult to leave".

26  For an argument that Plato's Atlantis owes a 'conceptual debt' to the real Egypt, see Gwyn Griffiths 1985. For its relationship to Athenian political ideology, see Morgan 1998.

27  See Harrison 2000b: 59–60. For the effortlessness of Egyptian agriculture, cf. Herodotus I.193; Aristophanes *Birds* 504–507; Diodorus Siculus I.36.4–5; contrast Strabo XVII.1.3. Herodotus' contrast is reflected at Aristophanes *Thesmophoriazusae* 855–857, with a character pretending to be Helen asserting (tr. Henderson): "These are the fair-maidened currents of the Nile, who in lieu of heavenly distilment floods the flats of bright Egypt for a people much given to laxatives (*melanosurmaion*)."

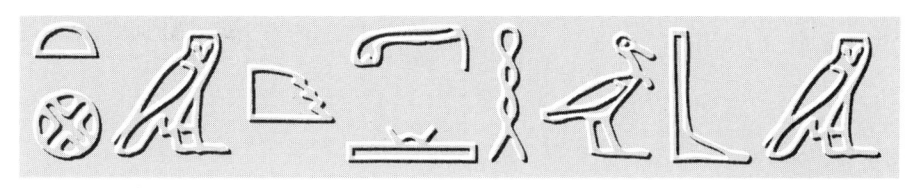

# CHAPTER 9

# ENCOUNTERS WITH ANCIENT EGYPT: THE HELLENISTIC GREEK EXPERIENCE

*Csaba A. La'da*

Encounters with foreigners, either as successful or unsuccessful invaders or as peaceful immigrants, were frequent experiences of the Ancient Egyptians and represent a crucially important force in the shaping of the history and culture of Egypt throughout the millennia. As a result, from the earliest times Egyptian outlook fundamentally divided the world into *kmt* and *dšrt*, that is, the nurturing and familiar black earth of Egypt and the hostile red earth of the desert, symbolizing the outside world. In this *Weltanschauung*, Egyptians (*rmṯ.w n*) *kmt* stood opposed to foreigners, usually referred to as *ḫ3sty.w* 'foreigners' or 'desert dwellers'[1] or, alternatively, by a large number of different ethnic designations (e.g. La'da 1996; Zibelius 1972).

Of all ancient peoples, the Greeks had probably the most extensive and fruitful encounter with Egypt. Documented contacts between Egypt and the Greeks span approximately two millennia, stretching from the Aegean Bronze Age to the loss of Egypt by the Byzantine empire to the Arabs in 641 AD. Here I survey and examine the nature of this interaction between Egyptians and Greeks in the hellenistic period, the period in which the two peoples and cultures experienced some of the closest and most enduring encounters with one another, which produced profound and long-lasting results for both civilizations.

A large number of aspects could be mentioned, encompassing practically all areas of life, a testimony to the extent and depth of the interaction between Greeks and Egyptians in the hellenistic period, e.g. the Greek impact on the Egyptian economy, for which there is evidence already from the first period of Persian domination in Egypt (Chauveau 1996a: 411, 1996b: 41–42 n. 14) and the introduction of Greek technological innovations and management techniques. Various areas of intellectual life could be discussed: cross-cultural influences in literature, sculpture (Ashton 2003), painting, medicine, astronomy and astrology, architecture and other branches of art and science. The problem of languages in contact forms another very important and large field. In this chapter, I concentrate on the key political and social factors of the encounter between Greeks and Egyptians, which created the essential framework for cross-cultural interaction and to a large extent predetermined its dynamics. I focus principally on theoretical questions, using examples from the sources to illustrate them, as it seems that there is a certain amount of confusion in this regard in the secondary literature and that, due to recent research and new sources, a major revision of current fundamental views of the society and culture of hellenistic Egypt has become inevitable.

Relations between Egypt and the areas of the Aegean and the Mediterranean settled by the Greeks are of great antiquity (Assmann 2000; Austin 1970; De Salvia 1989; Vercoutter 1997; and the exhibition catalogue Karetsou 1999). Contact with Minoan Crete and the Mycenaean Greeks is well attested. The image of Egypt is already firmly established in the Homeric poems and a plethora of Egyptian artefacts has been unearthed in Greece, the Aegean and even in western Greek colonies such as Cumae and Pithecusa in Italy from as early as the eighth century. The seventh century brought a significant broadening of relations: the first major Greek colony was established on Egyptian soil. Naucratis, founded in the Delta on the Canopic branch of the Nile in the reign of Psammetichos I (664–610), played a crucial role in channelling the flow of trade, people and ideas between Egypt and the Greeks. Besides merchants and their wares, an increasing number of mercenaries came from Greece to help to realize the political aspirations of the kings of the twenty-sixth Dynasty.

The late seventh century opened a qualitatively new chapter in relations. In addition to the tangible exchange of objects and goods, from the time of Solon there appears to have been a certain kind of abstract intellectual contact. There survive a growing number of works written in Greek which demonstrate some measure of familiarity with Egypt and Egyptian thought or at least claim to have been influenced by them. The list of the authors of such works is impressive: Solon, Hecataeus of Miletus, Herodotus, Euripides and Plato to name only the best known.

Finally, the fifth and especially the fourth century brought an intensification of military contacts. This took the form of anti-Persian co-operation between Greek city-states and, first, Egyptian rebels and then the pharaohs of the twenty-ninth and thirtieth Dynasties, who struggled, ultimately unsuccessfully, to preserve their independence in the face of the Persian threat.

It was against this historical background of Egypto-Greek relations that Alexander the Great and his army victoriously entered Egypt in December 332 BC. As the second period of Persian domination was particularly oppressive, the natives welcomed Alexander as their liberator. In the decades which followed, Alexander and his successors in Egypt, the Ptolemies, gradually built up a highly sophisticated and centralized state, which was to last for over three centuries until Octavian the later Augustus finally "added Egypt to the empire of the Roman people" (*Res Gestae* 27) in 30 BC.

One of the most immediate and tangible impacts on Egypt of Alexander's conquest and Ptolemaic rule was immigration. Although Egypt had always acted as a powerful magnet for invaders and immigrants alike, Alexander's conquest opened a new era in the history of the country from the point of view of immigration: a sustained period of mass immigration. Hundreds of thousands of foreign settlers poured into the country from practically all over the then known world, attracted by the prospect of employment, land and rich economic opportunities. In addition, a large number of foreign slaves and prisoners of war were brought to Egypt by its new rulers. For example, according to the *Letter of Aristeas*, Ptolemy I deported 100,000

Jewish prisoners from Palestine to Egypt, although the numbers in this report are greatly exaggerated (Modrzejewski 1991: 65).

The best and most reliable quantifiable evidence available for the history of immigration to Egypt in the hellenistic period are the ethnic labels referring to individuals in the papyrological and epigraphic source material (La'da 1996, the database of which is in preparation for publication). There are close to 150 different foreign ethnic terms attested in the Greek and demotic sources,[2] which demonstrates the ethnic and geographical heterogeneity of the immigrants. Although they originated from a large number of different ethnic groups inhabiting regions all over the Mediterranean, the Black Sea coast, Asia Minor, the Near East and north-eastern Africa, numerically the most dominant group was undoubtedly formed by the Greeks and the by then largely hellenized Macedonians. In addition, a significant number of immigrants arrived from other, previously more or less hellenized peoples in Europe and Asia Minor, such as the Thracians and the Carians. On the evidence of the ethnic designations found in the documents, Thracians seem to have constituted the third largest group of immigrants to the Egyptian *chora* after the Greeks and Macedonians. Other large immigrant groups were formed by the Jews, Arabs, Mysians and Syrians. Thus, in the hellenistic period the principal sources of immigration to Egypt were to some extent reorientated away from such traditionally important sources as Syria-Palestine, Libya and Nubia towards Greece, Macedonia, areas of the eastern and central Mediterranean inhabited by Greeks and to other parts of the Balkans and Asia Minor.

Ethnic designations in the documents can also provide information about the chronology of immigration to hellenistic Egypt. They suggest that immigration peaked in the third century, dramatically declining in the second and coming to a virtual halt in the first century, although there is very little evidence for the period before the 280s and for the first century.

Alexander's conquest was followed by a sustained period of mass immigration, the scale and ethnic and geographical diversity of which were unprecedented in Egyptian history. This process, which took place as part of a wider population movement from the north-eastern Mediterranean towards the Near East, seems to have lasted until about the end of the third century and brought in mostly Greeks, Macedonians and other peoples from the Balkans and Asia Minor, as well as smaller numbers of people from ethnic groups located in the Near East. As a consequence, a large proportion of the population of hellenistic Egypt was of foreign descent, although the exact numbers and proportions are ultimately indeterminable. These conclusions are unequivocally corroborated by other types of evidence, such as ancient Greek historians and archaeology.

It is particularly difficult to reconstruct what image of Egypt these Greek and Macedonian immigrants brought with them to their new country, apart from the fact that they must obviously have considered it an especially attractive destination from an economic point of view. The difficulty involved in this is due not only to a lack of direct sources but also to the fact that it is hard to gauge how much influence the ideas of Greek intellectuals exercised on ordinary people in the early hellenistic period. Nevertheless, in the light of the generally positive Greek intellectual approaches to Egypt and Egyptian civilization in the archaic, classical and early hellenistic periods (cf. Assmann 2000: 83–92), it seems reasonable to assume that these immigrants, and especially their more educated elite, arrived with a positive image of Egypt. Certainly, the intellectual attitude of the majority of Greco-Macedonian immigrants was in general open and receptive to at least some aspects of Egyptian culture. This is strongly suggested by the speedy adoption of particular Egyptian religious ideas and imagery by the new immigrants (e.g. Hölbl 1993, 1994: 256, 2001: 281; stela P. L. Bat. XX F). No doubt the ground had been prepared to some extent by the spread of the Isis cult to Greece early in the hellenistic period (Hölbl 1994: 78, 2001: 85) and by the participation of pre-hellenistic Greek immigrants to Egypt in native cults (Hölbl 1994: 93, 2001: 99; Thompson 1988: 96).

An important role must have been played in this regard by the example which Alexander's and the early Ptolemies' attitude towards Egyptian religion and their religious policies gave their Greek and Macedonian subjects. Alexander's attempt to win divine legitimacy through the oracle of Amun at Siwa, his respect for Egyptian religious and political traditions, his sacrifices to various Egyptian deities, his sacred building activity – especially his foundation of an Isis temple in Alexandria (Arrian *Anabasis* III.1.5, Hölbl 1994: 78, 2001: 85) – and possibly also his coronation in the traditional Egyptian manner (Q. Curtius Rufus IV.7.5; Hölbl 1994: 9, 69–70, 80; 2001: 9–10, 77–78, 88), all suggest wide-ranging co-operation with the Egyptian clergy, and set the tone for the rest of the hellenistic period. Whether inspired by mere political calculation, genuine religious devotion or perhaps by the appreciation generations of Greek intellectuals showed of Egyptian civilization, the Ptolemies followed Alexander's example through their active religious policy (see Hölbl 1994, 2001: chs. III (3), VI (6) and IX (9)). Numerous aspects of this policy seem to suggest not only that the Ptolemies were open and receptive to Egyptian culture, especially religion, but also that they had, obviously to a varying extent, a positive attitude towards it.[3] These aspects include, for example, the expensive temple building programme undertaken on a huge scale all over the country, the official acceptance and widespread application of Egyptian religious ideology and imagery, the increasing adoption of the Egyptian theory of kingship, the creation of the Serapis cult and the generous royal patronage it enjoyed, as well as Manetho's active involvement at the court in the shaping of this religious policy and the royal encouragement he received to write a history of Egypt and perhaps other works on Egyptian religion. This positive attitude undoubtedly reached its climax on both the ideological and artistic planes under Cleopatra VII.

The generally open and positive attitude that the Ptolemies and their Greco-Macedonian subjects appear to have had towards Egyptian religion and also to some other aspects of Egyptian culture no doubt had an important and beneficial influence upon the nature of interaction which developed between the Ptolemaic state and its native Egyptian subjects, on the one hand, and between Greeks and Egyptians, on the other.

Another factor which played a crucially important role in determining the dynamics of the interaction between Egyptians and Greeks was the political and strategic situation of Egypt in the hellenistic world.

Alexander the Great died suddenly in 323 BC and in the ensuing power struggle among his successors, one of his generals, Ptolemy, son of Lagos, secured Egypt for himself. Having victoriously defended his dominion from challenges several times on the battlefield, he made himself king and pharaoh of Egypt in 306/304 BC, founding the dynasty which was to be the most successful and long-lasting of all hellenistic royal dynasties. The fragmentation of Alexander's empire and the emergence of separate and often hostile hellenistic kingdoms from its ruins meant that the Ptolemies were forced to rely on Egypt as their one and only home base. Although they did possess territories outside Egypt proper, such as Cyrenaica, Cyprus, parts of the Aegean and the southern coast of Asia Minor, these possessions, which were entirely due to Egypt's economic and military might, were lost over time. This loss must obviously have hugely increased Egypt's strategic value to the Ptolemies. Immigration to Egypt declined sharply by the end of the third century and in the hostilities of this century Egypt was gradually cut off from its traditional recruiting grounds and sources of mercenaries in Greece and Macedonia. The emergency situation before the battle of Raphia in 217 BC, when an acute and dangerous shortage of Greek and Macedonian soldiers occurred, forced Ptolemy IV to arm for the first time large numbers of native and Libyan troops. This powerfully conveyed the message that the Macedonian monarchs of Egypt could no longer rely on foreigners and outside support to maintain their rule over the country in the face of both external and internal threats.

The fact that the Ptolemaic dynasty was forced by these political circumstances to make Egypt its sole power base represents another radically different characteristic of the Macedonian conquest and rule. In almost all previous and subsequent periods of foreign domination, Egypt was attached and subjected, as a vanquished province, to a foreign empire and ruled from outside. Its resources were channelled out of the country, draining it of its wealth. In the Ptolemaic period, however, a dynasty, which albeit foreign in origin came progressively to identify with Egypt, ruled the country from within. Although the Ptolemies spent vast sums on foreign campaigns and expensive gifts to further their political aims, the economic resources of the country substantially remained within it, benefiting the local population. This is in sharp contrast with the Roman period, for instance, when Egypt was gradually and ruthlessly bled of its wealth through the taxes it was forced to pay to its master. Thanks to the Ptolemies' efforts, in the third century Egypt regained its 'great power' status in the Near East and the eastern Mediterranean basin, which it had lost 700 years previously at the end of the New Kingdom. No power in the eastern and central Mediterranean and the Near East could afford to ignore Egypt any longer.

Thus, the scene is set: a country which was conquered by a foreign power but which eventually became an independent kingdom again, albeit under foreign monarchs. The ruling dynasty often had to struggle to protect its grip on power from both foreign threats and internal revolts. Large numbers of immigrants, probably in the hundreds of thousands, poured in and settled, making Egypt their permanent home. As a consequence, a significant proportion of the population came to be of foreign descent. After more than a century, however, large-scale immigration came to a halt. These are the key factors that had important consequences for the dynamics of the interaction between Egyptians and Greeks, the two largest ethnic groups sharing the country.

In any systematic analysis of the relations between different ethnic groups in any society, a fundamental distinction must be made between two large spheres of interaction: the official and the private. It is essential to realize that official or state policy, either openly declared or undisclosed, towards different ethnic groups is in most polities quite different from private attitudes. Nevertheless, it is obvious that official policy can and usually does have a strong influence upon ethnic interaction in the private sphere.

What kind of state and society was hellenistic Egypt from the perspective of ethnicity? What role did ethnic differences play and what significance did the Ptolemaic government attach to them in the distribution of political power and material wealth? To put it more abstractly, was hellenistic Egypt a stratified multi-ethnic polity which was characterized by differential control of power and wealth by different ethnic groups or, rather, did ethnicity play a minimal role, or no role at all, in social stratification?

And if ethnicity did play some role in the social stratification of hellenistic Egypt, precisely how important was this role? Was it an openly discriminatory state in which differentiation between the Greco-Macedonian immigrants and the natives was explicitly codified in the laws and expressed in the institutions of the state (type 1: openly discriminatory state)? To use a modern example, which has been referred to in recent research (see Ritner 1992: 290), was hellenistic Egypt a state similar to South Africa under the apartheid regime where the hierarchy and segregation of different racial groups were enshrined in the laws and strictly enforced?

Or was hellenistic Egypt a covertly discriminatory state, which, although it had no discriminatory laws and institutions, in practice had a discriminatory agenda and in its practical acts strengthened and promoted the immigrants at the expense of the natives (type 2: covertly discriminatory state)? Modern examples would be the former Soviet Union and Yugoslavia, where the laws guaranteed equality to all irrespective of ethnic background and where the governments claimed to uphold all human rights, but in reality both countries practised a deliberate policy of expulsion, discrimination and forced assimilation of ethnic groups they considered undesirable. Both of these states have recently been confined to history by internal ethnic strife as a direct consequence of precisely the ethnic inequalities they fostered.

Or, finally, was hellenistic Egypt a non-discriminatory state in which ethnicity played no role in governmental policy, the laws and the institutions of the state (type 3: non-discriminatory state)? This, however, would not necessarily mean that ethnicity had no role at all in social stratification: ethnic prejudice and discrimination between immigrants and natives may well have had some part in the structuring of society, even without an overt or covert discriminatory policy on the part of the Ptolemaic state. To understand how this could have been possible, the example of modern western Europe and North America may be helpful. There the equal rights of different ethnic and racial minorities are enshrined in the laws, and most states genuinely try to implement them, but there is more or less widespread prejudice by the majority ethnic group against minorities, resulting in various forms of discrimination and even racially motivated crime.

Different answers to these questions were provided by scholars working in different periods. Nineteenth and early 20th century scholarship conceptualized the hellenistic kingdoms of the Near East on the model of their own contemporary colonial experience. Thus, for them the conquering Macedonians and Greeks formed the ruling elite of society, a true ethno-class, which ruled the vanquished and exploited masses of the natives (type 1). This colonial model of the societies of the hellenistic Near East remained influential, albeit in a modified form, until as late as the 1970s.

It was replaced in the 1970s by a conceptual approach which emphasized not so much the hierarchical nature of society and culture in hellenistic Egypt along ethnic lines as the separateness (*étanchéité*) of the two ethnic groups and cultures. The central tenet of this approach was that the Greeks and the Egyptians led a separate coexistence in the same country with little interaction between them (a variant of type 1) (Préaux 1978, II: 588; Samuel 1989: 10, 35–49; cf. Goudriaan 1992: 95; and for a criticism, see Ritner 1992: 289–290). It seems hardly a coincidence that this theory was put forward and developed by scholars working in countries – Belgium and Canada – which experienced, in exactly this period, intense struggles for political power, cultural influence and territorial separation between the two main rival ethnic groups.

These two previous models of the society of hellenistic Egypt are invalidated not only by the obvious fact that they are unable to account for the complex and widely varied available evidence (see below) and prove inadequate for interpreting it meaningfully, but also by the fact that they appear to have been inspired to a large extent by the contemporary social and political contexts in which they were conceived (cf. Ritner 1992: 283–290).

I (1996: ch. 4) examined in great detail central aspects of the functioning of the Ptolemaic state, such as the administrative classification of the population, the taxation, the legal system, the use of different languages for official purposes and the role of native Egyptians in the state machinery and the upper classes. In none of these central areas was there any clear evidence for ethnic differences playing a fundamental or even a significant role. On the basis of this research, in the period for which there is evidence, there is no indication of systematic and institutionalized ethnic discrimination on the part of the central government in favour of the Greco-Macedonian immigrants and/or against the native Egyptians. Ptolemaic society cannot, therefore, be described as a poly-ethnic system which was based on, or even contained an element of, overt and institutionalized ethnic discrimination.[4] Thus, according to the broad typology sketched out above, in the period between the 280s and 30 BC hellenistic Egypt was not a type 1 state, although the possibility remains that in the period before the 280s it was, and that it gradually evolved into type 2 or 3.

The evidence available from hellenistic Egypt allows further refinement of our understanding of the role of ethnicity in the Ptolemaic state and society. On the basis of this evidence, it is possible to exclude not only the proposition that ethnicity played an open, codified and institutionalized role in the state (type 1) but also that it had a covert and uninstitutionalized, nevertheless significant, part (type 2). In other words, the Ptolemaic government was not covertly and consciously discriminatory towards its subjects of different ethnic backgrounds: it did not deliberately try to promote and strengthen the Greco-Macedonian immigrants as such at the expense of the Egyptians.

First, the Ptolemaic government's policy, predominantly in the fourth and third centuries, of attracting foreign soldiers and settling some of them on land as *cleruchs* principally in the Arsinoite and Oxyrhynchite nomes may be better understood in the light of security concerns rather than in terms of discrimination. It is understandable that, especially initially, foreign, mainly Greek and Macedonian, soldiers were expected to be more reliable and loyal to the Macedonian dynasty than native Egyptians. In addition, these Greco-Macedonian troops recruited by the Ptolemies represented the cutting edge of contemporary hellenistic warfare, a crucial consideration for the Ptolemies facing numerous threats from other hellenistic kingdoms with large Greco-Macedonian armies. In contrast, the military value of native Egyptian troops seems to have been quite modest. Finally, the areas of settlement of the foreign *cleruchs* suggest that the Ptolemaic government did its best to minimize ethnic tensions potentially generated by its settlement policy; the chief area of the settlement of foreign soldiers appears to have been the Arsinoite nome, the cultivable area of which was radically expanded by government land reclamation schemes in the early Ptolemaic period.

Further, although *argumenta ex silentio* are often questionable methodologically, it is still highly significant in this case, precisely because of the unusually large quantity of written sources from hellenistic Egypt, that there is not a particle of evidence in the surviving material to suggest that the Ptolemaic state had ethnic policies on the ground which were different from its laws. No dichotomy between laws and practical policies is detectable from the point of view of ethnicity, in direct contradiction to the characteristics of states falling into type 2 of the above general typology.

Furthermore, there is no evidence in the unusually large amount of source material for systematic, organized and widespread discrimination against ethnic Egyptians and/or in favour of Greco-Macedonian immigrants, which is, by definition, a hallmark of states practising covert ethnic discrimination. There is no evidence at all, for example, of expulsion of the natives from their land in order to settle immigrants, a common practice of discriminatory states. On the contrary, the Ptolemaic state preferred large-scale land reclamation schemes, principally in the Fayum, to expand the cultivable land available for the settlement of new immigrants. In addition, during the disturbances of the second half of the second century some of this land in the Fayum reclaimed by the early Ptolemies and originally settled by foreign immigrants was taken away and handed over to native soldiers loyal to the central power (Thompson 1994: 313).

The use of the language of the natives, demotic, was not pushed out of officialdom and relegated to the private sphere, as happened in discriminatory states. Although the upper levels of Ptolemaic administration functioned in Greek, demotic remained widespread and well entrenched at its lower and middle levels. It continued to be used also in the Egyptian administration of justice and in education.

Further, the Ptolemaic government did not impose a Greek legal system and Greek laws on the country. The Ptolemaic administration created a unique legal system which allowed a plurality of laws and judicial structures (Greek, Egyptian and

Jewish) to exist and function alongside each other. In this system of legal plurality, from 118 BC it was the language of the documents and not the ethnic background of the individuals involved in the case that decided which court adjudicated the case under which law (Modrzejewski 1984). The native Egyptian legal system not only continued to function under the Ptolemies but was expressly protected by royal legislation from encroachment upon its areas of competence, as is clear from the royal prostagma of 118 (*P. Tebt.* I 5 = C.Ord.Ptol.$^2$ 53; cf. Goudriaan 1988: 96–100).

Finally, and in part as a consequence of the above, there is surprisingly little obviously ethnic tension between the Greco-Macedonian immigrants and the natives perceptible in the extensive available source material (cf. Goudriaan 1988: 107–108; Ritner 1992: 289). Considering the volume of evidence, cases of ethnic friction and expressions of ethno-cultural prejudice on the individual level remain extremely rare until the late Ptolemaic and early Roman period, when the direct involvement of Rome in Egyptian matters and her introduction of a differential legal and tax system on the basis of legal and ethno-cultural criteria polarized the ethnic groups inhabiting Egypt.

In addition, most of the so-called 'native' rebellions have convincingly been shown to have been motivated mainly by economic and not ethnic grievances. Besides economic causes, political, religious and administrative (officials' abuse of their power) tensions also played a significant part (Goudriaan 1988: 108–115). In most of these uprisings both Egyptians and Greeks took part and/or were directed against not only Greeks but also Egyptians. There is no clear-cut divide along ethnic lines between the two opposing sides. In general, it may be argued that most of these uprisings were targeted not against one ethnic group by another but against the Ptolemaic state and its institutions and representatives by those who felt that the economic burden imposed on them by the state had become intolerable. Ethnic tensions and Egyptian 'nationalism' played no, or only a secondary, role here (Peremans 1978; Préaux 1936; cf. Hölbl 1994: 135–136, 2001: 153–154; McGing 1997: 282–283, 288, 292–293), which is why Greeks and Egyptians are found on both sides.[5] This probably accounts, for example, for native rebels attacking Egyptian temples, as well as their priests, in the Fayum in the 160s, as these temples in all likelihood played a key role in the economic and administrative life of the surrounding countryside (Hölbl 1994: 157, 2001: 181; McGing 1997: 289–293). In general, it seems that the term 'Egyptian rebellions' and other similar expressions have been misapplied by the sources, which are mainly Greek and among which Greek historians from outside Egypt tend to dominate, to describe not so much anti-Greek but rather anti-government uprisings. Since the Ptolemaic state projected a predominantly hellenic image abroad, and since these historians from outside Egypt tended to equate the Ptolemaic state with the Greek and Macedonian immigrants, by the force of this logic, those opposing it necessarily had to be cast as Egyptians.

From approximately the 280s onwards, the Ptolemaic state does not appear to have been a covertly discriminatory state in which the Greco-Macedonian immigrants would have enjoyed privileges over the natives merely by virtue of their ethnicity (type 2). Hellenistic Egypt was neither an openly nor a covertly discriminatory state in which ethnicity would have played a direct and significant role in social stratification, although the possibility cannot be excluded that it started as either of these two broad models.

These conclusions leave type 3, i.e. a non-discriminatory state, as the only possible model for hellenistic Egypt in this period. The fact that there does not appear to have been any overt or even covert ethnic discrimination on the part of the Ptolemaic state against the natives and/or in favour of the Greco-Macedonian immigrants does not, however, mean that there was full equality between these two ethnic groups. Despite the absence of discriminatory laws and policies, native Egyptians did suffer some discrimination and there are a few, though proportionately extremely rare, instances of prejudice expressed against them in the papyrological sources.

The clearest example of ethnic inequality in Ptolemaic society is the fact that it is not until the second century that a rising number of natives in the secular upper classes and in top jobs in the administration and the army are first found. The explanation for this, however, lies not in a systematic policy of discrimination, as previous research has argued (and for which, as has been seen, there is no evidence at all), but in the constraints which trust and language imposed, to a large extent, upon the structure of the court and administration, especially in the early hellenistic period. By the internal logic of a situation where a foreign court comes to rule a conquered foreign land, the practical constraints of language and trust predetermined the membership of the ruling elite (Peremans 1978: 48; cf. the royal court in early Norman England: Stenton 1971: 624–634, 637); Ptolemy I was forced to rely on his most trusted relatives and friends initially to consolidate his grip on the country and then to direct and run the state machinery. This is clearly reflected in the honorific aulic titulature in which the top ranks are based on the words συγγενής 'relative' and φίλος 'friend' (Heinen 1973: 95–96; Mooren 1977: 36).[6] These courtiers were obviously Greeks and Macedonians (only one, Manetho, of Soter's six closest confidants was Egyptian (cf. Turner 1984: 125)) and thus the Ptolemaic court, as with other hellenistic courts, was an overwhelmingly Greco-Macedonian court.

As Ptolemy's control over Egypt became more and more secure and he could set about the task of organizing and running the country, his *oikos* gradually grew into an administrative and military apparatus in which the highest positions were filled by his most reliable courtiers, with the exception of apparently very few cases in which the co-operation of Egyptians was essential. Thus, with the extension of the Ptolemaic court into the state machinery, the latter also came to be, at least at its highest levels, a predominantly Greek institution in which Egyptian collaboration was welcome but the most important positions were reserved for the king's Greek and Macedonian confidants.

The overwhelmingly Greek nature of the court and of the highest levels of the administration and the army which evolved during the reign of the first Ptolemy was largely preserved under his successors, despite the apparent lack of systematic ethnic discrimination against the natives and a gradual increase in both the number of Egyptians rising to top posts and a general Egyptian influence on the court (for the growing influence of the priesthood and of the Egyptian ideology of kingship, see Koenen 1983, 1993; Smith 1968). The reasons for the continuation of the predominantly Greco-Macedonian nature of the court and of the highest levels of the administration and the army were probably the sheer weight and inertia of tradition, which was much easier and safer to continue than to break, and also the fact that the very centre of the court, the monarch, remained firmly Macedonian,[7] and needed the expertise of those who could serve him in Greek, on the basis of essentially Greek values. Thus, even if there was no systematic ethnic discrimination, in practice there was at the court and at the highest levels of the administration and the army a natural selection process on the basis of language, cultural background and trust. Therefore, knowledge of Greek and a certain degree of hellenization were essential preconditions for obtaining a high position in the Ptolemaic state machinery. This, together with a certain measure of prejudice against the natives, rather than a putative system of ethnic discrimination, is the reason why the secular upper classes continued to be dominated by Greeks and Macedonians and why it was only in the second century that a gradually increasing number of ethnic Egyptians rose to top posts in the administration and the army.

From at least the 280s onwards, hellenistic Egypt was a poly-ethnic society which was not based on a system of ethnic discrimination, either open or covert, on the part of the government. This agrees well with, and is further supported by, the Ptolemies appearing to have had a generally open and positive attitude towards Egyptian religion and some other aspects of native culture. Nevertheless, there was a certain measure of prejudice and discrimination against the native Egyptians on the part of the incoming Greco-Macedonians, whose upper classes controlled the levers of power. This, coupled with the fact that the court, the higher administration and the army functioned overwhelmingly in Greek and on the basis of Greek cultural values, ensured that the upward social mobility of the natives remained slow.

These conclusions have far-reaching consequences for our understanding of the dynamics of interaction between Greeks and Egyptians. The Ptolemaic state, which from at least approximately the 280s onwards appears to have functioned on the non-discriminatory model, created the broader social context for a free and low-tension interaction between the various ethnic groups and their cultures settled in Egypt. This free and largely non-discriminatory social atmosphere facilitated a lively and intensive exchange of ideas, cultures and also genetic material between Greeks and Egyptians. Greco-Macedonian immigration to Egypt was predominantly military, and therefore male, immigration. As a consequence, a large number of mixed marriages between immigrant men and local Egyptian women is documented in the sources. The widespread practice of intermarriage between Greeks and Egyptians constitutes further proof of the correctness of the above analysis of the nature of the Ptolemaic state and society. It indicates clearly that no legal or institutional barriers were erected and maintained between these ethnic groups by the government. No such separation was enforced by the state as was the case between different legal status groups in Roman Egypt[8] or between different racial groups in apartheid South Africa.

Another phenomenon which is a clear indication of the free, close and widespread socio-cultural interaction between the natives and the Greco-Macedonian immigrants is provided by onomastics. It is striking how many individuals bear a Greek and an Egyptian double name not only in official but also in private documents. The same phenomenon can be observed in both Greek and demotic papyri. The conclusion from this must be that either these were individuals of mixed parentage, who wanted to express this with the names they used in the documents, or they were individuals who, although from one ethnic background, were assimilated to the other and were sufficiently at home in both cultures to use both kinds of names. The frequency of this practice in the sources suggests that it was a common form of cross-cultural interaction, which manifested itself in both the official and the private spheres of life.

Perhaps the best example for the far-reaching and administratively unhindered cross-cultural interaction between Greeks and Egyptians is religion in hellenistic Egypt. It was undoubtedly the most fertile and intense area of interaction. The cross-cultural exchange in this field was prolific and widespread. As already mentioned, in this domain the Greco-Macedonian immigrants seem to have mostly been the recipients. They appear to have been thoroughly fascinated by, and quite open to, Egyptian religion and thus either joined the ranks of its followers or readily assimilated some of its elements into their own cults. As a consequence, curious mixtures resulted with features often difficult to disentangle. Two of the most instructive examples follow.

In one of the earliest preserved Greek papyri from Egypt, from the late fourth century BC, a woman bearing the Greek name Artemisia invokes the Egyptian deity Oserapis (*Wsir-Ḥp*) to punish the father of her daughter, who has denied her a proper burial (UPZI 1=PGM XL). Although the language is Greek, the phraseology is clearly derived from Egyptian religious ideas, closely reflecting contemporary and earlier demotic petitions to gods (cf. Ritner 1992: 289).

Little more than two centuries later (98 BC), former *ephebes* and members of a Greek gymnasium, traditionally a bastion of hellenic identity, erected a stela in the Fayum, dedicating a plot of land to the Egyptian crocodile god Sobek. The top part of the stela is occupied by a winged sundisk protected by a pair of uraei below which lies a crocodile. The depiction of Sobek is entirely Egyptian without the slightest attempt at *interpretatio graeca* (I. Fayoum III, no. 200 = SB V 8885 = OGIS I 176; cf. Ritner 1992: 284).

These striking examples of close and pervasive ethno-cultural interaction between Greeks and Egyptians, the widespread practice of intermarriage, the use of double names and religious syncretism all strongly reinforce the above arguments against an ethnically discriminatory model for the Ptolemaic state, at least from the 280s onwards. In the face of these it seems impossible to maintain, as have advocates of previous models, that hellenistic Egypt was a state and society in which ethnicity played a pivotal role in social stratification and in which the two major ethnic groups and cultures lived in virtual separation from one another.

The ultimate proof of the non-discriminatory model for the state and society of hellenistic Egypt and of the resulting free and close cultural interaction between Greeks and Egyptians is provided, paradoxically, by the early Roman period. By the time the Romans arrived, the process of ethno-cultural integration between Greeks and Egyptians was so advanced that it was hardly possible any more to separate the bulk of the population in the countryside on an ethnic basis. Thus, when the new, Roman rulers of Egypt set about the task of dividing the population into status groups of varying legal and fiscal privilege, implementing their tried and tested principle of "*divide et impera*", they could no longer classify the Egyptian population into purely ethnic categories, as they had intended.[9] Instead, they had to content themselves with a mixture of legal, geographical and cultural principles, although they used literally ethnic terms for two of these status groups. This largely blurred ethno-cultural situation which the Romans found in Egypt was summed up famously by Livy (XXXVIII.17.11) in a statement condemning the descendants of Alexander the Great, which at the same time heralded the arrival of a new mentality of power in Egypt: *"Macedones … in … Aegyptios degenerarunt"*.

## Notes

References to Greek papyri adhere to the conventions of abbreviation employed in Oates *et al.* 1992. References to Greek inscriptions follow the system of abbreviation found in recent epigraphical publications.

1. Wb. V 126–128 and III 234–236; Faulkner 1991: 286 and 185. See also, for example, the military titles: *wr ꜥꜣ n ḫꜣsty.w* 'grand chef des contingents étrangers', *mr mšꜥ n ḫꜣsty.w* 'général des contingents étrangers'; Chevereau 1985: XVI–XVII. Cf. also *rwty* 'outsider', 'stranger' in Wb. II 405 and Faulkner 1991: 147.
2. This number, calculated on the basis of real ethnic designations occurring in official documents, is obviously subject to change as more material is published.
3. See, for example, the famous episode of Berenike II dedicating a lock of her hair for the safe return of her husband, which appears to have been influenced by the Egyptian Isis myths: cf. Hölbl 1994: 99, 2001: 105.
4. This conclusion, reached on the basis of the papyrological and epigraphical source material, agrees well with the evidence of Diodorus Siculus XVIII.14.1. See further Turner 1984: 123; Ritner 1992: 290.
5. A similar case – albeit on the individual level – is that of Ptolemaios, son of Glaukias, the most famous detainee of the Memphite Serapieion, whose conflicts with other characters in the society of the Serapieion probably had mainly economic and perhaps also personal and, despite Ptolemaios' misrepresentation of the situation, not principally ethnic causes. Cf. the interpretations of Goudriaan 1988: 52–57; McGing 1997: 293–294; Thompson 1988: 212–265, esp. 229–230. It is worth noting that the ethnic tensions alleged by Ptolemaios, who portrayed himself as a Greek, did not in any way prevent him from looking after the Egyptian twins and from forming friendly relations with a number of Egyptians.
6. For the Ptolemaic court titulature as a hellenistic Greco-Macedonian development independent of pharaonic Egyptian or other Near-Eastern influences, see Mooren 1975: 233–240, esp. 237.
7. Cf. Plutarch's (*Antony* XXVII.4–5) remark that only Cleopatra VII, the last Ptolemaic ruler of Egypt, took the trouble to learn Egyptian.
8. See the strict regulations concerning marriage between individuals from different status groups in the so-called *Gnomon of Idios Logos* = BGU V 1210.
9. This is revealed by the terminology they used to designate these status-groups, two of which were 'hellenes' and 'Egyptians'. Paradoxically, and characteristically of the by then largely blurred ethno-cultural boundaries in the Egyptian *chora*, especially to outsiders, and of the inadequacy of the Roman approach to the actual situation on the ground, the category designated as 'hellenes' formed the upper layer of the broader category 'Egyptians': cf. BGU V 1210 and Modrzejewski 1989: 241–280 = Modrzejewski 1990: ch. I.

## Acknowledgments

I am extremely grateful to Professor W. J. Tait for his invitation to present a paper at the conference 'Encounters with Ancient Egypt' held at the Institute of Archaeology, University College London between 16 and 18 December 2000, and to Professor C. Roemer for her valuable comments on this chapter. I should further like to thank Professors P. J. Frandsen, D. O'Connor and S. Walker for their comments during the conference.

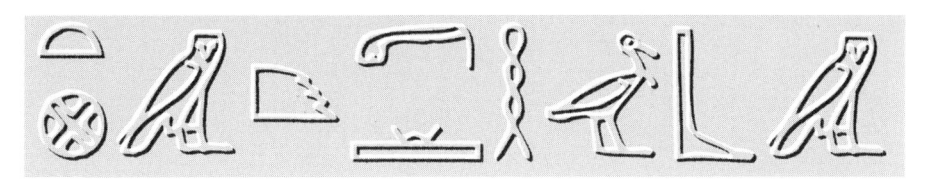

## CHAPTER 10

## PILGRIMAGE IN GRECO-ROMAN EGYPT: NEW PERSPECTIVES ON GRAFFITI FROM THE MEMNONION AT ABYDOS

*Ian Rutherford*

### Introduction

Of all encounters with Ancient Egypt, some of the most interesting are encounters with Egyptian religion. One important context for such encounters is pilgrimage. Some people argue that 'pilgrimage' is a medieval and modern category, difficult to transplant from the context of the salvation religions Christianity and Islam. I use pilgrimage in the broader sense of travel to a sacred place for a sacred reason (e.g. Bhardwaj 1973; Cohen 1992; Morinis 1992).

During the Greco-Roman period there is a wealth of evidence for visits made by people to sites of religious significance. These visits were of various types, not all of which correspond directly to modern categories: sometimes it seems to be something like tourism, for example the visitors who left graffiti on the walls of Theban tombs (Baillet 1920–1926: 6) or even casual visitors, such as soldiers of foreign descent who used sacred buildings as a barracks; in other cases, it seems to approach scientific enquiry, for example the fact-finding tour of Egypt made by the Greek historian Herodotus (Harrison Chapter 8, this volume; Tait 2003: 129, 131). In other cases, the visits seem to have a religious dimension. Sometimes the visit was a passing stop in a journey with another purpose, as in the case of the graffiti at the Paneia on the routes from the Nile in Upper Egypt to the Red Sea (Bernand 1972a, b: 15–16); in at least some of these cases the whole point of the journey was to visit the sacred place, and here the journey can be termed pilgrimage, using the modern term in its broadest sense.

Pilgrimage in Greco-Roman Egypt occurred in various forms (Bernand 1988; Volokhine 1998). People went to sanctuaries for the sake of healing (Deir el-Bahri) (Bataille 1951) or to consult oracles, often by way of the process of incubation (as at the Serapieion at Memphis).[1] People also went to sacrifice, like Herodotus' pilgrims to Bubastis, or much later the iron-workers of Hermonthis in the temple of Hatshepsut.[2] In other cases, the idea was to pay homage to a deity, for example at Philae (Rutherford 1998) or the recently published *proskunemata* in honour of the obscure deity Piuris at Ain Labakha in the Kharga Oasis (uniquely, Piuris is given the Egyptian epithet "*hesi*") (Wagner 1996; cf. Quaegebeur 1977). Finally, in some cases pilgrims expressed views that bordered on intellectual theological discourse, as in the case of the graffiti from the temple of Mandoules at Kalabsha (Nock 1972).

Most of the pilgrims and visitors were either non-Egyptians, or at least they commemorated their visits in languages other than Egyptian. Evidence for pilgrimage by Egyptians themselves is famously rare: the main sources are Herodotus' accounts of Egyptian pilgrimage to festivals, e.g. to Bubastis, and a hieroglyphic stela from Buto recording various forms of pilgrimage there (Drioton 1943).

In this chapter, I focus on one of the richest sources of data for pilgrimage and other forms of visitation, the Memnonion at Abydos. I begin with an account of the religious significance of Abydos in earlier periods of Egyptian culture, before moving on to survey the main evidence for pilgrimage and other activities in the Greco-Roman period. Finally, I suggest how to put the evidence for Greco-Roman pilgrimage in the context of Egyptian pilgrimage.

## Abydos in traditional Egyptian religion

Abydos (*'Ibjew*) was a centre of the worship of Osiris from the third millennium BC (Kemp 1975). Earlier still it had been the practice for Egyptians to seek burial there, probably because burial close to the seat of the god of the underworld was believed to yield positive benefits in the other world. Religious activity at Abydos was spread over a vast area: from the main town, together with the great temple of Osiris (Kom el-Sultan), and three major cemeteries at the northern extremity; an imposing barrier of cliffs to the south (Figure 10:1) and the uncanny landscape of the region may also

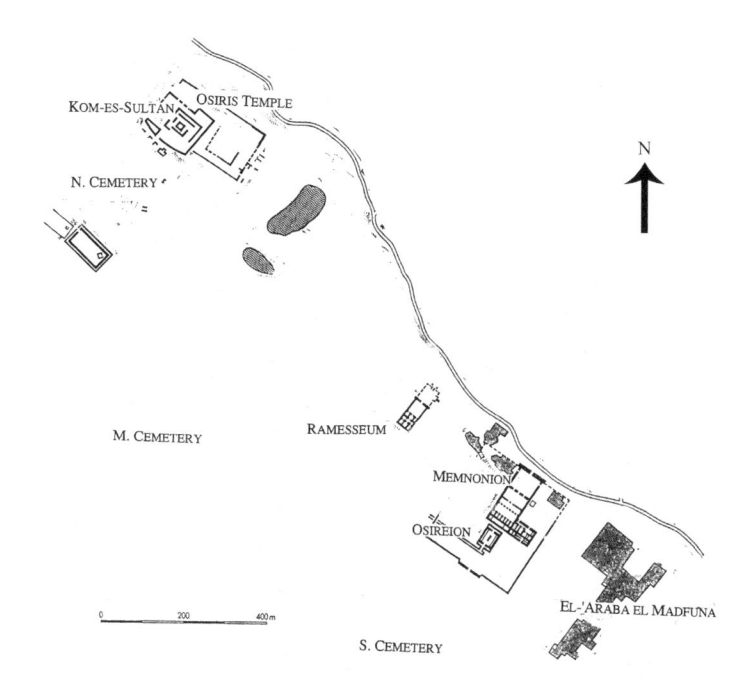

Figure 10:1 Religious activity at Abydos.

have made a contribution to the sanctity in which it was held (Richards 1999). The area between included the great cemetery known today as Umm-el-Qa'ab.

The history of pilgrimage at Abydos highlights two points in particular:

(i) There are huge numbers of brick cenotaphs and stelae at Abydos, dating from the Middle Kingdom and later. People must have visited Abydos to set the cenotaphs up, even if it would be incorrect to think of these journeys as pilgrimages (Lichtheim 1988). This practice continues into the Roman period. Verse inscriptions survive from Abydos, commemorating two people from Lycopolis (Asyut, about 100 km north of Abydos) buried there. One (Bernand 1969: 73) is for a 16 year old boy called Apollos, who died in the "Pharian land" (Alexandria). Another (Bernand 1969: n. 74) is for Elemon, who died at the age of 20, apparently a poet.[3] Based on this evidence, it appears that the erection of such stelae in the Roman period was reserved for people who died young.

(ii) Well-to-do Egyptians represented an imaginary journey to Abydos (the *Abydosfahrt*) on the walls of tombs. These first appear in the Middle Kingdom, in the early second millennium BC at Beni Hasan (Figure 10:2), in the tombs of Amenemhet and Khnumhotep (Altenmüller 1975). Such depictions are particularly common in Thebes, and during the New Kingdom. The journey is usually described as a "voyage in peace", and the activities of the voyagers at Abydos are said to include worshipping, kissing the ground before Osiris, ferrying the god across the Nile at the beginning of the year, taking part in the festival of Osiris, "seeing Osiris, and travelling in the sacred boat of Osiris, the Neshmet".[4]

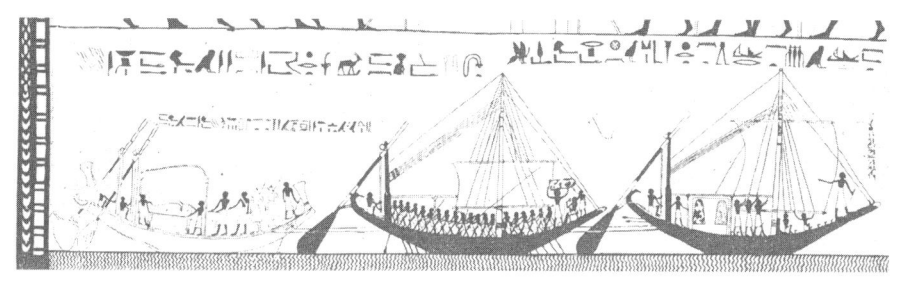

Figure 10:2    Tomb painting of imaginary journey to Abydos, Beni Hasan.

One might think that such depictions of pilgrimages to Abydos were records of pilgrimages that actually took place, but it is generally believed that they were entirely symbolic, perhaps a sort of substitute for burial at Abydos. They may continue an earlier tradition, dating back to the Old Kingdom, that when the Old Kingdom rulers at Buto in Lower Egypt died, their bodies were taken on a multi-stage journey to sacred places in the Delta, including Sais, Busiris, Behbeit-el-Haggar and Mendes (Spencer 1982: 51–52, 160–163).

What is much less clear is whether there was pilgrimage by living people to Abydos. Certainly there was much to see there, including a festival of Osiris, during which the statue of the god, and his sacred ship, were carried from the main temple in the city down to Poqer and back again (Schäfer 1904). Indeed, stelae record people's participation. The stela of Sehetep-ib-ra (Kamal 1938, 1940), an official who visited Abydos, talks about taking part in the "mystery of the lord of Abydos" (sšt3 n nb 3bḏw). Another official, a certain Moses (Varille 1930–1935: 39–43, pl. 1; Yoyotte 1960: 34) boasts that he took part in the festival, helping to carry the sacred bark of Osiris. But there is little direct evidence for pilgrimage to the festival, and it is uncertain whether this was, in practice, more than a local event.[5]

## The Memnonion and the Osireion

In the Greco-Roman period, the most conspicuous evidence for sacred encounters comes from the graffiti-laden buildings to the south-east of the main temple of Osiris, principally the Memnonion, and to a lesser extent the Osireion and the Ramesseum.

The building known to the Greeks as the Memnonion (identified as such by one graffito, PL (Perdrizet and Lefebvre 1919, hearafter PL) 563 and described by Strabo XVII.1.42) was originally the mortuary temple of the New Kingdom pharaoh Seti I.[6] The name 'Memnonion' is thought to imitate the throne name of the pharaoh Seti I, which was "Remain the Truth of the Sun" (Men-Mat-ra) (Kemp 1975: 39).

More commonly, the building, with its numerous chapels and sacred decorations, was approached as a divine temple, first as centre of the cult of Osiris, then Serapis, and finally as an oracle of the minor deity, Bes. The Memnonion continued as a centre of worship through the hellenistic and Roman periods. It was continuously active until a crisis in 359, when the Roman Emperor Constantine II closed it down, offended by people asking the oracle about the imperial succession (Ammianus Marcellinus XIX.12). But it seems to have revived after that, and was finally closed down by the Christian Copts in the late fifth century.

The unusual L-shaped structure was entered from the north-east, with a couple of courtyards preceding the main building. The wall paintings and inscriptions are well preserved, as is the ceiling (Neugebauer and Parker 1960: n. 1). There were several small chapels for Seti and a number of deities, as well as a false-chapel of Osiris, which is really a corridor that leads through to an inner sanctuary devoted to Osiris, Isis and Horus, the divine triad. To the east of this area was a corridor with a wall inscribed with representations of all the pharaohs of Egypt (the 'Table of the Pharaohs'), and a staircase leading to an upper terrace.

Immediately behind, to the south and set much lower, is another structure, of uncertain function. Frankfort (1933), who excavated it, called it a "Cenotaph of Seti", but today it is usually referred as an Osireion (Figure 10:3). The entrance was via a long passage from the north-west; there seems to have been no way in from the Memnonion, though the main staircase in the Memnonion would have led out into the area of ground above it. Inside was a chamber with a central area, perhaps meant to represent the primeval mound, surrounded by a channel of water. Strabo (XVII.42) seems to have interpreted it as a well.

The third building is the Ramesseum, a smaller structure, some 300 m to the north-west in the direction of the main temple. This building was originally the mortuary temple of Ramesses II (Kemp 1975: 39).

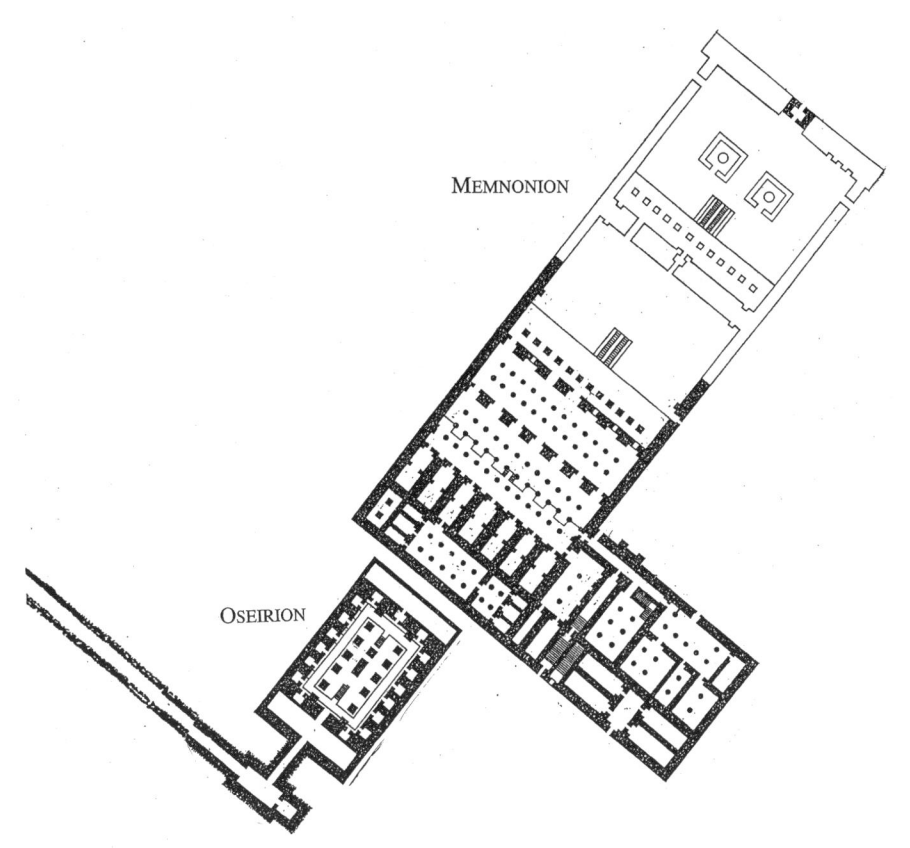

Figure 10:3 The 'Mortuary Temple' and 'Cenotaph' of Seti I, Abydos.

## Graffiti

The evidence for visitation to these structures is mostly graffiti, which survive all over the sanctuary. They are mostly in Greek, including some from Cyprus written in the Cypriot syllabary, but they are also in other languages, including Carian, Aramaic, Phoenician, and Coptic (Figure 10:4). They probably date from a thousand year period, from the sixth century BC to the fourth century AD. The good edition of the Greek graffiti in the Memnonion by Perdrizet and Lefebvre (1919) is not complete, and does not cover the Osireion or the Ramesseum.[7] No extant study takes account of the graffiti in all the different languages, and only one demotic graffito has been published (Farid 1995: 203–206), an unusual example written in Greek letters from the hellenistic period, as well as one or two hieratic ones from the twenty-second Dynasty (950–720 BC).

These data raise a number of problems. First, graffiti are very difficult to date, even within a century. And then again they are sometimes difficult to read, for example PL 334, which could be demotic in part (cf. PL 74; PL 313; and PL 385). Some include symbols, for example the palm-sign (PL 504, PL 526) (Rutherford

HBAΛΕΓ ΚΥΓΑΙ⌒⌒ΤΕΜΕ
ΙΕΓΝΕΜ
ΕΙΥΣΙΡΙΝΤΕΤ⌒ΣΡΙΑΝΟΙΤ ΙΙ
ΝΟΥΟΡΣΕΥ ΤΕΤ⌒ΣΡΙ ΕΝΤΕΜ ΠΡΕΤ
ΣΡΙΝ ΕΠΒΟΥ ΚΕΙΡΑΝ ΕΠ Ε⌒Ν hκs
ΟΣΤ ΟΣΤΟΙΑΥ ΤΑΣ    ΝΙ ΧΑΡΙΤΑΣ
ΑΝΤΑΠΟΔΩ

ΔΡπΚΟΑΡ

ΦΙΒΙΓΧ +

Figure 10:5 Graffito of a palm, a foot and a flask, Abydos (PL 325).

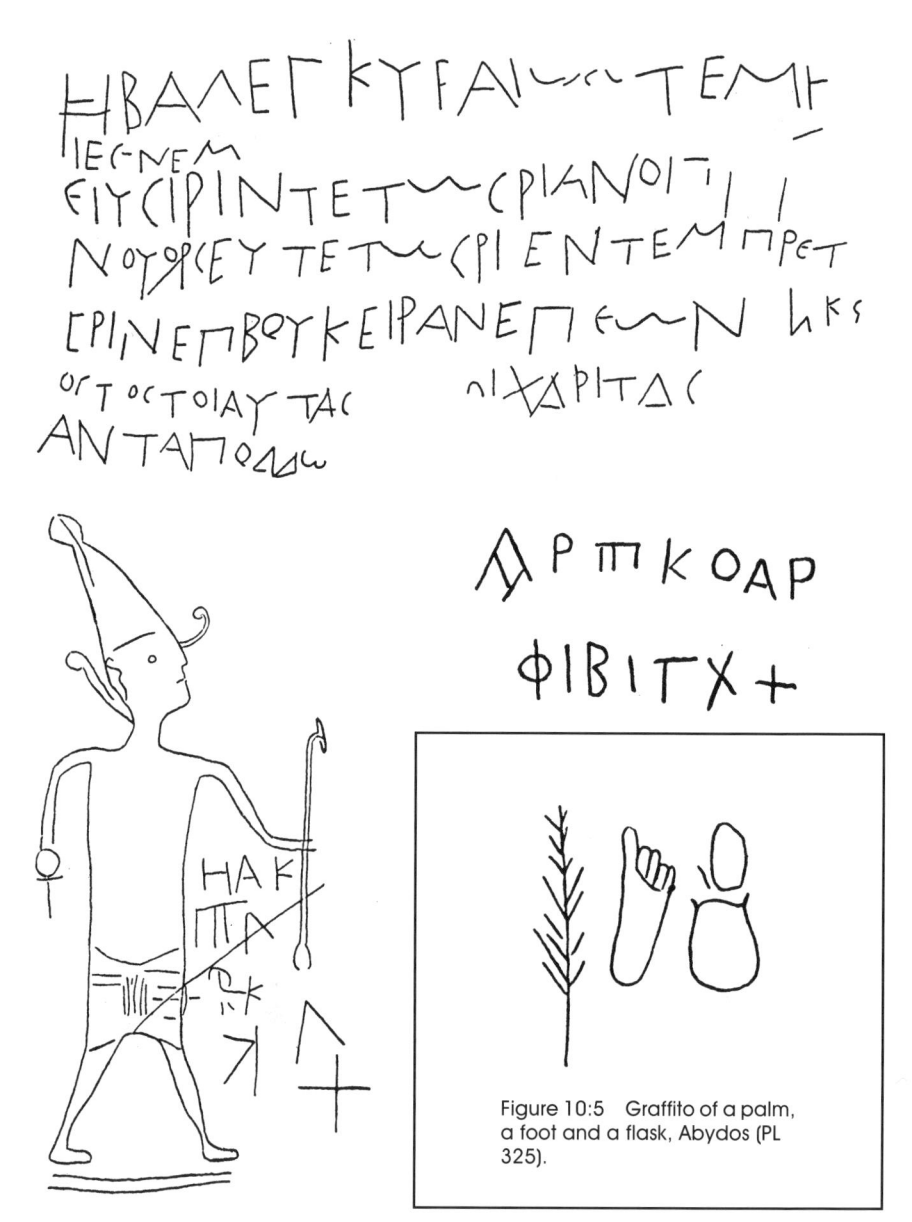

Figure 10:4 Graffiti of various types and different languages from the Ramesseum, Abydos (top: PL 334; left bottom: PL 313; right centre: PL 385).

forthcoming) and the ankh-sign (PL 465, 467, 468), and representations of feet (PL 325, 652, 657) (Guarducci 1942–1943: 312, no. 30). In one case, the graffito consists wholly of signs (unless the name "Leon" preceding is to be taken with it): a picture of a palm, a foot, and a flask (PL 325) (Figure 10:5). In one case there is a pair of ears (PL 306, in the Corridor of Kings; Wagner and Quaegebeur 1973). There are also a small number of magical symbols, and one horoscope (Rutherford 2000).[8]

## Reinterpretation in the context of pilgrimage

The history of the Memnonion involves multiple reinterpretations of the building: as the Memnonion itself, as a temple of Serapis and as an oracle of Bes. Diachronically, it is sometimes possible to ask to what extent religious perceptions attested in the Greco-Roman period represented innovations with respect to much older religious traditions. The great monuments of Ancient Egypt are continuously reinterpreted over the centuries. Such reinterpretations are particularly striking in the Greco-Roman period. There is naturally a high degree of overlap between the buildings that are reinterpreted and buildings that tend to attract visitors: for example the mortuary temple of Amenemhet III (twelfth Dynasty) was reinterpreted as the "Labyrinth" by Herodotus and others (Lloyd 1995); the statues of Amenophis III at Thebes, reinterpreted as statues of Memnon (Bowersock 1984); and the mortuary temple of Queen Hatshepsut at Deir el-Bahri, a lower terrace of which seems to have been reserved for a triad of healing deities: first, Imhotep, the deified architect from the third Dynasty, who became identified with Asclepius during the Greco-Roman period; second, Amenophis son of Hapu, another architect, this time of Amenophis III in the New Kingdom; and the Greek goddess Hugieia, completing a triad (Bataille 1950, 1951: XXIV–V; Bernand 1988: 53–54). This process of reinterpretation was underway much earlier; Yoyotte (1960: 50) describes how the Sphinx, originally a representation of the pharaoh Khephren, was reinterpreted as a colossal representation of the god Harmakhis, and became a frequent destination for pilgrims (Volokhine 1998: 80).

What is striking about the case of the Memnonion is that there seem to be two different reinterpretations: the name "Memnonion" represents an attempt to place the building in the context of the heroic past of Greece (Griffith 1998) but the graffiti on the walls for the most part show that the building had assumed a different significance in the Egyptian religion of the Greco-Roman period. Of all the graffiti surviving on the walls, only one identifies the building as the Memnonion (PL 563, left by a certain Menelaus). It thus seems to be popular tradition that prevails in the graffiti.

These two different interpretations find expression also in the graffiti left by a certain Philokles in the Chapel of Isis. In one he says he honours Sesostris, the semi-mythical Egyptian pharaoh. That one is in iambic metre (PL 31): "I, Philokles, making adoration to Sesostris, bid him rejoice." The other is a conventional homage to Serapis (PL 32): "Philokles, son of Hierokles, from Troizen, I arrived making adoration to Serapis." It looks as if they express two different aspects of sacred visitation: that of the learned tourist, and that of the pious worshipper.

## Early period

It makes sense to distinguish three broad phases of visitation represented by the Greco-Roman graffiti. The earliest period is from the sixth century BC when they are first attested, to some point in the hellenistic period, about the end of the third century BC. At the earlier end of that period, some Greek graffiti are certainly Archaic; Jeffery (1990) identified some as in the Aeginetan script of Cydonia in Crete. There are also the Carian graffiti, which probably date from between the early sixth century and mid-fifth (Ray 1990; listed in Adiego-Lajara 1993). The Syllabic-Cypriot graffiti are thought to be early fourth century (Masson 1983). There are also Aramaic and Phoenician graffiti, apparently to be dated to the period from the fifth to third centuries BC.

The graffiti are ambiguous: they often have merely the name, with patronym and sometimes ethnonym. It is often hard to tell if this is pilgrimage or tourism, or the record of soldiers of foreign descent visiting the area. In some cases, we can be reasonably certain that graffiti were left by mercenaries, such as those in Carian. And one of the Greek graffiti (PL 445, mentioning Amurtaios) is certainly by a soldier.

One apparent piece of evidence for pilgrimage in the classical period deserves special attention. In 417 BC two Phoenician pilgrims, brothers, are supposed to have left a papyrus-record of their visit to Osiris at Abydos, the so-called 'Madrid Papyrus' (Fitzmyer and Kaufmann 1992: B.3.f. 14; Teixidor 1964), which reads:

> The third of kislev of year 7, which is day 1 of Thoth of year 7 of King Darius, Abdba'al the Sidonian, son of Abdsedeq came with his brother Azarba'al to Abydos in Egypt before Osiris the great god.

One view is that this was written in Aramaic by a temple-scribe (Gibson 1975: n. 29, 148), Aramaic being the *lingua franca* in the eastern Mediterranean, and a common language in Egypt since the Persian takeover. Unfortunately, Naveh (1968) subsequently showed that this and a number of other recently discovered Aramaic documents were forgeries. One of his reasons is the dating formula, which he shows is (a) suspiciously like one in another Aramaic document and (b) inaccurate. Despite this, it may well be that the earliest evidence for pilgrimage to Abydos is indeed Aramaic. Aramaic graffiti tend to include the formula "May someone be blessed" (*brk*). Common formulas are: "may NN be blessed with Osiris" (*Brk NN l-Asry*) and "may NN be blessed before Osiris" (*Brk NN qdm Asry*).

They may date between the fifth and third centuries BC (Fitzmyer and Kaufmann 1992) and, of course, these do not have to have been made by pilgrims. They could be made either by Aramaic speakers visiting from outside Egypt, or by Aramaic speakers residing in Egypt (as many did). They may have made a proper pilgrimage, or they may have made a detour en route, a 'pilgrimage in passing' as it is sometimes termed (Yoyotte 1960: 24).

Some of the Phoenician graffiti could represent pilgrimage also, for example (from the stairs), "I, Paalobastos son of Sadyaton, son of Gersed, the Tyrian, an inhabitant ... in Egyptian Heliopolis ... in the freedom of Bodmelqert, the Heliopolitan". This could have been a Heliopolitan of Phoenician descent who came here on a pilgrimage (CISI.102a = Lidzbarski 1900–15, ESEAt).

It is possible that some of the earlier Greek graffiti could also represent pilgrimage or religious visitation. One particular example merits attention. In PL 424 three Ionian visitors left graffiti of the form "X *ethesato*", which means "X watched". One of the Cypriot-Greek graffito in Cypriote script reads "e-ta-we-sa-to" (= Greek *etheasato*). This sounds like the activity of "sacred contemplation" or *theoria* that Greek sources often mention in connection with pilgrimage[9] – in the sixth century BC Athenian politician Solon's journey of exploration and inquiry which took him to Lydia and Egypt was described as a *theoria* (Herodotus I.29–31). It may well be that when the three Ionian visitors viewed the sanctuary, it was a 'viewing' with sacred connotations.

## Second phase: Serapis

The second phase extends from the later hellenistic period into the Roman period, but, again, dating is imprecise. Even in the second century BC, many of the graffiti were by soldiers of foreign descent employed by the Ptolemies. It seems likely that the Memnonion was used as a barracks in the hellenistic period, if not all the time, at least during certain revolts that afflicted Upper Egypt in this period, for example in the first decades of the second century BC (Launey 1949–1950, I: 83.4).[10]

It is also true, however, that from the second century BC, the evidence for pilgrimage becomes more explicit. Pilgrims tend to identify the deity they worship as Serapis, who seems to have been 'invented' only around the end of the fourth century BC. He is a sort of syncretism between Osiris and the deity Apis, the sacred bull, often envisaged as a bearded god, reminiscent of the Greek Zeus.

The crucial aspect in this period is a change in the vocabulary employed to commemorate pilgrimage. Specifically, pilgrims commemorate their visits with graffiti which amount to a *proskunema*, or an act of adoration in honour of the deity (Geraci 1971).[11] This epigraphic habit seems to start around the end of the second century BC, and it is known from all over Egypt, and occasionally outside. Another idiom which seems to begin around the same time is the statement "I have come", using the verb *heko*. Other formulae are also found.[12]

We can deduce something of the motivation and behaviour of pilgrims from these graffiti. Some address "the gods in Abydos" in general (PL 80, 114, 279), but the gods most frequently mentioned are Serapis and Bes. Serapis is probably being honoured already in hellenistic times, pilgrimage in honour of Bes probably starts well into the Roman Empire. Apart from Serapis and Bes, there are a couple of graffiti that honour Amun-Ra, located close to the chapel of Amun-Ra (PL 218, 221), both by a Demetrios, who seems to have been a resident of the temple, an *enkatokhos*, perhaps with special knowledge of the place.

Pilgrims rarely mention their motivation for making a *proskunema* to Serapis, but sometimes they approach him as a healing deity. They were often accompanied by doctors, including Isidotos (PL 24, 256, 278, 473), and Theophilos (PL 354, 591), and Neoptolemos (PL 473).[13] Healing is a role Serapis frequently had elsewhere in Egypt. Some pilgrims ask for healing from illness, or announce that they have been healed (PL 114, 136, 156, 368, 377) – "I Spartakos, son of Phaidros, have come to Abydos; save me, Osiris!" – (PL 390, 414, 426).

Some ask for dream-oracles, implying the custom of incubation. A certain Achilles says that he has come to see a dream telling him about what he prays for (PL 298).

Visitors to Abydos sometimes specify that they come at the new moon (*noumeniai*) (PL 53, 567, 568); it is not clear what the significance of this was.[14] Some pilgrims say that they have made several visits (PL 227: six times; 207; 274; 420; 630). One pilgrim, a certain Sphex, announces that he is returning, this time healthy, to see the oracle for a second time (PL 107).[15] One visitor, Demetrius (probably from Ptolemais), who visited during the rule of Marcus Aurelius and Lucius Verus, said he came in Khoiak, when we know there was a festival of Osiris, and Khoiak seems to have been a common month to visit (PL 253).[16]

## Third phase: Bes

During the later Roman Empire, the sanctuary became an oracle of the popular god Bes (Dunand 1997; Frankfurter 1997). Bes, represented as a green dwarf, was a comparatively recent development in the Egyptian pantheon, not known before the Middle Kingdom (Malaise 1990; Meeks 1991). One source about the procedure for consulting him is the extraordinary account in Ammianus Marcellinus, who describes the crisis of 359 AD. He says that people sent in questions for the gods on paper, accompanied by prayers, and both were left written upon the walls of the temple, for everyone to see. (It was these that caught the attention of the Emperor.) A good example is a dedication by a certain Harpokras, son of a priest from a certain "city of Pan", who says in a metrical dedication that he has slept in the oracle many times, had many dreams, and wishes for omniscience (Bernand 1969: 131 (= PL 528)):

> Here slept and saw dreams Harpokras of holy Panias, a priest, dear descendant of Kopreias the priest, for Besas whose voice is all. And his gratitude is not small.
>
> (PL 528)

There is no reference to written documents here. A number of consultants seem to be athletes, victors at the Olympic Games or the Pythian Games, who come to Bes to ask his advice, or perhaps to thank him for victory.[17]

## Christian takeover

After the Christian takeover of Abydos, dramatized in the *Life of Apa Moses*, there are indications that the Memnonion was taken over and used as a nunnery. We have inscriptions from the walls of Mariette's room Z, the so-called Coptic Chapel (Murray 1904), but no sign of Christian pilgrimage. From the Osireion there are unusual Coptic graffiti, including images of boats, which Piankoff (1960) takes as a Christian symbol, though it is possible that it could be placed in the context of traditional Egyptian iconography as well.

## What sort of pilgrimage?

We have seen that pilgrims to Serapis went there for the sake of healing or to receive dream-oracles; pilgrims to Bes went for the oracle. Some pilgrims to Serapis came in Khoiak, at the time of a major festival of Osiris.

Most of the evidence from Abydos about the various forms of visitation to sacred places can be grouped into two classes: (i) casual visitation, for example by soldiers of foreign descent; and (ii) pilgrimage for specific purposes: healing, oracles and festivals. There is little evidence for tourism, and there is little evidence of 'intellectual pilgrimage' of the form found in places like Kalabsha (see above).

Out of 800 graffiti from the Memnonion, there seems to be only one example reflecting an intellectual or theological interest.

> Some say you are Asklepios, but I that you are Dionysus; others that you are Phoibos and Hermes and Harpokrates …
>
> (PL 498)

This discusses the identity of the god (presumably Bes) and resembles the famous graffito from a *proskunema* in which a Roman soldier speculates on the identity of the local god Mandoules in a way suggestive of the more or less contemporary syncretistic theologies emanating from Claros in Asia Minor.

Two out of 800 seems a pretty low proportion for 'intellectual' graffiti. There is a very clear contrast with other places, such as the statues of Memnon at Thebes or the Temple of Mandoulis at Kalabsha. It seems that in the hellenistic period the Memnonion did not attract visitors who were prepared to put interesting cultural or theological remarks into writing. Probably this means that it was not on the list of major sites to be visited by rich, educated foreigners or highly literate military officers.

## Catchment

It is possible to build up a sense of catchment (Figure 10:6). Some visitors give their nationality as non-Egyptian: from Greece, from Thrace, from south-west Asia Minor. Only a small minority give Egypt as a place of origin. Interestingly, most of these come from the *khora*: from Ptolemais (PL 222, 253, 269), from the Thebaid (PL 78), from Oxyrhynchus (PL 63), and from the Kunopolites Nomos just south of it (PL 510), from Khusai (PL 29, 244, 251, 358, 360–362, 392), from Antaioupolis (PL 27–28). In addition, the name Paniskos (PL 95, 96, 451, 574) has been linked to the worship of Min at Koptos.[18] Only two come from Alexandria (PL 10, 163), one from Pelusium (PL 621). The paucity of pilgrims from Alexandria is particularly striking in view of the size and affluence of its population. On this basis, we conclude that Alexandrians who wanted the services of Serapis would generally go to other centres of his worship, such as the centres at Menouthis near Alexandria or at Memphis. The catchment for the Bes-oracle is not well attested, but some individuals came from the Kunopolite Nome.[19]

Some of these visitors were probably soldiers or descendants of soldiers. For example, a certain Ablouthies (PL 229, 244, 251, 358, 360–362; 392), who makes about eight pilgrimages to Abydos, claims to come from Khusai in Middle Egypt. He may have been a Thracian soldier domiciled in some sort of colony there, since his name looks Thracian (Detschew 1957: 2–3) and there is independent evidence for Thracians at Khusai (see the commentary in Perdrizet and Lefebvre 1919).

One special problem concerns the stated ethnicity of pilgrims. In many cases they claim to come from Greece, Asia Minor and Thrace, but it is possible that their real point of origin is closer, and that they maintain a sentimental attachment to an older identity. Thus PL 300–301 is by a certain Pouarates who described himself as "Cyrenean, but now the land of Egypt holds him". In another case (PL 71), it seems

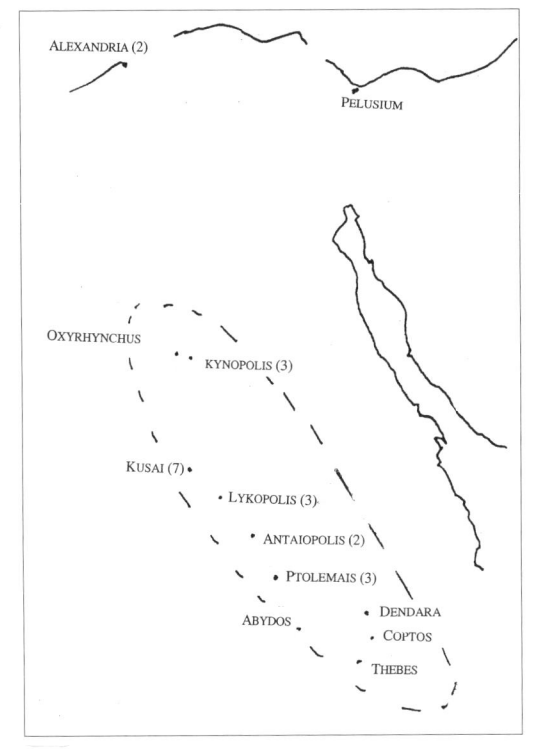

Figure 10:6  Abydos catchment area.

that we are dealing with a colony of soldiers from Arcadia living in Egypt. So it may be that other people who represent themselves as coming from Greece or Asia Minor were actually permanently established in Egypt too (Oates 1965).

## Space issues

### Change in position of Greek graffiti within the Memnonion

The positioning of the graffiti changes from phase to phase (Figures 10:7–10:10). In the earliest period, most of the graffiti come from two locations: either the staircase or the corridor that contains the King List. It is from the staircase that the Phoenician and Aramaic inscriptions come, and the archaic Greek graffiti likewise. It is appealing to think of early visitors being led to inspect the list of pharaohs, and being instructed, as Herodotus seems to have been, about the great antiquity of Egyptian civilization. It is not known why the staircase was a favoured location.

In the later stage, graffiti are found more generally in the sacred space of the building, including the more intimate spaces of the chapels of Isis, Osiris and Hours (O, N, M), and more public spaces, such as the Hypostyle Hall and the façade of the end Court. Many of the *proskunema* inscriptions come from these areas. Probably many pilgrims headed directly for the inner sanctuaries. Some of the areas used by pilgrims in the later period – the inner chapels, for example – may have been off limits

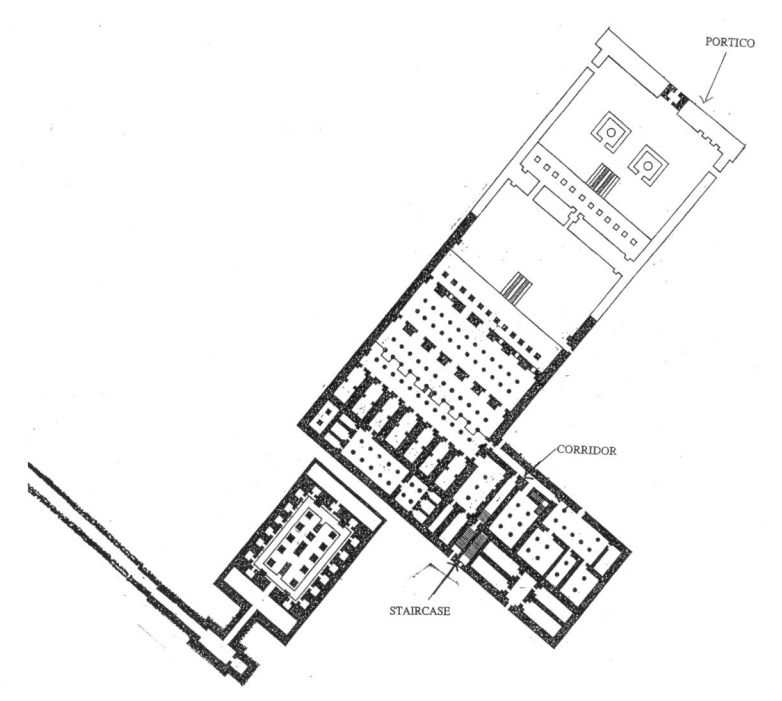

Figure 10:7  Distribution of Syllabic-Cypriot graffiti: classical period.

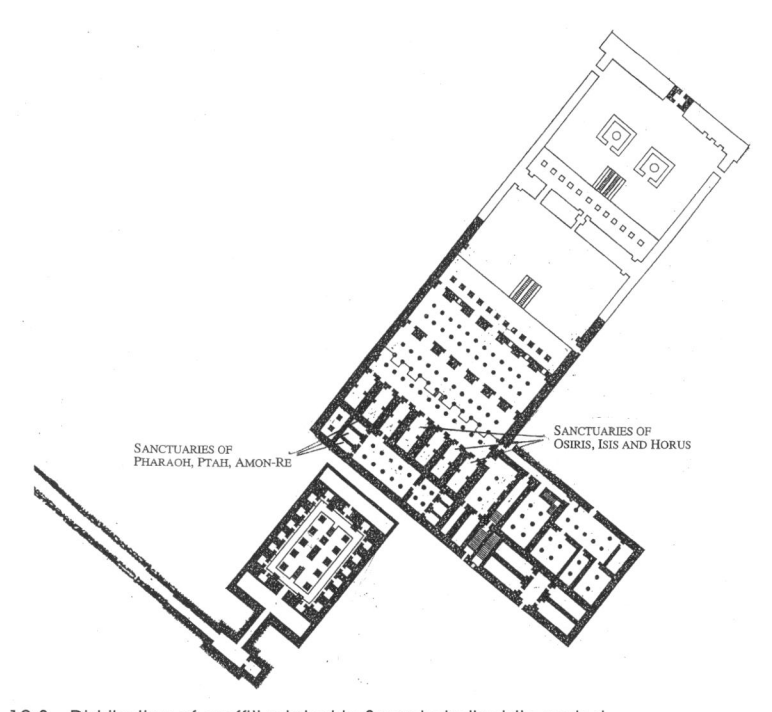

Figure 10:8  Distribution of graffiti related to Serapis: hellenistic period.

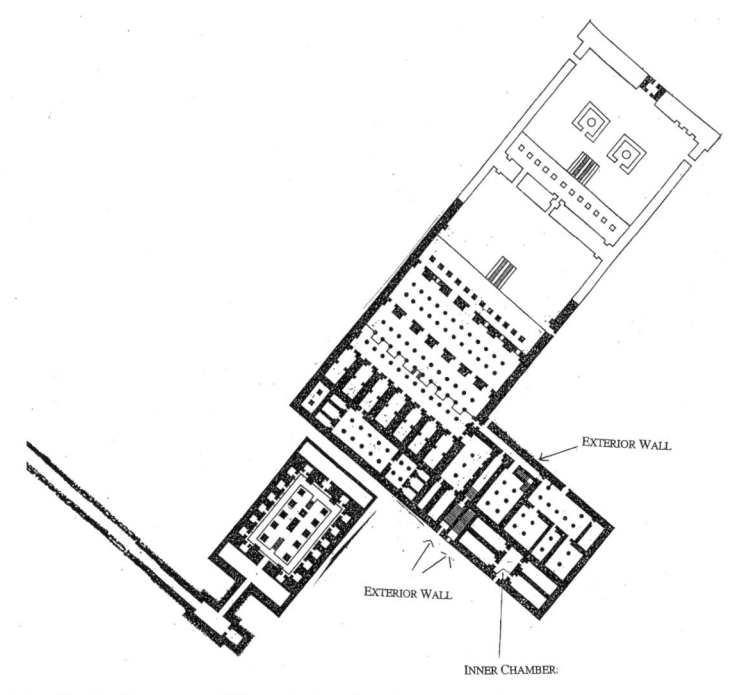

Figure 10:9  Distribution of graffiti related to Bes: Roman period.

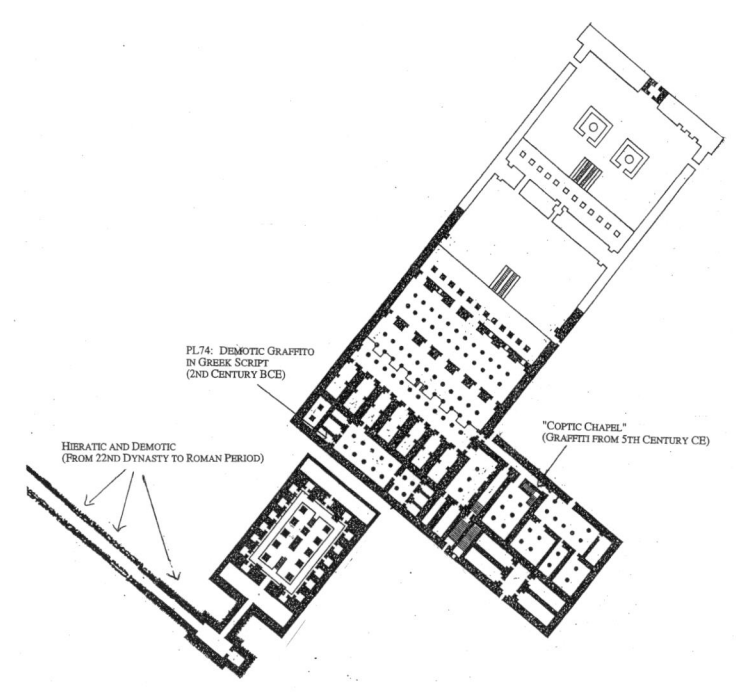

Figure 10:10  Distribution of Egyptian graffiti.

to earlier visitors. Perhaps what we are observing is a change in the way the Memnonion was administered.

Finally, inscriptions relating to Bes are almost all found on the external wall of the Memnonion, at the rear; rarely inside the building. One is found in the outer of the two courts; two in one inmost cell of Isis (1 and 22; perhaps this chapel was regarded as the oracle?); one on the Upper Terrace (PL 458). The 'poem of Harpokras' is in the so-called Chamber of Merenptah, which opens off the rear wall. The distribution of the inscriptions seems to argue against thinking that there were two clearly defined periods, one in which the object of pilgrimage was Serapis, another in which it was Bes. More probably, the two traditions overlap to some extent, while the temple is the centre for two different deities, one the more traditional and perhaps officially endorsed Serapis, and the other the less official Bes. It is possible that this grotesque popular god Bes was regarded as inappropriate to the more sacred environment of the interior. Perhaps he was regarded as more appropriate to the outer wall in so far as he is a mediating figure.

## Greek and Egyptian graffiti

In working on *proskunemata* at Philae, I noticed that the spatial distribution of the inscriptions is not random (Figures 10:7, 10:8), but rather influenced by language (Rutherford 1998: 250–253); for example, Greek ones appear on the pylons, while the 'Birth-House' is the place for the demotic ones. Again, demotic inscriptions appear in a group on their own on the roof of the temple at Edfu (Devauchelle 1983). Time is also a factor in the distribution of graffiti at Philae. The earliest Greek ones appear on free-standing monuments; then they appear on the 'South Pylon' in the first century BC; then they migrate nearer and nearer the main temple; and finally they appear on the roof of the temple.

At Abydos, similar, though not identical patterns are found. There are very few Egyptian graffiti in the Memnonion, at least before the Coptic ones in room Z (see above). The one demotic graffito that survives from the Memnonion deserves special attention because it is in Greek letters (PL 74); Pestman (1977: n. 11) takes it as a *proskunema*, although the crucial line is missing:[20]

> In year 6 of pharaoh Hr-wn-nfr
> beloved of Isis and Osiris beloved of Amun-Ra king of the gods the great god
> [X makes his *proskunema* before?]
> Osiris in Ta-wr

This text has been the subject of intense discussion; it may represent the presence of a southern pharaoh, perhaps a Nubian, during the southern revolt of the earlier second century BC (Préaux 1936; Turner 1984). If so, we can only guess why the writer chose to write in Greek letters; it is not what one would expect an Egyptian rebel to do, unless either (i) he was semi-literate, and demotic writing is hard; or (ii) he wanted to make sure that his use of demotic could be recognized as such by Greeks.

If there are few Egyptian graffiti in the Memnonion, there are rather more in the Osireion and in the passage leading to it, where there are hardly any Greek graffiti (Frankfort 1933, 1: 87–96). These Egyptian graffiti from the Osireion cover a wide chronological span, from the beginning of the first millennium BC until the end, including hieratic at one end of the scale to demotic at the other.

The writers of the Egyptian graffiti (Figure 10:10) may have been locals and not visitors of any sort. Nevertheless, the distribution of data still indicates that Egyptians, or rather people who wrote Egyptian (Egyptographs), attached sacred significance to different areas of the complex from the areas favoured by other (non-Egyptograph) visitors. One way of looking at this distribution would be to say that the non-Egyptian visitors made a mistake about the truly sacred parts of the temple, but it seems equally possible to say that different groups of people made their own decisions about what was and what was not sacred.

It has been argued that pilgrimage is a way to express a group allegiance, an identity (Elsner 1992), and in the case of pilgrimage to Abydos one motive may have been to identity oneself as a Greek, or at least a Greek-speaker, and to position oneself in the tradition of Greeks who had visited the building.[21] *Prima facie* that claim seems paradoxical, since to us the Memnonion looks like an uncompromisingly Egyptian edifice, and one imagines it would have done to Greeks living in Egypt as well. But over time the Egyptian origins of the building may have become of less importance than the living tradition of Greek visitors implied by the graffiti.

## Excursus: a prayer to Maia

Some of the most interesting graffiti in the complex are those that are out of place, such as the strange demotic graffito in Greek letters discussed above. An almost equally anomalous Greek graffito survives from the Osireion, anomalous both because it is in Greek and because its author was a fairly literate tourist or intellectual (Boyaval 1969).

It is impossible to produce a coherent translation of this text. It starts with an appeal to the "Daughter of Atlas", i.e. Maia, who is apparently asked to 'send' Hermes. Then there is an address to Hermes and reference to the episode on Circe's island and the drug "moly." And it ends with reference to the writers, Onesikrates and Dorotheos, who are apparently from Italy. If the text is complete, the metre is stichic pentameter, a rare form, but it seems possible, as Boyaval (1969: 356) has suggested, that every alternate line has been omitted for some reason.

The "daughter of Atlas" seems to be the goddess Maia, and the writer ask her to send her son Hermes to help him, as Hermes helped Odysseus when he was lost on Circe's island. Perhaps the writer thinks of Hermes (i.e. Hermes Trismegistos) as the Egyptian deity *par excellence*. As for Maia, it may be worth noticing that in the 'Oxyrhynchus Aretalogy of Isis' which lists the names under which Isis is worshipped in about a hundred different places, there are two places where she is worshipped as "Maia" (*P. Oxy.* 1380; included in Totti 1985). Or maybe the explanation is that the Osireion, designed apparently to resemble the island where the god was born, reminded the tourist of Circe's mysterious island in Homer's *Odyssey*.

There is a great difference between this and the simple graffiti left by the pilgrims who came to the Memnonion. It is true that the graffiti in the Memnonion often request salvation or announce that their writers have been saved (from illness or from the perils of the journey). But Onesikrates was a pilgrim, and a sophisticated one. He could be classed as an intellectual tourist. Perhaps any Greek could visit the Osireion or maybe this graffito is from a comparatively late period when Egyptian priests were no longer concerned to protect the god's sanctuary.

## The Memnonion as a peripheral site to the temple

It ought to be possible to speculate on the relation between the Memnonion and the main temple of Osiris at Abydos in the hellenistic and Roman periods. The main temple could have been expected to be the focus of interest among tourists and pilgrims, along with the sacred drama that was acted out between the temple and Poqer.[22] This interest would have been particularly great during the great festival of Osiris in the month of Khoiak (Altenmüller 1975: 176, 187 n. 85). As for pilgrimage by Egyptians, it may be that this took place as well, although there is no direct evidence for it. Some of the Greek graffiti indicate that their writers visited during Khoiak, which presumably implies that they came during the festival.

Why then did the Greek-speakers leave their records at the Memnonion? Perhaps they left graffiti on the walls of the temple of Osiris as well, though access inside would presumably have been forbidden. The difference with the Memnonion, of course, is that this was a structure of religious significance that they were able to have access to, and even sleep inside. The fact that the main temples tended to be blocked off to public access means that pilgrims gravitated toward secondary zones. This happened in a slightly different way at Karnak, where visitors and pilgrims seem to have been directed toward a small temple immediately to the east of the main temple (Yoyotte 1960: 43–44).[23] Thus, I would suggest that what we see in the Memnonion is a fragment of a bigger picture. In what I have called phase 2, the Memnonion was not a primary focus of activity, but it was at least accessible. In phase 3, the period of the oracle of Bes, the Memnonion acquired an independent status.

## Conclusions

Working with data like these makes one acutely aware of how far the picture we can construct is limited by the data that survive, here determined by the epigraphic habits of visitors to Abydos. There appear to be two conflicting patterns: on the one hand, the significance of Abydos in Egyptian religion continued more or less unchanged through the Roman period, along with the practice of erecting cenotaphs and stelae, and the great festival of Osiris, which arguably attracted pilgrims from the area. This pattern of continuity contrasts with the frequently changing significance of the Memnonion, originally a mortuary temple, then variously a tomb of Memnon, a temple of Serapis and an oracle of Bes. The surviving evidence allows us to reconstruct the broad outline of a pilgrimage-tradition in the hellenistic and Roman periods, in which Greek-speaking pilgrims came to Abydos, to pay respects to Serapis/Osiris, to be healed, and to receive oracles. They were in general not intellectual tourists of the sort who leave graffiti at other sites. Finally, one of the puzzles about Memnonion has always been why a comparatively peripheral structure attracted so much attention. An important factor in explaining this was that the pilgrims, finding themselves excluded from the main temple of Osiris, gravitated towards the Memnonion as a sacred space which they could appropriate for their own uses.

## Notes

1. A document from the archive of Hor of Sebynnitos recording incubation in the Hall of the Ibis at Saqqarah (Ray 1976: n. 13).
2. Bubastis: Rutherford forthcoming; Hermonthis: Lajtar 1991; sacrifice at the Serapieion at Memphis, 157 BC, Wilcken 1927: n. 122.
3. Other examples are collected in Abdalla 1992: 17–83, including several for young men from Lycopolis (cat. nos. 11; 20; 180); Bernand (1980) presents an inscription for a Tmous from Diospolis Parva (= Hiw, between Abydos and Dendara), who died aged 18.
4. Worshipping: tomb of Sennefer (TT96); see Virey 1899: 142; kissing the ground before Osiris: tomb of Antefoker (TT60); Davies and Gardiner 1920: 20 and Plate XVIII; ferrying the god across the Nile: tomb of Amenemhet = TT82; taking part in the festival of Osiris as in the tomb of Sen-nefer = TT96; "seeing Osiris": tomb of $P3iry$ (TT139; cf. Virey 1891: 582); travelling in the sacred boat of Osiris, the Neshmet, which has been taken to indicate a sort of mystical pilgrimage: TT96: "He descends in peace towards Abydos to make the festivals of Osiris, chief of the district of the South, Sennofri. Set off for the home of Osiris! May I follow the gods, may I lead my feet in the Neshmet ship with the great god."
5. Yoyotte (1960: 38) pointed out that almost all of the stelae are by local citizens of Abydos, and that there is no evidence for pilgrimage by anyone except government officials on official business (like the Moses mentioned above). However, David (1982: 108–109, 133) assumes that a pilgrimage took place, and Lichtheim (1988) allows for the possibility of at least some.
6. It should not be confused with the so-called statues of Memnon further south opposite Thebes (these were really statues of Amenophis III).
7. For graffiti in the Ramesseum, see Masson 1976. For a Greek graffito in the Osireion, Boyaval 1969, discussed below. Some additional examples of Aramaic and Phoenician graffiti in Kornmann 1978.
8. PL 557 has a pentagram, which seems to be a magical symbol; magic squares: PL 456 (on the terrace above the Table of the Kings).
9. Egyptians 'see' the gods: Van der Plas 1989; Volokhine 1998: 61, so some of the Phoenician graffiti use the verb *hzr*: see Rutherford 2000.
10. Later on Roman troops were stationed at Abydos, according to the *Notitia Dignitatum* (*In Partibus Orientis* XXVIII.11), but there is only one Latin graffito at the Memnonion: PL 569.
11. Common forms are … *proskunma* + genitive; they can also be with a nominative; sometimes abbreviated (PL 212); the verb *eproskunsa* is sometimes used.
12. In other cases, a prayer that someone is fortunate or lives well (*eutukhei*/ … *para*, $z\bar{e}s\bar{e}$ PL 67); … or statements that the deity rejoices: *khairein para* (PL 90). There are many statements that someone has arrived: usually $h\bar{e}k\bar{o}$, or other verbs (*elthe*: PL 88; *aphiketo*: PL 219; *paragignomai*). Sometimes people say they have been saved (*esōthē* etc. PL 91–92). The phrase *epi agathōi* ("for the good"): PL 504, in PL 524 at the end. On these formulae see Rehm 1940; Snell 1926.
13. Baillet (1920–1926) examines evidence of doctors sightseeing at the Theban tombs. Around the same time doctor Thessalus of Tralles represents himself as having gone to Egyptian Thebes in order to gain divine revelation ("to get close to god") (Totti 1985: n. 45) He represents his motives cynically: he desperately needed knowledge in order to avoid being humiliated in the eyes of his contemporaries. A priest tells him that he can reveal this knowledge, and he takes Thessalos into the desert, where Thessalos begs him for divine revelation. After a three day period of purification, the priest takes him to his house, he sits opposite the chair reserved for Asclepius, and Asclepius appears to him and reveals the nature of certain herbs, together with their relation to astrological signs. As Fowden (1986: 164) shows, this narrative should be read in the context of belief in the importance of Egypt as a repository of esoteric 'hermetic' doctrines.
14. Perdrizet and Lefebvre (1919: xvi) suggest that the first day of the month, being sacred to Thoth, was regarded as particularly suitable for oracles.
15. Perdrizet and Lefebvre (1919) point to a bilingual inscription from Copenhagen in honour of Pe-ti-min, son of Har-Khebis, which is written with the 'wasp' sign, and is transcribed by Paniskos, son of Horus, called 'Wasp': cf. Spiegelberg 1908/09: 101.

16  For Khoiak cf. also PL 2, 269, 510, 647. No other month is as common to visit. This Demetrius visited often; cf. also PL 630–631, two graffiti left on 28–29 Paophi 147 AD).
17  Demetrios, the famous *paradoxos*: PL 526; Aspidas, *Puthionikos*: PL 481, 580; Anoubion, *Olumpionikos*: PL 500). On the status of athletes in Greco-Roman Egypt see Perpillou-Thomas 1995.
18  Perhaps consider also PL 413; the father of this Euphris may have come from Tell Gurob.
19  PL 510 is by Apion, an arkhi-helmsman from the Kunopolite Nome; PL 502 is by Arouerios from Moukhent in the [Kuno?] polite Nome?
20  PL 295 and PL 334 are similar. The practice of writing Egyptian in Greek letters is well discussed in Quaegebeur 1982, and cp. "Old Coptic" script in magical papyri in Johnson (1986).
21  It is interesting that some Greek graffiti are written over Phoenician ones, as if declaring: 'this is Greek space, not Phoenician', e.g. PL 290, written over CSI 104.
22  Kemp (1975: 39) gives evidence for building work on the temple in the time of the Emperor Tiberius.
23  The building was the chapel of Amun-Ra "who hears prayers" (Porter and Moss 1974, II: 213).

## Acknowledgments

I thank B. Porten and J. Healey for a discussion of the issue of dating Aramaic documents. Thanks also to Susan Woodhouse for drawing my attention to the inscriptions on the roof at Edfu.

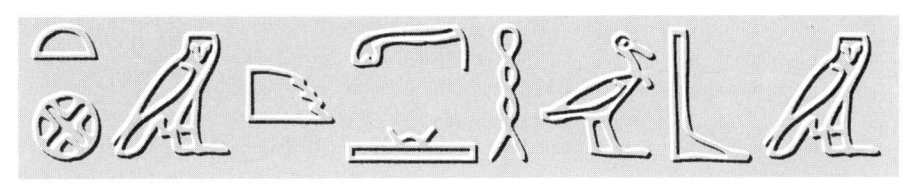

CHAPTER 11

# CARRY-ON AT CANOPUS: THE NILOTIC MOSAIC FROM PALESTRINA AND ROMAN ATTITUDES TO EGYPT

*Susan Walker*

## The caricatures

Among the large number of surviving works of art made in the first century AD to celebrate Roman interest in Egyptian culture and religion are some caricatures that deliberately recall – and subvert – elements of the famous Nilotic mosaic from Palestrina, near Rome. Three such images are described in some detail here, and are considered in relation to other works of art and opinions voiced in ancient literature which suggest a continued tension in Roman attitudes towards Egypt, even a century after the defeat of Cleopatra VII and the resultant conquest of Egypt in 30 BC.

No. 1 relief[1] (Walker and Higgs 2001: 336, no. 356) is decorated with a figured frieze framed above and below by *cyma reversa* mouldings. Below the lower moulding extends a plain fascia. The back of the relief is smoothly finished; perhaps it formed part of the revetment of the base of a large sculpture similar to the figures of the Nile and the Tiber now in the Vatican Museums (Lembke 1994: 214–216, pls. 19–22; Moltesen 1997: 111, fig. 6). The surviving figures comprise a naked couple engaged in sexual intercourse (Figure 11:1), the woman penetrated from the rear. The pair are caricatured pygmies, passengers in a sailing boat piloted by a fleshy man who takes no interest in their lovemaking. He wears a loincloth and an exaggerated version of the *pilos*, a pointed hat, in a Nilotic context usually of straw or papyrus and the typical headgear of poor Egyptian marsh-dwellers (Meyboom 1995: 247 n. 82). In his left hand is a paddle; his right holds an object now broken and unidentifiable. In front of the boat appears the rear of a hippopotamus, and in the water between it and the boat is a flower. Above the hippopotamus are the remains of two vertical bars, and attached to the left bar are horizontally engraved lines, these elements forming part of an ashlar masonry or brick structure with an open door or colonnaded porch, shown in profile to the right (Moltesen 1997: 115, fig. 9). Beside the boat a dolphin swims on the surface of the water, with the forked tail of another to the right, the dolphin's back curved as it leaps up against the side of the ship: dolphins accompanying boats at a greater distance appear on a sarcophagus now in Copenhagen, and on the floor mosaic of a Tunisian shipper's office in Piazzale delle Corporazioni, Ostia (Østergaard 1997: fig. 14 (mosaic at Ostia), fig.15 (sarcophagus in Copenhagen, Ny Carlsberg Glyptotek IN 1299)). Beneath the lovers, the edge of the boat is decorated with a scrolled panel. The

Figure 11:1 Fragment from a marble frieze: a couple make love in a boat in a Nilotic and Mediterranean setting (British Museum GR 1865.11-18.252). Height 38 cm; width 39 cm; thickness 5 cm.

sail, neither furled nor unfurled, is made to serve as a canopy over the couple. A similar arrangement of the sail appears in a painting of three pygmies in a boat, one perched on the prow with buttocks exposed to excrete on his animal enemies, from a *columbarium* (multiple tomb) in the Villa Pamphili at Rome, while the form of the vessel is recalled in a second century AD terracotta from the Fayum, now in Münster, showing Harpokrates travelling through a Nilotic landscape in a decorated boat (Cèbe 1966: 349–350, pl. IX,4 (sail as canopy); Pekáry 1982: 373, pl. 20 (boat), 1999: 298–299, V11, 38D–93). A grander sailing boat equipped with a cabin appears on the Palestrina mosaic: its position in the present reconstruction is incorrect, the surrounding water flowing at an unnatural angle (Meyboom 1995: 40).

Two fresco paintings from the plinth of an engaged colonnade in the *viridarium* (enclosed garden) of the House of the Doctor at Pompeii (VIII, 5, 24), cut from their context in the late 19th century and now in the collections of the Museo Archeologico Nationale, Naples (inv. no. 113195, ht. 43 cm, w. 126 cm (Walker and Higgs 2001: 338–339, no. 359); and inv. no. 113196, ht. 56 cm, w. 217 cm (De Caro 2000: 21, 45; Clarke 1998: 44–45)).

113195 (Figure 11:2 col. pl.) shows a nightmarish parody of a festival, while 113116 (Figure 11:3 col. pl.) illustrates a licentious outdoor drinking party. In both scenes, pygmies take the place of the Egyptian and Greek inhabitants of the Nile Delta and lower valley. In an interesting third scene from the plinth, not considered in detail here as it falls beyond the scope of this chapter, pygmies re-enact a scene of judgment before three judges in Greek dress. This last panel has attracted much comment from modern scholars (Cèbe 1966: 365–366, pl. XVIII.6; Eschebach 1984: 46, fig. 68 (judgment scene); Schefold 1962: 151, pl. 1444 (judgment and symposium scene)) who read it as a parody of the judgment of Solomon; and Cèbe (1966: 366–367, pl. XVIII.7) saw the symposium as a related parody of the Jonah story, reading the festival as a genre scene. McDaniel (1932: 266), who refused to discuss the symposium, saw both judgment and festival as parodying traditional Egyptian skills in law-giving and crocodile-hunting.

No. 2 comprises several lively episodes. To the upper right, a pygmy is drowned as his boat capsizes, while another clings perilously to the branch of a tree. A third is swallowed by a hippopotamus which has its eye on a fourth pygmy, standing with arms raised in the capsizing boat, as if paralysed with fear. A fifth pygmy from this ensemble vainly stabs the rear of the hippopotamus as it swallows his colleague. To the lower left of the panel, a pygmy attempts to frighten a menacing crocodile with clashing cymbals. To the lower right, in a vignette reminiscent of the entertainments provided at festivals, a pygmy rides a crocodile which is pulled to the shore by three colleagues. A bireme, shown at the top right of the scene, departs elsewhere at speed, its occupants displaying no interest in the fate of the pygmies. Behind the ship is an urban landscape comprising a long, perhaps colonnaded, building with a pitched red roof; a shrine with a triangular pediment and windows framing a curtained central door; above this, a monumental arch, and to the left, a long building with windows. It has been noted (Meyboom 1995: 309 n. 124) that the landscape of the foreground, with two shrines set on a platform in the waters of the Delta, the buildings surrounded by a glade, recalls that of the Palestrina mosaic. However, notwithstanding Cèbe's contention that scenes involving pygmies are set in the upper reaches of the Nile amidst Egyptian buildings, the architecture shown in the panel is Roman, not only lacking Egyptian features but also the curved pediments fashionable in Ptolemaic Egypt and a prominent feature of the Palestrina pavement (Cèbe 1966: 345–346; Meyboom 1995: 28, n. 83, 247–248 (pediments)). The thatched reed tower-house in the upper left of the painting is similar to the structures shown on Roman terracotta 'Campana' reliefs with Nilotic scenes (Moltesen 1997: 102–125). The black ibis flying into the scene from the left suggests that the Delta was intended as the setting (Pollard 1977: 66, quoting Aristotle *Historia Animalium* IX.617B29).

No. 3 (inv. no 113196) depicts an outdoor symposium, plentifully supplied with wine from a ship shown to the left, laden with amphorae, its prow decorated with an ass's head. On the shore below the boat, in a scene reminiscent of the pairing panel, a hippopotamus devours a pygmy, despite the efforts of one companion (dressed in a caricatured *pilos*) to pull the victim from the beast's mouth, while another – again, recalling festival entertainment – dances on its back. To the right, the symposium is set beneath a canopy hung from two trees. The shadowy drinkers (no food is shown) are served by a pygmy who has collapsed in a stupor beside the frame holding the serving amphora. No mixing bowls are present, indicating that the wine was served undiluted. The symposiasts watch an entertainment comprising a dark-skinned pygmy flautist accompanying a pale-skinned woman, naked but for a massive garland on her head, who squats on the phallus of a second pygmy, lying on the ground beneath her. Seen from the rear, she is turned away from his face. To the right, two clothed pygmies bearing staffs, one also carrying a pair of pipes, walk towards the scene, while another figure passes by. An ibis with white feathers struts in the foreground: this, together with the hilly reddish landscape, sets the scene in the Nile Valley rather than the Delta. Further to the right, two men, one perhaps wearing a Macedonian *kausia*, are absorbed in conversation before a building with a roofed corridor, most likely a shrine. They display no interest in the symposium. Beside the structure, in the crook of a tree, is a tall column on which is displayed a group of statues.

A related scene occurs on the wall of the *triclinium* of the House of the Ephebe at Pompeii (I, 7, 11) (Jacobelli 1995: 55, fig. 47). A woman and a man make love in similar fashion (though seen from a different angle) beneath an awning suspended from a tower. A female flautist and castanet-players provide a rhythm. In the background, a dark-skinned man carries an amphora, presumably of wine, while to the left of the tower, a pygmy operates a water-pump. A passer-by, dressed in a loincloth and carrying a staff, stops to watch.

Another pair of friezes from Pompeii (Naples inv. nos. 27698, 27702), as with the preceding example not evoking the scenery of the Palestrina mosaic, shows a woman performing fellatio on a reclining pygmy while she is penetrated from the rear by a second pygmy, who steers the boat through a marshy landscape, menaced by a crocodile and a hippopotamus; in a second scene a woman is penetrated from the rear while punting a raft through the same landscape, aided by a second pygmy who takes no part in the sexual congress. They drift towards a building of reeds with a triangular pediment (De Caro 2000: 46). Closer to the marble relief (no.1 above) is a mosaic panel featuring three pairs of lovers reclining in boats set in a Nilotic landscape. Discovered in Rome, the panel is now in Naples (inv. no. 122861). The setting is here adapted to a rectangular room, the boats drifting around the centre. On the fourth side are pygmy hunters (De Caro 2000: 46 (full view), 20 (details)).

## The format of the frieze and other Nilotic scenes

The marble relief no. 1 clearly formed part of a frieze, while the paintings from the 'House of the Doctor' nos. 2 and 3, though decorating the plinth of a colonnade, offer separate vignettes rather than a continuous narrative. The frieze was a popular format for Roman representations of life on the Nile, no doubt for its evocation of the length of the river and the narrow corridor of fertile landscape between the deserts to either side. Many vignettes were observed from the bank of the river, the figures seen from behind: however, this viewpoint was not used for no. 1, seen from the water itself, nor for nos. 2 and 3, in which a panoramic view akin to that of the Palestrina mosaic was attempted. The format of the frieze was well suited to wall and plinth decoration. In Nilotic floor mosaics the frieze format was used to decorate the thresholds of important reception or dining rooms, often in panels separated by columns (Lancha 1980: 265–267 n. 20; Righi 1984; Zevi 1998: 44, pl. 15.2).

Terracotta 'Campana' relief panels (Figure 11:4) also conform to the format of the frieze, in which life on the river is glimpsed through an architectural frame, placing

Figure 11:4  Terracotta 'Campana' relief: a parody of life on the Nile. Princeton University Art Museum. Gift of Edward Sampson, Class of 1914, for the Alden Sampson Collection.

the viewer indoors (the panels were used to decorate interior walls). Their vignettes recall the scenes of agricultural activity on the Palestrina mosaic. Some include an image of a woman reclining on a bed or couch, set outdoors. She is seen from the rear and turns to admire a herm of Priapus (Moltesen 1997: 105, fig. 2). Similar figures appear as appliqués, or were painted – again, in the form of a frieze – on ceramic vessels from Egypt of late hellenistic or Roman date (Guidotti 1980: 74). No scenes of sexual intercourse or excessive drinking appear in these caricatured images.

Some images of life on the Nile have survived from Egypt itself. These are models of decorum compared with the Roman caricatures: a banqueting scene on a Nilotic pavement from a late Roman villa at Thmuis shows the celebration of the inundations by humans of normal proportions amidst a panorama of natural life on the Nile, much in the manner of the Palestrina pavement (Alexandria, Greco-Roman Museum: inv. no. 21641) (Meyboom 1995: pl. 47), and tantalising fragments survive from Canopus of earlier pavements in which pygmies are naturalistically portrayed in a Nilotic landscape (Daszewski 1985: 139 no. 31, 167–168 no. 44).

Significantly, there are also Nilotic scenes from Roman contexts with no lampoon intended, such as the fragmentary mosaic *emblema* from the Esquiline, Rome, a noted centre of the Egyptian cults: the panel shows priests feeding crocodiles in a Nilotic landscape (Salvetti 2000: 235, no. IV.4). Indeed, the caricatures apparently exclude images of deities and priests, Egyptian and Greek, though some may have been aimed at profaning Egyptian religious practice. Among the latter may be counted a series of lamps made in Italy from about 40–80 AD, but mostly known from Roman military sites on the Rhine/Danube frontier and in the Rhône corridor. These depict on the discus a woman squatting on an outsized phallus set on a crocodile within a Nilotic landscape (e.g. Bailey 1980: Q900 = Walker and Higgs 2001: 337, no. 357; Grimm 2000: 129, fig. 3). It has recently been proposed that the phallus is that of the dismembered god Osiris, and the woman is enacting a perverse and disrespectful version of an Egyptian religious ritual (Etienne forthcoming).

## Roman orientalism?

Many Roman Nilotic scenes include grotesquely caricatured male pygmies engaged in sex with naked women, who are conventionally shown as white-skinned in the paintings, and whose hair is either gathered in a bun at the nape of the neck or in a topknot in hellenistic Greek style. Sexual scenes of similar liveliness occur in many other Roman contexts: among the best known is the series of heterosexual couplings portrayed on the walls above the lockers of the *apodyterium* (changing-room) of the Suburban Baths at Pompeii (Jacobelli 1995 *passim*). Here and in other instances sex takes place between individuals of normal human proportions (the genitals are sometimes exaggerated), and the protagonists are shown in bed, often with further indication that the scene is set indoors. The removal of clothing is also a significant element, both in the Suburban Baths sequence, and in the homosexual scenes on the silver Warren Cup, where abandoned clothes and softly cushioned beds fill the background (Clarke 1998: pls. 1–2).

Of what significance, then, is the shifting of sexual activity outdoors to the landscape of the Nile, and the substitution of individuals of normal proportions and western European appearance with caricatured pygmies? If any opinion is offered by modern commentators, it tends to assume that the scenes were intended to amuse if not arouse the ancient viewer (Jacobelli 1995: 88); the pygmies have also been understood as the embodiment of a (surely anachronistic) multi-cultural liberalism, the unexceptional occupants of a hellenistic landscape, members of an inclusive society in which their appearance did not invite ill-will (Clarke 1998: 46).

Egypt is thought to have evoked amongst the Romans a sense of fertility, both in its agricultural role as provider of grain for Rome, and in providing a landscape for exotic and highly sexed creatures offering a talisman of human fecundity. In the latter respect, Clarke (1998: 44–45) suggests that the outdoor Nilotic scenes of sexual engagement between pygmies were intended to serve as an amusing counterpoint to the indoor scenes between individuals of European origin and normal proportions. However, the displacement by pygmies of the Greek and Egyptian populations of the Nile Delta (as seen in the Palestrina and Thmuis mosaics) is worthy of comment. The pygmies have themselves moved from their natural habitat. This was variously perceived in antiquity, but the sources of the Nile (so in the Palestrina mosaic) (Meyboom 1995: 226–227 n. 17), or the shores of Ocean were preferred to the lower Nile Valley or the Delta region (Dasen 1993: 176, 1994). In Roman caricature, the myth associated with the pygmies, that of a mostly losing battle against crop-devouring flocks of cranes, is also transported to a Nile Delta setting, in which the cranes become observers; on terracotta 'Campana' reliefs, they are shown nesting on the pygmies' huts, even watching out for their young by holding a rock in one claw (Aelian III, 13, regarded with scepticism by Pollard 1977: 12). The cranes are replaced as the object of unsuccessful battle by the hippopotamus, almost invariably shown with its companion the crocodile, both creatures serving in hellenistic and Roman art as symbols of the Nile (Meyboom 1995: 255–256 n. 114). In orgiastic drinking and sex scenes the pygmies assume an identity close to that of satyrs and maenads, but there is no further evidence of Dionysiac or other religious activity, and it is reasonable to suppose that such scenes, along with acrobatic feats performed on crocodiles, do indeed lampoon the celebrations of the Nile flood, long regarded in the Greek world as licentious (e.g. Herodotus II.60, with reference to the festival of the Bubastia). Indeed, in plastic vases ascribed to the Athenian potter Sotades, active in the mid-fifth century BC, pygmies or dwarfs appear in the jaws of crocodiles. No blood is shed, and the vases may portray exotic entertainment. Most surviving examples were found in southern Italy, in the cemeteries and sanctuaries of Greek communities: the reason for their popularity in Italy is not understood (Williams forthcoming).

## The image of Egypt in Roman literature

Much Roman imperial literature offers a negative view of licentious behaviour in late Ptolemaic Egypt, the embodiment of excess at the table and in bed. Disapproving attitudes were occasioned by a campaign of propaganda against Rome's enemy Cleopatra VII, the last of the Ptolemaic monarchs of Egypt defeated by Octavian at the Battle of Actium in 31 BC (Williams 2001: 190–199). In the years leading up to the battle, and in the immediate aftermath of the consequent annexation of Egypt by Rome, Octavian unleashed a series of virulent personal attacks on Cleopatra, focusing upon her femininity and characterizing her as a dangerous woman of excessive habits, with insatiable appetites for alcohol and sex. Unable to cast a slur on his adoptive father Julius Caesar, whose alleged son by Cleopatra, her co-ruler Ptolemy XV Caesarion, was simply eliminated by Octavian's men shortly after they entered Alexandria, Octavian concentrated his wrath upon Cleopatra's later relationship with his former colleague, the experienced and widely admired Roman general Marc Antony. Surviving references in Roman literature make it clear that, in this light, Marc Antony was to be pitied as a weak man unable to resist the alluring but deadly charms of the Egyptian queen. Thus the historian Florus, writing in the second century AD, had Antony "forgetting his nation, his name, the toga, the axes of power, and degenerated wholly into the style of that monster (sc. Cleopatra) in mind, in dress and, above all, in his way of living" (II.21.2–3) (Pelling in Walker and Higgs 2001: 292–301, esp. 300). "That monster" was described by Octavian's court poet Propertius amidst other epithets in a tirade of abuse (III.29–56) as "the insatiable harlot of the Canopus", while, as late as the early third century AD, Antony was ridiculed by the historian Dio Cassius as Cleopatra's "cymbal player at Canopus" (Dio Cassius L.5.3). Significantly, war had been declared not on Antony but Cleopatra, who became for Octavian the personification of the other, the external threat to Rome, amongst whose citizens Antony still had to be counted, even though he had controversially celebrated a triumph in Alexandria and had orchestrated the divisions of the eastern territories amongst his and Cleopatra's children.

Meanwhile Canopus, a resort and religious centre located in the western Nile Delta and linked to Alexandria by canal, became synonymous in Roman eyes with licentious behaviour, for which the Greek term used by the Augustan geographer Strabo (XVII.1.16–17) was *kanobismos* (Meyboom 1995: 334 n. 196).

## The Palestrina mosaic

It has been argued (Meyboom 1995: 75–77) that Canopus was the setting of the principal scene of the mosaic at Palestrina, which is thought to portray the celebration of the Khoiak festival of the inundations of the Nile (Figure 11:5 col. pl.). In the central scene of the foreground, soldiers gather beneath an awning in front of a temple to drink through horns wine diluted in mixing bowls (the latter prominent in the scene), served to their commander by a female figure, perhaps a priestess (the figure is much restored). Behind the temple is a walled grove, and in front of the wall a quay. The quay turns by an elaborately arched gate, through which priests bear a coffin. In the water beside the quay is a galley manned by oarsmen; a man once dressed in a *kausia* (Macedonian cap) – the restoration is botched but the *kausia* is clearly shown in the drawing made for Dal Pozzo (Kingsly 1981: 39–46; Whitehouse 2001: 120–121, no. 17) – announces with a fanfare the arrival of the Ptolemaic royal patrons of the festival. Of the royal party nothing remains in the mosaic, which was heavily restored following both deliberate and accidental break-up in the 17th century AD. Fortunately one of the surviving drawings made for Dal Pozzo and now in the Royal Collections at Windsor Castle shows an elaborate red parasol with a gold fringe, clearly set above the water beside the quay; it has been conjectured (Whitehouse 2001: 114–115, no. 14) that the parasol protected the royal party, who were shown disembarking beside the galley that had been their naval escort. This piece was not restored to the pavement because the 17th-century restorer Calandra did not know whom to place beneath the parasol – the royal figures had long since vanished, and may have been deliberately removed from the pavement in antiquity.

Despite the vicissitudes of its recent history, the mosaic offers a detailed and carefully observed record of the festival and its participants: local inhabitants are shown watching the proceedings while carrying on with their fishing and farming activities, which were indeed dependent on the arrival of the floods. In the panoramic view of the Nile, the artist may have intended to show Ptolemaic dominance over Upper and Lower Egypt, the festival in the foreground demonstrating how all the population, even the humblest marsh-dwellers, benefited from the correct observance by royal patrons and their military enforcers of traditional Egyptian religious ritual.

It is generally assumed (Riemann 1986: 396, who however believed the Nile mosaic to be a later insertion) that the mosaic formed part of the original development of the lower building complex at Palestrina, which has been dated to the later second century BC by study of its architectural ornament. The great Nilotic landscape decorated the floor of the grotto-like apse of a large hall, linked by a colonnade to a similar structure decorated with a second mosaic, much less well-preserved but apparently contemporary, showing a columnar shrine and a granite altar by a shore, and the adjacent salt-water bay filled with fish (Gullini 1956: pls. II, VIII–XII; Meyboom 1995: 17). Both mosaics were submerged, the grottoes permitting water to flow from the spring-line of the steep escarpment against which the ensemble was built. The function of these buildings remains unclear: they were not necessarily connected with the famous sanctuary of Fortuna Primigenia constructed on the spectacular terraces of the hillside above. In the imperial period the hall with the Nilotic mosaic seems to have been the location of a cult of Isis, closely connected with Fortuna, but the scale of the hellenistic development seems much too grand for a Latin sanctuary of Isis at that date (Meyboom 1995: 8–16).

Though evidently Ptolemaic, it is not possible to offer a more precise date for the mosaic in the absence of the royal figures who were surely the focus of the principal scene. Nor is it clear why a mosaic so deferential to the Ptolemies should have been commissioned for Palestrina: the interest in Egypt of local businessmen (via the Greek island of Delos, where many Romans pursued commercial careers before the island was sacked in 69 BC) is usually cited (Meyboom 1995: 85, 89) as a pretext for the work, with emphasis placed on its religious character, on this reading a celebration of the state of *tryphe* or bliss conferred upon Egypt by the Nile and its gods. Though the sacred nature of the pavement is clear enough, the mosaic record clearly had a royal focus, now much diminished by the loss of the disembarking figures, but also evident in the scene of the hippopotamus hunt (see cover illustration, this volume), carried out from a royal boat and intended to recall the pursuit of Seth in vengeance for the murder of his brother Osiris, a hunt regularly re-enacted by the pharaohs of dynastic Egypt (Meyboom 1995: 31–32, 225 n. 114). Moreover the entire pavement appears to show the two kingdoms of Egypt, clearly differentiated by their wild and civilized natures, but both controlled by the Ptolemies, whose eagle appears on the walls of a temple built in Egyptian style, the object of curiosity on the part of passing travellers (Meyboom 1995: 30–31, fig. 18, 225–252 n. 103).

Palestrina did develop an interest in the Ptolemies in the 30s BC, when the city is known to have supported Antony over Octavian – like contemporary Athens, its population seems (Riemann 1985: 152 n. 12) to have displayed an unfortunate leaning towards successive losing sides in the civil wars of the late Roman republic. Its male population slaughtered by Sulla in 80 BC for supporting his enemy Marius, 50 years later Palestrina was evidently made to acknowledge the power of the victorious Octavian, whose massive portrait (inv. no. 141) is displayed in the local museum today amongst a number of altars enthusiastically celebrating the Augustan peace (Boschung 1993: 169, no. 141, pl. 159.1–3 (head of Augustus)). This may have been the occasion for removing the royal figures from the principal scene of the mosaic; it can only be conjectured that the missing figures might have represented not Ptolemy VIII and his entourage but Cleopatra VII and her co-ruler and alleged son by Caesar, Ptolemy XV Caesarion. Such a proposal involves a radical redating of the pavement, long ranked (Meyboom 1995: 18–19; Zevi 1998: 44–47) as the finest and earliest of the mosaics of Italy, and linked to the workshop responsible for the Nilotic threshold panel in the House of the Faun at Pompeii, set before the equally distinguished mosaic showing Alexander fighting the Persian king Darius at the Battle of the Issus. However, recent stratigraphic excavations at Pompeii (Fulford and Wallace-Hadrill 1998: 143) have called into question the sequence of dates for Pompeiian wall decoration, suggesting, for example, that the "second style" be placed in or extended to the reigns of Augustus or Tiberius. Moreover, the composition of the pavement resembles that of a lost painting from Rome, also drawn for Cassiano dal Pozzo and dated to ca. 40 BC (Whitehouse 2001: 202–208, nos. 48–49, and back cover). And Cleopatra's association with Canopus, if that is to be accepted as the location of the scene of the festival shown on the mosaic, is well established in Roman literature (see above).

## The mosaic as inspiration for Roman caricatures

Whatever the identity of the missing royal figures, there can be no doubt (Meyboom 1995: 60–62 (central scene of Nile mosaic), 173–176 (fish mosaic)) that the Nilotic and fish mosaics at Palestrina inspired a number of compositions in various media. Among these representations were caricatures of the sort that form the subject of this chapter. Thus, the erotic scene on the stone relief (no. 1) recalls the setting of the royal hunting scene on the Palestrina mosaic, but subverts its meaning by replacing a sacred act of vengeance enacted by the ruler's representatives with one of sexual pleasure enacted by pygmies. It has been suggested (Walker and Higgs 2001: 336) that the unnatural union of Nilotic flower and Mediterranean dolphins in the landscape of the relief may reflect the liaison of Antony and Cleopatra, both in a geographical sense and in suggesting an 'unnatural' relationship between the queen of Egypt and the distinguished general, who continued to describe himself as holder of the Roman republican office of tribune on the coins he shared with her.

The paintings from the House of the Doctor at Pompeii (nos. 2–3) offer a complex narrative. One of the two scenes is very closely related in its setting to the principal scene on the Palestrina mosaic, replacing the sacred festival with a burlesque in which everything goes wrong for the pygmies, while the other evokes a gross parody of the symposium scene (Figure 11:6 col. pl.).[2]

All three scenes include individuals who take no interest in the antics of the parodied pygmies: the pilot of the boat (no. 1), the sailors in the departing bireme (no. 2) and the figures, one perhaps wearing a *kausia*, talking near the shrine (no. 3). Could it even be suggested that the capsizing pygmies of the painting no. 2 were a joke at the expense of the royal party once shown disembarking in a very similar landscape on the Palestrina pavement, their naval escort fleeing rather than formally announcing their arrival?

## The date of the caricatures

The date of the caricatures is generally taken to be the mid–late first century AD, the paintings of the House of the Doctor and the lamps usually cited as 40–79 AD. It is of some interest that the proposed dates coincide with the reigns of the later Julio-Claudian emperors Gaius (Caligula: 37–41), Claudius (41–54) and Nero (54–68), and their successor, victor in the Year of the Four Emperors, Vespasian (69–79). All three later Julio-Claudians were directly descended from Antony by his Roman wife Octavia, and their reigns saw a significant spread of Ptolemaic Egyptian fashions in personal appearance and domestic decoration. The former were inspired by the hairstyles of women at court, such as Antonia, Agrippina and Messalina, whose influential positions reflected the distance Gaius and Claudius had travelled towards making the position of emperor a hereditary matter for one family (Levick 1993: 46. Hairstyle: Antonia pl. 3, Messalina pl. 6, Agrippina pls. 25–26). In terms of lifestyle, Gaius might be said (Syme 1984) to have put the clock back to July of 30 BC, reviving a court at which the celebrations of a well-connected nobility set the tone. He was also surrounded by an influential group of Alexandrian Greek freedmen and, like Caesar and Antony, was accused of ambitions to move the capital of the empire to Alexandria (Barrett 1989: 84). Claudius favoured Antony's memory, while Nero – though at first promising to restore executive power to the Senate – was fatally susceptible to Greek, especially Alexandrian Greek, adulation (Griffin 1984: 214 (Nero); Levick 1993: 46 (Claudius)). The family of his wife Poppaea owned several grand residences in Pompeii, which was granted the status of a colony in 63. When Poppaea died two years later, she was embalmed in the foreign (i.e. Egyptian) manner, and deified: her shrine was three years in the building (Griffin 1984: 102–103).

It could be (Levick 1999: 77, 208–209) that the caricatures represent some reaction to these developments, either contemporary or, perhaps more likely, during the reign of Vespasian, who encouraged a return to traditional Roman values well reflected in the personal appearance of the emperor and his imitators. The erotic paintings in the Suburban Baths at Pompeii were suppressed at this period (Jacobelli 1995: 82). Roman criticism of Cleopatra's behaviour remained prominent in the literature of the mid-later years of the first century AD, notably in the writings of the pro-Roman Jewish historian Josephus, who had Herod contemptuously refusing Cleopatra's offer of sex (*Jewish Antiquities* XV.97–8), while, in the tenth book of his *Pharsalia*, Lucan – now that sufficient time had elapsed – wittily captured Julius Caesar's indifference to her seductive persona.

## Conclusion

Roman caricatures of life on the Nile parody its inhabitants, who are, whatever their status, depicted as pygmies amidst a landscape bereft of the Alexandrian architecture that is so prominent a feature of the Palestrina mosaic. Displaced from their true origin, the pygmies fight hippopotamus, rather than their traditional enemies the cranes, and suffer for the most part a similar lack of success. They are also menaced by crocodiles, used for festive entertainment. The same pygmies energetically engage in outdoor heterosexual sex and drinking bouts, both activities the butt of Roman literary commentators who despised the Egyptian propensity for excessive behaviour in these respects. The female sexual partners are conventionally shown as white-skinned, their hair redolent of fashions of the last court of Ptolemaic Egypt, perhaps a visual reminder of the licentiousness of Alexandria under Cleopatra's rule.

Though in recent scholarship such images have been interpreted as no more than amusing or, at most, arousing, a more negative interpretation is offered here. This is not the first time that the caricatures have been seen in such a light – in 1932 McDaniel (1932: 270–271) read the hunting and judgment scenes in the House of the Doctor as racist examples of Roman contempt for the conquered Egyptians. However, whether from fear of offending his readers, personal prudery or editorial concerns about prosecution, McDaniel fatally weakened his case by refusing to treat the symposium scene, and by 1966 Cèbe (1966: 347 n. 1) was able to dismiss his interpretation and present the caricatures as unexceptional examples of gross Roman humour. Here it is suggested that Roman caricatures of licentious Egyptian behaviour were artistic expressions of the campaign to discredit Cleopatra, a theme of imperial literature for centuries after her death. Dated to the mid–late first century AD, the caricatures may represent a reaction against the Hellenizing and Egyptianizing courts of Antony's descendants through his Roman wife Octavia. The Palestrina mosaic presented to Italian viewers images of the settings of the religious rituals practised by Ptolemaic rulers to guarantee the prosperity of Egypt through the Nile floods; by lampooning excessive behaviour in those particular settings, any celebratory memory of Ptolemaic control of Egypt was profaned.

## Notes

1   Of unknown but probably Italian origin, formerly in the Witt Collection, and since 1865 in the British Museum, until recently in the *Museum Secretum*.
2   In the current state of the Palestrina mosaic, this vignette is completely restored and its correct location is not known; the original panel, following a complex collection history, is now in the Antikensammlung, Berlin (Meyboom 1995: 33–34; Whitehouse 2001: 124–126, no. 19).

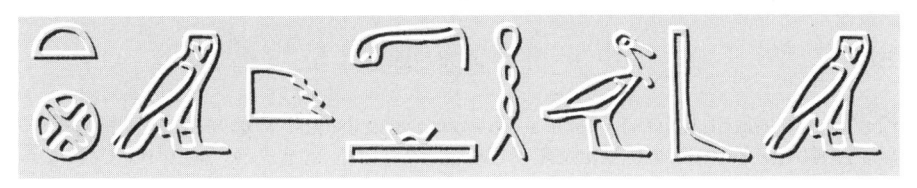

# CHAPTER 12

# ROMAN POETS ON EGYPT

*Herwig Maehler*

Until the end of the Republic, Roman public opinion took relatively little notice of Egypt. The Ptolemaic kingdom entered into sporadic contacts with the Roman Senate in the third century BC (such as in 273 when they exchanged trade delegations), and during Rome's showdown with Carthage, when one would have expected the Romans to have cultivated friendly relations with the Ptolemies in order to discourage them from supporting the Carthaginians, but there is no positive evidence to show that they did. The next contact we hear about (cf. Polybius IX.11a.1) comes in 215: there is a food shortage in Rome, caused, no doubt, by Hannibal's devastations in Italy; the Senate sent a delegation to Alexandria to ask for grain supplies. A few years later, in 210, we hear of another Roman embassy to Alexandria, headed by M. Atilius and Manlius Acilius, which brought presents "to king Ptolemy and queen Cleopatra [i.e. Arsinoe III] … to commemorate and renew their friendship" (Livy XXVII.44.10). At that time, the power of Carthage had not yet been broken, Hannibal remained as dangerous to Rome as ever, so the Romans had a strong interest in keeping the Egyptian kingdom neutral.

Rome's expansion into the eastern Mediterranean region began soon after Hannibal's final defeat at Zama in 202 BC. Two years later, when Philip V of Macedonia and Antiochos III had joined forces in order to attack the Ptolemaic kingdom, to seize Ptolemy V Epiphanes' overseas possessions and to divide them between themselves, Rome sent a delegation to Rhodes which told Philip very firmly to keep his hands off Ptolemy's affairs (cf. Polybius XVI.34.3). The same message was sent to Antiochos. In that year, 200 BC, the Romans attacked Philip V, and three years later Macedonia was on her knees. Rome's conquests in the east continued during the following decades. In 173 BC another Roman delegation arrived at Alexandria (cf. Livy XLII.6.4). Their aim was to find out about the intentions and preparations of the Ptolemies (Ptolemy VI Philometor and his sister, Cleopatra II) for another war against Syria, but their main objective was to make sure that both Antiochos and Ptolemy would remain neutral if Rome attacked Macedonia again. Under Philip's successor, Perseus, Macedonia had recovered some of her former military strength, so the Romans decided to crush Macedonia again, once and for all. This last showdown between Rome and Macedonia ended with the battle of Pydna in 168 BC. In that same year, the Romans also intervened, for the first time, in Egypt, where Antiochos had taken Memphis and was entering a suburb of Alexandria; there he met a Roman envoy, C. Popillius Laenas, who drew the famous circle in the sand and demanded that he get out of Egypt at once, and that he must give an answer to the Roman ultimatum before he would be allowed to leave the circle (see Polybius XXIX.23.9; Diodorus Siculus XXXI.2; Livy XLV.12). Needless to say, Antiochos obeyed.

168 BC marked Rome's double triumph over the Greek world, with the victory of Aemilius Paullus over Perseus at Pydna and with Antiochos' humiliating retreat from Egypt. The Romans had saved the Ptolemaic kingdom in its darkest hour; they now reminded the Ptolemies that they "should always consider the trust and good will of the Roman people the supreme defence of their kingdom" (Livy XLV.13.7). From now on, the Ptolemies regularly turned to Rome, not only for help against hostile neighbours, but also for arbitration and settlement of their internal disputes.

All these events concerned the Senate and the leading political class of Rome; they left no mark on Roman public opinion. Rome's expansion into the east did, nevertheless, have an impact on the public awareness of the newly conquered eastern provinces. Eastern cults began to penetrate Italy and Rome itself. During the second Punic war, in 205, with Hannibal still threatening, the Sibylline Books recommended the introduction of the Great Mother goddess of Pessinus, and in 204 Kybele appears in Italy (cf. Livy XXIX.11.5–8, 14.5–14; Ovid, *Fasti* IV.247–349), but the authorities bar their citizens from taking part in her cult (cf. Graillot 1912: 51–69). A major crisis came to a head in 186 BC with the *Senatus Consultum de Bacchanalibus* (*CIL* I$^2$ 581 = *ILLRP* 511); the Senate's decree was issued after secret religious associations had been denounced to the Praetor for alleged criminal actions under the cover of Dionysiac mysteries; these associations must have existed for quite some time before the authorities suppressed them (Latte 1960: 270–272).

Towards the middle of the second century, Egyptian cults arrive at Pozzuoli, brought there from Delos by Italian merchants; soon there were temples of Isis and Osiris at Pozzuoli and Pompeii. Here, far from Rome, their followers were not harassed by the authorities; provincial towns (*municipia*) were free to allow the formation of associations (*collegia*), while in Rome this was strictly regulated. Here, these things were handled differently: in 139 BC, the *praetor peregrinus* expelled the Jews from Rome on the grounds that they were trying to spread the cult of Sabazios and corrupting morality (Valerius Maximus I.3.3).

It seems, therefore, that the authorities in Rome were suspicious or even hostile to all 'Eastern' cults, no matter whether they were of Greek (Dionysos) or Oriental origin, because they felt that these were not compatible with the rational, juridical and utilitarian nature of Rome's very conservative religious traditions, which were a pillar of the political establishment. They feared not only the irrational elements of foreign cult practices, but also the danger of political opposition and subversion being fomented in foreign cult associations. The Senate's repeated attempts to ban Egyptian cults in Rome (but not in Pompeii, Beneventum, or other parts of Italy) suggest that the authorities were primarily suspicious of anything that they could not control and regulate. Their repression was not aimed at the Egyptian gods as such, but rather at the indigenous followers of foreign cults. This attitude is evident already in the *SC de Bacchanalibus*, and it is also the driving force in the persistent repression of Egyptian cults in Rome, which continued well into the Augustan period.

In the middle of the first century BC, Egyptian cults were still banned from the centre of Rome, the *pomerium*. By this time, however, the followers of the cults of Isis, Osiris, Horos/Harpokrates and Anubis had become very numerous and would no longer accept the ban on their cults. On 1 January 58 BC, Aulus Gabinius, one of the consuls for that year, was sacrificing to the gods on the Capitol, when the followers of the Egyptian cults arrived with images of Isis, Serapis, Harpokrates and Anubis, for which they tried to set up altars. The Senate, however, had these removed, but soon afterwards the crowd restored them "by force" (Tertullian, *Ad nationes* I.1.17–18). In 52 BC the Senate decided to demolish the temples of Isis and Serapis (see Cassius Dio XL.47.5–8), but this did not happen. (Already in the second century BC, Aemilius Paullus, as consul, had smashed the temple's door with an axe, as Valerius Maximus reports, I.3.4.) Four years later, the request of the official seers (*haruspices*) to have the temples of Isis and Serapis destroyed again was approved and carried out (cf. Cassius Dio XLII.26.2). Eventually, however, repression proved fruitless; in 43 BC, the Triumvirs decided to have another temple built in Rome for Isis and Serapis (see Cassius Dio XLVII.15.4).

In all this time, we find hardly any reference at all to Egypt, her gods, or her people in Roman literature. Egypt is mentioned once in Plautus' *Mostellaria*: old Theopropides, a merchant, has returned from a business trip to Egypt (*Most.* 440), but that can hardly count as a 'Roman' reference to Egypt because this play was modelled on a hellenistic comedy, Philemon's *Phasma*. Varro is quoted as having objected to the cult of Egyptian gods in Rome (Servius on Vergil *Aeneid* VIII.698), which may refer to the incident of 58 BC mentioned above. There is a passing reference to Serapis in Catullus X.25–27: Varus' girlfriend wants to be taken to the temple of Serapis in Rome – perhaps an indication that by the middle of the first century BC the cult was already popular among the *jeunesse dorée* of the capital.

It was the battle of Actium in 31 BC which brought about a dramatic change in the perception of Egypt and Egyptians among Rome's intellectuals. The growing confrontation between Marc Antony and Octavian, who both made every effort to win support in Rome, each for his cause, must have made an impact on public opinion; in their propaganda war, Egypt was a key element. Octavian's propaganda was more effective, because it was able to exploit two prejudices that were popular among the Roman public: (1) that Oriental influence corrupts even the best of men, and (2) that a powerful Oriental queen must be a threat to Rome. The way in which Antony behaved in Alexandria, his drunken excesses in the company of Cleopatra and their friends, who called themselves "The Inimitables" (ἀμιμητόβιοι, Plutarch *Antony* XXVIII.2), was seen as confirmation of the first of these prejudices, while Cleopatra's successes in regaining territories that had once belonged to the Ptolemaic kingdom seemed to confirm the second. These included Cyprus (which the Romans had annexed in 58 but which Julius Caesar had given back to her in 47) and parts of Lebanon, of the Phoenician and Cilician coasts and of Crete, which Antony gave back to her in 37, even though they were parts of Roman provinces and therefore under the Senate's jurisdiction. The alliance between Antony, who – despite his dissolute lifestyle – was popular with his troops and able to count on their loyalty, and the ambitious Cleopatra, who put the resources of her country at his disposal, must have been perceived in Rome as a real and very terrifying danger. Octavian himself made the Senate declare 1 August a feast day because on that day in 30 BC he had "liberated the state of that very depressing danger", as the *Fasti* record (cf. *CIL* I,1²: 214; also Fasti Amiterini 244). Contemporary poets, such as Propertius, refer to Rome's fear of Cleopatra (cf. Propertius III.11.58 *femineas timuit ... minas*; and see Hubbard 1974: 108; also Propertius IV.6.41 *solve metu*).

The first and most immediate reaction to Octavian's victory over Antony's and Cleopatra's fleet at Actium comes from Horace. In his ninth epode, which he probably wrote shortly after the battle (or, if he was not present, shortly after the news had reached him, cf. Paladini 1958: 13) he asks for the precious wine *Caecubum*, with which he wants to celebrate the victory together with Maecenas. Despite the victory, the mood of the epode seems strangely sombre. True, the enemy has been defeated, though not destroyed: where he will turn to is still unclear, so Octavian still has much to worry about and to fear. Cleopatra is not mentioned by name; the only reference to her comes in lines 12 (*feminae*) to 16: Roman soldiers have to serve her "withered eunuchs, and the legionary standards surround her canopy".[1] Here Horace simply expresses patriotic outrage at the degradation of Roman legionaries in the service of the lecherous Oriental queen who seduced and morally corrupted a great Roman general. We see here the earliest reflection in poetry of the most effective weapon of Octavian's propaganda: Cleopatra is a prostitute who will stop at nothing in her pursuit of power.

Octavian's victory at Actium on 2 September 31 BC and the final defeat of Antony and Cleopatra at Alexandria in August 30 BC changed the fear to jubilation; Horace's famous ode I.37, which begins with the same motif as epode 9, refers to the situation after Antony's and Cleopatra's death. It reflects the mood in Rome most vividly (trans. Shepherd 1983: 100–101; cf. Paladini 1958: 25–34):

|   | | |
|---|---|---|
|   | Nunc est bibendum, nunc pede libero | Friends, now is the time to drink, |
|   | pulsanda tellus, nunc Saliaribus | now tread the earth with our dancing, |
|   | ornare pulvinar deorum | now set Salian delicacies |
|   | tempus erat dapibus, sodales: | before the Gods' couches. |
| 5 | antehac nefas depromere Caecubum | Heretofore it had been a sin to produce |
|   | cellis avitis, dum Capitolio | Caecuban [wine] from ancient racks, |
|   | regina dementis ruinas | while a crazy queen was plotting, |
|   | funus et imperio parabat | with her polluted train |
|   | contaminato cum grege turpium | of evil debauchees to demolish |
| 10 | morbo virorum, quidlibet inpotens | the Capitol and topple the Empire – |
|   | sperare fortunaque dulci | a hopeful derangement drunk |
|   | ebria: sed minuit furorem | with its luck. But the escape |
|   | vix una sospes navis ab ignibus | from the flames of scarcely one ship |
|   | mentemque lymphatam Mareotico | dampened her fury, and Caesar |

| | | |
|---|---|---|
| 15 | redegit in veros timores | dragged back to fearful reality |
| | Caesar ab Italia volantem | her mind swimming in Mareotic [wine]: |
| | remis adurgens, accipiter velut | his galleys harried her fleeing from |
| | mollis columbas aut leporem citus | Italy (just as the hawk the mild dove, |
| | venator in campis nivalis | or the quick hunter the hare across |
| 20 | Haemoniae, daret ut catenis | Thessaly's plain of snow), in order |
| | fatale monstrum: quae generosius | to put the curs'd monster in chains. Yet |
| | perire quaerens nec muliebriter | she, seeking to die more nobly, showed |
| | expavit ensem nec latentis | no womanish fear of the sword nor retired |
| | classe cita reparavit oras, | with her fleet to uncharted shores. |
| 25 | ausa et iacentem visere regiam | Her face serene, she courageously viewed |
| | voltu sereno, fortis et asperas | her fallen palace. With fortitude |
| | tractare serpentes, ut atrum | she handled fierce snakes, her corporeal |
| | corpore combiberet venenum, | frame drank in their venom: |
| | deliberata morte ferocior: | resolved for death, she was brave indeed. |
| 30 | saevis Liburnis scilicet invidens | She was no docile woman but truly scorned |
| | privata deduci superbo | to be taken away in her enemy's ships, |
| | non humilis mulier triumpho. | deposed, to an overweening triumph. |

The first part of the poem is a rapidly moving invective, which contrasts Cleopatra's "mad" (*dementis*, 7) threats to destroy the Capitol and ruin the Empire, "a deranged hope", with the harsh reality of her defeat, the loss of nearly her entire fleet, and Octavian's pursuit as she fled from Italy. Here Horace boldly distorts the facts: it was Antony's ships which suffered the worst damage, while Cleopatra's fleet escaped more or less unharmed, and Octavian did not pursue her ships in order to capture her for his triumph. But Horace does not mention Antony; the whole poem focuses on Cleopatra, the queen (*regina*, 7) who had dared to threaten the Capitol. The invective moves towards and culminates in *fatale monstrum* (21): the Egyptian queen was a "deadly monster", "but *monstrum* is a 'miraculous portent' as much as a 'monster', and *fatale* is 'sent by destiny' as well as 'death-threatening'" (Pelling 2001: 295). At this point, however, the tone of the ode changes abruptly.[2] Cleopatra sought to perish nobly (*quae generosius perire quaerens* …), i.e. not paraded in chains in Octavian's triumphal procession in Rome and deprived (*privata*, 31) of her royal status. Her composure (*voltu sereno*, 26) and her courage in deciding to commit suicide, depriving Octavian of the greatest asset of his triumph, command admiration. In the face of death, Cleopatra has shown her strength of character. In the last stanza, Horace pays homage to the great Egyptian queen: she was "fiercer through her planned death" (*deliberata morte ferocior*), she refused (*invidens* = *recusans*) to be "lowered" (*deduci*) from her royal rank, "a not submissive woman" (*non humilis mulier*). Her greatness in death is thus impressively immortalized by the Roman poet. His ode, which began in a mood of noisy triumphalism, suddenly turned into a tribute of genuine admiration.

Vergil's vision of the battle of Actium is presented as the central part of the decoration of Aeneas' shield (Vergil *Aeneid* VIII.675–713) (Paladini 1958: 5–13; Pani 1984: 823). Here we see Augustus and Agrippa "with the Senate and the people [i.e. Roman troops], with the Penates and the great Gods" (Vergil *Aeneid* VIII.679), confronting Antony and his foreign troops from the East, from Egypt and remote Bactria, "and – shocking! – accompanied by an Egyptian wife" (*sequiturque – nefas – Aegyptia coniunx*, 688). While Cleopatra (*regina*, 696) spurs her troops with her "native" *sistrum* (*patrio vocat agmina sistro*), "all kinds of monstrous gods and barking Anubis" (*omnigenumque deum monstra et latrator Anubis*, i.e. the dog-headed messenger-god) fight the Roman gods: Neptune, Venus, and Minerva (698–700) …

In this passage, the Romans' contempt for the peoples of the east, including the Egyptians, combined with their prejudice against the ambitious "Oriental" queen, makes itself felt – not tempered, as in Horace's ode, by respect for Cleopatra's courageous attitude in the face of defeat and death. Here too, as in Horace's ninth epode (and in Ovid's *Metamorphoses* XV.826–828), we find echoes of Octavian's propaganda, which had been aimed at Cleopatra rather than Antony. Cleopatra presented herself as the "New Isis", and Isis was often shown with the *sistrum* (rattle); the reference to *patrio … sistro* therefore recalls Cleopatra posing as Isis in the great ceremony at Alexandria in 34 BC which so incensed the Romans, as Plutarch (*Antony* LIV.5–9; trans. Perrin 1920: 261) reports:

> He [Antony] was hated, too, for the distribution which he had made to his children in Alexandria; it was seen to be theatrical and arrogant, and to evince hatred of Rome. For after filling the gymnasium with a throng and placing on a tribunal of silver two thrones of gold, one for himself and the other for Cleopatra, and other lower thrones for his sons, in the first place he declared Cleopatra Queen of Egypt, Cyprus, Libya, and Koile Syria, and she was to share her throne with Kaisarion … In the second place, he proclaimed his own sons by Cleopatra Kings of Kings, and to Alexander he allotted Armenia, Media and Parthia (when he should have subdued it), to Ptolemy Phoinikia, Syria and Kilikia … Cleopatra, indeed, both then and at other times when she appeared in public, assumed a robe sacred to Isis, and was addressed as the New Isis.

Vergil's passage also reflects the Romans' dislike of animal-shaped or animal-headed deities, such as Anubis, which may have been one of the reasons for their early opposition to the "Alexandrian" (i.e. Egyptian) cults, against which Varro had already spoken out.

Some of the key elements of the Vergilian passage seem to be reflected in the anonymous *Carmen de Bello Actiaco*, an epic poem partially preserved in a papyrus from Herculaneum (*P. Herc.* 817, cf. Capasso 1998: 51–58; Immarco 1984: 583–590, 1989: 281–282). While the last eight columns deal with events from Octavian's capture of Pelusion to the fall of Alexandria and Cleopatra's suicide, the causes that led to the war and the battle of Actium were described in the first part of the roll, of which 15 fragments survive. Of these, the scanty remains of fr. 4 ( - - *i]n med[iis* - - - ] *veni[t] s[istr]um* [ - - - ] *manu [ut ag]mina [cogat]*) may refer to Cleopatra posing as Isis and calling on her troops by shaking her *sistrum*, as she does in Vergil *Aeneid* VIII.696, and the "Chinese and Indians" (*Seres et Indi*, fr. 4.9) are part of Antony's motley army of Oriental troops. Fr. 8, part of a dialogue between Antony and Cleopatra at Alexandria, speaks of the Nile which "opens a path, and streaming with all its water ..." (*pand]et i[t]er totoque tibi v[agus] aequor[e] Nilus ...*, fr. 8.7), which may be derived from Vergil's image of "the mourning Nile, of mighty frame, opening wide his folds and with all his raiment welcoming the vanquished to his azure lap and sheltering streams" (trans. Rushton Fairclough 1918: 109) (*maerentem ... Nilum | pandentemque sinus et tota veste vocantem | caeruleum in gremium latebrosaque flumina victos, Aeneid* VIII.711–713, cf. Propertius III.11.51 *fugisti tamen in timidi vaga flumina Nili*). Another passage of the anonymous poem refers to Cleopatra as "the main cause of the war, and part of the leadership" (*causa ... ma[xi]ma [be]lli,| pars etiam im[per]ii*), which is in line with Octavian's version that the war was declared on Cleopatra only, and that she played a leading role in the battle: a woman as leader in the army camp was a major scandal in Roman eyes – *nefas*, as Vergil (*Aeneid* VIII.688) says. Col. 7.6–9, describing Octavian's assault on Alexandria, stress that he came "with part of the Senate and with the army of his fatherland" (*cum parte se[n]atus | et patriae comitante suae cum milite Caesar*) "to take the walls of Alexander's people" (*gentis Alexan[d]ri ca[pi]en[da] ad moen[ia] venit*), which recalls Vergil's line *cum patribus populoque, penatibus et magnis dis* (*Aeneid* VIII.679). Here, too, the poet emphasizes, in line with Octavian's propaganda, that this was a war between Romans and Eastern barbarians, not a civil war (cf. Capasso 1998: 57).

Similar views are echoed, in contexts of a very different nature, in Propertius (ca. 48/7–3/2 BC; cf. Paladini 1958: 34–46). In Propertius' mind, Egypt seems inseparably linked to the battle of Actium, which he evokes in his imagination (IV.6.15–60). In another context he blames Antony's cowardice on his "infamous love" (*infamis amor*, III.16.39) which made him turn his ships and follow Cleopatra. In another poem he curses the Isis festival – by this time, the Alexandrian cults were well established even in Rome itself – because for 10 nights his beloved Cynthia has had to abstain from sex, and he threatens to drive "cruel" (*saeva*) Isis out of the city, "where Nile was never welcome to Tiber" (II.33.20). His most violent outburst against Cleopatra and Egypt comes in a poem (III.11) which pretends to answer the charge that he is enslaved (*addictum*) to a woman by listing examples of powerful women who subjected great mythical heroes or even Jupiter himself (cf. Pelling 2001: 295). "All of them were Eastern queens and princesses, and so was a contemporary figure, Cleopatra, to whom Propertius proceeds to devote the greater part of his poem" (Hubbard 1974: 108). Cleopatra is thus presented as the climax of this catalogue, and she is singled out for the most violent abuse (III.11.29–56; trans. Shepherd 1985: 114–115):

> What of her who lately heaped disgrace on our troops,
> a woman worn among her own household slaves?
> She claimed the walls of Rome and the Senate
> assigned to her rule as the fee for her filthy 'marriage'.
> Noxious Alexandria, land most skilled in guile,
> and Memphis so often bloody from our ills,
> where sand stripped off from Pompey his three triumphs!
> No day will take away that stigma, Rome ...
> Lecherous Canopus' prostitute queen, indeed,
> our one stigma branded by Philip's blood,

> dared to oppose her yapping Anubis against our Jove,
> to constrain the Tiber to tolerate Nile's threats,
> to usurp the Roman trump with a clattering rattle,
> to pursue Liburnian rams with punted barges,
> to spread her disgusting gauze on Tarpeia's rock,
> giving judgement amid Marius' arms and statues!
> What use now to have shattered Tarquin's axes …
> if a woman must be endured? Grasp at the triumph,
> Rome, and in safety beseech long life for Augustus!
> You fled to the wandering streams of cowardly Nile:
> Your hands accepted Romulus' fetters.
> I saw your arms all bitten by sacred adders,
> and limbs draw torpor in by secret paths.[3]
> 'With such a citizen, Rome, you had no cause to fear me!'
> So spoke even a tongue submerged by incessant wine.

Here the whole arsenal of slanderous allegations has been assembled: (1) The "woman" (*femina*), who put Rome's military might to shame, was a lecherous prostitute who had intercourse with her own slaves and demanded power over Rome as a "fee" (*pretium*) for her association with Antony. (2) Egypt is deceitful and "bloodstained" (*cruenta*) because Pompey was murdered there. (3) The harlot queen, "the unique disgrace branded [on Rome] by the blood of Philip",[4] dared to challenge Rome – here come the dog-headed Anubis again and the *sistrum* of Isis, both borrowed from Vergil (see above). (4) She threatened to set up her "gauze" (*conopia*, "canopy" of mosquito-nets: the word is borrowed from Horace, *Epode* IX.15). And then (5) the final taunt: her effrontery has been punished, she fled and was defeated, so her drunken tongue has to admit that "with such a citizen" [as Octavian] Rome has no reason to fear her. The charge of excessive and constant drinking may also be borrowed from Horace, who claimed that her mind was "swimming in Mareotic wine" (c. I.37.14: above). There is nothing original in this catalogue of taunts, each one of them being derived from either Vergil or Horace and ultimately, one may guess, from Octavian's propaganda before Actium. And yet, the focus of Propertius' poem (III.11) is not Cleopatra, or Actium, but his own torment, his infatuation with Cynthia and the suffering it causes him. His outburst against Cleopatra comes as the climax of his listing of powerful women who held men under their spell (as Cynthia has enslaved him); at the same time, it leads on to a highly patriotic image of Rome and ends with a panegyric of Augustus. "There is strong latent irony here, because Propertius knows (and knows that we know) that this world is not really one he could inhabit" (Shepherd 1985: 176).

Propertius' contemporary, Albius Tibullus (ca. 50–17 BC), was not interested in politics; his attitude to Augustus was detached, and the battle of Actium has left no trace in his surviving elegies. One of them (I.7) is a birthday poem written in or shortly after 27 BC for his patron, the senator M. Valerius Messalla Corvinus. It shows none of the disparaging views on Egypt expressed by Vergil, Horace and Propertius; on the contrary, in I.7.21–42 he praises the Nile which guarantees the country's fertility, and Osiris who is presented as inventor of agriculture and, above all, viticulture, as the Greeks had equated him with their Dionysos. Tibullus goes on to characterize Osiris as the god of feasting with songs, dancing and light-hearted love (*levis amor*). This image is, of course, very different from that of the Egyptian god of the dead, of whom the poets of the Augustan age seem to have known little or nothing, except that he was somehow connected to rebirth or life after death (cf. Merkelbach 1995: 133–134). Despite Augustus' and the authorities' disapproval, the Alexandrian cults appealed to the affluent middle class in Rome, not least because of their slightly exotic flavour, and so Tibullus mentions the Nile and "the foreign crowd that has been brought up to lament the [Apis] bull of Memphis" (I.7.27–28 *te canit atque suum pubes miratur Osirim | barbara, Memphitem plangere docta bovem*) without the usual gibe at Egypt's animal gods – not surprisingly, because this echoes not Augustus but a line in Kallimachos' elegiac epinician for Berenike II (the queen of Ptolemy III Euergetes) and her victory in the chariot race at Nemea (*SH* 254.16 εἰδυῖαι φαλιὸν ταυρον ιηλεμίσαι, cf. Cameron 1995: 477).

Among the poets and prose authors of the first century AD, the negative image of Egypt and her people prevails. Lucan (39–65 AD) takes up Vergil's view on Cleopatra and Egypt and adapts it to his own grand theme, the death of Pompey and the demise of the old republic. The motif of Egypt's animal gods recurs in Lucan's description of the banquet held by Julius Caesar and Cleopatra in Alexandria in 48 BC: "They served many birds and many beasts – the gods of Egypt" (X.158–159). Lucan's invective against Cleopatra echoes other elements of the propaganda war between Octavian and Antony before Actium: she entered the palace "without Caesar's knowledge – the disgrace of Egypt, deadly Erinys of Latium, promiscuous to the harm of Rome" (X.58–60) – here the charge of shamelessness crops up again, she acts like a prostitute. Later, at Actium, "with her rattle she alarmed the Capitol … and attacked the Roman standards with unwarlike Canopus [i.e. with Egyptian troops] in her intent to lead a Pharian [= Egyptian] triumph with Caesar [Octavian] as a captive" (X.63–65) – here Lucan is evidently indebted to Vergil's passage quoted above.

Lucan shares both Vergil's view of Cleopatra's moral depravity (she is incestuous because she is married to her brother: *incesta*, VIII.693) and his contempt for the "effeminate crowd of Canopus" (*mollis turba Canopi*, i.e. Egypt, VIII.543). Apart from these rather commonplace prejudices, however, Lucan's vehement aversion to Egypt has a very specific reason: Egypt is "a treacherous land" (*perfida tellus*, VIII.539), "guilty" (*noxia*, VIII.823) and "hated" (*invisa*, VIII.840), because his hero, the great Pompey, was murdered there, and now Egypt's sand retains Pompey's ashes, even though the Romans have admitted Isis and her *sistra* which bids the worshipper wail, the half-divine dogs (Vergil's "barking Anubis") and Osiris who is mortal because the Egyptians mourn him (VIII.831–834) – yet another reflection of the Roman authorities' longstanding dislike of Egyptian cults in general and animal cults in particular. The argument – Egypt, instead of showing gratitude for Rome's admission of her gods, has killed Pompey and keeps his remains – is weak on logic, but provides a rhetorically effective contrast. Lucan nowhere shows any knowledge of, or interest in, Egypt's religion or culture; he merely exploits the common preconceptions, which he shares with other Roman poets, in order to present Pompey as a great tragic hero.

By the time of Juvenal (67?–ca. 140 AD), the Romans' obsession with Actium and Cleopatra seems to have subsided, even though their popular prejudices about the "effeminate" Egyptians and their "barbarous" cult practices lived on. Juvenal certainly despised Alexandria as much as Egypt and her "unwarlike and useless crowd" (*inbelle et inutile volgus*, XV.126). To him, Alexandria is "notorious" (*famosa*) for its licentiousness, which is even worse than that of its fashionable coastal resort, Kanopos (VI.83–84), the cults of the Egyptian gods are ludicrous and their priests are swindlers who dress up as Anubis and "mock the crowd lamenting Osiris" (*plangentis populi ... derisor Anubis,* VI.534). Egyptians in Rome are targets of his scorn; one of them is a certain Crispinus, one of Domitian's protégés, "a slave from Kanopos (*verna Canopi*) from the Egyptian mob" (*pars Niliacae plebis,* I.26), who had made a fortune in Rome, "a monster not redeemed by any virtue from its vices" (*monstrum nulla virtute redemptum | a vitiis,* IV.2–3; he is also mentioned by Martial VII.99 and VIII.48).

It is in his fifteenth satire that Juvenal heaps all imaginable abuse on "deranged Egypt" (*demens | Aegyptos,* XV.1–2), which adores crocodiles, ibises, apes, cats, fishes, and dogs (XV.2–8). Her cult practices are absurd: while they forbid the slaughtering of young goats (kids, *fetum ... capellae*), they allow eating human flesh (*carnibus humanis vesci licet,* XV.12–13). This is, of course, a monstrous allegation; needless to say, Juvenal did not have a shred of evidence for it, except a gruesome scandal story about an incident of cannibalism in a fight between the inhabitants of Dendera (*Tentyra*) and Ombos (*Ombi,* modern Kôm Billâl opposite Qift), which he then describes in great detail. He claims that it happened "recently, when Iuncus was consul" (XV.27, i.e. in 127 AD); it started at a religious festival, when the crowd of Dendera was drunk and celebrating with African music (*nigro tibicine,* XV.49), and the people of Ombos attacked them. From a violent fist-fight it soon degenerated into a full-blown battle in which the attackers gained the upper hand (XV.72–76). One man stumbled, was captured and torn to pieces, and "the victorious crowd, gnawing his bones, ate all of him" (XV.80–81).

Whether this unsavoury incident really happened in the way Juvenal describes it is, of course, uncertain, although quarrels motivated by religious beliefs are attested between neighbouring towns, such as Oxyrhynchos and Kynopolis (Plutarch *De Iside et Osiride* 72 = *Mor.* 380 BC) and Hermonthis and Crocodilopolis in Upper Egypt (Wilcken 1912: no. 11). For Juvenal, the incident was a welcome pretext for castigating the depravity of society – in this case, Egyptian society. Hence his sweeping generalizations: it is not just the people of Dendera and Ombos who are "a barbarous mob" (XV.46), but Egypt as a whole is "demented", "rough" (XV.44), and "more cruel than the Tauric altar" (XV.115), i.e. than the Scythians. Juvenal, too, like other Roman poets, is not interested in Egypt as such; he picks up an alleged case of cannibalism, which had been reported from Upper Egypt,[5] because it gives him a pretext for combining the satirist's favourite theme – moral indignation about the decadence and immorality of his contemporaries – with the old prejudices about Egypt which had become commonplace among Rome's intellectuals since the time of Octavian's propaganda campaign against Cleopatra.

## Conclusions

None of the Roman poets, from Horace to Juvenal, seriously tried to understand Egypt's culture. They did not differentiate between Alexandrians and other 'Greeks' and the Egyptians who lived in the country, even though the official designation for Alexandria was *Alexandria ad Aegyptum,* which indicated that administratively the capital was not regarded as part of Egypt (cf. Bell 1946: 130–132). But this was just the official view; for the people of Rome they were all Egyptians, which is not surprising, given that right from the beginning of Roman rule in Egypt (30 BC) all inhabitants of the country other than those with Roman citizenship, in other words Greeks, Jews and Egyptians, were regarded as 'natives' or *provinciales* by the Roman authorities.

Rome's poets did not travel to Egypt; their knowledge of the country and its culture was based on hearsay and therefore extremely limited and superficial. Most of them may have heard of towns in Lower Egypt: Alexandria and Kanopos, Memphis and Pelusion; in addition, Juvenal mentions Dendera and Ombos, but even he is unlikely to have visited these places (see above). To the Romans, Egypt's gods are just bizarre; there is no attempt to understand the nature of Egyptian religion or the myths and religious concepts behind the rituals and cult practices.

Whenever Roman poets refer to Egypt and Egyptians, they do so in the contexts of their own agendas. For Horace and Vergil, the aim is to celebrate Augustus; Propertius sees Antony's infatuation with Cleopatra as a parallel to his own "enslavement" to Cynthia; Tibullus borrows a reference to Osiris from an *epinician* by Kallimachos because he is composing an analogous poem of praise; Lucan sees Egypt as a treacherous country, guilty of the murder of his great tragic hero, Pompey. Most of what these poets have to say about Egypt echoes Octavian's propaganda campaign against Cleopatra before the battle of Actium (31 BC), which had been deliberately targeted on the "Oriental" queen because Octavian was careful to present the coming war not as a conflict between Romans, i.e. as a civil war, but as a war against a foreign enemy. This is why Cleopatra appears as the main villain, while Antony tends to be presented as her slave, the victim of her seduction (Plutarch *Antony* LX; Florus II.21.1; cf. Scott 1933: 43) or even "witchcraft" (μαγγανεία, Cassius Dio L.5.3). Florus (early second century AD) clearly reflects the image of Cleopatra that Octavian's propaganda campaign had created (II.21.1; trans. Forster 1984: 323–325):

> After the Parthian expedition he [Antony] acquired a loathing for war and lived a life of ease, and a slave to his love for Cleopatra, rested in her royal arms as though all had gone well with him. The Egyptian woman demanded the Roman Empire from the drunken general as the price of her favours; and this Antonius promised her, as though the Romans were more easily conquered than the Parthians. He, therefore, began to aim at sovereignty – though not for himself – and that in no secret manner; but, forgetful of his country, his name, his toga and the emblems of his office, he soon completely degenerated into the monster which he became, in feeling as well as in garb and dress.

How much the generally negative image of Egypt, which prevails among Roman writers of the first century AD, owes to Augustus' negative propaganda is illustrated by a passage in Tacitus (55/6–ca. 120? AD, *Historia* I.11; see Jones 1942: 287–288):

> Egypt and the forces with which it has to be kept in subjection have been, ever since the days of the deified Augustus, ruled by Roman knights as vice-roys; it has been thought expedient thus to keep under home control a province difficult of access and productive of corn, distracted and excitable owing to its superstition and licence, ignorant of laws and unacquainted with magistrates.

But towards the end of the first century AD, Cleopatra and Actium had ceased to haunt the Romans. Statius (ca. 40–96 AD) in his *Silvae* (V.5.66–68) does speak of the "over-ready tongue and impudent wit" of the Egyptians, but this is his only polemical reference. The most venomous revilement comes from Juvenal, who detests Alexandria and Kanopos as much as the alleged cannibals of Upper Egypt. His insults are a combination of the old prejudices that had long been commonplace among Rome's intellectuals, and recent gossip about a particularly revolting incident which seemed to confirm not only the negative image of Egyptians, but above all the satirist's belief that, as Courtney (1980: 591) puts it, "human history has been essentially regression, not progress". On the other hand, it seems that this negative image was largely confined to the intellectuals in Rome. It did not prevent the "Alexandrian" cults of Isis, Osiris, Harpokrates, Anubis and Serapis from spreading and gaining popularity throughout the Empire, tolerated at first and soon actively promoted by the Emperors themselves: first by the notoriously 'Egyptophile' Caligula (Malaise 1972: 395–401), later by the Flavians and the Antonines, culminating in Commodus' unbridled enthusiasm for Oriental cults in general and for Serapis and Isis in particular (Malaise 1972: 407–436). Commodus was the first Roman emperor to put images of Serapis and Isis on his coins.[6] By his time, public opinion had changed radically: from the anti-Egyptian hostility of the Augustan age to general acceptance and even, in some cases, outright 'Egyptomania'.

When Apuleius (born at Madaura in Numidia in 125 AD) published his *Metamorphoses* (the *Golden Ass*) which happens to preserve the fullest description in Latin of the ideas and rituals of the Isis cult, he could count on a sympathetic audience. By the second century AD, the Isis cult had spread all over the Empire and enjoyed enormous popularity, as the numerous sanctuaries and countless statuettes of Isis and Serapis document. Yet, surprisingly, Apuleius is the only Latin author who had a genuine interest in Egypt's religion and culture. While authors like Juvenal who lived in Rome and wrote for a metropolitan audience continued to display hostility or, at best, indifference towards Egypt, Apuleius, being of north African origin and educated at Carthage (and later in Athens), was uninfluenced by their prejudices and remained open to the appeal of the Isiac religion. This religion was 'popular' also in the sense that, like early Christianity, its promise of divine protection and redemption appealed most to the common people, whom Apuleius, unlike Juvenal, did not despise – on the contrary, they are the main actors in his *Metamorphoses*, whose sufferings, passions and obsessions he observes sympathetically.

A contemporary author, the geographer Pomponius Mela, describes Egypt in his *Chorographia* (I.41–60). This work is a curious mixture of factual information, myth and fantasy; for example, in II.103 he derives the place name Canopos from that of Menelaos' steersman, who was said to have died there (Menelaos, according to Homer's *Odyssey* III.285 ff, was blown off course on his way back from Troy and forced to land in Egypt, but his steersman Canopos is a later invention). Pomponius also tells the fantastic story of the winged snakes that fly to Egypt in large numbers, where they are attacked and destroyed by ibises (III.82). This story is repeated by the historian Ammianus Marcellinus (XXII.15.26) in the later fourth century AD; in his digression on Egypt at the end of his 22nd book, Ammianus also mixes truth and fantasy in his account of Egypt's animals, such as the crocodile, the hippopotamus, and the manifold birds. For him, as for other writers of the later Roman period, Egypt is a land of strange and wondrous things and creatures. On the other hand, he is aware of Egypt's contribution to scholarship, wisdom and religious thinking: anyone, he (XXII.16.12–20) says, who studies religious writings will realise that this kind of knowledge originated and first developed in Egypt, whence it spread over the whole world; long before other peoples, the Egyptians "advanced to the various cradles of religions, as they say, and they cautiously guard the earliest beginnings of religious devotion laid down in secret writings". In the early fifth century AD, Macrobius (*Saturnalia* I.15.1) calls Egypt "the mother of sciences", because here the intercalary day was first added to the solar calendar.

Christian writers, by contrast, renew the traditional outbursts against Egypt's "idols", her animal-shaped gods. Tertullian (ca. 160–220 AD) in his *Scorpiace* ("Antidote to the scorpion's sting") links Aaron's Golden Calf (Exodus 32) with the Apis bull as examples of abominations. Hilarius of Poitiers (315–367 AD) quotes Vergil's line *omnigenumque deum monstra et latrator Anubis* (*Aeneid* VIII.698) in his polemic against the Egyptian *idola* (*In Matthaeum* I.6; cf. Monaco 1992: 262), and Paulinus of Nola (353–431 AD) claims in one of his poems that St Mark was "given" to Egypt "in order to defeat the [Apis] bull together with Jupiter, lest Egypt, crazy with Apis, worship cattle" (XIX.84–86).

The Romans knew little about Egypt and her ancient culture, nor did they want to know. They did not have Herodotus' inquisitiveness. Octavian's propaganda war against Antony, which targeted Cleopatra, without naming her, as a dangerous, power-hungry, shameless, oriental queen, Horace's *fatale monstrum*, who ruled over an effeminate and wicked populace, determined the Roman image of Egypt and Egyptians for more than a century. In a similar way, the images created in the sculpture of this period, the other powerful tool of Octavian's propaganda, determined the character of imperial portraits, and the iconography of imperial self-representation, for several generations. The power and persistent influence of images may act as a stabilizing force for governments, but it is also indicative of the loss of creativity and intellectual freedom.

## Notes

1 The charge came from Octavian himself: "In the account of his own life, Augustus reports that Antony ordered his troops to keep guard at Cleopatra's palace and to obey her wish and command" (Servius on Vergil *Aeneid* VIII.696).

2 Cf. Tarn 1931: 196–198, who argues that Cleopatra's alleged treachery at Actium was a myth, fabricated by hostile sources. He thinks that lines 23–24 *nec latentes | classe cita reparavit oras* may take up *Epode* IX.19–20 *portu latent | puppes sinistrorsum citae*; he sees a "second meaning behind the obvious one, echoing the epode, viz.: 'Antony's ships were traitors to him (*latent – citae*); but she was not a traitor as the ships were' (*nec latentis – cita*) ... I wonder whether this be not his way of indicating that the charge of treachery was equally unfounded" (198). See also Chauveau 1998: 99–100; Monaco 1992: 263–264; Scott 1933: 45–46.

3 Propertius' claim that he "watched" (*spectavi*) Cleopatra being bitten by adders may imply that he watched Augustus' triumphal procession in which an image of Cleopatra with the asp was carried, as Plutarch (*Antony* LXXXVI.6) reports.

4 Cf. Butler and Barber 1933: 290. The phrase '*Philippeo sanguine*' refers to an allegation that the founder of the Macedonian dynasty in Egypt, Ptolemy I son of Lagos, was in reality a son of Philip II of Macedonia.

5 Juvenal *Satires* XV.46 *quantum ipse notavi* "so far as my personal observation goes", i.e. 'to judge by the Egyptians I have met' (cf. Courtney 1980), should not be taken to mean that he had been an eye-witness.

6 Serapis as *CONSERU(ATOR) AUG(USTI)* (Mattingly 1940: 834, no. 684, pl. 110.3) Commodus, crowned by Victory, clasping hands with Serapis and Isis (Mattingly 1940: 751, no. 335, pl. 99.15).

# References

Note: references to chapters and books in the *Encounters with Ancient Egypt* series are denoted in bold type.

Abdalla, A. 1992, *Graeco-Roman Funerary Stelae from Upper Egypt*. Liverpool: Liverpool UP

Adam, S. 1966, *The Technique of Greek Sculpture in the Archaic and Classical Periods*. London: Thames and Hudson

Adams, B. 1975, Petrie's Manuscript Notes on the Koptos Foundation Deposits of Tuthmosis III. *Journal of Egyptian Archaeology* 61, 102–113

Adiego-Lajara, I-J. 1993, *Studia Carica. Investigaciones sobre la escritura y lengua carias*. Barcelona: Promociones y Publicaciones Universitarias

Albright, W. F. 1964, The Eighteenth Century Princes of Byblos and the Chronology of Middle Bronze. *Bulletin of the American Schools of Oriental Research* 176, 38–46

Alexiou, S. 1967, *Hysterominoikoi Taphoi Limenos Knosou (Katsamba)*. Athens: Bibliotiki Archaiologikis Etaireias

Algaze, G. 1993, *The Uruk World System. The Dynamics of Expansion of Early Mesopotamian Civilization*. Chicago: University of Chicago Press

Alon, D. 1972, Lahav. *Hadashot Arkheologiyot* 41, 34–35

Altenmüller, H. 1975, Abydosfahrt, in W. Helck and E. Otto (eds), *Lexikon der Ägyptologie I*, 42–47. Wiesbaden: Harrassowitz

Amiran, R. 1969, *Ancient Pottery of the Holy Land*. Jerusalem: Massada

Amiran, R. 1974, An Egyptian Jar Fragment with the Name of Narmer from Arad. *Israel Exploration Journal* 24, 4–12

Amiran, R. 1976, The Narmer Jar Fragment from Arad: An Addendum. *Israel Exploration Journal* 26, 45–46

Amiran, R. 1978a, Excavations at Tell Ma'ahaz 1975, 1976, *Israel Museum News* 12, 63

Amiran, R. 1978b, *Early Arad*. Jerusalem: Israel Exploration Society

Amiran, R. 1985, Canaanite Merchants in Tombs of the Early Bronze Age I at Azor. *'Atiqot* (English Series) 17, 190–192

Amiran, R. 1992, *Arad: eine 5000 Jahre alte Stadt in der Wüste Negev, Israel*. Neumünster: Karl Wachholtz

Amiran, R. and R. Gophna 1993, Ma'ahaz, Tel, in E. Stern (ed.), *The New Encyclopedia of Archaeological Excavations in the Holy Land 1–4*, 919–920. Jerusalem: Israel Exploration Society

Amiran, R. and O. Ilan 1993, Malhata, Tel (Small), in E. Stern (ed.), *The New Encyclopedia of Archaeological Excavations in the Holy Land 1–4*, 937–939. Jerusalem: Israel Exploration Society

Amiran, R. and O. Ilan 1996, *Early Arad. The Chalcolithic and Early Bronze IB Settlements and the Early Bronze II City: Architecture and Town Planning II*. Jerusalem: Israel Museum

Amiran, R., O. Ilan and C. Arnon 1983, Excavations at Small Tel Malhata: Three Narmer *Serekhs*. *Israel Museum Journal* 2, 75–83

Amiran, R. and E. C. M. van den Brink 2001, A Comparative Study of the Egyptian Pottery from Tel Ma'ahaz, Stratum I, in S. R. Wolff (ed.), *Studies in the Archaeology of Israel and Neighboring Lands in Memory of Douglas L. Esse*, 29–58. Chicago: Oriental Institute

André-Salvini, B. 1995, Les Pierres précieuses dans les sources écrites, in F. Tallon (ed.), *Les pierres précieuses de l'orient ancien*, 71–88. Paris: Réunion de Musées Nationaux

Andrews, A. 1956, *The Greek Tyrants*. London: Hutchinson

Anthes, R. 1963, Affinity and Difference between Egyptian and Greek Sculpture in the Seventh and Sixth Century BC. *Proceedings of the American Philosophical Society* 107, 60–81

Armayor, O. K. 1978, Did Herodotus Ever Go to Egypt? *Journal of the American Research Center in Egypt* 15, 59–73

Armayor, O. K. 1985, *Herodotus' Autopsy of the Fayoum: Lake Moeris and the Labyrinth of Egypt.* Amsterdam: Gieben

Arnold, D. 1993, *An Introduction to Ancient Egyptian Pottery: Fascicle 1 – Techniques and Traditions of Manufacture in the Pottery of Ancient Egypt.* Mainz: von Zabern

**Ashton, S-A. 2003, Foreigners at Memphis? Petrie's Racial Types, in J. Tait (ed.), 'Never had the like occurred': Egypt's view of its past, 187–196. London: UCL Press**

Assmann, J. 2000, *Weisheit und mysterium. Das bild der Griechen von Ägypten.* Munich: C. H. Beck

Aston, B. G. 1994, *Ancient Egyptian Stone Vessels: Materials and Forms.* Heidelberg: Heidelberger Orient

Aston, B. G., J. A. Harrel and I. Shaw 2000, Stone, in P. T. Nicholson and I. Shaw (eds), *Ancient Egyptian Materials and Technology*, 5–77. Cambridge: CUP

Astour, M. C. 1992, The Date of the Destruction of Palace G at Ebla, in M. W. Chavalas and J. L. Hayes (eds), *New Horizons in the Study of Ancient Syria*, 23–39. Malibu: Undena Publications

Astour, M. C. 1995, Overland Trade Routes in Ancient Western Asia, in J. M. Sasson (ed.), *Civilizations of the Ancient Near East*, 1,401–1,420. Peabody: Henrickson

Austin, M. M. 1970, *Greece and Egypt in the Archaic Age.* Cambridge: Cambridge Philological Society

Austin, M. M. 1981, *The Hellenistic World from Alexander to the Roman Conquest. A Selection of Ancient Sources in Translation.* Cambridge: CUP

Bailey, D. M. 1980, *A Catalogue of the Lamps in the British Museum ii: Roman Lamps made in Italy.* London: British Museum Press

Baillet, J. 1920–1926, *Inscriptions Grecques et Latines des tombeaux des rois ou syringes.* Cairo: Institut Français d'Archéologie Orientale

Baines, J. 1988, Literacy, Social Organization, and the Archaeological Record: the Case of Early Egypt, in J. Gledhill, B. Bender and M. T. Larsen (eds), *State and Society. The Emergence and Development of Social Hierarchy and Political Centralization*, 192–214. London: Routledge

Baines, J. and N. Yoffee 1998, Order, Legitimacy and Wealth in Ancient Egypt and Mesopotamia, in G. M. Feinman and J. Marcus (eds), *Archaic States: A Comparative Perspective*, 199–260. Santa Fe: School of American Research Press

Baines, J. and N. Yoffee 2000, Order, Legitimacy and Wealth: Setting the Terms, in J. Richards and M. van Buren (eds), *Order, Legitimacy and Wealth in Ancient States*, 13–17. Cambridge: CUP

Bammer, A. 2001, Der Ephesische peripteros und die Ägyptische architektur, in M. Bietak (ed.), *Archaische Griechische Tempel und Altägypten*, 71–82. Vienna: Austrian Academy of Sciences

Barrett, A. A. 1989, *Caligula: the Corruption of Power.* London: Batsford

Basch, L. 1991, Carènes égénnes à l'Age du Bronze, in R. Laffineur (ed.), *Thalassa. L'Égée préhistorique et la mer*, 43–50, Liège: Université de Liège

Bass, G. F. 1995, Sea and River Craft in the Ancient Near East, in J. M. Sasson (ed.), *Civilizations of the Ancient Near East*, 1,421–1,431. Peabody: Henrickson

Bataille, A. 1950, Aménouthès fils de Hapou à Deir el-Bahari. *Bulletin de la Société Française d'Egyptologie* 3, 6–14

Bataille, A. 1951, *Les Inscriptions grecques du temple de Hatshepsout à Deir el Bahari.* Cairo: Institute Français d'Archéologie Orientale

Beck, P. 1985, An Early Bronze Age "Family" of Bowls from Tel Aphek. *Tel Aviv* 12, 17–28

Beck, P. 2000, Area B: Pottery, in M. Kochavi, P. Beck. and E. Yadin (eds), *Aphek-Antipatris I: Excavations of Areas A and B. The 1972–1976 Seasons*, 93–112. Tel Aviv: Tel Aviv University

Beck, P. and M. Kokhavi 1993, Aphek (in Sharon), in E. Stern (ed.), *The New Encyclopedia of Archaeological Excavations in the Holy Land 1–4*, 62–72. Jerusalem: Israel Exploration Society

Beckerath, J. von 2002, Nochmals die eroberung Ägyptens durch Kambyses. *Zeitschrift für Ägyptische Sprache und Altertumskunde* 129, 1–5

Beckman, G. 1996, *Hittite Diplomatic Texts.* Atlanta: SBL

Beit-Arieh, I. and R. Gophna 1999, The Egyptian Protodynastic (Late EB I) Site at Tel Ma'ahaz: A Reassessment. *Tel Aviv* 26, 191–207

Bell, H. I. 1946, Alexandria ad Aegyptum. *Journal of Roman Studies* 36, 130–132

Ben-Tor, A. 1975, Two Burial Caves of the Proto-Urban Period at Azor, 1971. *Qedem* 1, 1–54, Jerusalem: Hebrew University

Ben-Tor, D. 1997, The Relations between Egypt and Palestine in the Middle Kingdom as Reflected by Contemporary Canaanite Scarabs. *Israel Exploration Journal* 47, 162–189

Ben-Tor, D., S. J. Allen and J. Allen 1999, Seals and Kings. *Bulletin of the American Schools of Oriental Research* 315, 47–74

Bernal, M. 1987, *Black Athena: The Afroasiatic Roots of Classical Civilization. Vol 1, The Fabrication of Ancient Greece, 1785–1985.* London: Free Association Press

Bernal, M. 1995, Review of Sarah P. Morris: Daidalos and the Origins of Greek Art. *Arethusa* 28, 113–135

**Bernal, M. 2003, Afrocentrism and Historical Models for the Foundation of Ancient Greece, in D. O'Connor and A. Reid (eds), *Ancient Egypt in Africa*, 23–30. London: UCL Press**

Bernand, A. 1972a, *Le Paneion d'El-Kanais: les inscriptions grecques*. Leiden: Brill

Bernand, A. 1972b, *De Koptos à Kosseir.* Leiden: Brill

Bernand, E. 1969, *Inscriptions métriques de l'Égypte gréco-romaine. Recherches sur la poésie épigrammatique des Grecs en Égypte.* Paris: Belles Lettres

Bernand, E. 1980, Sur une stèle d'Abydos. *Zeitschrift für Papyrologie und Epigraphik* 40, 213–214

Bernand, E. 1988, Pelerins, in M-M. Mactoux and E. Geny (eds), *Mélanges Pierre Leveque 1*, 49–63. Paris: Université de Besançon

Betancourt, P. P. 1987, Dating the Aegean Late Bronze Age with Radiocarbon. *Archaeometry* 29, 45–49

Bevan, A. H. 2001, Value Regimes in the Eastern Mediterranean Bronze Age: a Study through Stone Vessels, unpublished PhD thesis, University of London

Bhardwaj, S. M. 1973, *Hindu Places of Pilgrimage in India. A Study in Cultural Geography.* Berkeley: University of California Press

Bianchi, R. S. 1991, Egyptian Metal Statuary of the Third Intermediate Period (ca 1070–656 BC), from its Egyptian Antecedents to its Samian examples, in *Small Bronze Sculpture from the Ancient World*, 61–84. Malibu: J. Paul Getty Museum

Bietak, M. 1995, *Avaris: the Capital of the Hyksos.* London: British Museum Press

Bietak, M (ed.) 2001, *Archaische Griechische Tempel und Aaltägypten.* Vienna: Austrian Academy of Sciences

Bisset, N. G., J. G. Bruhn, S. Curto, B. Holmstedt, U. Nyman and M. H. Zenk 1996, Was Opium known in 18th Dynasty Egypt? An Examination of Materials from the Tomb of the Chief Royal Architect Kha. *Ägypten und Levant* 6, 199–201

Bissing, F. W. von 1940, Ägyptische und Ägyptisierende alabastergefäße aus den Deutschen ausgrabungen in Assur. *Zeitschrift für Assyriologie* 46, 149–182

Blanton, R. E., G. M. Feinmann, S. A. Kowalewski and P. N. Peregrine 1996, A Dual Processual Theory of the Evolution of Mesoamerican Civilisation. *Current Anthropology* 37, 1–14 (commentary: 49–71)

Boardman, J. 1967, *Pre-Classical: from Crete to Archaic Greece.* Harmondsworth: Penguin

Boardman, J. 1980, *The Greeks Overseas: Their Early Colonies and Trade.* London: Thames and Hudson

Boardman, J., J. Dörig, W. Fuchs and M. Hirmer 1967, *The Art and Architecture of Ancient Greece*. London: Thames and Hudson

Bordreuil, P. and D. Pardee 1989, *Ras Shamra-Ougarit V. La Trouvaille épigraphique de l'Ougarit. Vol. 1: concordance*. Paris: Editions Recherche sur les Civilisations

Bosanquet, R. C. 1904, Some 'Late Minoan' Vases found in Greece. *Journal of Hellenic Studies* 24, 317–335

Boschung, D. 1993, *Die Bildnisse des Augustus. Das römische Herrscherbild I*. Berlin: Mann

Bourriau, J. 2000, The Second Intermediate Period (c. 1650–1550 BC), in I. Shaw (ed.), *The Oxford History of Ancient Egypt*, 185–217. Oxford: OUP

Bowen, J. 1989, Education, Ideology and the Ruling Class: Hellenism and English Public Schools in the Nineteenth Century, in G. W. Clarke (ed.), *Rediscovering Hellenism: the Hellenic Inheritance and the English Imagination*, 161–186. Cambridge: CUP

Bowersock, G. W. 1984 The Miracle of Memnon. *Bulletin of the American Society of Papyrologists* 21, 21–32

Boyaval, B. 1969, Graffite Grec d l'Osireion d'Abydos. *Chronique d'Égypte* 44, 353–359

Boyd Hawes, H., B. E. Williams, R. B. Seager and E. H. Hall 1908, *Gournia, Vasiliki and Other Prehistoric Sites on the Isthmus of Ierapetra*. Philadelphia: American Exploration Society

Brandl, B. 1989, Observations on the Early Bronze Age Strata of Tel Erani, in P. de Miroschedji (ed.), *L'urbanisation de la Palestine à l'Age du Bronze ancien: bilan et perspectives des recherches actuelles*, 357–388. Oxford: British Archaeological Reports

Brandl, B. 1992, Evidence for Egyptian Colonization in the Southern Coastal Plain and Lowlands of Canaan during the EB I Period, in E. C. M van den Brink (ed.), *The Nile Delta in Transition: 4th–3rd Millennium BC. Proceedings of the Seminar Held in Cairo, 21–24 October 1990, at the Netherlands Institute of Archaeology and Arabic Studies*, 441–477. Tel Aviv: E. C. M. van den Brink

Brandl, B. and R. Gophna 1994, Ashkelon, Afridar. *Excavations and Surveys in Israel* 12, 89

Braudel, F. 1972, *The Mediterranean and the Mediterranean World in the Age of Phillip II*. London: Collins

Braudel, F. 2001, *The Mediterranean in the Ancient World*. Harmondsworth: Penguin

Braun, E. 2000, Area G at Afridar, Palmahim Quarry 3 and the Earliest Pottery of Early Bronze I: Part of the Missing Link, in G. Baird and D. Baird (eds), *Breaking with the Past: Ceramics and Change in the Early Bronze Age of the Southern Levant*, 113–128. Sheffield: Sheffield Academic Press

Braun, E. 2001, Proto and Early Dynastic Egypt and early Bronze I–II of the Southern Levant: Some Uneasy $^{14}$C Correlations. *Radiocarbon* 43, 1,202–1,218

Braun, E. 2002a, Egypt's First Sojourn in Canaan, in E. C. M. van den Brink and T. E. Levy (eds), *Egyptian-Canaanite Interaction: from the 4th through Early 3rd Millennium BCE*, 173–189. Leicester: Leicester UP

Braun, E. 2002b, Post Mortem: A Late Prehistoric Site at Palmahim Quarry. *Bulletin of the Anglo-Israel Archaeological Society* 18, 17–30

Braun, E. forthcoming, Who's Who and What's What? Interpreting Ethnicity from Prehistoric Pottery in Ancient Egypt and the Southern Levant (or: Little pot who made thee? Dost thou know who made thee?). Paper presented at the Transmission and Assimilation of Culture in the Near East conference, Jerusalem, 2000

Braun, E., R. Gophna, E. C. M. van den Brink and Y. Goren 2001, New Evidence for Egyptian Connections during the latter part of Early Bronze I, from the Soreq Basin in South-Central Israel, in S. R. Wolff (ed.), *Studies in the Archaeology of Israel and Neighboring Lands in Memory of Douglas L. Esse*, 51–92. Chicago: Oriental Institute

Braun, E. and E. C. M. van den Brink 1998, Some Comments on the Relative Dating of Tomb U-j at Umm el Ga`ab and Graves 330 and 787 from Minshat Abu Omar with Imported Ware: Views from Egypt and Canaan. *Egypt and the Levant* 7, 71–94

Breasted, J. H. 1906–1907, *Ancient Records of Egypt, Historical Documents from the Earliest Times to the Persian Conquest*. Chicago: University of Chicago Press

Broodbank, C. 2000, *An Island Archaeology of the Early Cyclades*. Cambridge: CUP

Brown, J. 1998, *Painting in Spain, 1500–1700*. New Haven: Yale UP

Bryan, B. M. 1991, *The Reign of Tuthmose IV*. Baltimore: Johns Hopkins UP

Bryan, B. M. 2000, The Eighteenth Dynasty Before the Amarna Period (c. 1550–1352 BC), in I. Shaw (ed.), *The Oxford History of Ancient Egypt*, 218–271. Oxford: OUP

**Butler, B. 2003, 'Egyptianizing' the Alexandrina: The Contemporary Revival of the Ancient Mouseion/Library, in J-M. Humbert and C. Price (eds), *Imhotep Today: Egyptianizing architecture*, 257–282. London: UCL Press**

Butler, H. E. and E. A. Barber 1933, *The Elegies of Propertius*. Oxford: Clarendon

Cameron, A. 1995, *Callimachus and his Critics*. Princeton: Princeton UP

Capasso, M. 1998, L'Egitto nei Papiri Ercolanesi: il Carmen de Bello actiaco e il de signis di Filodemo, in N. Bonacasa, M. C. Naro, E. C. Portale and A. Tullio (eds), *L'Egitto in Italia dall'Antichità al Medioevo*, 51–64. Rome: Consiglio Nazionale delle Ricerche

Carter, J. B. 1987, The Masks of Ortheia. *American Journal of Archaeology* 91, 355–383

Cartledge, P. 1993, *The Greeks*. Oxford: OUP

Casson, L. 1995, *Ships and Seamanship in the Ancient World*. Baltimore: Johns Hopkins UP

Caton-Thompson, G. and E. W. Gardner 1934, *The Desert Fayum*. London: Royal Anthropological Institute

Caubet, A. 1991, Répertoire de la vaisselle de Pierre, Ougarit 1929–1988, in M. Yon (ed.), *Arts et industries de la Pierre*, 205–264. Paris: Editions Recherche sur les Civilisations

Cèbe, J-P. 1966, *La Caricature et la parodie dans le monde Romain antique des origines à Juvenal*. Paris: Bulletin de l'Ecole Française à Rome

Černý, J. 1943, Philological and Etymological Notes. *Annales du Service des Antiquités de l'Égypte* 42, 346–348

**Champion, T. C. 2003, Egypt and the Diffusion of Culture, in D. Jeffreys (ed.), *Views of Ancient Egypt since Napoleon Bonaparte: imperialism, colonialism and modern appropriations*, 127–146. London: UCL Press**

Chauveau, M. 1996a, in M. Wuttmann, B. Bousquet, M. Chauveau, P. Dils, S. Marchand, A. Schweitzer and L. Volay, Premier rapport préliminaire des travaux sur le site de 'Ayn Manawir (oasis de Kharga). *Bulletin de l'Institut Français d'Archéologie Orientale du Caire* 96, 385–451

Chauveau, M. 1996b, Les Archives d'un temple des oasis au temps des Perses. *Bulletin de la Société Française d'Égyptologie* 137, 32–47

Chauveau, M. 1998, *Cléopâtre au-delà du Mythe*. Paris: Liana Levi

Chevereau, P-M. 1985, *Prosopographie des cadres militaires Égyptiens de la basse époque; carrières militaires et carrières sacerdotales en Egypte du XI$^e$ au II$^e$ siècle avant JC*. Antony: Façonnage

Ciasca, R. 1962, Scavi e esplorazioni: Tell Gat. *Oriens Antiquus* I, 23–39

Clarke, J. R. 1998, *Looking at Lovemaking. Constructions of Sexuality in Roman Art*. Berkeley: University of California Press

Cline, E. H. 1987, Amenhotep III and the Aegean: a Reassessment of Egypto-Aegean Relations in the 14th Century BC. *Orientalia* 56, 1–36

Cline, E. H. 1994, *Sailing the Wine-Dark Sea: International Trade and the Late Bronze Age Aegean*. Oxford: Tempus Reparatum

Cline, E. H. 1995, Egyptian and Near Eastern Imports at Late Bronze Age Mycenae, in W. V. Davies and L. Schofield (eds), *Egypt, The Aegean and the Levant. Interconnections in the Second Millennium BC*, 91–115. London: British Museum Press

Cline, E. H. and D. O'Connor 2003, The Mystery of the 'Sea Peoples', in D. O'Connor and S. Quirke (eds), *Mysterious Lands*, 107–138. London: UCL Press

Cohen, E. 1992, Pilgrimage and Tourism: Convergence and Divergence, in E. A. Morinis, *Sacred Journeys: the Anthropology of Pilgrimage*, 47–61. New York: Greenwood

Cook, R. M. 1967, Origins of Greek Sculpture. *Journal of Hellenic Studies* 87, 24–32

Coulton, J. J. 1977, *Greek Architects at Work: Problems of Structure and Design*. London: Granada

Courtney, E. 1980, *A Commentary on the Satires of Juvenal*. London: Athlone

Dalley, S. 1998, Occasions and Opportunities. 1, To the Persian conquest, in S. Dalley (ed.), *The Legacy of Mesopotamia*, 9–33. Oxford: Clarendon

Dasen, V. 1993, *Dwarfs in Ancient Egypt and Greece*. Oxford: Clarendon

Dasen, V. 1994, Pygmaioi, in *Lexicon Iconographicum Mythologiae Classicae*, 594–601. Zurich and Munich: Artemis

Daszewski, W. 1985, *Corpus of Mosaics from Egypt I. Hellenistic and Early Roman Period*. Mainz: von Zabern

David, A. R. 1982, *The Ancient Egyptians. Religious Beliefs and Practices*. London: Routledge and Kegan Paul

Davies, N. and A. Gardiner 1920, *The Tomb of Antefoker*. London: Allen and Unwin

Davis, W. 1981, Egypt, Samos and the Archaic Style in Greek Sculpture. *Journal of Egyptian Archaeology* 67, 61–81

Davison, J. A. 1968, *From Archilochus to Pindar*. London: Macmillan

De Caro, S. 2000, *Il Gabinetto Segreto*. Naples: Electa

De Marrais, E., L. J. Castillo and T. Earle 1996, Ideology, Materialisation and Power Strategies. *Current Anthropology* 37, 15–31

De Miroschedji, P. and M. Sadek 1999a, Informations about a New Franco-Palestinian Archaeological Project: Excavations at Tell Sakan, an Early Bronze Age Site in the Gaza Strip. *Posting: Ancient Near East List* (ane@oi.uchicago.edu), 28 December

De Miroschedji, P. and M. Sadek 1999b, The Frontier of Egypt in the Early Bronze Age: Preliminary Soundings at Tell Sakan (Gaza Strip). Paper presented at the Transmission and Assimilation of Culture in the Near East conference, Jerusalem

De Miroschedji, P. and M. Sadek 2000a, Travaux archéologiques à Tell Sakan (Bande de Gaza) en 1999. *Orient Express* 2, 30–32

De Miroschedji, P. and M. Sadek 2000b, Tell es-Sakan 2000. *Orient Express* 2, 30–32

De Polignac, F. 1992, Influence extérieure ou évolution interne: l'innovation culturelle en Grèce géometriquet archaique, in G. Kopcke and I. Tokumaru (eds), *Greece between East and West: 10th–8th Centuries BC*, 114–127. Mainz: von Zabern

De Salvia, F. 1983, La Problema della reazione culturale egea all' influenza della civiltà Egizia durante l'Età Arcaica. *Orientalia* 52, 201–214

De Salvia, F. 1989, Cultura Egizia e cultura Greca in Età Pre-ellenistica: attrazione e repulsione. *Egitto e Vicino Oriente* 12, 125–138

De Salvia, F. 1991, Stages and Aspects of the Egyptian Religious and Magic Influences on Archaic Greece, in *Akten des Vierten Internationalen Ägyptologen Kongresses, München 1985, Vol 4*, 335–343. Hamburg: Helmut Buske

Desroches-Noblecourt, C. 1956, Interprétation et datation d'une scène gravée sur deux fragments de récipient en albatre provenant des fuilles du Palais d'Ugarit, in C. F. A. Schaeffer (ed.), *Ugaritica III*, 179–220. Paris: Paul Geuthner

Dessel, J. P. 1991, Ceramic Production and Social Complexity in fourth Millennium Canaan: a Case Study from the Halif Terrace, unpublished PhD thesis, University of Arizona

Detschew, D. 1957, *Die Thrakischen sprachreste*. Vienna: Österreichische Akademie der Wissenschaften

Devauchelle, D. 1983, Les Graffites démotiques du toit du temple d'Edfu. *Bulletin de l'Institut Français d'Archéologie Orientale du Caire* 83, 123–131

Dickers, A. 1995, Spätbronzezeitliche steingefässe des Griechischen festlandes. *Studi miceni ed egeo-anatolici* 92, 125–223

Dickinson, O. 1994, *The Aegean Bronze Age*. Cambridge: CUP

Dihle, A. 1994, *Die Griechen und die Fremden*. Munich: C. H. Beck

Donadoni, S. F. 1980, Gli Egiziani e le lingue degli altri. *Vicino Oriente* 3, 1–14

Dothan, M. and Y. Porath 1993, Ashdod V: Excavation of Area G. *'Atiqot* 23, 1–296

Drioton, E. 1943, Les Fêtes de Bouto, *Bulletin de l'Institut d'Egyptologie* 25, 1–19

Dunand, F. 1997, La Consultation oraculaire en Egypte tardive: l'oracle de Bès à Abydos, in J. G. Heintz (ed.), *Oracles et propheties dans l'antiquité. Actes du Colloque de Strasbourg, 15–17 juin 1995*, 65–84. Paris: De Boccard

Dunand, M. 1939, *Fouilles de Byblos 1, 1926–1932*. Paris: Geuthner

Dunand, M. 1958, *Fouilles de Byblos 2, 1933–1938*. Paris: Geuthner

Dunbar, N. 1995, *Aristophanes' Birds*. Oxford: OUP

Duncan C. and A. Wallach 1980, The Universal Survey Museum. *Art History* 3, 448–469


Edel, E. 1949, KBo 15+19, ein Brief Ramses' II mit einer Schilderung der Kadešschlacht. *Zeitschrift für Assyriologie* 15, 195–212

Edel, E. 1976, *Ägyptische Ärtzte und Ägyptische medizin am hethitischen Königshof: neue funde von Keilschriftbriefen Ramses' II aus Bogazköy*. Düsseldorf: Akademie der Wissenschaften

Edel, E. 1978, *Der Brief des Ägyptischen wesirs pasijara an den hethiterkönig Hattusili und verwandte Keilschriftbriefe*. Göttingen: Akademie der Wissenschaften

Edel, E. 1983, Zwei steinschalen mit Ägyptischen inschriften aus dem palast von Kamid el-Loz, in R. Hachmann (ed.), *Frühe Phöniker im Libanon – 20 jahre Deutsche ausgrabungen in Kamid el-Loz*, 38–39. Mainz: von Zabern

Edwards, I. E. S. and T. G. H. James 1984, Egypt, in J. Boardman (ed.), *The Cambridge Ancient History, Plates to Vol. III. The Middle East, the Greek World and the Balkans to the Sixth Century AD*, 125–147. Cambridge: CUP

El-Khouli, A. 1978, *Egyptian Stone Vessels, Predynastic Period to Dynasty III*. Mainz: von Zabern

El-Khouli, A. 1993, Stone Vessels, in J. Baines (ed.), *Stone Vessels, Pottery, and Sealings from the Tomb of Tut'ankhamun*, 5–35. Warminster: Aris & Phillips

Elsner, J. 1992, Pausanias: A Greek Pilgrim in the Roman World. *Past and Present* 135, 3–29

Eschebach, H. 1984, Die Arzthäuser in Pompeji. *Antike Welt* 15, Sondernummer

Etienne, M. forthcoming, in S. Walker and S-A. Ashton, *Cleopatra Re-assessed*. London: British Museum Press

Evans, A. J. 1905, The Prehistoric Tombs of Knossos. *Archaeologia* 59, 526–562

Evans, A. J. 1928, *Palace of Minos at Knossos vol. 2*. London: Macmillan

Evans, A. J. 1935, *Palace of Minos at Knossos vol. 4*. London: Macmillan


Fadinger, V. 1993, Griechische Tyrannis und Alter Orient, in K. Raaflaub (ed.), *Anfänge Politischen Denkens in der Antike*, 263–316. Munich: R. Oldenbourg

Faltings, D. 1998, Canaanites at Buto in the Early Fourth Millennium BC. *Egyptian Archaeology* 13, 29–32

Farid, A. 1995, *Fünf Demotische stelen aus Berlin, Chicago, Durham, London und Oxford mit zwei Demotischen Türinschriften aus Paris und einer Bibliographie der Demotischen Inschriften*. Berlin: Achet

Faulkner, R. O. 1991, *A Concise Dictionary of Middle Egyptian*. Oxford: Griffith Institute

Fehling, D. 1989, *Herodotus and His "Sources". Citation, Invention and Narrative Art*. Leeds: Francis Cairns

Fehr, B. 1996, The Greek Temple in the Early Archaic Period. *Hephaistos* 15, 165–191

Fitton, J. L., M. Hughes and S. Quirke 1998, Northerners at Lahun. Neutron Activation Analysis of Minoan and related pottery in the British Museum, in S. Quirke (ed.), *Lahun Studies*, 112–140. Reigate: SIA

Fitzmyer, J. A. and S. A. Kaufmann (eds) 1992, *An Aramaic Bibliography*. Baltimore: Johns Hopkins UP

Fornara, C. W. 1971, *Herodotus: An Interpretative Essay*. Oxford: OUP

Fornara, C. W. 1983, *Archaic Times to the End of the Peloponnesian War. Translated Documents of Greece and Rome 1*. Cambridge: CUP

Forster, E. S. 1984, *Lucius Annaeus Florus, Epitome of Roman History*. Cambridge, Mass: Harvard UP

Fowden, G. 1986, *The Egyptian Hermes. A Historical Approach to the Late Pagan Mind*. Princeton: Princeton UP

Fowler, B. H. 1983, The Centaur's Smile: Pindar and the Archaic Aesthetic, in W. G. Moon (ed.), *Ancient Greek Art and Iconography*, 159–170. Madison: University of Wisconsin Press

Fowler, R. 1996, Herodotus and his Contemporaries. *Journal of Hellenic Studies* 116, 62–87

Francis, E. D. and M. Vickers 1984a, Green Goddess: a Gift to Lindos from Amasis of Egypt. *American Journal of Archaeology* 88, 68–69

Francis, E. D. and M. Vickers 1984b, Amasis and Lindos. *Bulletin of the Institute of Classical Studies* 31, 119–130

Frankfort, H. 1933, *The Cenotaph of Seti I at Abydos*. London: Egypt Exploration Society

Frankfort, H. 1941, The Origin of Monumental Architecture in Egypt. *American Journal of Semitic Languages and Literatures* 58, 329–358

Frankfurter, D. 1997, Ritual Experts in Roman Egypt. The Problem of the Category "Magic", in P. Schäfer and H. Kippenberg (eds), *Envisioning Magic*, 115–135. Leiden: Brill

Froidefond, C. 1971, *Le Mirage Egyptien dans la littérature Grècque d'Homere à Aristote*. Aix-en-Provence: Université d'Aix-en-Provence

Fulford, M. and A. Wallace-Hadrill 1998, Unpeeling Pompeii. *Antiquity* 72, 128–145

Funari, P. P. A., M. Hall and S. Jones (eds) 1999, *Historical Archaeology: Back from the Edge*. London: Routledge

Fyfe, G. 1996, A Trojan Horse at the Tate: Theorizing the Museum as Agency and Structure, in S. MacDonald and G. Fyfe (eds), *Theorizing Museums: Representing Identity and Diversity in a Changing World*, 203–298. Oxford: Blackwell

Gamer-Wallert, I. 1978, *Ägyptische und ägyptisierende Funde von der Iberischen Halbinsel*. Wiesbaden: Tübinger Atlas des Vorderen Orients

Gasche, H., J. A. Armstrong, S. W. Cole and V. G. Gurzadyan 1998a, *Dating the Fall of Babylon: A Reappraisal of Second-Millennium Chronology*. Ghent: Mesopotamian History and Environment

Gasche, H., J. A. Armstrong, S. W. Cole and V. G. Gurzadyan 1998b, A Correction to Dating the Fall of Babylon: A Reappraisal of Second-Millennium Chronology. *Akkadica* 108, 1–4

Gebhard, E. R. 2001, The Archaic Temple at Isthmia: Techniques of Construction, in M. Bietak (ed.), *Archaische Griechische Tempel und Altägypten*, 41–61. Vienna: Austrian Academy of Sciences

Gee, J. L. 1998, The Requirements of Ritual Purity in Ancient Egypt, unpublished PhD thesis, Yale University

Geraci, G. 1971, Ricerche sul Proskynema. *Aegyptus* 51, 3–211

Gibson, J. C. L. 1975, *Textbook of Syrian Semitic Inscriptions, vol. 2*. Oxford: OUP

Gikandi, S. 1996, *Maps of Englishness. Writing Identity in the Culture of Colonialism*. New York: Columbia UP

Goldwasser, O. 1984, Hieratic Inscriptions from Tel Sera' in Southern Canaan. *Tel Aviv* 11, 77–93

Goody, J. 1997, *Representations and Contradictions: Ambivalence Towards Images, Theatre, Fiction, Relics and Sexuality*. Oxford: Blackwell

Gophna, R. (ed.) 1995, *Excavations at `En Besor*. Tel Aviv: Ramot

Gophna, R. 1996, *Excavations at Tel Dalit: An Early Bronze Age Walled Town in Central Israel*. Tel Aviv: Ramot

Gophna, R. 1998, Early Bronze Age Canaan: Some Spatial and Demographic Observations, in T. E. Levy (ed.), *The Archaeology of Society in the Holy Land*, 269–280. Leicester: Leicester UP

Gophna, R. and E. Buzaglo 2000, A Note on an Egyptian Pottery Basin from 'En Besor. *Tel Aviv* 27, 26–27

Gophna, R. and D. Gazit 1985, The First Dynasty Egyptian Residency at 'En Besor. *Tel Aviv* 12, 9–16

Gorelick, L. and A. J. Gwinnett 1983, Ancient Egyptian Stone-Drilling: an Experimental Perspective on a Scholarly Disagreement. *Expedition* 25, 40–47

Goudriaan, K. 1988, *Ethnicity in Ptolemaic Egypt*. Amsterdam: J. C. Gieben

Goudriaan, K. 1992, Ethnical Strategies in Graeco-Roman Egypt, in P. Bilde, T. Engberg-Pedersen, L. Hannestad and J. Zahle (eds), *Ethnicity in Hellenistic Egypt*, 74–99. Aarhus: Aarhus UP

Graillot, H. 1912, *Le Culte de Cybèle, mère des dieux, à Rome et dans l'Empire Romain*. Paris: Fontemoing

Grayson, A. K. 1981, Assyria's Foreign Policy in Relation to Egypt in the Eighth and Seventh Centuries BC. *Journal of the Society for the Study of Egyptian Antiquities* 11, 85–88

Grayson, A. K. 1995, Assyrian Rule of Conquered Territory in Ancient Western Asia, in J. M. Sasson (ed.), *Civilizations of the Ancient Near East*, 959–968. New York: Charles Scribner's Sons

Griffin, M. T. 1984, *Nero: the End of a Dynasty*. London: Batsford

Griffith, R. D. 1998, The Origin of Memnon. *Classical Antiquity* 17, 212–234

Grimm, G. 2000, Regina Meretrix oder Kleopatra als Königliche Hure? *Antike Welt* 31, 127–133

Guarducci, M. 1942–1943, Le Impronte del quo vadis e monumenti affini, figurati ed Epigrafici. *Rendiconti della Pontificia Accademia di Archeologia* 19

Guidotti, M. C. 1980, Alcuni Vasi dipinti da Saqqara. *Egitto e Vicino Oriente* 3, 65–81

Gullini, G. 1956, *I Mosaici di Palestrina. Archeologia Classica, Supplemento 1*. Rome: University of Rome

Gunter, A. 1990, Models of the Orient in the Art History of the Orientalising Period. *Achaemenid History* 5, 131–147

Guralnick, E. 1978, The Proportions of Kouroi. *American Journal of Archaeology* 82, 461–472

Guralnick, E. 1981, The Proportions of Korai. *American Journal of Archaeology* 85, 269–280

Guralnick, E. 1982, Profiles of Korai. *American Journal of Archaeology* 86, 173–182

Guralnick, E. 1985, Profiles of Kouroi. *American Journal of Archaeology* 89, 399–409

Guralnick, E. 1996, The Monumental New Kouros from Samos: Measurements, Proportions and Profiles. *Archäologischer Anzeiger* 4, 505–526

Guralnick, E. 1997, The Egyptian-Greek connection in the 8th to 6th centuries BC: an Overview, in J. E. Coleman and C. A. Walz (eds), *Greeks and Barbarians: Essays on the Interactions between Greeks and Non-Greeks in Antiquity and the Consequences for Eurocentrism*, 127–154. Ithaca: Cornell UP

Guralnick, E. 2000, Near Eastern and Egyptian Bronzes in Greece, in C. Mattusch, A. Brauer and S. E. Knudsen (eds), *From the Parts to the Whole: Acts of the 13th International Bronze Congress, vol. 1*, 35–39. Portsmouth: Rhode Island

Gwyn Griffiths, J. 1970, *Plutarch: De Iside et Osiride*. Cardiff: University of Wales Press

Gwyn Griffiths, J. 1985, Atlantis and Egypt. *Historia* 34, 3–28

Hall, E. 1989, *Inventing the Barbarian. Greek Self-Definition Through Tragedy*. Oxford: OUP

Hall, J. M. 1997, *Ethnic Identity in Greek Antiquity*. Cambridge: CUP

Hannerz, U. 1992, *Cultural Complexity: Studies in the Social Organisation of Meaning*. New York: Columbia UP

Hansen, D. P. 1998, Art of the Royal Tombs of Ur: a Brief Interpretation, in R. L. Zettler and L. Horne (eds), *Treasures from the Royal Tombs of Ur*, 43–72. Philadelphia: University of Pennsylvania Museum

Harrell, J. A. 1989, An Inventory of Ancient Egyptian Quarries. *Newsletter of the American Research Center in Egypt* 146, 1–7

Harrison, S. J. 2000, *Apuleius: a Latin Sophist*. Oxford: OUP

Harrison, T. 1998, Herodotus' Conception of Foreign Languages. *Histos* 2

Harrison, T. 2000a, *The Emptiness of Asia. Aeschylus' Persians and the History of the Fifth Century*. London: Duckworth

Harrison, T. 2000b, *Divinity and History. The Religion of Herodotus*. Oxford: OUP

Harrison, T. (ed.) 2002a, *Greeks and Barbarians*. Edinburgh: Edinburgh UP

Harrison, T. 2002b, The Persian Invasions, in E. Bakker, I. de Jong and H. van Wees (eds), *Brill's Companion to Herodotus*, 551–578. Leiden: Brill

Harrison, T. forthcoming, The Place of Geography in Herodotus' *Histories*, in C. Adams and J. Roy (eds), *Travel in the Ancient World*. London: Routledge

Hartog, F. 1988, *The Mirror of Herodotus. The Representation of the Other in the Writing of History* (trans. J. Lloyd). Berkeley: University of California Press

Hartog, F. 2002, The Greeks as Egyptologists, in T. Harrison (ed.), *Greeks and Barbarians*, 211–228. Edinburgh: Edinburgh UP

Hassan, F. A. 1995, Egypt in the Prehistory of Northeast Africa, in J. M. Sasson (ed.), *Civilizations of the Ancient Near East*, 665–678. Peabody: Henrickson

Hayes, W. C. 1959, *The Sceptre of Egypt II – The Hyksos Period and the New Kingdom*. Cambridge, Mass: Harvard UP

Heinen, H. 1973, Heer und Gesellschaft im Ptolemäerreich. *Ancient Society* 4, 91–114

Helck, W. 1971, *Die Beziehungen Ägyptens zu Vorderasien in 3 und 2 Jahrtausend v. Chr*. Wiesbaden: Harrassowitz

Held, T. 1997, Shaping Eurocentrism: the Uses of Greek Antiquity, in E. Coleman and C. A. Walz (eds), *Greeks and Barbarians: Essays on the Interactions between Greeks and Non-Greeks in Antiquity and the Consequences for Eurocentrism*, 255–272. Ithaca: Cornell UP

Helms, M. 1988, *Ulysses' Sail: An Ethnographic Odyssey of Power, Knowledge and Geographical Distance*. Princeton: Princeton UP

Hendrickx, S. 1996, The Relative Chronology of the Naqada Culture: problems and possibilities, in A. J. Spencer (ed.), *Aspects of Early Egypt*, 36–69. London: British Museum Press

Hendrickx, S. and P. Vermeersch 2000, Prehistory: from the Palaeolithic to the Badarian Culture, in I. Shaw (ed.), *The Oxford History of Ancient Egypt*, 17–44. Oxford: OUP

Higginbotham, C. R. 1996, Elite Emulation and Egyptian Governance in Ramesside Canaan. *Tel Aviv* 23, 154–169

Higginbotham, C. R. 2000, *Egyptianization and Elite Emulation in Ramesside Palestine. Governance and Accommodation on the Imperial Periphery.* Leiden: Brill

Hoffmann, H. 1953, Foreign Influence and Native Invention in Archaic Greek Altars. *American Journal of Archaeology* 57, 189–195

Hölbl, G. 1979, *Beziehungen der Ägyptischen Kultur zu Altitalien. Études Préliminaires aux Religions Orientales dans l'Empire Romain.* Leiden: Brill

Hölbl, G. 1993, Aussagen zur ägyptischen Religion in den Zenonpapyri, in M. Capasso (ed.), *Papiri documentari greci,* 7–36. Lecce: Congedo Editore

Hölbl, G. 1994, *Geschichte des Ptolemäerreiches; Politik, Ideologie und religiöse Kultur von Alexander dem Großen bis zur Römischen Eroberung.* Darmstadt: Wissenschaftliche Buchgesellschaft

Hölbl, G. 2001, *A History of the Ptolemaic Empire* (trans. T. Saavedra). London: Routledge

Holzberg, N. 1995, *The Ancient Novel: an Introduction.* London: Routledge

Hornung, E. 2001, *The Secret Lore of Egypt: its Impact on the West.* Ithaca: Cornell UP

Hout, Th. P. J. van den 1994, Der Falke und das Kücken: der neue Pharao und der hethitische Prinz? *Zeitschrift für Assyriologie* 84, 60–88

Hubbard, M. 1974, *Propertius.* London: Duckworth

**Humbert, J-M. 2003, The Egyptianizing Pyramid from the 18th to the 20th Century, in J-M. Humbert and C. Price (eds),** *Imhotep Today: Egyptianizing architecture,* **25–40. London: UCL Press**

Hurwit, J. M. 1985, *The Art and Culture of Early Greece, 1100–480 BC.* Ithaca: Cornell UP

Immarco, R. 1984, Per una Nuova Edizione del *P. Herc.* 817, in *Atti del XVII Congresso Internazionale di Papirologia,* 583–590. Napoli: Centro Internazionale per lo studio dei papiri ercolanesi

Immarco, R. 1989, Sul *P. Herc.* 817. *Cronache Ercolanesi* 19, 281–282

Iversen, E. 1957, The Egyptian Origins of the Archaic Greek Canon. *Mitteilungen des Deutschen Archäologischen Instituts, Kairo* 15, 137–147

Iversen, E. 1968, *Obelisks in Exile 1: The Obelisks of Rome.* Copenhagen: Gad

Izre'el, Sh. and I. Singer 1990, *The General's Letter from Ugarit: A Linguistic and Historical Re-evaluation of RS 20,33 (Ugaritica V, No. 20).* Tel Aviv: Tel Aviv UP

Jacobelli, L. 1995, *Le Pitture Erotiche delle terme suburbane di Pompei. Soprintendenza Archeologica di Pompei.* Rome: "L'Erma" di Bretschneider

Jacobsson, I. 1994, *Aegyptiaca from Late Bronze Age Cyprus.* Stockholm: Paul Åströms

James, F. 1966, *The Iron Age at Beth Shan: A Study of Levels VI–IV.* Philadelphia: University of Pennsylvania Press

Jantzen, H. 1972, *Samos, Band VIII: Ägyptische und Orientalische Bronzen aus dem Heraion von Samos.* Bonn: Rudolf Habelt

Jécquier, M. G. 1934, Vases de Pierre de la VI$^e$ dynastie. *Annales du Service des Antiquités de l'Égypte* 34, 97–113

Jécquier, M. G. 1935, Vases de Pierre de la VI$^e$ dynastie: note additionelle. *Annales du Service des Antiquités de l'Égypte* 35, 160

Jeffery, L. H. 1990, *The Local Scripts of Archaic Greece: a Study of the Origin of the Greek Alphabet and its Development from the Eighth to the Fifth Centuries BC.* Revised edition, Oxford: OUP

**Jeffreys, D. (ed.) 2003a,** *Views of Ancient Egypt since Napoleon Bonaparte: imperialism, colonialism and modern appropriations.* **London: UCL Press**

Jeffreys, D. 2003b, Introduction – Two Hundred Years of Ancient Egypt: Modern History and Ancient Archaeology, in D. Jeffreys (ed), *Views of Ancient Egypt since Napoleon Bonaparte: imperialism, colonialism and modern appropriations*, 1–18. London: UCL Press

Jeffreys, D. 2003c, All in the Family? Heirlooms in Ancient Egypt, in J. Tait (ed.), *'Never had the like occurred': Egypt's view of its past*, 197–212. London: UCL Press

Jenkins, I. 1992, *Archaeologists and Aesthetes in the Sculpture Galleries of the British Museum, 1800–1939*. London: British Museum Press

Joffe, A. H. 2000, Egypt and Syro-Mesopotamia in the 4th millennium: Implications of the New Chronology. *Current Anthropology* 41, 113–123

Johnson, J. H. 1986, Introduction to the Greek Magical Papyri, in H. D. Betz (ed.), *The Greek Magical Papyri in Translation Including the Demotic Spells*, lv–lviii. Chicago: University of Chicago Press

Jones, A. H. M. 1942, Egypt and Rome, in S. R. K. Glanville (ed.), *The Legacy of Egypt*, 283–299. Oxford: OUP

Jones, S. 1997, *The Archaeology of Ethnicity*. London: Routledge

Joyce, A. A. and M. Winter 1996, Ideology, Power and Urban Society in Prehispanic Oaxaca. *Current Anthropology* 37, 33–47

Kaelin, O. 1999, *Ein Assyrisches bildexperiment nach Ägyptischem vorbild*. Münster: Alter Orient und Altes Testament

Kaiser, W. 1957, Zur inneren Chronologie der Nakadakultur. *Archaeologia Geographica* 6, 69–77

Kamal, M. 1938, The Stela Sehetep-ib-re' in the Egyptian Museum. *Annales du Service des Antiquités de l'Égypte* 38, 266–283

Kamal, M. 1940, The Stela Sehetep-ib-re' in the Egyptian Museum. *Annales du Service des Antiquités de l'Égypte* 40, 209–233

Kannicht, R. 1969, *Euripides, Helena*. Heidelberg: Winter

Kantor, H. J. 1947, *The Aegean and the Orient in the Second Millennium BC*. Bloomington: American Institute of Archaeology

Kantor, H. J. 1992, The Relative Chronology of Egypt and its Foreign Correlations before the First Intermediate Period, in R. W. Ehrich (ed.), *Chronologies in Old World Archaeology*, 3–21. Chicago: University of Chicago Press

Kaplan, J. 1959, The Connections of the Palestinian Chalcolithic Culture with Prehistoric Egypt. *Israel Exploration Journal* 9, 134–136

Kaplony, P. 1968, *Steingefässe mit inschriften der frühzeit und des Alten Reichs*. Brussels: Monumental Aegyptiaca

Karetsou, A. (ed.) 1999, *Crete – Egypt, 3 Millennia of Cultural Interaction*. Heraklion: Archaeological Museum

Karetsou, A. (ed.) 2000, *Kriti-Egyptes Politismiki Desmi train Chiliebtion*. Katalogois, 31–37. Athens: Kapon

Karetsou, A., M. Andreadaki-Blazan and N. Papadaki (eds) 2000, *Kriti-Aigyptos*. Heraklion: Archaeological Museum

Keel, O. 1997, *Corpus der Stempelsiegel-Amulette aus Palästina/Israel. Von den Anfängen bis zur Perserzeit. Katalog Band I: von Tell Abu Farag bis 'Atlit*. Freiburg: Vandenhoeck and Rupprecht

Kemp, B. J. 1975, Abydos, in W. Helck and E. Otto (eds), *Lexikon der Ägyptologie, vol. 1*, 28–42. Wiesbaden: Harrassowitz

Kemp, B. J. 1989, *Ancient Egypt. Anatomy of a Civilization*. London: Routledge

Kempinski, A. and I. Gilead 1991, New Excavations at Tel Erani: A Preliminary Report of the 1985–1988 Seasons. *Tel Aviv* 18, 164–192

Kienast, H. J. 2001, Samische Monumental Architektur: Ägyptischer Einfluss?, in M. Bietak (ed.), *Archaische Griechische Tempel und Altägypten*, 35–39. Vienna: Austrian Academy of Sciences

Kingsly, B. M. 1981, The Cap that Survived Alexander. *American Journal of Archaeology* 85, 39–46

Kitchen, K. A. 1969, Interrelations of Egypt and Syria, in M. Liverani (ed.), *La Siria nel Tardo Bronzo*, 70–95. Rome: Orientis Antiqui

Kitchen, K. A. 1979, *Ramesside Inscriptions II*. Oxford: Blackwell

Kitchen, K. A. 1982, *Pharaoh Triumphant: The Life and Times of Ramesses II*. Warminster: Aris & Phillips

Kitchen, K. A. 1995, Pharaoh Ramesses II and His Time, in J. M. Sasson (ed.), *Civilizations of the Ancient Near East*, 763–774. New York: Charles Scribner's Sons

Kitchen, K. A. 1998, Amenhotep III and Mesopotamia, in D. O'Connor and E. H. Cline (eds), *Amenhotep III: Perspectives on his Reign*, 250–261. Ann Arbor: University of Michigan Press

Kitchen, K. A. 2000, The Historical Chronology of Ancient Egypt: A Current Assessment, in M. Bietak (ed.), *The Synchronisation of Civilisation in the Eastern Mediterranean in the Second Millennium BC*, 39–52. Vienna: Austrian Academy of Sciences

Klemm, R. and D. Klemm 1993, *Steine und Stein-Brüche im Alten Ägypten*. Berlin: Springer

Klengel, H. 1992, *Syria 3000 to 300 BC: A Handbook of Political History*. Berlin: Akademie

Koenen, L. 1983, Die Adaptation Ägyptischer Königsideologie am Ptolemäerhof, in E. Van't Dack, P. Van Dessel and W. Van Gucht (eds), *Egypt and the Hellenistic World, Proceedings of the International Colloquium, Leuven, 24–26 May 1982*, 143–190. Leuven: Studia Hellenistica

Koenen, L. 1993, The Ptolemaic King as a Religious Figure, in A. Bulloch, E. S. Gruen, A. A. Long and A. Stewart (eds), *Images and Ideologies, Self-definition in the Hellenistic World*, 25–115. Berkeley: University of California Press

Koenen, L. 2002, Die Apologie des Töpfers an König Amenophis oder das Töpferorakel, in A. Blasius and B. U. Schipper (eds), *Apokalyptik und Ägypten* 139–187. Leuven: Peeters

Kornmann, W. 1978, Neues über die Phönikischen und Aramäischen Graffiti in den Tempeln von Abydos. *Anzeiger der Philosophischen-Historischen Klasse de Öster. Akademie der Wissenschaft* 115, 193–204

Kuhrt, A. 1995, *The Ancient Near East c. 3000–330 BC*. London: Routledge

Kyrieleis, H. 1990, Samos and Some Aspects of Archaic Greek Bronze Casting, in M. True and J. Podany (eds), *Small Bronze Sculpture from the Ancient World*, 15–30. Malibu: J Paul Getty Museum

Kyrieleis, H. 1993, The Heraion at Samos, in N. Marinatos and R. Hägg (eds), *Greek Sanctuaries: New Approaches*, 125–153. London: Routledge


La'da, C. A. 1996, Ethnic Designations in Hellenistic Egypt, unpublished PhD thesis, University of Cambridge

La'da, C. A., in preparation, Database of La'da 1996. *Studia Hellenistica*

Lajtar, A. 1991, Proskynema Inscriptions of a Corporation of Iron-Workers from Hermonthis in the Temple of Hatshepsut in Deir El-Bahri: New Evidence for Pagan Cults in Egypt in the 4th Cent. AD. *Journal of Juristic Papyrology* 21, 53–70

Lambdin, T. O. 1953, Another Cuneiform Transcription of Egyptian *msh*, 'crocodile'. *Journal of Near Eastern Studies* 12, 284–285

Lamprichs, R. 1995, *Die Westexpansion des neuassyrischen Reiches: eine Strukturanalyse*. Neukirchen-Vluyn: Alter Orient und Altes Testament

Lancha, J. 1980, Deux fragments d'une frise Nilotique inédite au Musée de Naples, *Mélanges de l'Ecole Française de Rome* 92, 249–276

Largacha, A. P. 1993, Relations between Egypt and Mesopotamia at the End of the Fourth Millennium. *Göttinger Miszellen* 137, 59–76

Larsen, M. T. 1976, *The Old Assyrian City-State and its Colonies*. Copenhagen: Akademisk

Larsen, M. T. 1979, The Tradition of Empire in Mesopotamia, in M. T. Larsen (ed.), *Power and Propaganda. A Symposium on Ancient Empires*, 75–103. Copenhagen: Akademisk

Latacz, J., P. Blome, J. Luckhardt, H. Brunner, M. Korfmann and G. Biegel (eds) 2001, *Troia: Traum und Wirklichkeit*. Darmstadt: Wissenschaftliche Buchgesellschaft

Latte, K. 1960, *Römische Religionsgeschichte, Handbuch der Altertumswissenschaft, Abt. 5, 4*. Munich: C. H. Beck

Lattimore, R. 1958, The Composition of the *History* of Herodotus. *Classical Philology* 53, 9–21

Launey, M. 1949–1950, *Recherches sur les Armées hellenistiques*. Paris: De Boccard

Laurens, A-F. 1986, Bousiris. *Lexicon Iconographicum Mythologiae Classicae*, 147–152

Lawrence, A. W. 1983, *Greek Architecture*. Harmondsworth: Penguin

Leeds, E. T. 1922, Alabaster Vases of the New Kingdom from Sinai. *Journal of Egyptian Archaeology* 8, 1–4

Lembke, K. 1994, *Das Iseum Campense in Rom. Studie über den Isis Kult unter Domitian*. Heidelberg: Archäologie und Geschichte

Leoussi, A. S. 1998, *Nationalism and Classicism: the Classical Body as National Symbol in Nineteenth Century England and France*. London: Macmillan

Levick, B. 1993, *Claudius*. London: Batsford

Levick, B. 1999, *Vespasian*. London: Routledge

Levy, S. n. d., unpublished Excavation Report, el-Maghar. Israel Antiquities Archive

Levy, T. E. *et al.* 1997, Egyptian-Canaanite Interaction at Nahal Tillah, Israel (ca. 4500–3000 BCE): An Interim Report on the 1994–1995 Excavations. *Bulletin of the American Schools of Oriental Research* 307, 1–52

Levy, T. E., E. C. van den Brink, Y. Goren and D. Alon 1995, New Light on King Narmer and the Protodynastic Egyptian Presence in Canaan. *Biblical Archaeologist* 58, 26–35

Lichtheim, M. 1988, *Ancient Egyptian Autobiographies, Chiefly of the Middle Kingdom. A Study and an Anthology*. Göttingen: Vandenhoeck & Ruprecht

Lidzbarski, M. 1900–1915, *Ephemeris für Semitische Epigraphik*. Giessen: Topelmann

Lilyquist, C. 1993, Objects Attributable to Kamid el-Loz and Comments on the Date of Some Objects in the 'Schatzhaus', in R. Hachmann (ed.), *Das 'Schatzhaus' im Palastbereich. Die Befunde und ihre Deutung*, 207–220. Bonn: R. Habelt

Lilyquist, C. 1994, Granulation and Glass: Chronological and Stylistic Investigations at Selected Sites, ca. 2500–1400 BCE. *Bulletin of the American Schools of Oriental Research*, 290–291

Lilyquist, C. 1995, *Egyptian Stone Vessels: Khian Through Tuthmosis IV*. New York: Metropolitan Museum

Lilyquist, C. 1996, Stone Vessels at Kamid el-Loz, Lebanon: Egyptian, Egyptianizing, or Non-Egyptian? A Question at Sites from the Sudan to Iraq to the Greek Mainland, in R. Hachmann (ed.), *Kamid el-Loz 16: 'Schatzhaus' – Studien*, 133–173. Bonn: R. Habelt

Lilyquist, C. 1997, Egyptian Stone Vases: Comments on Peter Warren's Paper, in R. Laffineur and P. P. Betancourt (eds), *Techne: Craftsmen, Craftswomen and Craftmanship in the Aegean Bronze Age*, 225–228. Liège: Université de Liège

Livingstone, N. 2001, *A Commentary on Isocrates' Busiris*. Leiden: Brill

Lloyd, A. B. 1975–1989, *Herodotus Book II*. Leiden: Brill

Lloyd, A. B. 1988, Herodotus' Account of Pharaonic History. *Historia* 37, 22–53

Lloyd, A. B. 1990, Herodotus on Egyptians and Libyans, in W. Burkert, *Herodote et les peuples non-Grecs*, 171–214. Geneva: Fondation Hardt Entretiens

Lloyd, A. B. 1995, Herodotus on Egyptian Buildings: a Test Case, in A. Powell (ed.), *The Greek World*, 273–301. London: Routledge

Lloyd, A. B. 2002, Egypt, in E. Bakker, I. de Jong and H. van Wees (eds), *Brill's Companion to Herodotus*, 415–435. Leiden: Brill

Long, T. 1986, *Barbarians in Greek Comedy*. Carbondale: Southern Illinois UP

Lucas, A. and J. R. Harris 1962, *Ancient Egyptian Materials and Industries*. London: E. Arnold

Lumsden, S. 2000, On Sennacherib's Nineveh, in P. Matthiae, A. Enea, L. Peyronel and F. Pinnock (eds), *Proceedings of the First International Congress on the Archaeology of the Ancient Near East*, 815–834. Rome: La Sapienza


Macalister, R. A. S. 1912, *The Excavation of Gezer vol I*. London: Palestine Exploration Fund

Macdonald, E. 1932, Prehistoric Fara, in *Beth-Pelet II*, 1–21. London: British School of Archaeology in Egypt

Macqueen, J. G. 1995, The History of Anatolia and of the Hittite Empire: An Overview, in J. M. Sasson (ed.), *Civilizations of the Ancient Near East*, 1,085–1,105. New York: Charles Scribner's Sons

Malaise, M. 1972, *Les Conditions de pénétration et de diffusion des cultes Égyptiens en Italie*. Leiden: Brill

Malaise, M. 1990, Bes et les croyances solaires, in *Studies in Egyptology Presented to M. Lichtheim*, 680–729. Jerusalem: Magnes

Malek, J. 2000, The Old Kingdom (c. 2686–2160 BC), in I. Shaw (ed.), *The Oxford History of Ancient Egypt*, 89–117. Oxford: OUP

Manning, S. 1999, *A Test of Time*. Exeter: Oxbow

Marcus, E. 1998, Maritime Trade in the Southern Levant from Earliest Times through the Middle Bronze IIA Period, unpublished D Phil thesis, University of Oxford

Marfoe, L. 1987, Cedar Forest to Silver Mountain: Social Change and the Development of Long-Distance Trade in Early Near Eastern Societies, in M. Rowlands, M. Larsen and K. Kristiansen (eds), *Centre and Periphery in the Ancient World*, 25–35. Cambridge: CUP

Mark, S. 1998, *From Egypt to Mesopotamia. A Study of Predynastic Trade Routes*. London: Chatham

Masson, O. 1976, Nouveaux Graffites Grecs d'Abydos et de Bouhen. *Chronique d'Égypte* 51, 305–313

Masson, O. 1983, *Les Inscriptions Chypriotes syllabiques: recueil critique et commente*. Paris: De Boccard

Matthews, R. J. 2002, *Secrets of the Dark Mound. Jemdet Nasr 1926–1928*, Warminster: British School of Archaeology in Iraq

Matthews, V. J. 1974, *Panyassis of Halikarnassos*. Leiden: Brill

Mattingly, H. 1940, *Coins of the Roman Empire in the British Museum, vol. 4*. London: Trustees of the British Museum

Mayer, W. 1995, *Politik und Kriegskunst der Assyrer*. Münster: Abhandlungen zur Literatur Alt-Syrien-Palästinas und Mesopotamiens

Mazar, A. and P. De Miroschedji 1996, Hartuv, an Aspect of the Early Bronze Culture of Southern Israel. *Bulletin of American Schools of Oriental Research* 302, 1–40

McDaniel, W. B. 1932, A Fresco Presenting Pygmies. *American Journal of Archaeology* 36, 260–271

McGeehan-Liritzis, V. 1996, *The Role and Development of Metallurgy in the Late Neolithic and Early Bronze Age of Greece*. Stockholm: Paul Åströms

McGing, B. C. 1997, Revolt Egyptian Style. Internal Opposition to Ptolemaic Rule. *Archiv für Papyrusforschung und Verwandte Gebiete* 43, 273–314

Meeks, D. 1991, Dieu masqué, Dieu sans tête. *Archéo Nil* 1, 5–15

**Meeks, D. 2003, Locating Punt, in D. O'Connor and S. Quirke (eds), *Mysterious Lands*, 53–80. London: UCL Press**

Meiggs, R. and D. M. Lewis 1988, *A Selection of Greek Historical Inscriptions*. Oxford: OUP

Mercer, S. A. B. 1952, *The Pyramid Texts vol. 1*. New York: Longman

Merkelbach, R. 1995, *Isis Regina – Zeus Sarapis: die Griechisch-Ägyptische Religion nach den Quellen dargestellt*. Leipzig: Teubner

Meskell, L. 2002, *Private Life in New Kingdom Egypt*. Princeton: Princeton UP

Meyboom, P. J. P. 1995, *The Nile Mosaic of Palestrina. Early Evidence of Egyptian Religion in Italy*. Leiden: Brill

Midant-Reynes, B. 2000, The Naqada Period (c. 4000–3200 BC), in I. Shaw (ed.), *The Oxford History of Ancient Egypt*, 44–60. Oxford: OUP

Miller, M. C. 1997, *Athens and Persia in the Fifth Century: A Study in Cultural Receptivity*. Cambridge: CUP

Minault-Gout, A. 1997, Sur les vases jubilaires et leur diffusion, in C. Berger and B. Mathieu (eds), *L'Ancien Empire et la Nécropole de Saqqâra dédiées à Jean-Philippe Lauer*, 305–314. Université Paul Valéry: Orientalia Monspeliensia IX

Modrzejewski, J. M. 1984, Droit et justice dans le monde hellénistique au III$^e$ siècle avant notre ère: expérience Lagide, in A. Biscardi, J. M. Modrzejewski and H. J. Wolff (eds), *MNHMH Georges A. Petropoulos vol. I*, 55–77. Athens: N. Sakkoulas

Modrzejewski, J. M. 1989, Entre la cité et le fisc: le statut Grec dans l'Égypte romaine, in F. J. F. Nieto (ed.), *Symposion 1982; Vorträge zur griechischen und hellenistischen Rechtsgeschichte (Santander, 1–4 September 1982)*, 241–280. Vienna: Böhlau

Modrzejewski, J. M. 1990, *Droit Imperial et traditions locales dans l'Egypte romaine*. Aldershot: Variorum

Modrzejewski, J. M. 1991, *Les Juifs d'Egypte de Ramsès II à Hadrien*. Paris: Editions Errance

Möller, A. 2000, *Naukratis, Trade in Archaic Greece*. Oxford: OUP

Moltesen, M. 1997, Hvor Nilen vander Aegypterens tord. *Medelser fra Ny Carlsberg Glyptotek* 53, 102–125

Monaco, G. 1992, Connotazioni dell'egitto negli autori Latini, in G. Pugliese Carratelli (ed.), *Roma e l'Egitto nell'Antichità Classica*, 261–264. Rome: Istituto Poligrafico

Mond, R. and O. H. Meyers 1940, *Temples of Armant*. London: Egypt Exploration Society

Montet, P. 1928, *Byblos et L'Egypte*. Paris: Paul Geuthner

Mooren, L. 1975, Die Angebliche Verwandtschaft zwischen den Ptolemäischen und Pharaonischen Hofrangtiteln, in *Proceedings of the XIV International Congress of Papyrologists, Oxford, 24–31 July 1974*, 233–240. London: Egypt Exploration Society

Mooren, L. 1977, *La Hiérarchie de cour Ptolémaïque; contribution à l'étude des institutions et des classes dirigeantes à l'époque hellénistique*. Leuven: Studia Hellenistica 23

Moorey, P. R. S. 1987, On Tracking Cultural Transfers in Prehistory: the Case of Egypt and Lower Mesopotamia in the Fourth Millennium BC, in M. Rowlands, M. Larsen and K. Kristiansen (eds), *Centre and Periphery in the Ancient World*, 36–46. Cambridge: CUP

Moorey, P. R. S. 1998, Did Easterners Sail Round Arabia to Egypt in the Fourth Millennium BC?, in C. S. Phillips, D. T. Potts and S. Searight (eds), *Arabia and its Neighbours. Essays on Prehistorical and Historical Developments Presented in Honour of Beatrice de Cardi*, 189–206. Turnhout: Brepols

Moorey, P. R. S. 2001, The Mobility of Artisans and Opportunities for Technology Transfer between Western Asia and Egypt in the Late Bronze Age, in A. J. Shortland (ed.), *The Social Context of Technological Change: Egypt and the Near East, 1650–1550 BC*, 1–14. Exeter: Oxbow

Moran, W. L. 1992, *The Amarna Letters*. Baltimore: Johns Hopkins UP

Moretti, L. 1953, *Iscrizione Agonistiche Greche*. Rome: A. Signorelli

Morgan, K. A. 1998, Designer History: Plato's Atlantis Story and Fourth-Century Ideology. *Journal of Hellenic Studies* 118, 101–118

Morinis, E. A. 1992, *Sacred Journeys: the Anthropology of Pilgrimage*. New York: Greenwood

Morris, I. 1997, The Art of Citizenship, in S. Langdon (ed.), *New Light on a Dark Age: Exploring the Culture of Geometric Greece*, 9–43. Columbia: University of Missouri Press

Morris, I. 2000, *Archaeology as Cultural History: Words and Things in Iron Age Greece*. Oxford: Blackwell

Morris, S. P. 1992, *Daidalos and the Origins of Greek Art*. Princeton: Princeton UP

Morris, S. P. 1997, Greek and Near Eastern Art in the Age of Homer, in S. Langdon (ed.), *New Light on a Dark Age: Exploring the Culture of Geometric Greece*, 56–71. Columbia: University of Missouri Press

Moyer, I. S. 2002, Herodotus and an Egyptian Mirage: The Genealogies of the Theban Priests. *Journal of Hellenic Studies* 122, 70–90

Murray, M. A. 1904, *The Osireion at Abydos*. London: Quaritch

Murray, O. 1980, *Early Greece*. Cambridge, Mass: Harvard UP

Naveh, J. 1968, Aramaica Dubiosa. *Journal of Near Eastern Studies* 27, 317–329

Naville, E. 1922, Le Vase a parfum de Byblos. *Syria* 3, 291–295

Nelson, H. 1934, Fragments of Old Egyptian Stone Vases from Byblos. *Berytus* I, 19–22

Neugebauer, O. and R. A. Parker 1960, *Egyptian Astronomical Texts I. The Early Decans*. Providence: Brown UP

Niemeyer, H-G. (ed.) 1982, *Phönizier im Westen*. Mainz: von Zabern

Nock, A. D. 1972, A Vision of Mandulis Aion, in Z. Stewart (ed.), *Essays on Religion and the Ancient World, vol 1*, 357–400. Oxford: Clarendon

**O'Connor, D. 2003, Egypt's Views of 'Others', in J. Tait (ed.), 'Never had the like occurred': Egypt's view of its past, 155–186. London: UCL Press**

O'Connor, D. and E. H. Cline (eds) 1998, *Amenhotep III: Perspectives on his Reign*. Ann Arbor: University of Michigan Press

Oates, J. F. 1965, The Status-Designation *Perses Test epigones*. *Yale Classical Studies* 18, 1–127

Oates, J. F., R. S. Bagnall, W. H. Willis and K. A. Worp 1992, *Checklist of Editions of Greek Papyri and Ostraca*. Atlanta: Scholars Press

Onasch, H-U. 1994, *Die Assyrischen Eroberungen Ägyptens*. Wiesbaden: Ägypten und Altes Testament

Onians, J. B. 1999, *Classical Art and the Cultures of Greece and Rome*. New Haven: Yale UP

Oren, E. D. and Y. Yekutieli 1992, Taur Ikhbeineh: Earliest Evidence for Egyptian Interconnections, in E. C. M van den Brink (ed.), *The Nile Delta in Transition: 4th–3rd Millennium BC. Proceedings of the Seminar Held in Cairo, 21–24 October 1990, at the Netherlands Institute of Archaeology and Arabic Studies*, 361–384. Tel Aviv: E. C. M. van den Brink

Osborne, R. 1993, A la Grècque. *Journal of Mediterranean Archaeology* 6, 231–237

Osborne, R. 1996, *Greece in the Making 1200–479 BC*. London: Routledge

Osborne, R. 1998, *Archaic and Classical Art*. Oxford: OUP

Ostby, E. 2001, Der Ursprung der griechischen Tempelarchitektur, in M. Bietak (ed.), *Archaische Griechische Tempel und Altägypten*, 17–33. Vienna: Austrian Academy of Sciences

Østergaard, J. S. 1997, Navigare Necesse Est! En Romersk Sarkophag med Skibsfart. *Medelser fra Ny Carlsberg Glyptotek* 53, 81–102

Overbeck, J. 1868, *Die Antiken Schriftquellen zur Geschichte der Bildenden Künste bei den Griechen*. Leipzig: Wilhelm Engemann

Özgüç, T. (ed.) 2002, *Die Hethiter und ihr Reich*. Darmstadt: Wissenschaftliche Buchgesellschaft

Paladini, M. L. 1958, *A Proposito della Tradizione Poetica Sulla Battaglia di Azio*. Brussels: Latomus

Palagia, O and R. S. Bianchi 1994, Who Invented the Claw Chisel? *Oxford Journal of Archaeology* 13, 185–197

Pani, M. 1984, Cleopatra, in *Enciclopedia Virgiliana, vol. I*, 822–825. Rome: Istituto della Enciclopedia Virgiliana

Pasztory, E. 1989, Identity and Difference: the Uses and Meanings of Ethnic Styles, in S. J. Barnes and W. S. Melion (eds), *Cultural Differentiation and Cultural Identity in the Visual Arts*, 17–37. Washington: National Gallery

Pekáry I. 1982, Cheniscus. Zu einem Tongefäss mit Schiffsdarstellung. *Boreas* 5, 273–279

Pekáry, I. 1999, *Repertorium der Hellenistischen und Römischen Schiffsdarstellungen*. Münster: Archäologisches Seminar der Universität (Boreas Beiheft 8)

Pelling, C. 2001, Anything Truth Can Do, We Can Do Better: the Cleopatra Legend, in S. Walker and P. Higgs (eds), *Cleopatra of Egypt: from History to Myth*, 292–301. London: British Museum Press

Perdrizet, P. and G. Lefebvre 1919, *Inscriptiones Graecae Aegypti III*. Nancy: Berger-Levrault

Peremans, W. 1978, Les Revolutions Égyptiennes sous les Lagides, in H. Maehler and V. M. Strocka (eds), *Das Ptolemäische Ägypten, Akten des Internationalen Symposions, 27–29 September 1976 in Berlin*, 39–50. Mainz: von Zabern

Perpillou-Thomas, F. 1995, Artistes et athlètes dans les papyrus Grecs d'Égypte. *Zeitschrift für Papyrologie und Epigraphik* 108, 225–251

Perrin, B. 1920, *Plutarch's Lives, vol. 9*. Cambridge, Mass: Harvard UP

Perrot, J. 1959, Statuettes en ivoire et autres objets en ivoire et en os provenant des gisements préhistoriques de la région de Beersheba. *Syria* 36, 6–19

Perrot, J. 1961, Une Tombe à Ossuaires du iv$^e$ millénaire à Azor près de Tel Aviv. *'Atiqot*, 1–83

Pestman, P. 1977, *Recueil de textes demotiques et bilingues avec la collaboration de J. Quaegebeur et R. L. Vos*. Leiden: Brill

Petrie, W. M. F. 1902, *Abydos: Part I*. London: Egypt Exploration Fund

Petrie, W. M. F. 1937, *The Funeral Furniture of Egypt with Stone and Metal Vases*. London: British School of Archaeology in Egypt

Petrie, W. M. F. 1953, *Corpus of Proto-Dynastic Pottery*. London: British School of Archaeology in Egypt

Petrie, W. M. F. and G. Brunton 1924, *Sedment I*. London: British School of Archaeology in Egypt

Phillips, J. 1991, The Impact and Implications of the Egyptian and Egyptianizing Material found in Bronze Age Crete ca. 3000–ca. 1100 BC, unpublished PhD thesis, University of Toronto

Phillips, J. 1992, Tomb-robbers and their Booty in Ancient Egypt, in S. E. Orel (ed.), *Death and Taxes in the Ancient Near East*, 157–192. Lewiston: Edward Mellon

Phillips, J. 1996, Aegypto-Aegean Relations up to the 2nd Millennium BC, in L. Krzyzaniak, K. Kroeper and M. Kobusiewic (eds), *Interregional Contacts in the Later Prehistory of Northeastern Africa*, 459–470. Poznan: Studies in African Archaeology

Piankoff, A. 1960, The Osireion of Seti I at Abydos during the Greco-Roman Period and the Christian Occupation. *Bulletin de la Société d'Archéologie Copte* 15, 127–149

Pinch, G. 1993, *Votive Offerings to Hathor*. Oxford: Griffith Institute

Pinnock F. 1988, Observations on the Trade of Lapis Lazuli in the IIIrd Millennium BC, in H. Waetzoldt and H. Hauptmann (eds), *Wirtschaft und Gesellschaft von Ebla*, 107–110. Heidelberg: Heidelberger Orient

Pittman, H. 1996, Constructing Context: the Gebel el-Arak knife. Greater Mesopotamian and Egyptian Interaction in the Late Fourth Millennium BCE, in J. S. Cooper and G. M. Schwartz (eds), *The Study of the Ancient Near East in the Twenty-First Century*, 9–32. Winona Lake: Eisenbrauns

Pollard, J. 1977, *Birds in Greek Life and Myth*. London: Thames and Hudson

Pollitt, J. J. 1990, *The Art of Ancient Greece: Sources and Documents*. Cambridge: CUP

Pomerance, L. 1973, The Possible Role of Tomb Robbers and Viziers of the 18th Dynasty in Confusing Minoan Chronology. *Antichità Cretesi: Studi in onore di Doro Levi 1, Chronache di Archeologia* 12, 21–30

Pomerance, L. 1984, A Note on the Stone Ewers from the Khian Lid Deposit, in P. Aström, L. R. Palmer and L. Pomerance, *Studies in Aegean Chronology*, 15–25. Stockholm: Paul Åströms

Porat, N. 1992, An Egyptian Colony in Southern Palestine during the Late Predynastic/Early Dynastic Period, in E. C. M van den Brink (ed.), *The Nile Delta in Transition: 4th–3rd Millennium BC. Proceedings of the Seminar Held in Cairo, 21–24 October 1990, at the Netherlands Institute of Archaeology and Arabic Studies*, 433–440. Tel Aviv: E. C. M. van den Brink

Porat, N. 1996, Appendix B. "Egyptian" Pottery from Hartuv: A Petrographic Description. *Bulletin of the American Schools of Oriental Research* 302, 34–35

Porter, B. and R. Moss 1974, *Topographical Bibliography of Ancient Egyptian Hieroglyphic Texts, Reliefs, and Paintings*. Oxford: Griffith Institute

Potts, A. 1982, Winckelmann's Construction of History. *Art History* 5, 377–407

Potts, D. T. 1986, The Booty of Magan. *Oriens Antiquus* 25, 271–285

Potts, D. T. 1995, Distant Shores: Ancient Near Eastern Trade with South Asia and Northeast Africa, in J. M. Sasson (ed.), *Civilizations of the Ancient Near East*, 1,451–1,463. Peabody: Henrickson

Potts, T. F. 1989, Foreign Stone Vessels of the Late Third Millennium BC from Southern Mesopotamia: their Origins and Mechanisms of Exchange. *Iraq* 51, 123–164

Prag, K. 1986, Byblos and Egypt in the Fourth Millennium BC. *Levant* 18, 59–74

Préaux, C. 1936, Esquisse d'une histoire des révolutions Égyptiennes sous les Lagides. *Chronique d'Égypte* 11, 522–552

Préaux, C. 1978, *Le Monde hellénistique*. Nouvelle Clio 6. Paris: Presses Universitaires de France

Preston, L. 1999, Mortuary Practices and the Negotiation of Social Identities at LMII Knossos. *Annual of the British School at Athens* 94, 131–144

Pritchard, J. B. (ed.) 1969, *Ancient Near Eastern Texts Relating to the Old Testament*. Princeton: Princeton UP

Pritchett, W. K. 1993, *The Liar School of Herodotus*. Amsterdam: J. C. Gieben

Quaegebeur, J. 1977, Le Saints Égyptiennes prechrétiens. *Orientalia Lovaniensia Periodica* 8, 129–143

Quaegebeur, J. 1982, De la préhistoire de l'écriture Copte. *Orientalia Lovaniensia Periodica* 13, 125–136

Ray, J. D. 1976, *The Archive of Hor*. London: Egypt Exploration Society

Ray, J. D. 1990, An Outline of Carian Grammar. *Kadmos* 29, 54–83

Reade, J. 1998, *Assyrian Sculpture*. London: British Museum Press

Reade, J. 2001, Assyrian King-lists, the Royal Tombs of Ur, and Indus Origins. *Journal of Near Eastern Studies* 60, 1–29

Redfield, J. 1985, Herodotus the Tourist. *Classical Philology* 80, 97–118

Redford, D. B. 1965, The Coregency of Tuthmosis III and Amenophis II. *Journal of Egyptian Archaeology* 51, 107–122

Redford, D. B. 1992, *Egypt, Canaan, and Israel in Ancient Times*. Princeton: Princeton UP

Reeves, N. 1990, *The Complete Tutankhamun*. London: Thames and Hudson

Rehm, A. 1940, MNHSQH. *Philologus* 94

Reisner, G. A. 1931, *Mycerinus: the Temple of the Third Pyramid at Giza*. Cambridge, Mass: Harvard UP

Renfrew, A. C. 1972, *The Emergence of Civilisation: the Cyclades and the Aegean in the Third Millennium BC*. London: Methuen

Rhodes, P. J. 1994, In Defence of the Greek Historians. *Greece and Rome* 41, 156–171

Richards, J. 1999, Conceptual Landscapes in the Egyptian Nile Valley, in W. Ashmore and A. B. Knapp (eds), *Archaeologies of Landscape: Contemporary Perspectives*, 83–100. Oxford: Blackwell

Richter, G. 1960, *Kouroi: Archaic Greek Youths. A Study of the Development of the Kouros Type in Greek Sculpture*. London: Phaidon

Ridgway, B. S. 1977, *The Archaic Style in Greek Sculpture*. Princeton: Princeton UP

Riemann, H. 1985, Zur Südmauer der Oberstadt von Praeneste. *Mitteilungen des Deutschen Archäologischen Instituts, Römische Abteilung* 94, 151–168

Riemann, H. 1986, Zum Forumstempel und zum unteren Heiligtum der Fortuna Primigenia zu Praeneste. *Mitteilungen des Deutschen Archäologischen Instituts, Römische Abteilung* 95, 357–404

Righi, R. 1984, Nuove ricerche e rinvenimenti nel Lazio costiero meridionale. *Archeologia Laziale* 6, 178–185

Ritner, R. K. 1992, Implicit Models of Cross-Cultural Interaction: A Question of Noses, Soap, and Prejudice, in J. H. Johnson (ed.), *Life in a Multi-Cultural Society: Egypt from Cambyses to Constantine and Beyond*, 283–290. Chicago: Oriental Institute

Rizkana, I. and J. Seeher 1987, *Maadi I: The Pottery of the Predynastic Settlement*. Mainz: von Zabern

Roaf, M. 1973, The Diffusion of the Salles à Quatre Saillants. *Iraq* 35, 83–91

Roberts, O. T. 1991, The Development of the Brail into a Viable Sail Control for Aegean Boats of the Bronze Age, in R. Laffineur (ed.), *Thalassa. L'Égée préhistorique et la mer*, 55–60. Liège: Université de Liège

Roberts, O. T. 1995, An Explanation of Ancient Windward Sailing. Some Other Considerations. *International Journal of Nautical Archaeology* 24, 307–315

**Robinson, P. 2003, "As for them who know them, they shall find their paths": Speculations on Ritual Landscapes in the 'Book of the Two Ways', in D. O'Connor and S. Quirke (eds), *Mysterious Lands*, 139–160. London: UCL Press**

Romm, J. 1989, Herodotus and Mythic Geography: the Case of the Hyperboreans. *Transactions of the American Philological Association* 119, 97–113

Rosen, S. 1988, A Preliminary Note on the Egyptian Component of the Chipped Stone Assemblage at Tel Erani. *Israel Exploration Journal* 38, 105–116

Roshwalb, A. F. 1981, Protohistory in the Wadi Ghazzeh: A Typological and Technological Study Based on the Macdonald Excavations, unpublished PhD thesis, University of London

Roth, A. M. 1992, The *Psš-kf* and the 'Opening of the Mouth' Ceremony. *Journal of Egyptian Archaeology* 78, 113–147

Roth, M. T. 1997, *Law Collections from Mesopotamia and Asia Minor*. Atlanta: SBL

Rushton Fairclough, H. 1918, *Virgil's Aeneid vol. II*. London: William Heinemann

Rutherford, I. C. 1998, The Island at the Edge. Space, Language and Power in the Pilgrimages Traditions of Philai, in D. Frankfurter (ed.), *Pilgrimage and Holy-Space in Late Antique Egypt*, 229–256. Leiden: Brill

Rutherford, I. C. 2000, The Reader's Voice in a Horoscope from Abydos. *Zeitschrift für Papyrologie und Epigraphik* 130, 149–150

Rutherford, I. C. forthcoming, Down-stream to the Cat Goddess. Herodotus on Egyptian Pilgrimage to Bubastis, in J. Elsner and I. Rutherford (eds), *Seeing the Gods. Patterns of Pilgrimage in Antiquity*

Rutter, J. B. 1993, Review of Aegean Prehistory II: Prepalatial Bronze Age of the Southern and Central Greek Mainland. *American Journal of Archaeology* 97, 745–797

Ryholt, K. S. B. 1997, *The Political Situation in Egypt During the Second Intermediate Period, c. 1800–1550 BC*. Copenhagen: Museum Tusculanum Press

Ryholt, K. S. B. 1998, Hotepibre, a Supposed Asiatic King in Egypt with Relations to Ebla. *Bulletin of the American Schools of Oriental Research* 311, 1–6

Saghieh, M. 1983, *Byblos in the Third Millennium BC. A Reconstruction of the Stratigraphy and a Study of the Cultural Connections*. Warminster: Aris & Phillips

Said, E. W. 1978, *Orientalism: Western Conceptions of the Orient*. Harmondsworth: Penguin

Saïd, S. 2002, Greeks and Barbarians in Euripides' Tragedies: The End of Differences?, in T. Harrison (ed.), *Greeks and Barbarians*, 62–100. Edinburgh: Edinburgh UP

Saidah, R. 1993–1994, Beirut in the Bronze Age: The Kharji Tombs. *Berytus* 41, 137–210

Sakellarakis, J. A. 1976, Mycenaean Stone Vases. *Studi Miceni ed Egeo-anatolici* 17, 173–187

Samuel, A. E. 1989, *The Shifting Sands of History: Interpretations of Ptolemaic Egypt*. New York: University Press of America

Sasson, J. M. 1995, King Hammurabi of Babylon, in J. M. Sasson (ed.), *Civilizations of the Ancient Near East*, 901–915. New York: Charles Scribner's Sons

Savage, S. H. 2001, Some Recent Trends in the Archaeology of Predynastic Egypt. *Journal of Archaeological Research* 9, 101–155

Scandone Matthiae, G. 1982, Inscriptions royales égyptiennes de l'ancien empire à Ebla, in H. J. Nissen and J. Renger (eds), *Mesopotamien und seine Nachbarn, vol. 1 part 1*, 125–130. Berlin: Reimer

Scandone Matthiae, G. 1988, Les Relations entre Ébla et l'Égypte au IIIème et au IIème millénaire av. J-C., in H. Waetzoldt and H. Hauptmann (eds), *Wirtschaft und Gesellschaft von Ebla*, 67–73. Heidelberg: Heidelberger Orient

Scandone Matthiae, G. 1979, Vasi Iscritti di Cefren e Pepi I Nel Palazzo Reale G di Ebla. *Studi Eblaiti* 3, 33–43

Scandone Matthiae, G. 1981, I Vasi Egiziani in Pietra dal Palazzo Reale G. *Studi Eblaiti* 4, 99–127

Schaeffer, C. F. A. 1949, *Ugaritica II (Missions de Ras Shamra V)*. Paris: C. Klincksieck

Schaeffer, C. F. A. 1954, Les Fouilles de ras Shamra-Ugarit quinzième, seizième et dix-septième campagnes (1951, 1952 et 1953). *Syria* 31, 14–67

Schaeffer, C. F. A. 1956, *Ugaritica III*. Paris: Paul Geuthner

Schäfer, H. 1904, *Die Mysterien des Osiris in Abydos unter König Sesostris III*. Leipzig: Hinrichs

Schefold, K. 1962, *Vergessenes Pompeji*. Bern: Francke

Schneider, H. D. 1996, *The Memphite Tomb of Horemheb – Commander in Chief of Tutankhamun. Vol II. A Catalogue of the Finds*. London: Egypt Exploration Society

Schulman, A. R. 1988, Catalogue of the Egyptian Finds, in B. Rothenberg, *The Egyptian Mining Temple at Timna*, 114–147. London: Institute for Archaeo-metallurgical Studies

Schulman, A. R. and R. Gophna 1981, An Archaic Egyptian *Serekh* from Tel Ma'ahaz. *Israel Exploration Journal* 31, 165–167

Schwab, K. 1996, Stone Vessels, in J. W. Shaw and M. C. Shaw (eds), *Kommos I. The Kommos Region and Houses of the Minoan Town*, 271–282. Princeton: Princeton UP

Scott, K. 1933, The Political Propaganda of 44–30 BC. *Memoirs of the American Academy in Rome* 11, 7–49

Seger, J. D. 1990, The Bronze Age Settlements at Tell Halif: Phase II Excavations, 1983–1987, in *Preliminary Reports of ASOR-Sponsored Excavations*, 1–32. Baltimore: Johns Hopkins UP

Seger, J. D. 1996, The Point One Principle: A Case Study from the Halif Terrace, in J. D. Seger (ed.), *Retrieving the Past: Essays on Archaeological Research and Methodology in Honor of Gus W. van Beek*, 245–268. Mississippi State University: Cobb Institute of Archaeology

Seidl, U. 2000, Babylonische und Assyrische kultbilder in den Massenmedien des 1 jahrtausends v. Chr, in Ch. Uehlinger (ed.), *Images as Media*, 89–114. Fribourg and Göttingen: Orbis Biblicus

Shaw, I. 2000, Egypt and the Outside World, in I. Shaw (ed.), *The Oxford History of Ancient Egypt*, 314–329. Oxford: OUP

Shaw, I., E. Bloxham, J. Bunbury, R. Lee, A. Graham and D. Darnell 2001, Survey and Excavation at Gebel el-Asr Gneiss and Quartz Quarries in Lower Nubia (1997–2000). *Antiquity* 75, 33–34

Shepherd, W. G. 1983, *Horace: The Complete Odes and Epodes*. Harmondsworth: Penguin

Shepherd, W. G. 1985, *Propertius: The Poems*. Harmondsworth: Penguin

Sherratt, A. G. 1993, What Would a Bronze Age World System Look Like? *Journal of European Archaeology* 1, 1–57

Sherratt, A. G. and S. Sherratt 1991, From Luxuries to Commodities: The Nature of Bronze Age Trading Systems, in N. H. Gale (ed.), *Bronze Age Trade in the Mediterranean*, 351–381. Stockholm: Paul Åströms

Sherratt, S. and A. G. Sherratt 1993, The Growth of the Mediterranean Economy in the Early First Millennium BC. *World Archaeology* 24, 361–378

Shipley, G. 1987, *A History of Samos, 800–188 BC*. Oxford: Clarendon

Simpson, W. K. 1960, Papyrus Lithgoe: A Fragment of a Literary Text of the Middle Kingdom from El-Lisht. *Journal of Egyptian Archaeology* 46, 65–70

Singer, I. 1988, Merenptah's Campaign to Canaan and the Egyptian Occupation of the Southern Coastal Plain of Palestine in the Ramesside Period. *Bulletin of the American Schools of Oriental Research* 269, 1–10

Skon-Jedele, N. J. 1994, Aigyptiaka: A Catalogue of Egyptian and Egyptianising Objects from Greek Archaeological Sites, ca. 1100–525 BC, with Historical Commentary, unpublished PhD thesis, University of Pennsylvania

Smelik, K. A. D. and E. A. Hemelrijk 1984, Who Knows Not What Monsters Demented Egypt Worships? Opinions on Egyptian Animal Worship in Antiquity as part of the Ancient Conception of Egypt. *Aufstieg und Niedergang der römischen Welt* 17, 1,852–2,000

Smith, H. S. 1968, A Note on Amnesty. *Journal of Egyptian Archaeology* 54, 209–214

Snell, B. 1926, Antiker Besucher des tempels von Sunion. *Athenische Mitteilungen* 51, 159–172

Snodgrass, A. M. 1980, *Archaic Greece: the Age of Experiment*. London: Dent

Snodgrass, A. M. 1986, Interaction by Design: the Greek City State, in C. Renfrew and J. F. Cherry (eds), *Peer Polity Interaction and Socio-Political Change*, 47–58. Cambridge: CUP

Snowden, F. M. 1981, Aithiopes, in *Lexicon Iconographicum Mythologiae Classicae*, 413–419

Soldt, W. von 2000, Syrian Chronology in the Old and Early Middle Babylonian Periods. *Akkadica* 119/120, 103–116

Soles, J. S. 1992, *The Prepalatial Cemeteries at Mochlos and Gournia*. Princeton: American School of Classical Studies at Athens

Sommerfeld, W. 1995, The Kassites of Ancient Mesopotamia: Origins, Politics and Culture, in J. M. Sasson (ed.), *Civilizations of the Ancient Near East*, 917–930. New York: Charles Scribner's Sons

Spalinger, A. 1974, Esarhaddon and Egypt: An Analysis of the First Invasion of Egypt. *Orientalia* 43, 295–326

Spalinger, A. 1977, Egypt and Babylonia: A Survey (c. 620–500 BC). *Studien zur Altägyptischen Kultur* 5, 221–244

Spalinger, A. 1978, The Foreign Policy of Egypt Preceding the Assyrian Conquest. *Chronique d'Égypte* 53, 22–47

Sparks, R. 1998, Stone Vessels in the Levant During the Second Millennium BC. A Study of the Interaction between Imported Forms and Local Workshops, unpublished PhD thesis, University of Sydney

Spencer, A. J. 1982, *Death in Ancient Egypt*. Harmondsworth: Penguin

Spiegelberg, W. 1908–1909, Neue Demotische Inschriften. *Zeitschrift für Ägyptische Sprache und Altertumskunde* 45, 97–102

Stenton, F. M. 1971, *Anglo-Saxon England, The Oxford History of England vol. II*. Oxford: OUP

Steuernagel, D. 1991, Der Gute Staatsbürger: zur Interpretation des Kuros. *Hephaistos* 10, 35–48

Stewart, A. F. 1986, When is a Kouros not an Apollo? The Tenea Apollo revisited, in M. del Chiaro (ed.), *Corinthiaca: Studies in Honour of Darrell A. Amyx*, 54–70. Columbia: University of Missouri Press

Stocks, D. A. 1988, Industrial Technology at Kahun and Gurob: Experimental Manufacture and Test of Replica and Reconstructed Tools with Indicated Uses and Effects upon Artefact Production, unpublished Masters thesis, University of Manchester

Stocks, D. A. 1993, Making Stone Vessels in Ancient Mesopotamia and Egypt. *Antiquity* 67, 596–603

Stolper, M. 1985, *Entrepreneurs and Empire*. Istanbul: Nederlands Historisch-Archaeologisch Instituut

Sulek, A. 1989, The Experiment of Psammetichus: Fact, Fiction, and Model to Follow. *Journal of the History of Ideas* 50, 645–651

Syme, R. 1984, *Princesses and others in Tacitus. Roman Papers III, 1364–1375*. Oxford: OUP

**Tait, J. 2003, The Wisdom of Egypt: Classical Views, in P. J. Ucko and T. C. Champion (eds), *The Wisdom of Egypt: changing visions through the ages*, 23–38. London: UCL Press**

Takács, S. A. 1995, *Isis and Sarapis in the Roman World*. Leiden: Brill

Tanner, J. 2001, Nature, Culture and the Body in Classical Greek Religious Art. *World Archaeology* 33, 257–276

Tarn, W. W. 1931, The Battle of Actium. *Journal of Roman Studies* 21, 173–199

Teissier, B. 1987, Glyptic Evidence for a Connection between Iran, Syro-Palestine and Egypt in the Fourth and Third Millennia. *Iran* 25, 27–53

Teixidor, J. 1964, Un Nouveau Papyrus Araméen du règne de Darius II. *Syria* 41, 285–290

Thomas, R. 2000, *Herodotus in Context. Ethnography, Science and the Art of Persuasion*. Cambridge: CUP

Thompson, D. J. 1988, *Memphis under the Ptolemies*. Princeton: Princeton UP

Thompson, D. J. 1994, Egypt, 146–31 BC, in J. A. Crook, A. Lintott. and E. Rawson (eds), *The Cambridge Ancient History IX*, 310–326. 2nd edition, Cambridge: CUP

Tomlinson, J. A. 1997, *Painting in Spain: El Greco to Goya, 1562–1828*. London: Weidenfeld and Nicholson

Totti, M. 1985, *Ausgewählte Texte der Isis- und Sarapis-Religion*. Hildesheim: G. Olms

Trigger, B. G. 1993, *Early Civilizations. Ancient Egypt in Context*. Cairo: American University in Cairo Press

Tufnell, O. 1969, The Pottery from Royal Tombs I-III at Byblos. *Berytus* 18, 5–33

Turner, E. G. 1984, Ptolemaic Egypt, in F. W. Walbank, W. A. E. Astin, M. W. Frederiksen and R. M. Ogilvie (eds), *The Cambridge Ancient History, VII*, 118–174. 2nd edition, Cambridge: CUP

Van de Mieroop, M. 1999, *Cuneiform Texts and the Writing of History*. London: Routledge

van den Brink, E. C. M. 1998, Late Protodynastic–Early First Dynasty Egyptian Finds in Late–Early Bronze Age I Canaan: an Update, in C. J. Eyre (ed.), *Proceedings of the Seventh International Congress of Egyptologists* (*Orientalia Lovaniensia Analecta* 82), 215–225. Leuven: Peeters

van den Brink, E. C. M. forthcoming, Late EB I Settlements and Sporadic Chalcolithic–PNA Remains at the Tel of Lod, Central Coastal Plain. *'Atiqot*

van den Brink, E. C. M. and E. Braun 2002, Wine Jars with *Serekhs* from Early Bronze Lod: Appellation Controlée Région le Nile, but for Whom?, in E. C. M. van den Brink and E. Yannai (eds), *In Quest of Ancient Landscapes and Settlements*, 167–192. Tel Aviv: Ramot

Van der Plas, D. 1989, 'Voir' Dieu. Quelques observations au sujet de la fonction des sens dans le culte et la dévotion de l'Égypte ancienne. *Bulletin de la Société Française d'Égyptologie* 115, 4–35

Van Dijk, J. 2000, The Amarna Period and the Later New Kingdom (c. 1352–1069 BC), in I. Shaw (ed.), *The Oxford History of Ancient Egypt*, 272–313. Oxford: OUP

Vannicelli, P. 1997, L'Esperimento linguistico di Psammetico (Herodot. II.2): c'era una volta il frigio, in *Frigi et Frigio. Monografie scientifiche – Serie Scienze umane et sociale*, 201–217. Rome: Centro Nationale di Ricerche

Varille, A. 1930–1935, La Stèle Égyptienne n° 1175 du Musée de Toulouse. *Kémi* 3, 39–43

Vasunia, P. 2001, *The Gift of the Nile. Hellenizing Egypt from Aeschylus to Alexander*. Berkeley: University of California Press

Veenhof, K. 1995, Kanesh. An Assyrian Colony in Anatolia, in J. M. Sasson (ed.), *Civilizations of the Ancient Near East*, 859–871. New York: Charles Scribner's Sons

Venit, M. S. 1988, *Ancient Naukratis, Vol. 6: Greek Painted Pottery from Naukratis in Egyptian Museums*. Winona Lake: Eisenbrauns

Vercoutter, J. 1945, *Les Objets Égyptiens et Égyptisants du mobilier funéraire Carthaginois*. Paris: Bibliothèque Archéologique et Historique

Vercoutter, J. 1997, Égyptiens et préhellènes: nouveaux points de vue. *Revue d'Égyptologie* 48, 219–226

Vidal-Naquet, P. 1964, Athènes et l'Atlantide. Structure et signification d'un mythe Platonicien. *Revue des Études Grecques* 77, 420–444

Virey, P. 1891, *Sept Tombeaux Thébaines de la XVIIIe dynastie*. Paris: Ernest Lerioux

Virey, P. 1899, La Tomb des vignes en Thèbes. *Recueil de travaux relatifs à la philologie et à l'Archéologie Égyptienne et Assyrienne* 21, 137–149

Volokhine, Y. 1998, Les Déplacements pieux en Égypte pharaoniques. Sites et pratiques culturelles, in D. Frankfurter (ed.), *Pilgrimage and Holy-Space in Late Antique Egypt*, 51–97. Leiden: Brill

Vos, M. de 1980, *L'Egittomania in Pitture e Mosaici Romane-Campani della Prima Età Imperiale*, 84, Leiden: Brill

Wace, A. J. B. 1921–1923, Excavations at Mycenae. *Annual of the British School at Athens* 25, 1–402

Waelkens, M., P. De Paepe and L. Moens 1990, The Quarrying Techniques of the Greek World, in M. True and J. Podany (eds), *Marble: Art Historical and Scientific Perspectives on Ancient Sculpture* 47–72. Malibu: J. Paul Getty Museum

Wagner, G. 1996, Les Inscriptions Grecques d'Ain Labakha. *Zeitschrift für Papyrologie und Epigraphik* 111, 97–114

Wagner, G. and J. Quaegebeur 1973, Une Dédicace Grecque au dieu Égyptian Mestasymtis de la parte de son synode. *Bulletin de l'Institut Français d'Archéologie Orientale du Caire* 73, 41–60

Walker, S. and P. Higgs 2000, *Cleopatra Regina d'Egitto*. Milan: Electa

Walker, S. and P. Higgs 2001, *Cleopatra of Egypt: from History to Myth*. London: British Museum Press

Warburton, D. A. 2000a, Stratigraphy: Methodology and Terminology, in P. Matthiae, A. Enea, L. Peyronel and F. Pinnock (eds), *Proceedings of the First International Congress on the Archaeology of the Ancient Near East*, 1,731–1,750. Rome: La Sapienza

Warburton, D. A. 2000b, Synchronizing the Chronology of Bronze Age Western Asia with Egypt. *Akkadica* 119/120, 33–76

Warburton, D. A. 2001, *Egypt and the Near East: Politics in the Bronze Age*. Neuchâtel: Civilisations du Proche-Orient

Warburton, D. A. 2002, Eclipses, Venus-Cycles and Chronology. *Akkadica* 123, 108–114

Ward, W. A. 1971, *Egypt and the East Mediterranean World 2200–1900 BC*. Beirut: American University of Beirut

Ward, W. A. 1993–1994, Egyptian Objects from the Beirut Tombs. *Berytus* 41, 211–222

Warren, P. 1969, *Minoan Stone Vases*. Cambridge: CUP

Warren, P. 1981, Knossos and its Foreign Relations in the Bronze Age. *Pepragmena ton Diethnous Kritologikon Sinedrion* 4, 628–637

Warren, P. 1989, Egyptian Stone Vessels from the City of Knossos: Contributions towards Minoan Economic and Social Structure. *Ariadne* 5, 1–9

Warren, P. 1995, Minoan Crete and Pharaonic Egypt, in W. V. Davies and L. Schofield (eds), *Egypt, the Aegean and the Levant. Interconnections in the Second Millennium BC*, 1–18. London: British Museum Press

Warren, P. 1996, The Lapidary Art: Minoan Adaptations of Egyptian Stone Vessels, in R. Laffineur and P. P. Betancourt (eds), *Techne: Craftsmen, Craftswomen and Craftmanship in the Aegean Bronze Age*, 209–223. Liège: Université de Liège

Warren, P. and V. Hankey 1989, *Aegean Bronze Age Chronology*. Bristol: Bristol Classical Press

Watrous, L. V. 1987, The Role of the Near East in the Rise of the Cretan Palace, in R. Hägg and N. Marinatos (eds), *The Function of the Minoan Palace*, 65–70. Stockholm: Paul Åströms

Webb, V. 1978, *Archaic Greek Faience: Miniature Scent Bottles and Related Objects from East Greece, 650–500 BC*. Warminster: Aris & Phillips

Webb, V. 1980, Phoenician Anthropomorphic Flasks: a reply. *Levant* 12, 77–89

Weeks, K. R. 1997, History of the Field: Archaeology in Egypt, in E. M. Meyers (ed.), *The Oxford Encyclopedia of Archaeology in the Near East, Vol 3*, 67–70. Oxford: OUP

Weinstein, J. M. 1975, Egyptian Relations with Palestine in the Middle Kingdom. *Bulletin of the American Schools of Oriental Research* 217, 1–16

Weinstein, J. M. 1981, The Egyptian Empire in Palestine: A Reassessment. *Bulletin of the American Schools of Oriental Research* 241, 1–28

Weinstein, J. M. 1992, The Collapse of the Egyptian Empire in the Southern Levant, in W. A. Ward and M. S. Joukowsky (eds), *The Crisis Years: The 12th Century BC. From Beyond the Danube to the Tigris*, 142–150. Dubuque, Iowa: Kendall Hunt

Wenke, R. J. 1989, Egypt: Origins of Complex Societies. *Annual Review of Anthropology* 18, 129–155

Wente, E. F. 1995, The Scribes of Ancient Egypt, in J. M. Sasson (ed.), *Civilizations of the Ancient Near East*, 2,211–2,221. New York: Charles Scribner's Sons

West, S. 1984, Io and the Dark Stranger (Sophocles, *Inachus* F 269a). *Classical Quarterly* 34, 292–302

West, S. 1991, Herodotus' Portrait of Hecataeus. *Journal of Hellenic Studies* 111, 144–160

West, S. 1992, Sesostris' Stelae (Herodotus 2,102–2,106). *Historia* 41, 117–120

White, H. 1978, Historical Text as Literary Artifact, in R. Canary and H. Kozicki (eds), *The Writing of History*, 41–72. Madison: University of Wisconsin Press

Whitehead, D. 2000, *Hypereides. The Forensic Speeches*. Oxford: OUP

Whitehouse, H. 2001, *The Paper Museum of Cassiano dal Pozzo. Series A, Part 1: Ancient Mosaics and Wallpaintings*. London: Harvey Miller

Whiting, R. 1995, Amorite Tribes and Nations of Second-Millennium Western Asia, in J. M. Sasson (ed.), *Civilizations of the Ancient Near East*, 1,231–1,242. New York: Charles Scribner's Sons

Wilcken, U. 1912, *Grundzüge und Chrestomathie der Papyruskunde, vol. 1 part 2: Chrestomathie*. Leipzig: Teubner

Wilcken, U. 1927, *Urkunden der Ptolemäerzeit (Ältere Funde). 1, Papyriaus Unterägypten*. Berlin: Mouton de Gruyter

Williams, D. forthcoming, Sotades Plastic and White, in S. Keay and S. Moser (eds), *Greek Art in View. Studies in Honour of Brian Sparkes*. Exeter: Oxbow

Williams, J. H. C. 2001, Spoiling the Egyptians. Octavian and Cleopatra, in S. Walker and P. Higgs (eds), *Cleopatra of Egypt: from History to Myth*, 190–199. London: British Museum Press

Wilson, J. A. 1941, The Egyptian Middle Kingdom at Megiddo. *American Journal of Semitic Languages and Literature* 58, 225–236

Winckelmann, J. J. 1784, *The History of Ancient Art* (trans. G. H. Lodge 1888). London: Sapson, Low, Manston, Seale and Rivington

Woolf, G. 1990, World-Systems Analysis and the Roman Empire. *Journal of Roman Archaeology* 3, 44–58

Woolley, C. L. 1955, *Alalakh: An Account of the Excavations at Tell Atchana*. Oxford: OUP

Wright, M. 1988, Contacts between Egypt and Syro-Palestine during the Old Kingdom. *Biblical Archaeologist* 51, 143–161

Yannai, E. and O. Marder 2001, Lod. *Hadashot Arkheologiyot* 112, 63–65

Yeivin, S. 1960, Early Contacts between Canaan and Egypt. *Israel Exploration Journal* 10, 193–203

Yeivin, S. 1961, *First Preliminary Report on the Excavations at Tel "Gat" (Tell Sheykh 'Ahmed el-'Areyny): Seasons 1956–1958*. Jerusalem: Hebrew University

Yekutieli, Y. 1991, The Early Bronze IA of Southwestern Canaan: Settlement, Economy and Society, unpublished MA thesis, Tel Aviv University

Yekutieli, Y. and R. Gophna 1994, Excavations at an Early Bronze Age Site near Nizzanim. *Tel Aviv* 21, 162–185

Yoyotte J. 1960, Les Pélerinages dans l'Égypte ancienne, in *Sources Orientale. vol 3*. Paris: Editions de Seuil

Yoyotte, J. and S. Sauneron 1952, La Campagne Nubienne de Psammétique II et sa signification historique. *Bulletin de l'Institut Français d'Archéologie Orientale du Caire* 50, 157–207

Yule, P. 1980, *Early Cretan Seals: A Study of Chronology*. Mainz: von Zabern

Zaccagnini, C. 1983, Patterns of Mobility among Ancient Near Eastern Craftsmen. *Journal of Near Eastern Studies* 42, 245–264

Zevi, F. 1998, Die Casa del Fauno in Pompeji und das Alexandermosaik. *Mitteilungen des Deutschen Archäologischen Instituts, Römische Abteilung* 105, 21–65

Zibelius, K. 1972, *Afrikanische Orts- und Völkernamen in Hieroglyphischen und Hieratischen Texten*. Wiesbaden: Ludwig Reichert

# Index 1: place names

**Note: figure numbers are denoted in bold type.**

'En Besor **2:1**, 26, 31, 34–35

Abu Simbel 12, 93, 126

Abydos 7, 12, 32, 68, 171–189

Actium 205–206, 208–211, 213–214

Aegean 9, 10, 32, 57–73, 78–79, 86, 90–92, 97, 99–100, 107, 149

Aegyptisches Museum, Berlin 2

Afghanistan 6, 8, 106

Africa 5, 10, 19

Afridar/Ashqelon **2:1**, 26, 33, 37

Agade 79

Agia Triada **4:2**, 71

Ain Labakha 171

Alalakh 71, 77, 82

Aleppo 77–80, 99

Alexandria 12, 14, 16–17, 181, 197–198, 213; library 16–17; foundation 12; Greco-Roman museum 195

Amarna, *see* Tell el-Amarna

Amasis 14

Amurru 84, 88, 94

Anatolia 9, 40, 57, 70, 78–80, 82–83, 87, 90–91, 97, 99, 104, 107, 111

Antaioupolis 181

Arad **2:1**, 32, 35, 37

Archanes 71

Arzawa 90–91, 99, 104

Ashdod 43

Ashqelon, *see* Tel Ashqelon

Asia Minor 15

Assur 3, 79–80, 97, 104–105, 112–113

Assyria 1, 9, 75, 77–80, 82–84, 89–90, 92, 96–101, 103–109, **6:2**, 111–113

Aswan High Dam 3

Athens 13–16, 214; theatre of Dionysus 15

Azor **2:1**, 32

Baalat-Gebal, *see* Byblos

Babylon 3, 77–80, 82–83, 87, 89–91, 99–100, 103, 106, 109, 111

Babylonia 9, 10, 75, 78–80, 82–84, 89–91, 96–97, 100–101, 103–107, 109, 111–112

Beirut **3:1**, **3:4**, 51, 56, 88

Beneventum 204

Beqa'a 87

Beth Shan 43, 87–88

Boğazköy 49; *see also* Hattusha

British Museum, London 2

Bubastis 171–172

Buto 172–173

Byblos 7–9, 12, **3:1**, 45, 47–56, **3:4**, 58–59, **4:1**, 63–66, 69, 71, 87–88, 99; Baalat-Gebal, temple of at Byblos 48, 53–55, 63

Canopus 195, 198, 200, 211, 213–214

Carchemish 78, 80, 85, 99

Carthage 107, 203, 214

Cilicia 71, 78

Cnidos 16

Corinth 131

Cos 16

Cretans 13, 125

Crete 9–10, 12–13, 40, 49, 57–59, **4:1**, **4:2**, 62–63, **4:4**, 65–72, **4:5**, 90, 97, 205; Kaptara 9–10; Keftiu 10; Minoan 9–10, 58; Prepalatial 57, 59, 62, 65; Protopalatial 65; Neopalatial 66–67, 69–70, 72; post-Neopalatial 70

Crocodilopolis 212

Cumae 158

Cyprus 10, 12, 40, 49, 57, 70–71, 92, 104, 205

Cyrene 126

Damascus 87, 89, 94

Deir el-Bahri 131, **7:6**

Delos 132, 135

Delta, *see* Nile, Delta

Dendera 212–213

Diospolis Parva **4:2**

Dur Kurigalzu 83

Ebla 8, **3:1**, 47–48, 63–64, 69, 79; Palace G 8, 47–48, 53–54, 63–64; cuneiform archives 8, 63
Elam 42, 77, 107–109, **6:2**, 111
El-Maghar 30, 34
Emar 77, 99
Enkomi 71
Ephesus 90–91
Euphrates river 6, 77–80, 90, 96, 99
Europe 3, 10
European museums 3

Fayum 97

Gaza 21, 33
Gebel el-Asr 72
Gezer 33, **3:1**, **3:4**, 51, 56
Givat Ha-esev 30
Giza 8
Gournia **4:2**
Greece 1, 19, 79, 90, 112, 115–155
Gurob 97, 99

Halif Terrace 25, 34, 37
Haraga **4:2**
Hartuv 31–32, 37
Hattusha 82–83, 97, 99, 104; *see also* Boğazköy
Heliopolis 89, 149
Hermonthis 211
Horvat 'Illin Tahtit **2:1**, 29–31, 35–37

Iberian peninsula 107
India 11, 79
Iran 7, 75, 111
Iraq 80
Isopata 70–71, 73
Israel 21, **2:1**, 26, 33, 37
Italy 17–18

Jemdet Nasr 7
Jordan 87–89
Judah 109, 112

Kadesh 75, **5:1**, 77, 87–89, 94, **5:3**, 109
Kahun 66
Kamid el-Loz 46, 48
Kamilara 66
Kamiros on Rhodes 121, **7:4**, 132
Kanesh 79, 107
Kaptara, *see* Crete
Karnak 93, **5:2**
Katsamba 70–71
Khusai 180
Knossos 46, 49, 58–59, 62–65, **4:3**, **4:4**, 67–72, 91
Kommos **4:2**, 66
Koumasa **4:2**
Kynopolis 212
Kynopolites Nomos 181

Lachish 32–33
Lebanon 51, 87, 90, 205
Lefkadi on Euboia 125, 127
Levant 5–9, 12, 21–25, 27–29, 31–37, 39–40, 42–45, 47, 49–52, 57–58, 62–63, 65–66, 67, 70–71, 79, 87, 97, 100, 104, 107–108, 112
Libya 97
Lindos 141
Litani river 87, 90
Lod, *see* Tel Lod
Louvre Museum, Paris 2
Lower Egypt 5–6
Luxor **5:3**

Ma'adi 33
Macedonia 203–204
Magan 42
Mari 9
Mavro Spelio 69
Mediterranean 10–14, 17, 19, 21, 24, 29, 52, 57–58, 62, 65, 67–70, 72, 78–80, 84, 91, 107–108, 111
Memphis 14, 16, 131, 137, 181, 211, 213
Menouthis 181
Merimda Beni Salama 5
Mersa Matruh, *see* Umm ar-Rakhkham
Mesara 59, **4:2**, 65–66

# Index 1: place names

Mesopotamia 3, 5–9, 40, 42, 71–72, 79–80, 83, 100, 101–113, **6:1**

Miletus 90–92

Mochlos 59, **4:1**, 65–66, 72

Mycenae 69–72, 77, 90–92, 97, 99–100, 112

Mykene 127, **7:7**, 129

Nahr al-Kabir 87

Naples, Museo Archeologico Nazionale 192

Naqada 3, 24, 37

Naucratis 12, 125–126, 129, 131, 137–138, 146, 158

Nawar 79

Negev 21, 31–32

Nile 16, 18–19, 32, 78, 96–97, 210–211; Delta 6, 9, 12–13, 49, 89, 97, 112, 125, 148–149, 173, 192; flood 14, 16 154, 197; Valley 4–5, 12–15, 21–22, 25, 29, 31, 33, 35–36, 79, 89, 112

Nineveh 105, **6:2**

Nippur 112

Nizzanim 32–33

Nubia 1, 4, 62, 111–112

Ombos 212–213

Orontes river 75, 77, 82, 84, 87–89, 92, 97, 106

Ostia 191

Oxyrhynchus 181, 212

Palestine 10, 43, 80–81, 87, 89, 97, 107, 109

Palestinian Autonomous Zone 21, **2:1**, 33

Palmahim Quarry **2:1**, 29–30, 35–37

Paris 15

Pelusium 181, 208, 213

Persian Gulf 111–112

Phaistos 66

Pharos 13, 17

Philae 185

Philistia 109

Phoenicia 108

Piramesse 9

Pithecusa 158

Platanos **4:1**, **4:2**

Pompeii 17–18; House of the Doctor 192, 200–201; House of the Ephebe 194; House of the Faun 199; suburban baths 201

Pozzuoli 204

Punt 8

Pydna 203–204

Pylos 99

Qarqar, battle of 106

Raphia 161

Ras Shamra **3:1**, 49, **3:4**, 55–56

Red Sea 8, 12

Rhodes 121–122

Rome 1, 18–19; Esquiline at 195; Villa Pamphili at 191; temple of Isis at 18

Sahara 5

Sais 12, 14, 137–138

Samos 121, 125, 129, 136–137, 147

Sardes 14

Sidon 12

Sinai 87

Siwa 16

Small Tel Malhata 26, 34

Somalia 8

Sparta 15

Sudan 8

Syria 8, 10, 50–52, 75, 77–82, 84–88, 90–92, 94, 96–97, 100, 107

Syro-Palestine 45, 47, 49, 51

Taur Ikhbeineh 24, 33–36

Tel Apheq/Rosh Ha-Ayin 32, 35–36

Tel Ashqelon 25–26, 32, 99

Tel Aviv 29, 32

Tel Dalit 29, 35–36

Tel el-Ajjul 24, 44, 67

Tel Erani **2:1**, 23–26, 33–35, 37

Tel Halif **2:1**

Tel Lod **2:1**, 26–29, **2:2**, 34–37

Tel Ma'ahaz **2:1**, 31, 34–35

Tell ed-Dab'a 3, 9

Tell el-Amarna 3–4, 99, 104; workmen's village 4
Tell el-Shihab 87
Tell es-Sakan **2:1**, 24–25, 34–36
Thebes (Egypt) 10, 13, 70, 91, 104, 108
Thmuis, Roman villa at 195
Tigris river 104
Til-Tuba, battle of 109, **6:2**
Tod, temple of Montu 10
Troy 15, 91–92, 99
Turkey 10
Tyre 87–88

Ugarit 9, 40, **3:1**, 45–46, 50–52, 70–71, 73, 77, 79, 82, 84, 88, 90, 92, 96, 99
Uluburun shipwreck 10

Umm ar-Rakhkham (Mersa Matruh) 97, 99
Upper Egypt 6–7, 10, 16–17
Ur 7; royal cemetery 7; third Dynasty of 79
Ura 71
Urartu 109
Urkish 79
Uruk 6–8; Uruk expansion 6–8

Wady Ghazzeh Site H 31, 33

Yarmuk river 87, 89

Zagros 80
Zakros 69
Zama 203

# Index 2: names of people, peoples and deities

Abdi-Ashirta 84, 88

Achilles 13

Adad-Nerari I 90

Aemilius Paullus 204

Aeschylus 146

Agrippa 208

Ahhotep 86

Ahmose 49

Akhenaten 4, 10, **3:3**, 51, 82–84, 86, 97–98, 101, 103–104

Akkadian 75, 79, 91–93, 98–99, 104–105

Alexander the Great 12, 16, 112; conquest of Egypt 145, 158

Alkmaionids 142

Alyattes 147

Amasis 126, 137, 140–141, 149, 154

Amenemhet III 177

Amenhotep II 81

Amenophis II 10, 46, **3:3**, 50–52, 55, 84

Amenophis III 44, **3:3**, 51, 55, 68, 81–82, 84, 104, 177

Amun 16

Amun-Ra 87, 93, 179

Antiochos III 203–204

Antony, *see* Marc Antony

Anubis 17, 205, 208, 211–212, 215

Aphrodite 17–18

Apis bull 211, 215

Apollo, sanctuary of at Didyma 126; statue of at Samos 136; temple of at Corinth 129; temple of at Delphi 142

Apries 126, 140, 149

Apuleius 17, 19

Arabs 159

Arinna 86, 89

Aristeas, letter of 158

Aristotle 16

Arnuwanda 80

Arsinoe II 203

Artaxerxes I 112

Artemisia, curse of 168

Assurbanipal 104, 107–109

Assur-Uballit 83, 96, 103

Athena, sanctuary of, Rhodes 126

Augustus, *see* Octavian

Aulus Gabinius 205

Aya 82, 85–87

Aziru 84, 88


Bernal, Martin 116

Bes 121, 179, 185

Burnaburiash 83, 101


Caesar 205, 211

Caesarion 199

Caius Cestius Epulo 18

Caligula (Gaius) 18, 200–201, 214

Cambyses 12, 111, 147, 154

Canaanite 45, 52, 105

Carians 159

Cicero 17

Claudius 18, 200–201

Cleopatra III 203

Cleopatra VII 17–18, 160, 197, 199–200, 205–215

Commodus 214

Constantine II 174

Copts 174

Cyclops 13

Cyrus 111


Daidalos 136, 145

Dakhamunzu 85–86, 98

Danaos 126

Darius 111

Deioces 150

Demeter 18

Dionysiac mysteries 204

Dionysos 210

Dipoinos 141

Djer/Zer 32, 37, 68

Domitian 212

Esarhaddon 107–108, 111–112
Euripides 15, 145, 151

Great Mother goddess of Pessinus 204
Greeks 11–19, 112, 145–155, 157–169

Hammurabi 79
Hannibal 203–204
Haremhab **3:3**, 51, 56, 87
Harpokrates 191, 205, 214
Hathor 17
Hatshepsut 8; temple of 171, 177
Hatti 75–100, **5:1**, 108; *see also* Hittites
Hattushili 80, 89–90, 92, 94, 96
Hekataios of Miletus 14, 149
Helen of Troy 13, 15, 151
Hellanicus of Lesbos 146
Heracles 151
Herodotus 11–16, 19, 106, 145–155
Hetepheris 53
Hittites 9, 51–52, 70, 75–101, 103–104; *see also* Hatti
Homer 13–16
Horace 11, 206–208
Hor-Aha 37
Horus 174, 182, 205
Horus Ka 27
Horus Narmer 26–27
Hotepibre 8
Hugieia 177
Hurrian 77, 104
Hyksos 9, 42–43, 46, 49, 72, 80, 86, 91, 112

Ibis 214
Imhotep 177
Inarus 146
Indo-European 79, 104
Irj-Hor 37
Isches 141–142
Isis 14, 17–19, 159, 173, 181, 198, 204–205, 208, 211, 214

Isocrates' *Busiris* 149, 153

Jews 159, 204
Josephus 201
Jupiter 215
Juvenal 211–212

Kafra (Khephren) 8, 48, 53
Ka-Narmer 37
Kashkeans 87
Kassites 9, 80, 82–83, 101, 104–105
Kha 70
Kheops 53
Khephren, *see* Kafra
Khian 46, 49, 72
Kleoboulos 126
Kroisos 14, 131, 140
Kurushtama 81–82
Kypselos 131

Livia 18
Lucan 211
Lykurgos 150

Macedonians 2, 99, 111–112
Maecenas 206
Maia 186
Mandoules, temple of 172, 181
Manetho 160
Marc Antony 18, 196, 199–203, 205–211, 213–214
Medes 110
Melampos 151
Memnon 181
Menelaus 13, 15, 121, 214
Merenptah **3:3**, 51, 77, 97
Merenra Nemtyemsaf I 55
Meritytis 53
Minoan 9–10, 91
Mitanni 9, 52, 77–78, 80–82, 84–85, 87, 89–91, 97, 99–100, 103–104, 108–109
Murashu archive 112
Murshili 79–80, 82, 87, 96

Murshili II 89–91
Musri 106
Muwatalli 75, 88–89, 94
Mykerinos 53, 149
Mysians 159

Naram-Sin 79
Narmer 23, 26–27, **2:2**, 32
Nebuchadrezzar 111
Necho 126
Neferirkare Kakai 53
Nefer-Seshem-Ra 56
Nefertiti 10, 46, 55
Neit 63
Neith, sculpture of **7:2**; temple of 137
Nero 18, 200–201
Neuserre Ini 53
Nikandre from Delos **7:11**, 139
Nubians 121

Octavian 158, 197, 199, 205, 207, 210–213, 215
Odysseus 13–14
Oserapis (Serapis) 17–18, 160, 177, 179, 185, 205, 214
Osiris 14, 17–19, 40, 68; cult of 172, 174, 178, 182, 204–205, 210–211, 213–214; festival of 173, 187, 192, 198, 201

Padukhep 89, 96
Pelusium, battle of 111
Pepi I 8, 48, 53–54, **4:1**
Pepi II 48, 54–55, 63
Periander 126
Persians 1, 11, 15, 111–112
Petrie, Flinders 2, 3
Philip of Macedonia 112
Phrynichus 146
Piyamaradu 90–92
Plato 14, 145, 154
Plutarch 17, 19, 151
Polycrates 126, 132, 141, 154
Pompey 210, 213
Popillius Laenas 203

Poppaea 201
Poseidon, temple of at Isthmia 129
Posidippus 17
Priapus 194
Propertius 209–210
Proteus 13, 15
Psammenitus 149
Psammetichos 109
Psammetichos I 12, 125, 129, 137, 140, 141, 158
Psammetichos II 126, 146
Ptolemies 145, 158–170, 179, 199
Ptolemy IV Philopator 203
Ptolemy V Epiphanes 203
Ptolemy VI Philometor 203

Ra 89
Ramesses II 12, 46, **3:3**, 50–52, 56, 75, 77, 82, 87–90, 92–94, 96–98, 109, 174
Ramesses III **3:3**, 99
Ramesses IV **3:3**
Rhampsanitos 149
Rhodopis 148
Rhoikos 131, 136, 142
Romans 2, 11–12, 17–19, 112, 168

Sabacus 150
Sabazios 204
Sargon 109
Scyllis 141
Scythians 212
Sea Peoples 91, 97, 99
Sennacherib 105, 108–109, **6:2**
Serapis (Oserapis) 17–18, 160, 177, 179, 185, 205, 214
Sesostris 149–150, 153, 177
Seti I 12, **3:3**, 87–88, 90, 173; cenotaph of 174
Seti II **3.3**
Shalmaneser I 90
Shalmaneser III 106
Shamshi-Adad 79
Shattiwaza 89
Shuppiluliuma 78, 81–87, 89–91, 96, 98
Simonides 139

Smenkhara 82
Solon 13–14, 145, 151, 178
Sophocles 152
Souchos 17
Sphinx 177
St Augustine 19
Stesichoros 15
Sumerians 6
Syrians 159

Telemachus 13
Teti 53
Theodoros of Samos 131, 140
Thracians 159
Tibullus 210–211
Tiglath-Pileser I 79, 104
Tiglath-Pileser III 109
Tiy 55
Tudkhaliya 80, 96
Tukulti-Ninurta I 96–98
Tutankhamun 42, 44, 46, 82, 85
Tuthmosis I 99

Tuthmosis II 81
Tuthmosis III 44, 49, 70, 77, 80, 84, 92
Tuthmosis IV 84
Twosret **3:3**

Unis 53
Urkhi-Teshup 89–90, 92, 96

Valerius Messalla Corvinus 210
Venus 19
Vergil 208
Vespasian 200

Winckelmann 116

Xenophon 112

Yahweh 113
Yantin 49

Zeus 17

# Index 3: topics

Abydos ware 32
*Abydosfahrt* 173
Aeginetan script 177
Aegyptomania 214
afterlife 39
Amarna Letters 45–46, 82, 84, 104
Amarna period 70, 84
animal worship 147, 152, 211–212
animal-shaped gods 215
archaeology 7, 9–11, 13; Egyptian 2–5, 12
architecture 5, 13, 23–24, 26, 31, 47, 51, 107, 115, 127, 141; sand bed foundation 130
art 13, 20, 45, 96
Artemision at Ephesus 129, **7:8**, 131, 140
artistic motifs 5–6
aulic titulature 166

barbarians 11–12, 15–16, 18, 20
*barbaros* 118, 145–146, 148, 153
Bronze Age 7, 42, 44–45, 57, 62, 65, 72, 82, 94, 99, 108–109

Campana reliefs 193–194, **11:4**, 196
cannibalism 212
caricatures of Egypt 191–203
*Carmen de Bello Actiaco* 208–209
carnelian 65
cartouche, on stone vessels 39–40, 42–52, **3:4**
chalcolithic 24–25
chariot, horse-drawn 9
claw-chisel 138
coins 214
copper 7, 10
Corinthian *aryballoi* 121
crocodile 146, 148, 193–194, 197, 201, 214
cuneiform 45, 91–92, 104–105
cylinder seals 5–6, 33

discrimination 162–169

Early Bronze Age 7, 9, 21–37, 47–48, 58, 65–66
Early Iron Age 123, 125
ebony 8, 10
Egyptian canon 136, 138–139
Erani C phase 25–26, 31, 33–34, 37
ethnicity 162–169, 181; ethnic tensions 164–165; multi-ethnic polity 162

faience 8, 13, 51, 115, 118, 121, **7:4**, 122
First Intermediate Period 42, 59, **4:2**, 62, 65–66
first millennium BC 99, 107–108
fourth millennium BC 3, 5–7, 9, 21, 101
frankincense 8

Gebel el-Arak knife handle 6
geography of Egypt 148
German archaeologists 3
gift exchange 126, 141–142
glass 10
gold 7–8, 10, 82, 84, 111
graffiti 12, 171–189; Aramaic 178, 182; Carian 177; Coptic 185; demotic 185–186; Egyptian 185–186; Greek 174–189; Phoenician 177–178, 182
Greek archaeology 13
Greek art 11, 13
Greek-Persian wars 145, 150
gymnasium 168

Hathor locks 122
Heraia on Samos 119, **7:1**, 126, 129–132, 136, 141–142
hippopotamus 191, 193–194, 197, 199, 201, 214

*Iliad* 13
immigration to Egypt 158–162
incubation 171, 179–180
Iron Age 101–113
ivory 8, 65, 107

Kamares ware 9, 66

kingship of Ptolemies 160
kitchen ware 36
Kouroi 132, **7:10**, 136, **7:12**, 138, 141–142
Kushite period 118

labyrinth 148
languages: Aramaic 175; Carian 175; Coptic 175, 178; demotic 164, 175; Phoenician 175
lapis lazuli 6–9, 44, 82–83, 106
Late Bronze Age 9–10, 40, 42, 45, 48, **4:3**, 67, 69–70, 75–113, 123
Late Uruk period 6
legal system 164–165
lost-wax process 118

materialization of power 142
medicine, Egyptian 147
Memnonion at Abydos 172–189
memory 154
mercenaries 12, 179; Carian 125–126, 178; Greek 12, 125–126, 129, 146, 158, 178; Ionian 125–126, 140
metalwork, Egyptian 120
Middle Assyrian period 104
Middle Bronze Age 8, 58, **4:3**, 66, 107
Middle Kingdom 10, 45, 47–48, 52, 59, **4:2**, 65–66, 79
monarchy 150, 152
mummification 147
museum displays 116
myrrh 8

Napoleonic expedition 2
Neolithic 5, 58
New Kingdom 5, 9, 39, 45, 49, 52, 62
Nilotic landscape 191–203
Nilotic scenes 193–203
Nubian Salvage Campaign 3

obelisk 148
Old Babylonian period 78
Old Kingdom 24, 39, 45, 47, 52–53, 59, **4:1**, 62–63, **4:3**, 68–69, 71–72, 173
Old Testament 106

onomastics 167
oracles 171, 179–180, 187; Amun at Siwa 160; Bes at Abydos 173, 177, 180
orientalism 117
orientalizing period in Greek art 117, 123
orientalizing 112
Osireion 174, 185–186
Oxyrhynchus Aretalogy of Isis 186

palaces 11, 15, 41–45, 50, 55–57, 67, 69–70, 104–105, 107, 109, **6:2**
Palaeolithic 5
Palestrina mosaic 192–203
Paneia 171
papyri 11, 42, 94; *P. Herc.* 208; *P. Köln* 17; *P. Oxy.* 186; *P. Tebt.* 165
Peloponnesian War 112
Persian rule of Egypt 14
Persian wars 11
Phoenician traders 125
*Poikilia* 120
potters 33–34
pottery 5, 9, 11–12, 23–33, 36, 67, 99–100
prejudice, popular 153
priests, Egyptian 149, 151–152
*Proskunema* 179, 181–182, 185
Ptolemaic fashions 200
pygmies 191–197
pyramids 8, 14, 17–18, 148

quarrying techniques 129

Ramesseum 174
religion 4, 11, 13–20, 43, 105, 112; Egyptian 160, 167–168, 171, 214; Egyptian cults 204, 211–212
religious policy of Ptolemies 160
renaissance, Egyptian 118
reversal of customs 152
revolts in Egypt 161, 165, 179, 185
Roman citizenship 213
Roman Empire 11, 18, 179, 180
Roman gods 208
Roman Republic 18

# Index 3: topics

Rosetta Stone 2

sacrifice 171
sailing ship 58, 63, 65–66
Saite art 121
Saite period 12, 14, 107, 118, 126,
Saitic Dynasty 119–120
scarab 10, 43–44
scaraboid beads 8
scholarship, Greek 215
sculpture 13, 51; bronze 115, 118–119, 122; Daidalic 132, 138, 139, 141; marble 115, 138; stone 132, 141
seals 6, 9, 43–44, 92, 107
Second Intermediate Period 42, 48–49, 62, 67
second millennium BC 8–9, 40, 52, 57, 62–63, 65–66, 68, 70, 78–79, 91, 99, 103, 107–108
*Senatus Consultum de Bacchanalibus* 204
Serapieion at Memphis 171
*serekh* 24–27, **2:2**, 29–32, 34–35, 37
silver 8, 92
sixth millennium BC 5
slaves 8
social complexity 6, 57, 72
solar calendar 215
soldiers 179–182
sources 1–2, 11, 20, 104–105; archaeological 1–2, 7, 11–12, 20–21, 23, 29, 35–36, 42–44, 46, 57, 67, 77, 100, 103–105, 107; textual 1–2, 11, 20, 44, 77, 100, 103, 106–107, 145–189, 203–216

stepped altars 131
Stoic philosophy 18
stone vessels 7–9, 12, 39–56, 57–73
syllabic-Cypriot script 177

technological transfers 124, 139
temples 2–4, 8, 10–11, 13, 17–18, 39–40, 42–44, 46–48, 53–56, 78, 93–94, **5:2**, **5:3**, 104–105
*Theoria* 178
Third Intermediate Period 68, 119, 121,
third millennium BC 7–8, 21, 40, 57–58, 63–65, 69, 101, 107
timber 7, 9
tin 9–10
tombs 2–3, 5, 7, 10, 39–40, 42, 44, 46, 49, 51, 55–56, 59, 62–63, 68–73
trade 6–8, 12, 20, 33–34, 39, 41–42, 45, 49, 51–52, 57–59, 63, 65–66, 69–72, 79, 106–108
travellers to Egypt 145, 153, 158, 171, 178
treaties 75, 80–82, 87, 89, 92–94, **5:2**, 97, 105
Trojan War 125
tyrants 131–132, 140, 142

Unesco 3

wall painting 9–10, 107, 191–201
wine 7, 24, 29
wisdom 215
wonders of Egypt 147–149
world systems 115, 124, 144
writing 6, 9, 11, 57, 91, 104–105, 107